Russia and Beyond

Margaret Zarudny Freeman

Russia and Beyond

One Family's Journey,
1908 – 1935

IMPALA
2006

Published by
Impala
(International Media Publication and Literary Associates) Ltd
Registered Office:
c/o Davenport Lyons
30 Old Burlington Street
London W1S 3NL

Copyright © Margaret Zarudny Freeman 2002, 2006

First published in 2002 in Russian by Novoe Literaturnoe Obozrenie (Moscow), as *Mchalis' gody za godami: Istoriia odnoi sem'i* ['Years Chasing Years: The Story of One Family'].

Front cover illustration and author photograph © Ed Freeman 2006

Every effort has been made to trace possible copyright holders and to obtain their permission for the use of any copyright material. The publishers will gladly receive information enabling them to rectify any error or omission for subsequent editions.

ISBN 1 905530 03 X

All rights reserved. No part of this publication may be reproduced, stored in a retrieval system, or transmitted in any form or by any means, electronic, mechanical, photocopying, recording or otherwise, without the prior permission of the publishers.

Contents

Part IV

Illustrations

The section titles show the author in 1911, 1920 (watercolor by Evgenii Cavos), 1924, and 1957 (portrait by Ed Freeman).

The photograph on the back cover was taken by Ed Freeman in April 2005.

Acknowledgements

Of the many friends, colleagues, and volunteer readers who helped me during my work on this memoir – over some eighteen years – I can list only a few. Others will have to believe that I am grateful to them too! First I must mention Beatrice Kleppner, without whose generous invitation to spend summers at her Vermont home I would not have even started to write. Not only were there ideal conditions for work but both Bea and her daughter-in-law Amy Kleppner read my chapters as I wrote them, correcting my English and commenting on my text.

I am deeply grateful to Elena Bonner, who overcame great difficulties getting the entire case of my mother from the KGB archives: the actual copies of her interrogations, several letters that related to her case, statements concerning the verdict and the carrying out of the sentence, Mother's last photograph, and, finally, the document concerning her rehabilitation. Mr. Pihoia of the Central Russian Archives in Moscow arranged for me to have photocopies of various notes and letters from the Zarudny archives. My relatives in Russia also supplied me with copies of notes and photographs.

My sister Elena Levin spent many hours with me making the manuscript more concise, and helping me to express my thoughts more clearly. My sister Tanya Hull supplied me with many of the photographs that I needed, while my sister Katerina Singleton made copies from documents and from old books and journals she dug out in various libraries. My son Edward restored my old photographs and digitized them, and also helped with computer problems, answering my numerous questions by telephone from California. My son Arthur, and his wife Janet Ing Freeman, went over the English version word by word, helped to put it into its final form, and oversaw this publication.

The work of Maria Shaskolskaya deserves special gratitude. She looked over all my archives and, being herself one of the Brullov descendants, was able to add information and illustrations of her own. She translated my first English version into Russian, was closely involved with the publication of the memoir in Moscow in 2002, and helped to edit my final English text.

The English edition also greatly benefitted from the efforts of Serge Karpovich, who offered linguistic assistance that only a native American Russian could provide.

I received comments and encouragement from many Russian friends here in the Boston area. Peter Zug arranged my illustrations, scanned them into my computer, and printed them for me; Misha Kruk helped constantly with computer problems; and Alexander Gorfunkel added many valuable corrections. The maps are largely the work of Mary Parkin.

Some quotations are taken from the diary of John Crane, the son of Charles R. Crane, who traveled with his father through Siberia in 1921. These diaries are located in the Bekhterev Archives at Columbia University in New York City.

Foreword

On a warm late May afternoon in 1992 I sat in my living room in Belmont, Massachusetts, looking through a picture window at the blooming horse chestnut. I transplanted it forty years ago, when it was six feet high and had a single pink blossom on the top – now it is an enormous tree covered with hundreds. That spring everything seemed to flower at the same time. The red, pink, and lavender azaleas and the tender pink rhododendrons started opening just before the apple tree lost its blossoms. The house – an old carriage house rebuilt by my husband and me over the years – seemed comfortably cozy in spite of its rather stately dimensions. It was so peaceful to sit inside and look out, now that all the pictures of an art exhibition had been removed, and the living room had reassumed its usual aspect. The outdoor modern sculptures were gone too, taken away by their maker, a bearded Russian, and the terrace was back to its umbrella and white furniture. The crowds of visitors were gone and I was finally left alone, to contemplate the last winter's activities, and all the long way which had led to this day.

Ever since I retired as Associate Professor from the Massachusetts Institute of Technology more than twenty-five years ago, my house has been a place where lectures, music recitals, and art exhibitions often take place. I started it for the Russian émigrés, to help them feel at home in America. Having spent more than forty years in the USA by then, I felt thoroughly American and I hoped I could spare them some of the displacement and loneliness I experienced when starting my life in the USA. My own desire in meeting these newly arrived "future Americans" was to show them how one can become American and be able to contribute to the wealth and multiculturalism of America without losing those liberal principles that caused my parents as well as many of the "Russian dissidents" to be in opposition to any form of suppression.

My brother, four sisters, and I all ended up in America; three of us graduated from MIT, two from Radcliffe. We all married Americans, all produced American children, who speak little or no Russian. Spread among many of the states they teach, write, and produce American music and art. One of my two sons lives on the West Coast, the other in England. Yet my sisters' and my own native tongue remained Russian, and as I get older I seem to have some kind of cultural affinity with the new Russian émigrés.

The long route my family traveled from the intellectual and artistic circles of old St. Petersburg in Russia through the First World War, two Russian revolutions, a Russian civil war, the Old Russian World enclave in China, on the road that in the course of twenty-seven years took us by train across Russia, the Urals, Siberia, Manchuria, and finally by a Japanese steamer across the Pacific to the United States, will seem like ancient history – or even fiction – to the new generations. But I hope it will still interest them.

I

CHILDHOOD

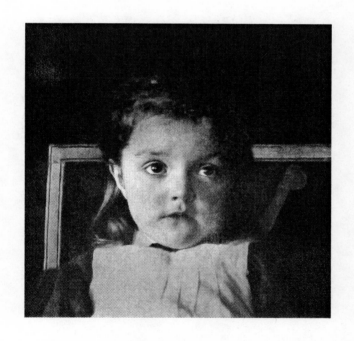

1

Our Family

One day when I was about ten years old someone at school told me that my great-grandfather was very famous. I came home excited, and asked my mother about it. She replied: "I shall tell you a story. Once a flock of geese was being herded by a boy with a big stick. One of the geese turned to him, objecting: 'How dare you strike us with a stick! After all, we are famous – our ancestors saved Rome!' To this the boy answered, 'I care nothing about your ancestors, what is important here is my stick!'"

Mother's parable evoked the old legend of the sacred geese whose honking alerted the sleeping Romans to a night-time attack, but she meant that family history should never be an end in itself: "You see," she added, "what matters is not who or what your ancestors were, but what you yourself can accomplish in your life." After that, our response to anyone who boasted about forebears or relatives was, usually, "Oh we know! Your ancestors saved Rome!"

My own story, however, is not only of myself, but of my sisters and brother, my mother, my father, and our lives as a family in the early twentieth century. And so something must be said – just to begin with – about where we all started.

Mother's Family

My great-great-great-grandfather Georg Bruello moved to Russia from Germany with all his family in 1773. Russian royalty always imported European talents to decorate the capital and its palaces, and Georg Bruello, a skilled artisan in porcelain, was one of them. He came from a French Huguenot family that had fled France for Germany a hundred years earlier, because of religious persecution. As artists and architects his descendants left their mark on St. Petersburg. His famous grandsons Karl, the Romantic painter, and Alexander, portrait painter and architect (my great-grandfather), changed their original name to a russified form, Brullov; Alexander was granted gentry status for "service to Tsar and Fatherland." Karl Brullov died in Rome, where he had painted his most famous canvas, "The Last Day of Pompeii," and is buried in the Monte Testaccio cemetery below a monument designed by his brother Alexander. Alexander is now best known for his many architectural achievements in St. Petersburg, and for his rich re-decorations of the great rooms in the Hermitage Palace.[1]

My maternal grandfather, Pavel Brullov, was born in St. Petersburg in 1840. He was a landscape painter, a member of a group of painters called "The Itinerants,"[2] a member of the Academy of Arts, and curator of paintings in the Museum of Alexander III (now the Russian Museum) in St. Petersburg. Pavel was a broadly educated man: artists used to say he was a mathematician, since he had graduated from the mathematics department of the University and could always be called on to help with the accounts; mathematicians called him a musician, since he graduated from the Conservatory in piano and cello and loved to participate in amateur chamber orchestras; musicians knew him as an artist since he was a graduate of the Academy of Arts and his main occupation was painting in oils. Perhaps they were hinting that he was a "jack of all trades"!

Grandfather's paintings of trees, mountains, and seascapes covered the walls of homes that our family occupied during my early childhood. One that I remember well was of a huge oak tree in the middle of a meadow with small woods on the distant horizon. It seemed to me that my grandfather must have painted each leaf of the huge oak tree and every crevice in its gnarled trunk. I often wondered at the patience it took to do that. The picture occupied most of the wall of our living room, and I loved to finger the deeply sculptured design of its heavy gold frame. Another painting, somewhat smaller in a wide black frame, was of large round rocks on the shore of the Black Sea, with little boys leaping from them into the calm blue waters below. It was entitled "Gursuf," the name of a seaside resort in Crimea. I remember how my brother, still in my mother's arms, reached out to the little boys in the picture, wanting to pick them off the rocks.

There were also paintings by our aunt, my father's older sister, Ekaterina Zarudnaya Cavos (Aunt Katya), who was primarily a watercolorist. Some portraits painted by my mother hung in Father's study. But for me the most intriguing of all was Grandfather's picture of a railway steam engine, smoke rising from its stack and a train of cars snaking behind it, as it moved straight at the onlooker. The painting was not quite finished but it had an interesting story behind it: grandfather and Aunt Katya loved to go together into the country to paint. One day they wanted to represent a train head on, and placing their easels between two tracks they waited for one to approach. But when it was already near them, they suddenly realized that another train was coming up behind them, on the opposite track, which they had not heard because of the noise of the first. There was no time to escape to either side of the tracks. Aunt Katya, a frail, rather nervous woman, panicked, but Grandfather seized her by the shoulders and held her steadily between the two moving trains until they had passed.

I remember my grandfather as an active, strong person, dedicated to his work. On one of his visits to us he was painting outside and someone called him to come in because it had started to rain. He answered, "My oil paints are not hurt by water!" and continued to paint. When he was in his sixties, he broke his right arm jumping onto a moving streetcar. While his arm was in a cast, he tried to paint with his left hand, and learned to do it so well that after his right arm healed, he continued to alternate hands as he worked. The short biographies of him that I have read are full of amusing stories about his absent-mindedness. Apparently the activities he loved absorbed him completely: when he was painting or listening to music or playing a chess game or just deep in his thoughts, the rest of the world simply ceased to exist.

Grandfather died in December 1914, a widower four times. He had eight children by his four wives. His first wife, Sofia Kavelina, daughter of a famous historian and a historian herself, had two sons, Vadim and Alexander. Sofia died in 1877, when Alexander was two years old, and in 1879 Grandfather married Margarita Likhonina, my grandmother. With her he had three children, Lyubov, Boris, and my mother, Elena. Margarita Likhonina died of consumption when my mother was two years old.

A widower now, with five children, two years later Grandfather married Elizaveta Noskova, with whom he had two more daughters, Lydia and Margarita; Elizaveta died giving birth to their second daughter, who lived only two years herself. The Russian church did not permit a fourth marriage, so Grandfather married his fourth wife, Ksenia Minina, in a civil ceremony. She and their son Pavel – Grandfather's eighth child – were not permitted to bear his surname. Grandfather loved Pavel deeply, and was very proud of him when in World War I he volunteered and served in the air force. Pavel emigrated after 1917 and died in Paris in 1938.

All the children received university educations, spoke both French and German, and traveled in Europe. From his first wife, Sofia Kavelina, Grandfather inherited an estate in the Tula District called Ivanovo, where his children spent many summers, and he often went there himself. A few of his paintings are now in the Russian Museum in St. Petersburg; others are in the Irkutsk Museum in Siberia. Some of his sketches can be found in the civic museum of Belyov, the nearest town to Ivanovo.

Elena, My Mother

Living through early losses of several family members, and brought up by governesses, Mother and her siblings were very close to each other. In winter they lived in St. Petersburg in an apartment adjacent to but separate from that of their father, and they summered at the Ivanovo estate. During the summers, for lack of other ideas, the governess had the children work through the whole course of high school study for the following school year, so that Mother claimed she never learned anything new at school except a special kind of darning. But she was fond of her governess.

She was fond of her father too, but she became close to him only when she was older. As a child she loved to steal into his library, where she could pick books from the bookshelves and read them by the light of a candle, hiding under the library table covered with a low-hanging green cloth.

What Mother missed most as a child were parental affection and free time, and as a mother she always tried to give us what she herself had missed. But I think the physical expression of affection did not come easily to her. She was more concerned with "educating" us. I remember how I enjoyed being sick, because only then could I get from her all the loving attention I craved.

Mother graduated from the Petersburg Girls' Gymnasium in 1899 (a "gymnasium" in pre-revolutionary Russia was an academic high school on the German model). Graduation was a festive affair. The Dowager Empress herself, the patroness of the school, awarded medals to the best students. Mother's sister Lyubov graduated one year earlier and received the highest award – a gold medal. Mother was awarded a silver medal.

After Gymnasium Mother studied history at the Bestuzhev Courses[3] in St. Petersburg, the first institution of higher learning for women in Russia. Many of the students there in her day were fired by a revolutionary spirit, and with her passionate nature, Mother was strongly drawn to political activities. Her contemporaries were reading and discussing Nietzsche, Karl Marx, Karl Kautsky,[4] Russian philosophers such as Vladimir Soloviev[5] and Nikolai Berdyaev,[6] radical journalists, and Russian Symbolist poets. Some of these poets lived right there in Petersburg: Dmitri Merezhkovsky,[7] Zinaida Gippius,[8] and Alexander Blok.[9] The historical seminars of Professor I. M. Grevs[10] were particularly popular and often extended long beyond the formally assigned time. It was a time of intoxicating intellectual and creative ferment.

At some point while Mother was a student she joined the Social Democratic Party (SD), which adhered to Marxist ideology and was oriented towards industrial workers' interests. In 1903 this party split into two factions, the more radical Bolsheviks (majority) led by Lenin, and the more conciliatory Mensheviks. In 1905 Mother left the SD and joined the Socialist Revolutionary Party (SR), and after her marriage in 1911 left the SR and joined the Society for the Dissemination of Mass Education instead. From that time on she did not belong to any political party.

Together with her brother Boris and her younger sister Lydia, Mother was much influenced by her favorite cousin, Nadezhda Brullova Shaskolskaya, who was three years younger. Nadenka, as we knew her, was a brilliant woman and an ardent SR member. Her husband, Peter Shaskolsky, a historian, died of influenza in 1918 while hiding from the Cheka, or "Extraordinary Commission," the secret political police, and Nadenka herself was arrested in 1922, like many other SRs, released, arrested again, and finally shot in 1937. Her three children survived her.

I heard from my parents of only one dramatic incident during Mother's student life: a confrontation with Lev Trotsky.[11] After the notorious "Bloody Sunday" of 1905, when police opened fire on a huge demonstration of workers, killing and wounding several hundred of them, the police had orders to treat any student demonstrations outside the University grounds in the same way. Trotsky, a fiery speaker, came to a big student meeting, and urged everyone to take to the streets, with the idea that the more harshly they were treated, the more sympathy they and their cause would generate. Roused by the speech, the students started to get up and obey. But Mother, who had just been a witness to the Bloody Sunday massacre, knew that many could be killed or wounded if they demonstrated, and was appalled by Trotsky's reasoning. She leaped up on the podium and shouted: "Comrades! We promised that we wouldn't go out unarmed! We have no arms, so we won't go!" Startled, the students hesitated, and in the end no one went out to demonstrate.

Because of her revolutionary friendships and activities, the police kept Mother under surveillance. Sometime later in 1905 she was forbidden to stay in St. Petersburg, and so left the city and spent a winter at Ivanovo. The estate had a large house with many outbuildings and a village adjacent, but in summer only a horse carriage could reach it over the unpaved country roads, and during the winter months travel was by sleigh over packed snow. Anyone who ventured outside the roadway on foot could sink waist deep in snow.

During that winter Mother developed a vital interest in the local school, which she helped to establish and where she taught. Since she was the only one of the family living at the big house, the village peasants would turn to her in any emergency. There was no doctor in the vicinity, and she had to minister to all sorts of medical problems. Frostbite was very frequent. One man who came asking for her help had frozen his hand some time earlier and the flesh on his fingers had begun to decay. Bones were visible where the flesh had started to fall off. Mother knew from her sister, who was studying medicine, that in such cases the only way to prevent gangrene from spreading was to amputate the fingers. Of course Mother had never done such a thing, and had never seen it done. She had no choice, however, so she did it right there and then. Eventually the man's hand healed and he lived.

The next winter Mother returned to her studies in St. Petersburg, where the university, now "autonomous," permitted women students to attend lectures. Students now gathered frequently in various halls of the University to express protests or demands and to start demonstrations; intellectual and political activity was even more frantic than before. Numerous groups met in private homes to discuss literature, philosophy, and above all politics. Having missed one school year while at Ivanovo, Mother had to study hard. But she could not help being involved in some of the intellectual turmoil around her. The stories about those years that I heard from Mother when I was a child, few as they were, made me feel later that my own youth lacked the intellectual intensity and excitement that I assumed were a necessary part of being young.

Mother graduated on October 16, 1907, her diploma certifying her as a "home instructor in subjects in which she received a grade of good or higher." For a while she still was under suspicion by the police for her revolutionary activities, but it was personal relations, rather than politics, that were most important to her now. The time had come to find a life partner, and it is clear from her diary, which I still possess, that this was a period of soul-searching for her. Here are a few entries, written between August 1906 and December 1907:

> My head is spinning over the same kind of questions: not those confounded general questions of life, but specific, pressing, personal questions. It annoys me to realize their personal character. Sometimes I wonder, is it a sign of moral degradation to think only of personal problems? But on the

other hand, how can one not think about them when they concern other human beings, their happiness, their lives.

What causes more grief: terrible living conditions and social inequities, or the absence of warmth in human relations, including love and the response to it?

Why am I loved? I see nothing in myself. I find it burdensome sometimes. Five men have told me that I am the dearest person in their life. Now three of them are asking me to marry them. I don't need them. I don't know what to do with them.

Her next entry four months later sounds a different tune:

I'm getting married. I am used to it. ... I am calm and happy. My happiness is not the intense kind, it is not as if the whole world has suddenly bloomed before my eyes. I am calm.

Many years later Father added a note of his own to Mother's diary:

We were married on the evening of December 7, 1907. My sister Katya and Pavel A. Brullov were present. We went to Imatra [a resort in south Finland] for 10 days; skied and played chess. I was checkmated 16 times.

I know that the last sounds very much like a *double entendre*, but somehow I don't think it was. Father often talked about Mother's skill at chess, of which he was very proud – as he was of all her abilities.

The last entry in Mother's diary was written after she had married my father. It is subdued. She is staying at home while expecting me, her first child. She has no outside occupation.

Sometimes I am sorry that there is so little beauty and poetry in our life. Fatigue after a day's work, rest together and that is all. If only it were spring now! But by the time spring arrives, and he has a chance to get a proper rest, the honeymoon period will be over, and "normal" times will prevail.

"Only the morning of love is beautiful!" I did not have this "morning." I started at once at noon, or am I too sensual?

I am terribly afraid of banality and spiritual degradation. I feared them in my childhood and adolescence, I read about them all the time, and meet them in real life.

Sometimes the thought strikes me: are we really just ordinary people? After all, Zarudnys and Brullovs are not born by the dozens, and somehow their spirit is in us. This thought is the straw I clutch to. But then, one should work, and I sit here doing nothing – this is degradation.

Mother's diary ends here.

Father's Family

My grandfather, Sergey Ivanovich Zarudny, was a descendant of Zaporozhye Cossacks, a community of freedom-loving Ukrainian warriors on the Dniepr River. The Cossacks pledged their allegiance to the Russian emperors in the seventeenth century and helped them to expand and defend Russia's borders. One of Grandfather's ancestors was granted gentry status, but Grandfather was no pampered aristocrat. He was born on the family estate in Ukraine, one of nine children of a comparatively impoverished landowner. From the age of fourteen he lived alone and almost penniless in the city of Kharkov, preparing himself for the university without tutors. At the University of Kharkov he studied mathematics as his specialty, and read voraciously in other subjects, not only in Russian but also in French, German, English, and Italian. After graduating in 1842, he went to St. Petersburg, intending to work as an astronomer at the Pulkovo observatory. However, as a member of the gentry he was expected to work for the state, and he accepted a post in the Ministry of Justice when it was urged upon him.

At that time the Russian emperor was Nicholas I, the most autocratic and repressive Tsar of the nineteenth century. Still, the capital, St. Petersburg, was caught up in the turmoil of developing social consciousness. Progressive ideas spread among enlightened liberal officials under the influence of European social philosophy. Many voices called for the abolition of serfdom. Even Nicholas understood that it was an evil and a threat to the country's stability, but he feared the consequences of abolition even more. No real reform of serfdom took place during his reign.

Pavel Brullov (1840-1914)

Alexander Brullov
Portrait by Karl Brullov

Sergey Ivanovich Zarudny
(1821-1887)

The first document Grandfather had to prepare was a request by the Minister of Justice addressed to Russian judges and prosecutors to report deficiencies in Russian civil laws, with a view to possible future revisions. Grandfather had to forward the answers to this request to the Minister, and reading these reports was the beginning of his legal education. Nobody else paid much attention to them, but he did, with mounting interest, and as a result he became passionately interested in law.

While in Europe for treatment of his eye problems, he studied the legal systems of many Western countries and later published a number of scholarly articles on the subject. He also organized seminars for lawyers and law graduates who worked in the ministry, thus laying a foundation for a school of practical jurisprudence. He had a remarkable ability to organize his thoughts and express them clearly in writing, and as he gained authority on problems of the law his talents were recognized and he was promoted rapidly in the ranks of the civil service.

After the death of Nicholas I and the accession of his son Alexander II in 1855, the economic development of the country and the pressure of public opinion made the abolition of serfdom a top priority for the new government. One of the first assignments Grandfather received from the new administration was to serve on the commission investigating corruption and the misappropriation of government funds that had occurred during the Crimean War. The investigation was carried out in a number of southern cities and in Moscow, and revealed to Grandfather the appalling state of local administration, with its arbitrary court decisions, graft, and bribery. This strengthened his conviction that law reform was essential, and that the judiciary branch of government must be independent of the executive.

Later, Grandfather also served on the commission preparing the reform of 1861 that emancipated the serfs, and received a gold medal for his service. I remember a framed lithograph on the wall of my father's study: Tsar Alexander II surrounded by the portraits of all his collaborators in that crucial reform, and at the bottom, slightly bigger than the others, a portrait of Grandfather. Subsequently

Grandfather participated in another major commission, appointed to prepare a complete revision of civil and criminal law. Grandfather's responsibility was in the area of civil law, but in the end he worked on all the sections addressed. The revision of Russian law was his most sacred dream, and he worked day and night without sparing himself.

In 1864 the Tsar proclaimed a reform of the legal system based on the new revisions. Among many other innovations that were introduced for the first time in Russia were trial by jury, separation of administrative and judicial powers, and creation of an independent association of defense lawyers. But the effects of the reform of 1864 turned out to be more radical than the government expected. In several political trials the prosecution failed to get convictions, and this caused the government to modify some of the articles of the new legal code. Grandfather, who in 1866 published an important monograph, *The Codex of Laws and the Deliberations on which It Is Based*, did his best to resist these reversals. In 1869, however, he was made a Senator, technically another promotion in rank, but effectively a sequestration, for he was moved to a part of the Senate quite remote from legal work. This was a bitter pill for him to swallow.

He continued to write on problems of law, and also occupied himself with translating from Italian to Russian. He translated Cesare Beccaria's *Essay on Crime and Punishment,* [12] and a few years before his death he published a translation of Dante's *Inferno* with an extensive commentary, relating to the judgment of sinners. This may have been, incidentally, the first appearance of Dante in the Russian language. Grandfather Zarudny married Zoya Myasnovo in 1859, and they had eight children: Maria, Ekaterina, Alexander, Anastasia, Sergey, Zoya, Varvara, and the last, Ivan – my father, who was born in 1875.[13]

Grandmother was a kindhearted woman and she was much more ready than her husband to use her position (as the wife of a Senator) in appeals to the authorities, so that Grandfather often referred people needing help to her. At the same time, she was more conventional than her husband and did not always approve of his ideas, or of the radical behavior of her children. But she was an admiring wife and devoted mother.

The children were also devoted to their father and his work, and sympathized with his frustration when the implementation of his life's work seemed to fall short of its goal; a strong sense of social responsibility figured in most of their lives as they grew up. Even while busy with his work at the Ministry, Grandfather had taken an active part in his children's education. He himself taught them to read and write, selected their tutors, and supervised their program of studies. His children at different times had English, French, and German governesses, and each of them, like my father, became relatively fluent in all three languages. The girls also studied piano and painting, while my father received violin lessons. All, even the girls, completed their higher education, except the second son Sergey, who could not finish his course at the Agricultural Academy, having been arrested for political activity after just two years there.

The Zarudnys spent their winters in St. Petersburg, and their summers on the family's estate, Kolodezhnoye, near the city of Kharkov in Ukraine. Grandfather saw to it that each child had his own flower and vegetable bed and learned something about the nature of plant life, thus acquiring respect for the labor necessary to work the land. The children participated in some of the events of village life.

After being sidelined from legal work Grandfather spent long periods at his estate, often long after the family returned to St. Petersburg in the fall, working in his greenhouse and spending quiet evenings on his translations and reading. He would start flowers, shrubs, and exotic fruit trees from seed. His wife did not quite approve of her husband's "exchanging his pen for the gardener's shovel." He bought a large stock of medications at his own expense, and treated peasants, since the local doctor lived far away and was available only in serious cases.

He was already quite ill with what was probably stomach cancer in 1887. He had remained on the estate alone with his son Sergey, who was then under house arrest there, in connection with the assassination of Alexander II,[14] but illness forced Grandfather to leave Sergey alone and go back to the city, where his doctors advised him to seek medical help in Europe. He died in December 1887, *en route* to Nice, where he is buried. At the time his eldest son Alexander was twenty-four, and my father, the youngest, was twelve.

Ivan, My Father

At the age of thirteen my father was enlisted in the St. Petersburg Cadet Corps, part of a system of elite military schools on the Prussian model. The one in St. Petersburg, a naval school, was the first cadet corps in Russia, established in 1731.

I remember only a few stories told by Father about his school days. One of his classmates was Alexander Kolchak,[15] who later became an admiral and a famous Arctic explorer, before heading the breakaway White Russian government in Siberia in 1920. In the cadet corps Father competed with Kolchak for the title of fastest man up the mast. Father reached the top first but had to catch his breath, and Kolchak was the first back on the deck.

When their graduation was approaching, it became known that the ten best students would get a round-the-world trip as a graduation present. Father's grades were very good, except for "behavior," which was mediocre at best. However, this could have been overlooked if his boat, of which he was coxswain, finished near the top in the sculling races.

Just before the beginning of the races, it became known that a Grand Duke, a member of the Royal family, would take part in the races, and the cadets were told to let him win. It seemed quite unfair to the cadets, some of whom agreed among themselves that they would row as best they could, and if they were ahead of the Grand Duke near the finish line, they would all stop just short of it, lift their oars in a salute, and let him pass them – which was indeed what they did. Unfortunately, this was taken as an intentional affront to royalty, and to punish them, the Academy's administration reduced the behavior grades of all the coxswains on the sculls that participated in this demonstration. So Father did not get to go round the world.

Father graduated on September 20, 1893 with the rank of naval cadet, was assigned to one of the sailing vessels of the Russian navy, and went to sea. I think that this was a very important part of my father's character formation, and his vivid stories of life at sea, with its dangers and adventures, certainly influenced my brother Sergey's imagination as well.

Father sailed both in the interior of Russia and in foreign seas until 1899, when after spending a whole night on watch in a cold rain, he came down with rheumatic fever, which affected his heart. At the age of twenty-four he was forced to leave active duty and become a reservist.

His life had been planned around naval service, and now it took some soul-searching, and consultation with friends and relatives, before he could decide what to do instead. He chose to study engineering, having had good training in technical subjects in the cadet corps. Metallurgy and mining specialists were particularly needed in Russia then, so he settled on studying at a well-known industrial mining school in Mons, Belgium, where he could obtain a diploma in a short time. He had no funds, so he asked his older sister Ekaterina and her husband, the architect Evgenii Cavos, for a loan. Cavos gave him the money and said the words that Father always remembered as the most encouraging advice of his youth: "Go ahead, jump! If you break your leg, we'll fix it!"

In Belgium he lived like any other native student. While he worked on tedious drawings, his Belgian roommate used to sing arias from many French operas, and to the end of his days Father remembered in French arias from Gounod's *Faust*, Bizet's *Carmen*, and others, as they were rendered at Mons by his musical friend.

Before graduating, Father contracted a troubling eye infection, which blinded him for some time. He changed his concentration to electrical engineering, which required less reading, and found someone to read aloud to him to prepare for examinations. In 1901 he passed with honors, and graduated with a diploma as an electrical engineer.

Upon his return to Russia later that year Father worked on the construction of an electrical streetcar line and a power station in St.

Petersburg. Before that time the local streetcars went on rails, but were pulled by horses; I remember still seeing the old horse-drawn cars in 1914 when we went to St. Petersburg.

Once the construction was over, Father did not want to continue working for the streetcar system, so he found a position in Kerch, on the Azov Sea, at the construction of an electric station. The engineer whom Father was to replace met him at the station, having just come from church after performing a penance. This was the seventh penance to which he had been sentenced, each time because one of the men working for him had been killed by accidental electrocution. Father immediately called together all the employees and gave them instructions on the safety precautions around live wires, and on artificial respiration in case of a shock.

As it turned out, Father himself was the first one to benefit from these instructions, for while showing the distribution panel at the station to some visitors, his left hand behind his back as it was supposed to be, Father turned and brushed the panel with his elbow, thus closing the circuit. According to his previous instructions, the men switched the power off immediately, saving his life. During his administration there were no cases of accidental electrocution.

In 1904 Father, now in somewhat better health, returned to the navy as a navigator second class, and was assigned to the imperial yacht *Tsarevna* (Princess), one of six royal yachts used within Russia's domestic waterways. Father enjoyed telling us about his encounters with royalty while sailing on that ship. When Tsar Nicholas II was aboard he dined with the officers, and as a newly appointed officer, Father was seated next to the Tsar. He noticed that while all the officers were served one kind of wine, Nicholas had a special bottle set in front of him. Father stared at the label trying to find out just what it was, and the Tsar noticed this. "Would you like to try it?" he asked the embarrassed young officer. Father made his flustered excuses.

Father also sailed as an officer on the larger royal yacht, *Standart*, used in international waters. The royalty of other nations visited this ship and Father remembered once catching the Queen of Denmark as she fell down the stairs, and shaking hands with Kaiser

Wilhelm II, of the famous mustache, when all the officers lined up on the deck to greet him.

In the summer of 1904 the *Tsarevna* was at the dock in Petersburg. Empress Alexandra was about to give birth to her fifth child. A fast and nimble officer, Father was sent up the mast to watch for a signal from the palace that would tell whether a boy or a girl was born. He was then supposed to have the men fire the salute: 100 salvos for a girl or 101 salvos for a boy. After four daughters, the Tsar and the whole country were hoping for a male heir to the Russian throne. In his excitement at the news of a boy, Father was afraid of confusing the count, but the cannons fired the correct 101 times. The new-born boy was Alexis, the youngest child and only son of Nicholas II, the boy whose hemophilia led to Rasputin's disastrous influence on later events in Russia. Alexis was shot with the rest of the family after the Bolshevik revolution.

Earlier in 1904, Japanese armed vessels had attacked Russian armed vessels in the harbor of Port Arthur, built by the Russians on Chinese territory. This created a great patriotic response in Russia, and by the end of the year, war was in progress. The Russian Baltic fleet was to be sent by a roundabout route to the Far East; Father wanted to take part in the naval campaign and applied for a transfer to the fleet, but the Admiral refused to grant it to him, on the grounds that he was already "an officer on the Emperor's yacht, which is a great honor."

Father was deeply upset by the fact that in the Admiral's eyes, service on the Emperor's recreational yacht was more important than defending the country. He resigned from the navy on January 3, 1905 for "health reasons," as the Admiral advised him to do. He was lucky, in spite of himself, for in May 1905 the antiquated Russian fleet was annihilated in the battle of Tsushima Straits and many of Father's naval school classmates perished.

After leaving the navy, Father returned to his engineering profession. He was offered a position in the Urals, at Nadezhdensky Zavod (now renamed Serov), a small mill town connected to the main railroad by a narrow-gauge railway, where he was to take charge of the construction of an electric power station. Prior to going to a place where many of the country people were illiterate, he wanted to produce a good poster that would warn people about the danger of electric shock. Existing posters usually showed a skull and crossed bones of very poor artistic quality, and were not nearly frightening enough to suit Father. He knew that a group of well-known artists gathered weekly at the studio of his artist sister, Ekaterina Cavos, to paint a common subject, and so he went there on the day and suggested that they all try their hand at creating an appropriate poster.

Each of them painted one, and Father then made a composite poster, using elements from every painting. The result was a skull with lightning entering the left eye socket and emerging below on the right, with crossed bones below the skull completing the picture – not very original, but very well drawn. Father took this to a lithographer to draw it on stone, and had a number of posters printed to take with him. He left the stone with the lithographer for safekeeping. Months later, when he returned from the Urals, he discovered his posters all over St. Petersburg: it turned out that the lithographer had printed and sold them in large quantities. That particular "danger" poster became universally used in Russia, and appears in textbooks on electrical installations, but no one knows that it was designed by famous artists. Father was always quite proud of his contribution to that familiar image.

When Father arrived at the mill town he rented a room and started work on the construction. At first everything went smoothly. With his gregarious and friendly nature he got along well with the rest of the staff and the workers. But 1905 was a year of great unrest among the populace of Russia. After "Bloody Sunday" there were protests, demonstrations, and strikes throughout the country, forcing the Tsar to make some concessions; in his Manifesto of October 17, 1905 he agreed to have a popularly elected Duma with real legislative functions.[16] During the entire previous year workers' organizations had operated actively in many mill towns, and at Nadezhdensky Zavod they achieved a number of improvements in the working and living conditions of the workers. Their workday was reduced from twelve to eleven and a half hours, medical care was extended to their families, and a worker's hall was created, with a library, newspaper subscriptions, and a tearoom. Father sympathized with all these improvements, and apparently had friendly relations with some of the labor organizers, although the administration itself resisted such activities whenever it could. The police watched warily as demonstrators carried signs with slogans like "Down with monarchy, long live the constitution!" Demands for an eight-hour workday were frequently heard.

Inevitably there were many conservative workers who viewed with suspicion the new achievements of the labor organizers. When the first rumors of the Tsar's Manifesto arrived, the conservatives did not believe them. To verify the news they even went to church officials, whose answer was "We'll believe it when we see it." It took some days before a copy arrived, and in the meantime tension between the two groups of workers continued, with several violent confrontations.

A riot and an anti-Jewish pogrom followed, several labor organizers were killed and others badly beaten up, and the workers' hall, tearoom, and library were demolished. A special train was ordered for people trying to escape the violence, but a furious mob arrived at the station before the train left. Father was there seeing off the family of a Jewish colleague, when the rioters began to pull people off the train. Father tried to defend the victims against the mob, so the mob attacked him too. He had an explosive temper and fought back, striking attackers with his cane. This enraged them still further.

Father's galoshes were brought back to his landlady with the words, "This is all that is left of Zarudny!" But Father was soon carried in by friends: unconscious, bruised and bloodied, but alive. Meanwhile, some of the attackers gathered outside the house, demanding their prey. It was then that the police intervened and arrested Father for "disturbance of the peace," perhaps as a pretext to place him in protective custody. Hardly able to walk, he was taken to the next town and placed in solitary confinement in the local prison.

Father asked his friends to bring him a sketchbook, pencils, and a comfortable chair, for he still suffered from the vicious beating.

The prison allowed him what he asked for – at that time the attitude of prison officials towards their well-born prisoners was usually deferential – and while he remained there, Father filled the sketchbook with various views of his cell. It took some time for his appeals to reach the capital, but eventually an executive order came to release him immediately. He was not tried on any charge.

While he was in prison his arthritis and eye problems flared up, and his back hurt so badly that he could not walk. When released, he moved into a hotel and sent telegrams to his sister Ekaterina in St. Petersburg, asking her to come get him. It took her several days of travel to reach him, but finally she arrived with a doctor and took Father back to Petersburg, where she nursed him until he recovered.

In Petersburg Father was met with great warmth by his family and friends as a hero who had endured unjust treatment from the authorities while defending helpless victims. His sketchbook was passed from hand to hand. My mother's father, Pavel Brullov, was one of those artists who painted at the weekly gatherings in my aunt's studio, and it was there that my mother met my father, as Ekaterina's brother Ivan. She saw his prison sketchbook and almost envied him for suffering while protesting injustice. It was there too that she fell in love with him.

I think this episode at Nadezhdensky Zavod had a tremendous influence not only on Father's health but on his outlook. He had experienced for himself the cruelty of a mob easily swayed by propaganda and attacking its own benefactors. He never lost his compassion for simple people, but he stopped idealizing them. I think it also influenced the thinking of my mother, mitigating her idealism.

Father had simply been trying to save an innocent family from a mob, not cure the ills of society. Mother also would come to the defense of an unjustly treated person, but beyond that she saw the larger problem of an unjust system and wanted to change it. They suited each other admirably, but she had the more analytical mind, and always sought a general solution to a systemic problem, while

Mother, 1910
(Elena Brullova Zarudnaya)

Ekaterina Zarudnaya Cavos, 1915

he was more concerned with the particular instance. As I read stories together with Mother, about the tragedy of a drunken peasant for instance, she taught me to look not only at the peasant's despair but also at the cause of it – the helpless frustration of a person struggling in an unjust society. She seemed always to be battling against windmills, while Father was likely to assume that such battles were nearly hopeless, and looked instead for specific opportunities to help effectively. Like his own father, he believed in the possibility of fair laws and their proper implementation. And he would never jeopardize the safety of his family and children.

[1]   Karl Brullov (1799-1852) was perhaps the first Russian painter of international standing. For a discussion of his work see Galina Leontyeva, *Karl Briullov: The Painter of Russian Romanticism* (Bournemouth, England, 1996), which includes a portrait by Karl of his brother Alexander (1798-1877).

[2]   The Itinerants (Peredvizhniki – "Community of Itinerant Artistic Exhibitions"), started in 1870, were a large group of Russian artists who renounced the old academic principles of art and turned to more democratic ideals and to a more realistic style of art.

[3]   Bestuzhev Courses was the unofficial name of the first Russian higher educational institution for women, after the name of their founder, K. N. Bestuzhev-Ryumin. The courses were opened in St. Petersburg in 1878.

[4]   Karl Kautsky (1854-1938): one of the leaders and main ideologists of the German Social Democrats.

[5]   Vladimir Soloviev (1853-1900): a famous Russian philosopher and lector at Moscow University; poet and author of many books.

[6]   Nikolai Berdyaev (1874-1948): religious philosopher and a strong opponent of Marxism and communism. In 1922 he was sent out of Russia with several other important Russian philosophers aboard the so-called "philosophers' ship," and then lived in Paris. Founder of the religious-philosophical magazine *Put* (The Way).

[7]   Dmitri Merezhkovsky (1866-1941): philosopher, writer, and critic; author of many historical novels and plays; one of the founders of the "decadent" movement in Russia. In 1920 he emigrated to France.

[8]   Zinaida Gippius (1869-1945): writer and poet, one of the ideologists of the "decadents" in Russia.

[9] Alexander Blok (1880-1921): one of the greatest Russian poets of the twentieth century.

[10] Ivan Mikhailovich Grevs (1860-1941): historian, professor of Bestuzhev courses and at St. Petersburg University. A specialist in ancient Rome, he often took his students on his famous summer tours to Italy.

[11] Lev Trotsky (Lev Davidovich Bronstein, 1879-1940): one of the leaders of the Russian revolution and terror; later a great opponent of Stalin. He was killed in exile in Mexico by the order of Stalin.

[12] Cesare di Beccaria (1738-1794): Italian jurist.

[13] Maria (1860-1942) married Professor Grevs and died during the siege of Leningrad.

Ekaterina (1861-1917), an artist, married the architect Evgenii C. Cavos.

Alexander (1863-1934), a lawyer (see Chapters 2 and 18).

Anastasia, a teacher, died in a nursing home in the twenties.

Sergey (1866-98): see following note.

Zoya (1867-1942) acted as her brother Alexander's secretary; she died during the siege of Leningrad.

Varvara (1872-1940s) married the architect Lisovsky.

Ivan (1875-1933), my father.

[14] Sergey Zarudny (Father's brother) was arrested in April 1887 as a person connected to the assassination of Alexander II on March 1. In May 1887 Sergey was sent to his father's estate to stay there under house arrest until further orders. Left alone on the country estate after his father's departure, Sergey fell in love and married a peasant girl who was his mother's helper, without asking his parents' consent. Soon after that, in July 1888, he was exiled to Siberia where he went with his wife and small child. After his mother's appeals he was allowed to stay in Siberia in the large city of Omsk. He spent almost four years there. From 1892, after being allowed to leave Siberia, he worked as a bookkeeper in a bank in Nizhni Novgorod. There he was put into prison for several months for "offending an official," and while in prison he developed tuberculosis. Hoping to improve his health, he moved with his family to Crimea in 1896 and died there in 1898, leaving his wife with five children. One of his grandsons, Nikolai N. Zarudny, now in Moscow, has collected much information about the Zarudny family and their fates.

[15] Alexander Vasilievich Kolchak (1874-1920): see below, Chapters 7-12.

[16] The Manifesto of October 17, 1905 also proclaimed freedom of assembly and freedom of speech.

2

The Children

Margarita

I was born in St. Petersburg on November 11, 1908[1] and was named after my maternal grandmother, Margarita. Once when I was sick and my mother was carrying me, walking back and forth to stop my crying, Father heard her chanting to comfort me: "milya, malya, mulya." The first two words were abbreviations of *milaya* (dear one) and *malenkaya* (little one), and the third was just a nonsense word added for rhythm. After that Father called me Mulya.

My parents settled in an apartment on Vassilievskii Ostrov in Petersburg. There was a high diapering table there, thickly upholstered in padded white oilcloth. All Father's brothers and sisters and Father himself had been diapered on that table – all of them tightly swaddled, as was I. I remember that table very clearly: after me it was used for my brother and all of my sisters except the youngest.

My nurse Anastasia was a woman of considerable experience: she had been Mother's wet nurse. When Mother was born, her own mother had tuberculosis, and nursing the baby was out of the question for her. It was usual at that time to find a strong and healthy peasant girl who had recently had a baby to be a wet nurse. In her childhood Anastasia was a serf, and after the emancipation of the serfs she had moved from her village to the city and worked in a laundry under very hard conditions. She gave birth to an illegitimate child, who was adopted by another family, and she became a wet nurse for my mother.

After Mother was weaned, Anastasia remained part of Grandfather's household, taking care of his younger children. When the children grew, she helped in the kitchen and became quite skilled as a cook. When my parents were married Anastasia moved in with them as their cook, bringing with her the traditional recipes of the Brullov family. Father told us that when he and Mother would go out for dinner, they would tell Anastasia afterwards about the dishes they ate, and the next day she would produce the same dish for them. This was pretty good for a completely illiterate person, with no written recipes to guide her! As far as I know, Mother herself knew absolutely nothing about cooking.

When I was born Anastasia became my nurse. Later she took care of my brother and all my sisters one after another, and she remained with our family until 1935. We called her Nanny ("Nyanya" in Russian), but Father and others always called her respectfully by her first name and patronymic, Anastasia Pavlovna. Her own daughter, who was brought up elsewhere, occasionally corresponded with Nanny, but we never met her. It was an early duty for us, when we learned to write, to take Nanny's dictation of her letters, which always started: "Dear daughter, how are you? I am well and wish you the same."

Sergey

From the scant notes about this period that my father left, I can surmise that Mother again had problems with the police, which forced them to move out of St. Petersburg. Apparently Mother was banned from St. Petersburg for three years. First they moved to a *dacha*, a country house, and then to the Brullovs' villa in Pavlovsk. On June 28 (July 10), 1910 a new baby was born – a boy named Sergey, after Father's father, but called Seryozha by all of us.[2] I think Mother was very happy to have a boy – she always felt that women did not have full rights as citizens, and she hated to think what kind of frustrations lay ahead for her daughters.

Father soon received a position in Tula, at the munitions factory: Tula has long been famous for its manufacture of arms and samovars. Father thus returned to his original interest, metallurgy, but when I was three and Seryozha was one a quarrel of some kind with the administration of the factory forced Father to leave. This is my earliest memory, very vague – some sort of noise and shouting. Mother was still not allowed in St. Petersburg, so the family went to stay at Ivanovo, the Brullovs' estate south-east of Moscow.

Father must have gone to St. Petersburg to look for new

employment, because I do not remember him being there at all. I remember a large house with the kitchen downstairs and wide stairs to the second floor. Upstairs there was a spacious room, with a big round brick stove in the corner covered with black painted metal reaching almost to the ceiling. But the most remarkable place to me was the little house nearby, where an old retired cook of my grandfather's lived.

She was old and weak and was attended by a young girl. I remember so well the room where she spent all her time: the high narrow bedstead with a featherbed on it, the icon with its icon lamp in the corner, a chair and a small table on which the girl served her meals. The old woman was very heavy and could hardly move, but there was something about her that attracted me. I loved to slip away from the house to go visiting her, although this sometimes caused great anxiety at home, since no one knew where I was.

While we lived at Ivanovo an important new member joined our household – Manya. As the family grew bigger, Mother began to realize that Nanny needed help. From the time when she taught at the village school, Mother remembered a healthy and intelligent young girl, whose stuttering created problems for her there. The girl's parents had large apple orchards and exported apples to a number of cities; they knew Mother and they sent their daughter to school, which was rather unusual at that time. Her full name was Maria Kuzminichna Yurkina, but she was always called Manya.

By now Manya was fifteen years old and helped her illiterate grandfather with the accounting in his apple trade. Mother asked her to come live with us and help with the children and housekeeping as a second maid. As there were other children in their family, Manya's parents let her go. She joined our household and became part of our family for the rest of her life.

So now we were six: Mother, Father, me, my brother Seryozha, Nanny, who took care of the youngest and cooked, and Manya. I think that I must have been very jealous of Seryozha. He was a boy and I knew that this pleased Mother. So much attention was paid to him! I remember him crawling among the ashes of the big black stove upstairs. He was eating the ashes and his mouth was black

Father, 1912
(Ivan Sergeyevich Zarudny)

Manya, 1912
(Maria Kuzminichna Yourkina)

with charcoal. I think I called someone to take care of him, as I was always made to feel responsible for him, but I do not remember a sense of worry or even pity – rather a sense of disdain, or even disgust, for the "stupid baby." Now I wonder whether in fact my forays into the surrounding country or my visits to the old cook were not a way of making Mother worry about me instead.

At Libava

I don't remember at what time of the year we moved from Ivanovo to Libava (now called Liepaja) in Latvia, which at that time was part of Imperial Russia. Father was appointed manager of the metal processing section of a factory that made strings for the famous German Becker pianos that were manufactured in St. Petersburg.

Libava was a small city on the shores of the Baltic Sea. It had clean, neatly paved streets with sidewalks, elegant shops, and modern brick apartment buildings in the center. Streetcars ran in the streets. One could see old stone gothic churches, synagogues, and narrow streets that we, as children, never visited. Libava had a European character and a mixed population of Latvians, Germans, and Russians. Just outside the city stood a Russian naval fort.

I remember the beautiful sandy beach with little straw or canvas cabins in which we could change into bathing suits, and a kind of restaurant where one could buy lemonade. There was a long line of seaweed piles at the edge of the water. We looked there for little pieces of amber and found many. Occasionally a fishing boat would come very close to the beach and we could see nets being hoisted, full of fluttering silver herring.

We were always taken to the beach under the supervision of a grown-up, often with picnic supplies. We bathed in the shallow water near the shore. I wore a blue and white striped bathing suit with little pants and short sleeves, all in one piece. It came rather high at the neck, but it was much more open than the bathing suits of young women.

Our first apartment was at the center of the city, but soon we moved to a more spacious one near Father's factory. It had a glassed-in balcony where we often ate. Some of our furniture had come out from St. Petersburg, and a number of pictures, mostly painted by my grandfather, hung on the walls. There were polished mahogany tables in the living room and chairs with bright green plush seats and carved polished arms, and a small desk at which Mother often sat reading. In Mother's study there was an enormous Turkish sofa, the pride of my parents and a joy for the children, with soft pillows for the back and long bolsters for the arms. It was covered with something that resembled rather crude needlepoint. Two adults could sleep on it with their heads on the opposite ends of the sofa and their feet just touching in the middle. On that sofa we built houses with chairs and pillows, we jumped on it, and we played on it with our dachshund, which liked to lie there curled up. In short, it was our best place to play.

There was a big field on one side of the house, and a highway leading to the naval port in front of it. The factory where Father worked was a short walking distance from the house.

The life of the family assumed a different, more urban, character. Now we had a Latvian cook, Susanna (Zuza). She did all the cooking and all the marketing, so my Mother never even walked into the kitchen. Zuza was extremely neat: she would not leave the kitchen at the end of the day without polishing all the brass pans that hung on the walls. She shared the servants' quarters with Manya, and they became good friends. After a while, Manya learned some Latvian from Zuza, so that now there was another language in which adults could communicate without the children understanding. My parents always used French for that purpose.

Father and Mother occasionally went out in the evenings. I loved to see Mother all dressed up in her beautiful black velvet dress, with her hair piled up high on her head and wearing some very pleasant fragrance that I could smell when she bent down to kiss me good-night before leaving. I also loved to see Manya all dressed up when she was going out. She was very pretty, I thought, in her dark red dress with high collar and amber beads.

At that time I was usually called Rita, short for Margarita. But now I heard this word constantly when Manya and Zuza spoke

Latvian. It bothered me: were they talking about me? When I finally asked them why they were talking about me all the time, they said that in Latvian *rita* means "tomorrow." I then announced that my name was Mulya, and from that time on I refused to answer if anyone called me Rita. I was very firm about that, and nobody called me Rita anymore.

I was obviously a headstrong girl, and sometimes got into trouble. One day I was walking with Nanny and Seryozha on the sidewalk of a wide street in the city. Nanny was pushing Seryozha's carriage, a kind that I have never seen anywhere else: the small wooden chair was mounted on the axle between two large wheels with two long handles, like those of a wheelbarrow, so that the sitting child faced the person who was pushing the carriage. If that person were to let go of the handles, the child would fall out.

On this occasion I was walking next to Nanny, holding on to one of the carriage's handles. Suddenly I saw a girl I knew walking with her mother on the other side of the street, and I dropped my handle and rushed across the wide street with its streetcar tracks. The street was full of horse and carriage traffic, and poor Nanny was helpless to stop me, being unable to let go of the carriage without losing Seryozha. She called out to me in vain, and before my friend's bewildered mother could catch me I dashed back again to the other side. There was a streetcar moving on the tracks and I ran straight into its path. Amidst the screech of the wheels and the screams of bystanders, the streetcar stopped — almost touching me. The passengers piled out, and someone grabbed me and led me back to Nanny, scolding her for letting me go. But I felt like a hero. I don't remember any remorse at all, perhaps just a little guilt about getting Nanny in trouble.

If guests arrived, it was usually in the evening. Before going to bed we might be allowed to come out to the living room to greet them: I with a quick curtsy, or *kniksen*, and Seryozha clicking his heels. I remember how once I embarrassed my Mother when a friend visited her in the afternoon. I liked to undress Seryozha when we played alone, so on that occasion I brought him in stark naked to greet the adults. Another time my misdeed was much more serious.

I decided to play doctor, so I undressed Seryozha, put him on the Turkish sofa, and proceeded to treat him by pouring cod liver oil all over him. I was sure it did not do *him* any harm, but the adults thought differently about the sofa; no cleaning efforts could get rid of the smell, and it had to be reupholstered.

Once we went to visit the estate of a "baron" (I cannot remember his name) just outside Libava. I was dressed in a white dress with eyelets, over a pink silk slip with a wide silk sash tied into a big bow behind: I think I still have that sash. I was carefully instructed in good manners, and felt pretty confident. While the grown-ups took their tea, I was offered a walk with the maid to the pigpen, to look at some newly-born piglets. The pigpen was a model of neatness, the pride of the owner. The big mother pig was lying on her side nursing her many little piglets, who looked so clean and so inviting that I could not resist picking up one. It did not prove to be as clean as I thought, and my pretty party dress was badly soiled. I remember a terrible sense of embarrassment when I had to return to the company dressed only in my pink slip, while the maid washed and ironed my dress.

Our apartment windows opened on the inner court, facing the windows of other apartments. In one of them lived a little girl who was my friend. One rainy day I wanted to invite my friend to play but did not know how to do it. So Father suggested that we could communicate across the inside yard. He took sheets of white writing paper and carefully drew a single large letter on each; as I watched, fascinated, he put one of the sheets in each windowpane to form a message of invitation. I don't remember if the girl did come as asked, but I do remember that her mother responded to this message, and that she, as well as I, thought it a very ingenious form of communication.

Some cousins visited us during their school vacations. They were older and much more fun to play with than Seryozha, though, when he could, Seryozha would join us. I watched in awe my nine-year-old cousin, a student in the Ballet School of St. Petersburg, do her exercises every morning, even though she was on vacation. Grandfather Pavel Brullov too came to stay with us during the summer, with his paints, brushes, and palettes, setting up his easel outside as we watched, and painting most of the day. Alexander Zarudny (my Uncle Sasha) also visited, between his appearances in the court in Kiev during the Beilis trial.

Uncle Sasha, Father's older brother, was a lawyer. He lived in St. Petersburg, but spent most of his time traveling all over Russia, defending people involved in political cases. This time he was one of the defense attorneys in the famous trial of Mendel Beilis. Beilis, a Jew, had worked as a watchman at a brick factory in Kiev, where it was his duty to chase away the boys who – taking a shortcut through the factory yard – often disturbed the piled stacks of bricks. The dead body of one of these boys was found in a cave near the city with a number of peculiar wounds. The local anti-Semitic groups spread a rumor that some Jews had killed him in order to obtain a Gentile boy's blood for some ritual purpose. They accused Beilis and he was arrested. The absurdity of the accusation attracted the attention of the entire world, and in Russia several of the most distinguished liberal attorneys volunteered their services for his defense. Uncle Sasha was one of the three principal defenders.

At Kiev demonstrations by anti-Semitic groups greeted the trial; the infamous "Protocols of the Elders of Zion" were reprinted and distributed all around the country, and the government itself and many Russian churchmen supported the prosecution. In his rousing speech to the jury Uncle Sasha said, "Gentlemen of the jury! It is not Mendel Beilis but Russian justice that is on trial here!" Beilis was finally acquitted, in what turned out to be the last case of "ritual murder" ever tried. He left Russia, immigrated to the United States, published a well-known autobiography, and died in Boston. Years after the trial the real murderers were found: they were the parents of a friend of the murdered boy. Thieves and burglars, they were afraid that the boy knew too much about their activities.

The adults in my family avidly followed the trial, appalled at the position taken by the government. The children, however, were never invited to hear the adults' discussions and I learned about it only when I was a student in Harbin, Manchuria, and Uncle Sasha came there to lecture about it.

Our apartment house was a short walk from the steel mill where my father worked. He often took me there to see the pouring of the molten steel from the furnaces and its processing. I was fascinated by the stream of liquid, bright as the sun, which you could look at only through a dark blue glass held in a wooden frame. The huge rollers were fed with enormous lumps of red-hot steel on one side, and on the other a thin sheet of metal emerged, moving along a long flat table, or else a thin wire, which was stretched a long way and wound up on enormous spools. It was like an illustrated fairy tale of magical transformations.

Elena

My sister Elena was born on the day after Christmas 1912, old style – January 8, 1913 by the new calendar. I do not recall either that Christmas or the event of her birth. There must have been several very anxious days, because Mother, as I learned later, had hurt herself lifting Seryozha, and Elena was born two months early. The children were kept away from Mother and the baby, since the baby was not expected to survive and Mother was very sick. The household was totally preoccupied with their care, and a local doctor visited Mother daily. Nanny and even Manya spent much of their time with the tiny baby, who was wrapped in cotton, constantly tended, and kept warm. The room in which she was kept was full of mysterious equipment, and was off limits for the children.

One day as Manya was carrying a burning alcohol lamp used to warm something for the baby, our cat ran into her path; Manya stumbled and the alcohol lamp fell on the cat. The poor cat, with flames on its back, dashed in fright under the window drapes, with Manya trying desperately to catch it, for fear it might run into the baby's room and set her basket alight. The drapes caught fire, and I remember the commotion, the panicky screams, and the pitiful howls of the cat. Somehow the cat was caught and the flames put out, but Manya was sick with nervous shock for several days afterwards, and the drapes had to be replaced.

The attending doctor reported that Mother would not be able to have any more children, which was sad news for both my parents, who desired many more. The baby was named Elena after our mother; she was and is always called Lena (pronounced L'yena) by family and close friends. She became stronger, and after a while passed into Nanny's care. Mother too soon recovered, and the doctor's prediction turned out to be wrong.

I was now approaching five and Seryozha three, and my parents began to think about our education. Mother taught me some drawing, but there was a more serious question: which foreign language should we learn? French was the language of society, and with their liberal tendencies my parents did not feel it was a proper language for us to start with. So the choice was between English and German. I protested against English, because for some reason I visualized an English governess as a stiff, strict "blue stocking." My parents did not insist, since German was the language of a large part of the population of Libava and it was probably much easier to find a German governess there. My mother did not speak English herself.

My first governess, Frau Walle, was middle-aged and very imposing, and I felt quite intimidated by her. She started speaking German to us from the very beginning; I remember her walking around the room, pointing at different objects and naming them. She walked with us along the streets, corrected our manners, and took us to the beach, but I never warmed to her. Seryozha was indifferent as well, and Frau Walle soon left us – I don't know just why. Our second governess was the young, cheerful, and very warm Fräulein Marie. I loved her at once, and German now came very easily to me. We walked, played, sang songs, and simply had fun.

Little Lena was still in Nanny's charge, but Seryozha and I felt that we were "big children." Some lessons began, mostly in drawing. At just four, Seryozha exhibited a remarkable talent for drawing, already depicting whatever he chose quite recognizably. As for me, I was given pencil-sketching books, ordinary soft pencils, and instructions to draw simple objects from observation. I was also taught some rules of shadow and perspective. Mother showed me, for example, how to make objects seem round by shading them: she herself painted in oils, and I remember her very nice portrait of Nanny with her peasant face, wrinkles, and brushed-back hair. That hung for some years in Father's study, together with other paintings by Mother.

But Seryozha began to be very sure of himself after making a large drawing of the face of one of our parents' friends. It was a big round face, with sleek black hair parted on the side, eyeglasses, and a small mustache, and everyone at once recognized who it was. Now Seryozha claimed that he drew better than I. What arrogance! After all, I was almost six and he was only four, and I had had instruction. So we decided on a contest: we would each draw a bucket. I put all my skill into shading a trapezoid with a bow handle above. Seryozha, of course, did not know how to shade, but he drew an oval for the top, two slanted lines for the sides and a half oval below with the same bow of a handle as I. I was mortified. I had to admit that his was better, and from that moment on I stopped drawing for fun.

All through the winter of 1913-14 I had bronchitis and, as was customary then, was kept in bed for months. Mother paid a lot of attention to me, so that I don't remember being too unhappy about it, but I definitely became weaker during that winter. During the first part of the summer I recuperated, spending time on the beach, and wading in the warm shallow waters near the shore. I was not aware that a complete change in our way of life, and everyone else's, was rapidly approaching.

---

[1]   In this book some of the dates before 1918 are given in two versions: according to the old (Julian) calendar, which was used as the official calendar in pre-revolutionary Russia, and the new (Gregorian) calendar. A date on the old calendar occurs thirteen days later than on the new one. For example, November 11, 1908 in Russia was already November 24, 1908 in London or New York. The old calendar was in official use in Russia until 1918; it is still used there by the Russian Orthodox Church.

[2]   Russians use a variety of nicknames. Nearly every name has at least one or two nicknames: Ivan – Vanya, Elena – Lena, Margarita – Rita, Maria – Masha or Manya, Sergey – Seryozha, Tatiana – Tanya, Ekaterina – Katya, Evdokia – Dunya, Alexander – Sasha, Lidia – Lida, Lyubov – Lyuba, Evgenii – Zhenia, Pavel – Pavlik, Varvara – Varya.

They also use various endearing endings: Vera – Verochka, Margarita – Margaritochka, Manya – Manechka, Anna – Annushka, etc.

Besides the first name (always only one) they also use a patronymic, which is the first name of the father with an added ending: *-ovich* or *-evich* for boys, and *-ovna* or *-evna* for girls. Thus Elena daughter of Pavel is Elena Pavlovna, Ivan son of Sergey is Ivan Sergeyevich. Both first and patronymic names together are used as a sign of respect. The younger people thus address the elders, and the not too familiar adults use this form when addressing each other.

3

War

World War I began on July 28, 1914. The mood in Libava was tense, for a naval attack from the Baltic was expected, and the fort near us was on alert. Men in uniforms walked the streets. Seryozha, dressed in his sailor suit, exhibited a lot of patriotism. He saluted everybody in uniform, and refused to speak German, "the language of our enemies." This upset me because I loved Fräulein Marie, and could not think of her as an "enemy."

Family life was maintained on an even keel, though the adults anxiously read the newspapers, and correspondence with Petersburg became quite intense. Father's factory changed from producing piano strings to making barbed wire for military fortifications.

To relieve the tension Father used to fly kites in a nearby field. Once he made a very large kite out of cloth with a wooden frame. It was about five feet tall and could fly so high that you could not even see the string attached to it. Father would amuse us by encircling the tail-end of the string with a piece of paper, which would then slide all the way up to the kite itself, as we watched. He called this "sending a telegram," and it was great fun.

But soon we saw many people had gathered along the road, watching our kite, with some agitation among them. The city police next appeared, asked Father a lot of questions, and then advised him not to fly kites any more, because doing so created disturbing rumors. It turned out that some people suspected that Father was using the kite to communicate with the Germans, or even that it was really a German airplane. Aircraft had never been used in war before, and most people had never seen one.

The Germans started to bombard the city from ships at sea. I don't know what damage they did or how far into the city the bombardment reached, but it rattled the dishes on the table set for dinner on our balcony. We children found all this exciting. The adults must have been anxious, but concealed it in order not to worry us. At its very beginning, no one knew how different from previous wars this one would be as a result of the powerful new cannons, machine guns, airplanes, radio communication, and even tanks, none of which had been used in previous European conflicts.

The Russians began to withdraw, and for a while abandoned the naval fort. But there did not seem to be any German army approaching Libava. That news quickly spread throughout the city, and we began to see a strange procession of people on the highway in front of our house, walking from the fort towards the city, carrying buckets of oil, furniture, and various objects taken from the fort. This lasted all day long and into the next day, when announcements on posters appeared, hung up all over the city, that anyone found in possession of property from the fort would be subject to martial law. Now we saw the procession reversed: hundreds of people marching with the same items from the city towards the fort, but not bothering to take them all the way back. For days afterward we saw the looted materials lying along our roadside, with nobody daring to touch them.

Several days later it became known that the German army was indeed approaching Libava, and the Russians began to prepare for evacuation, for it was assumed that the city would be occupied soon. Some of our possessions were already packed, but it was obvious that we could not take everything with us: the trains were overcrowded, and it was difficult to obtain passage even for people, let alone a great deal of baggage. Finally one night Father took Mother, Nanny, Manya, and the three children to the station and put us on the train for St. Petersburg, while he stayed behind to arrange the factory's affairs and to ship what he could of the rest of our belongings. But some remained in Libava long afterward.

I vaguely remember the crowded train, the high berths on which we had to sleep, and the excited, worried crowd of passengers, all fleeing the Germans. When we arrived in St. Petersburg it was crowded with refugees. Fortunately we had many relatives there, and were able to stay first with Mother's sister Lydia, and then with her brother Vadim. Father soon arrived, and now we were installed in a single big room of Uncle Vadim's apartment, with Manya and Nanny sleeping elsewhere in the apartment, probably in the servants' quarters.

The name of St. Petersburg had just been changed to Petrograd, a russified alternative, because Petersburg *sounded* German, though actually it had a Dutch origin and had been selected by Peter the Great himself. The fact that the present Tsarina, Alexandra Feodorovna, was German had fuelled rumors that the royal family was sympathetic to the enemy, so the change in the name of the capital was in fact a political move on the part of the government, to offset such suspicions. A fine was imposed on people who used the old name in public. I was proud that I remembered the new name better than the adults could, and that I was often able to correct them.

I remember only a few things about Petrograd. Once I was left in our room alone. I think that Mother had to take Seryozha to a doctor, and the baby Lena was being tended somewhere else. My parents were careful not to inconvenience Uncle Vadim's family, so I was told that the room would be locked on the outside and that I should be a good girl and not make any noise. They promised to return in a couple of hours. Just before they left we had been busy cutting out paper doilies, and the floor of the room was covered with innumerable tiny pieces of white paper. I remember thinking of how to reduce the tedium of waiting and deciding that picking up some of these pieces, one by one, would be a good way to fill up the time, and besides, it would be a real surprise for Mother. I spent all two hours picking up every scrap of paper until none remained on the floor. I learned two things I never forgot: that one should occupy oneself while waiting, with nothing else to do, and that a seemingly impossible task can be accomplished if one goes at it patiently and systematically.

Father had to look for another job, and Mother spent a lot of time with us. She loved her native city and wanted us to know and remember it. As we walked the streets with her she pointed out the famous statues and buildings. The statue of Peter the Great on his horse impressed me greatly: it seemed enormous to me when I played near it. Mother read me Pushkin's poem *The Bronze*

Horseman, and I could vividly imagine how this horse with its rider might thunder through the streets of Petersburg chasing poor mad Evgenii. The statue of Peter building a boat, and one of him saving a drowning sailor, gave me a different picture of him, and when I learned that he became sick and died after that rescue he became my hero. I remember being disappointed by the Winter Palace: I expected a castle, and what I saw was a long straight rectangular building whose only embellishments were sculptural relief on the front and numerous statues along the top of the roof, which I could not even see in any detail. The Tsar's gilded carriage, which passed us on the street with white horses pulling it, was more to my liking, and the old, horse-drawn streetcars, called *konki*, also amused me.

Only a few visits to relatives remain in my memory. One day we were invited to dinner by my mother's brother Boris. We sat at a long table covered with a white tablecloth. At the end of the dinner the maid came in with a whiskbroom and a little scoop to remove the crumbs from the table, but Uncle Boris stopped her. Evidently to amuse us children, and to the consternation of his wife, he brought in a pair of his pet white mice and let them run around on the table picking the crumbs up themselves. Seryozha and I found it very amusing, but I think the adults were shocked.

It may have been to retaliate for this surprise that my Father and Mother decided to play a trick on Uncle Boris. They went into his apartment when Boris and his wife were out, and pasted an irregular star of black paper on the beautiful mirror in the front hall, and then drew long lines from each point of the star with a piece of soap. When they had finished it looked just like a broken mirror. We all hid in the other room of the apartment, waiting for Uncle and his wife to return. Their maid was very agitated and begged my parents not to leave such a frightening sight on the wall. And I think she was right, because when Uncle Boris and his wife returned she almost fainted, and the way they scolded my father showed that they did not think it funny at all.

A number of times we visited Father's brother, Uncle Sasha, who was always a great deal of fun: he performed all kinds of magic tricks, alone or with his beautiful, big, black French poodle, who jumped through hoops and located hidden objects. Uncle Sasha's son, also called Seryozha, was about a year younger than my brother, and for some reason he became very attached to me, following me about like a puppy, repeating "Margaritochka!" (Dear little Margaret!), which quite annoyed me. His daughter, granddaughter, and even great-granddaughter still lived in St. Petersburg in 1995, when I met them all.

A visit with my father to his Aunt Dunya, Princess Golitzina, was memorable in a different way. She lived in an apartment with her maid. She was terribly old, it seemed to me, and her maid was almost as ancient as she. She was dressed in something dark with a lot of lace, with more lace on her head. Father had warned me to be very careful, because Aunt Dunya should not have to worry about a boisterous child running around her apartment, which was full of fragile things. After I greeted her with the usual curtsy I was allowed to walk about and look at these: innumerable statuettes, some in glass cabinets, music boxes, and other ornamental filigreed objects, all with special histories, all untouchable by me, but nonetheless fascinating. Our visit did not last long, but it left an indelible impression.

With the usual help of his brother-in-law Cavos, Father obtained a position directing a steel mill in a small town called Vyksa, southeast of Moscow. The nearest railroad station was in the provincial city of Murom; from there one traveled on about twenty miles by horse. Murom is built on the Oka River, a tributary that merges with the Volga at the city of Nizhni Novgorod (it was renamed Gorkii during the Soviet period), about one hundred miles north of Murom. The materials needed for the mill and its production were shipped in and out on river barges. A small electric station installed at the dam on the river supplied electricity.

There were several advantages for my parents in accepting a position in such a remote place. Being manager of the whole mill, my father would have more freedom in dealing with the personnel and in other aspects of his work. In addition, there was a larger salary, with a house, garden, horses, gardener, and coachman provided. The house was located in a special compound for the staff of the mill, which included a park maintained by the mill's funds, at Father's discretion. My parents could put up visitors for the long summer months, as if they were living on a family estate.

Mother, who was a member of the National Education Organization, was interested in schools for children and for adults, and looked forward to organizing an evening school for the adult workers and a children's summer program. She undertook this work as soon as we settled there. Mother planned for us to get our own education at home, which she thought she could carry out by herself, with the help of some tutors in foreign languages.

As usual, Father went on ahead to prepare the house for the family, and in the fall of 1914 Mother with Manya, Nanny, and we three children traveled by train to Moscow, where we changed for Murom. Father met us there with several horse carriages, and we arrived in Vyksa late in the evening, in the rain. The carriages had their protective curtains down, so we saw little of our new countryside on the way.

4

Vyksa, 1914-15

The Vyksa mill was one of a number of steel mills in the center of European Russia built between the end of the seventeenth century and the middle of the eighteenth. They were located near iron ore deposits, on the banks of navigable rivers, which were used for transportation before any railroads existed. The dams on the rivers and the wood and charcoal from the dense forests of the region, as well as the local deposits of turf, satisfied the mills' energy needs. The majority of the labor force consisted of serfs from nearby estates. The management, having available a work force that was tied to the land first by law and later by tradition, cared little for improving working conditions. When the railroad was built through Murom it bypassed Vyksa, and the rivers remained the connecting link to the markets.

After the emancipation of the serfs the struggle between labor and management of the mills intensified. Management shifted to foreign investors, who leased the land around the mills and mercilessly exploited the forests. By the time my father went to Vyksa the mills could no longer depend entirely upon wood for their fuel, and had to import oil using river barges.

The Vyksa mills were owned by a Corporation of sixteen members, of which the principal stockholder was a German family named Lessing. Russian subjects owned a very small portion of the stock, but among the latter was Mechislav Buinevich, a Pole by origin, and a mining engineer. At the beginning of the war the Lessings returned to Germany, so Buinevich became responsible for the overall operation of the Corporation's mills, including Vyksa.

Father's position was rather difficult: he was employed by the Corporation and was charged with the efficient and profitable management of the mills. But the workers were underpaid and working conditions were deplorable, especially in the mines, and this troubled him. In order to survive, many of the workers had to supplement their meager earnings with work in the fields, and by cultivating garden crops. As the war increased demands on the productivity of the mills, the labor force became increasingly restless.

Country Living

When we arrived in Vyksa, we found the house already fully furnished: some of it with our own furniture, which Father had rescued from Libava. The pictures were hung and the beds were made. To my great delight, one of the people who greeted us was Fräulein Marie. I had not seen her since we left Libava, and I did not know that Father had succeeded in getting her out. Anti-German sentiment was very strong, but Father felt confident that in this quiet and remote place she would be safe from both the police and the hostility of the local population. Still, we had to be careful.

Tired and sleepy, we were immediately put to bed. The next day we ran around investigating the house, the large garden, and the backyard. The house was big and sprawling, with many rooms. On the first floor, to the left of the entrance, was Father's study. On the right was the dining room, which opened into the large living room, with our own red mahogany furniture (the big Turkish sofa had been left in Libava, sadly) and Grandfather's pictures on the walls, and then came Mother's small study. It was here that Mother would spend many hours reading or working at her big desk. This was the room where we made Christmas tree decorations together, and where mother would fix various donated mechanical toys, replacing springs and painting them so that they could be used as Christmas presents for the workers' children, or at the orphanage.

The large, light corner room beyond mother's study was the children's room, with windows opening onto the garden. Fräulein Marie, Seryozha, and I had our beds there. It also had shelves for toys, a low table with small chairs, and chests of drawers, but even with all these furnishings there was still plenty of room to play. Our parents' bedroom was across the corridor, with the room for the baby and Nanny adjoining it. Lena, who was now just a year and a half old, slept there with Nanny until the next baby arrived.

A corridor ran through the whole house all the way to the front hall, interrupted only by the bathroom, with a toilet, a washstand, a big tub, and a special boiler for hot water, heated by wood. This was fired whenever someone planned to take a bath – once a week, for us children. Upstairs were several rooms, some of them with washstands. Manya had a room there, among several guestrooms and our future "classroom," and there was also some attic space. The kitchen wing, with its pantry and other service rooms, was at the side of the house, but this was generally off limits for us.

Our house was the largest house in the compound, which was surrounded by a low fence and had a gate at its entrance. Within the compound were the houses of the other managers of the mill, and a park for our use. Other houses in the compound had children too, whom we soon met, but I believe as a rule the workers' children were not allowed to enter the compound. After we finally settled in I cannot remember going out of our compound, and except for coming into Vyksa, and leaving our home later on journeys, we never even saw the river: it was not a part of our life, although it was a very important part of the existence of the village. The nearest town was Murom, where fairs were held and where some shopping could be done, but it took almost a day's travel by horse to reach it, so again we children never saw it except when passing through it to and from somewhere else.

Father also invited our Latvian cook Zuza to Vyksa. She was married, so he had to arrange some employment for her husband, and found him a position at the mill. I believe he was a carpenter. They lived nearby, and Zuza spent most of the day at our house. She had a helper, a local girl Annushka, who cleaned the kitchen and the floors in the house, and I think milked the cow and fed the chickens. The coachman looked after the horses, the carriages, and the winter sleighs, and also acted as a gardener.

The garden surrounding our house was quite large, with a row of maple trees along the fence, and acacia bushes. There were many flowerbeds, a vegetable garden, and a row of cold frames. A stable for horses was located in the backyard, and there were stalls for two cows, from which we got our milk. Chickens ran freely in the backyard, but we seldom walked into it, except maybe to give the horses lumps of sugar on the open palms of our hands. The horses with the carriage were brought to the front of the house whenever my parents went anywhere.

On our first walk to the park Father inspected the playground equipment, which was minimal. He asked me to raise myself on the parallel bars and was shocked when I could not. He immediately ordered a lot of gymnastic equipment for the park and had a trapeze hung in the children's room at home. Within a year I was like a monkey, climbing ropes, swinging upside down from the trapeze and the rings, and sometimes frightening my parents by my daring.

The war was far away, as was the political turmoil shaking the big cities. As a child, I was virtually unaware of these problems, and our stay in Vyksa remained for me the model of a perfectly balanced existence, through all the turmoil and uprootings of the following years.

ൠ

After waking at eight, dressing, washing, and braiding my hair into two pigtails with ribbon bows, I would go with Seryozha to the breakfast table. A simple breakfast and seeing Father off to the mill started our day. In summer we played in the garden if the weather was good; in the winter we took walks with Fräulein Marie, which I hated, because my feet were always so cold that I would return home in tears. Then the shoes would be taken off my blue and painful feet while I was crying, and Mother or Fräulein Marie would rub them with alcohol. Once they wrapped my feet with newspapers inside the shoes, but they froze even worse. This remained a real problem for me until we moved to Siberia. There we had no shoes, so we started wearing felt boots over feet wrapped in strips of old sheets, and my feet never froze any more.

Fräulein Marie sewed a complete wardrobe for my doll, and with a scroll saw and thin plywood she cut out a set of furniture for the doll's room. These pieces had a lace-like design, the drawers of the chest opened, and there was even a grand piano. It was a marvel to everyone who saw it, but I did not know how to play with it. Nonetheless I was very proud of it, and when children came to visit me I immediately led the girls to my dollhouse, and then skipped out into the garden to play with the boys. We built forts of sticks; we built tree houses; we played something like cops and robbers; we ran, climbed trees, and just chatted. Somehow it was more fun than playing with the girls.

At home we most liked to play with a set of wooden blocks that Father had had made for us by a carpenter. They were all the same size and shape – about one inch thick, two inches wide and four inches long – but the wonderful part was that we had hundreds of them, which meant we could build a great number of things and never run out of blocks. We built bridges and infinitely long rows of standing bricks like great dominos. You could touch one end and have them all fall, one after another, which took a long time. On long winter evenings we built towers, lined them with colored tissue paper and lit them inside with a candle – after turning off the lights in the room for greater effect.

We also had a collection of stuffed animals. This was our zoo since, of course, there was no real zoo anywhere nearby, and we were very proud of it. For music, besides a piano, we had a music box with several metal records. During our first fall at Vyksa our coachman started teaching us to ride. He insisted that at first we must ride without a saddle to "get the feel of the horse," which frightened me, and I never dared let the horse trot, only walk. Seryozha was even more timid.

A few details of our everyday life stand out in my memory: the whole process of going to bed, for instance. The clothes that I took off had to be neatly folded and the silk ribbons from my two pigtails had to be wetted and wound around the glass door handle, so that in the morning they would be as smooth as if ironed. I can still see those glass door handles – sapphire-blue glass cylinders attached to the door by metal brackets above and below. This habit of compulsory neatness sometimes irked even my Mother, for I insisted on folding my clothes when I took them off at the dressmaker's, and when I walked into the bedroom of my visiting cousin in the morning I proceeded to fold his clothes, which were lying on the chair, while he was still in bed.

To "clean one's plate," to eat everything that was served on it, was obligatory, and I was not allowed to leave the table until I had done so, even if everyone else had gotten up. Once, at the midday meal, I refused to eat a meatball. I was left at the table and not allowed to leave my chair. I was stubborn, however: dusk arrived, and I still sat in front of my cold plate. Finally, Manya came and offered me a glass of cold water, urging me to try at least to eat my meatball with water. It was so typical of Manya, who really cared for us children without any pedagogical theories. I broke my meatball into small pieces and swallowed them one by one with water, without chewing. That way I proved to myself that I did not give in and actually *eat* it. After that I never had any problems swallowing pills.

One day I went into the kitchen where Zuza was preparing meatballs. She let me shape the prepared meat mixture into balls and roll them in crumbs. When they were served at dinner, I was excited and asked Mother how she liked them. Puzzled, Mother replied: "Why do you ask?" I proudly announced: "I made them!" To this Mother's only reply was, "They are fine, but you must not go to the kitchen and bother Zuza!" The adult world still was quite separate from ours.

There was a man living very near by who interested himself in our physical development, and generally had great influence on me. His name was Josif Ignatievich Volodzko, but we always called him Yuzya. I think he was a younger brother of Mother's governess, who had died many years earlier. My father gave him a position – maybe a bookkeeping job – at the mill. Yuzya must have been of Polish origin. His wife was a quiet, shy, and rather frail woman whom we knew only slightly. His sons were considerably older than I. The younger son, Genik, was thin and pale and looked like his mother; he played the violin, and was considered very musical. The older, Vladek, was a healthy, strong young man, like his father.

Yuzya loved children. He was interested in yoga, showed us many exercises, and encouraged us to do them by ourselves. He talked to us often about yoga philosophy, and told us about the reincarnation of souls, love for animals, and control of bad impulses. He was the kindest man I can remember, but he used to say that he had many wild desires he had to control, which meant that his soul needed more reincarnations to be perfected. He said that he had dreamed more than once that he was a bear during the ice age, or perhaps during the time when mountain ranges were formed. He dreamed that he was running away in panic, alarmed by the thunder and roar of what was happening around him, and he believed that this was a memory of one of his past lives. My parents never commented on his stories, but they left a strong impression on me. I don't know how much we believed in them, but in general we trusted Yuzya implicitly. He remains in my memory as a wonderfully compassionate man, who would excuse anyone's aggressive act by trying to understand the reason for it, and who was always ready to blame himself. He was humble without being sanctimonious, something I have remembered all my life. We lost touch with him during the Civil War, but in 1921 while we were in Omsk, Yuzya stopped to see us on his way home to Staraya Russa, a city in the European part of Russia. We never learned what later happened to him and his family, but I still have several of his warm and informative letters to Father.

Father and Mother soon developed a circle of friends: Father's boss, Buinevich, and his wife, the local doctor and his wife, some engineers whom I don't remember at all, Yuzya, and Evgenii (Zhenia) Cavos, my cousin – Aunt Katya's son – with his wife Verochka. They were all people of the same political views – liberal, but not radical, all great readers, and lovers of long philosophical discussions in the evenings.

Zhenia and Verochka were the youngest among them. Zhenia had gone to the "Corps of Pages" school, where he studied drawing, music, humanities, languages, and horseback riding, in general being groomed for life in high society. He played the violin and painted with watercolors, like his mother. He showed no specific talent, however, and was prepared only for some more or less social appointment in the government or army. But instead he fell in love with Verochka, a young girl of very simple background, and married her, against his parents' wishes. Rebelling against their disapproval of the match, he decided that he should work and earn his own living to support his family. He appealed to my Father, who suggested that mechanical drafting was something he could learn quickly, and that a draftsman was needed at the mill. Zhenia accepted that offer and soon moved to Vyksa, where he and Verochka took a house within the compound very near to us; they became effectively a part of our family, Mother playing a role of older sister to the young and inexperienced Verochka.

Christmas

In 1915, our first year in Vyksa, Mother was expecting another child and had plenty of time to spend with us on preparations for Christmas. She made all of our Christmas tree decorations. We watched her draw the elements of different polyhedrons on thin cardboard, which she would then cut out, bend into shapes, glue together and cover with bright, glossy colored paper; finally, she would line their edges with thin strips of gold paper. To me, even now, they seem more interesting and attractive than the plain glass spheres we use for tree-trimming today. She also made paper chains, each link of which was lined with contrasting paper. Little pails, wheelbarrows, and drums were all constructed from cardboard covered with bright paper and gold edging. There was a miniature book, with well-known children's poems written on its pages in her small but very legible handwriting. I particularly admired a little house with mica windows, through which one could see a clock on the wall and a table with vegetables dancing on it: this was an illustration of a popular children's rhyme. Mother also covered walnuts with gold leaf and attached thin strings for hanging them.

The tall tree, which reached to the ceiling, was trimmed in secret by our parents on Christmas Eve. The living room was declared off limits for us until the evening. Dressed in our Sunday outfits, with several invited friends, we had to stay in the children's room in excited anticipation. It was already quite dark outside when we were finally allowed out. The doors to the living room were opened triumphantly, while Father played a loud march on the piano, and we saw the tree all lit up with real candles. The sight was overwhelming. We marched round the tree and sang some Christmas songs in

German, taught to us by Fräulein Marie. Then we examined the beautiful decorations in detail, locating our favorite ones to admire in the light of the candles. We picked edible sweets off the tree. We each got one present, a toy or a book, with the warning that we must share it with others. Each adult received a present from us, which was usually a piece of our own handiwork.

On Christmas day Manya and Nanny went to church, but for us the church would come by itself, that is, the priest would visit us after the service in the church. Dressed in his holiday robes with a big golden cross on a chain around his neck, he would swing his censer and intone some prayers, while we stood quietly by. He then walked around the house, sprinkling it with holy water, and afterward joined us for tea. Father and Mother treated him respectfully, but I had the impression that he visited us without being specifically invited; rather, because it was expected of him by tradition. I felt a little uncomfortable, perhaps because I was never taught how to behave at such a ceremonious performance, or perhaps because I sensed Mother's ambivalent attitude toward it. Father appeared to be more at ease.

Was Mother's ambivalence due to the fact that her father, although married to Russian Orthodox wives, had been and continued to be a Lutheran protestant, however inobservant? All his children, however, were baptized into Russian Orthodoxy, as was the rule when one of the parents was Orthodox. Or was it due to her resentment of the total loyalty of the Russian church to the monarchy? She was certainly not an atheist, she was willing to go through the motions of the rituals, and seemed to enjoy following all the traditions during the holidays. But she never taught me to pray before going to bed, and never mentioned the name of God or Christ or the Holy Mother: rather, she taught me to think over my day, my good or bad deeds, and resolve to improve my behavior, before going to sleep. Later she did buy a beautifully illustrated children's Bible for us, with Old and New Testament stories, and let us read it without any comment on her part. Perhaps this was because she knew that religion was an obligatory subject in the schools, and that sooner or later we would be examined in it. But for now, the only thing we knew was how to make the sign of the cross, and I don't know who taught us that, probably either Nanny or Manya. Soon after our first Christmas in Vyksa, however, I was exposed to more of the traditional religious observances.

∞

As usual, the delivery of the baby was to take place at home. The village had a doctor, and I think there was a small village hospital, but births were supposed to occur in the family home. The first sign of the expected event was the arrival of "Babushka." After the trouble Mother had had with the birth of Lena, she was not expected to have any more children, and the approaching birth was cause for concern. She had gained a lot of weight – proper dieting was quite unknown then – and was now far too heavy. Under the close observation of the newcomer she tried to walk away some of the pounds.

Babushka (or "Grandmother") was in fact the mother of Mother's close friend Tonya, who had died before Mother was married. After that Babushka treated Mother almost like her own daughter, and since she was a midwife by profession she tried to be present at the birth of Mother's children. Neither of our own grandmothers was alive when we were born, and she was the closest replacement we had, so we all called her that.

The birth of the new baby was in fact easy, Mother having no trouble. She was born on January 12, 1915, Saint Tatiana's day (or simply, "Tatiana's Day," the traditional students' day of Moscow University),[1] and was named Tatiana. This meant that her birthday and her name-day coincided, and that unlike the rest of us she had only one day a year to celebrate – but at least everyone knew her saint's day.

Tanya, as she was always known, was baptized in our house, as was customary. We were all baptized soon after birth, since the baptismal certificate was the only record of birth that was issued in Russia. The priest and his assistant came with their regalia and a big basin on a stand. All the family, servants, and friends stood at one end of the living room, while candles were lit, the smoking censer was swung, and prayers were intoned. The tiny baby was undressed;

the priest took her in his hands and dipped her completely into the tepid water of the basin, as I gasped. She was crying, of course, but when quickly wrapped in a warm blanket and cuddled in the arms of her godmother she calmed down. Everyone was congratulated and we all joined with the priest in a festive dinner. This is the first baptism I remember.

My First Confession and Communion

Lena moved into the room with Seryozha and me, leaving Nanny totally occupied with the new baby. Babushka stayed with us through Lent, and before Easter decided – presumably with my parents' consent – that I should go to my first confession during the Holy Week. The Russian church gives communion freely to children until the age of six, but after that it may be received only after confession. Mother never spoke of my going to confession, and I was only vaguely aware of what it was all about. Babushka decided that we would spend the entire Holy Week at a nearby women's convent.

The convent, the Iversk-Vyksa Women's Monastery, was situated within a short ride from Vyksa. It was founded in 1864 as a shelter for old and disabled monks, and became a commune and then a convent in 1888. The grounds were extensive, with four churches in them, one of which had just been completed, a nursing home for old nuns, a hospital, a school for orphan girls, two hotels or guesthouses, and a pilgrims' house, which accommodated 250 people. There were various workshops, for painting icons, for gold thread embroidery, for house and furniture painting, for making *rizas* (the metalwork covering icons), and for tailoring. There was a food shop, a shop where the icons and embroidery were sold, and a vegetable garden. There was also a retreat for some hermit nuns who took vows of total silence and, I believe, slept in coffins so as to be ready to die. Outside the tall, whitewashed brick enclosure of the convent there were stables for horses, a pond, a brick-making factory, an apiary, and about four hundred acres of woods.

As our carriage approached the convent I felt rather intimidated by the thought of what lay ahead. The snow still lay on the ground among the dark pines surrounding the tall white wall of the enclosure. The buildings inside were all whitewashed, the few nuns who were walking soundlessly outside wore black, and it seemed that the only colors, except for the gold cupolas of the churches with their gold crosses, were black and white. It created a somber atmosphere.

Babushka had rented a room for us in the guesthouse, to which the orphanage was attached. We could eat with the nuns and go across the yard to a church where the long Lenten services were held twice a day. On the first morning I opened the door and walked out into the corridor. To my amazement, I found it full of young girls dressed in dark uniforms, some of them my own age, some older, walking up and down very quietly. If they spoke to each other at all, it was in such low voices that when I was in our room I could not even hear them: I had never known children to be so quiet. Babushka told me that they were the girls from the orphanage on their recess between classes. I was desperately sorry for them, for their lack of family, and for their having to behave in so inexuberant a fashion – apparently by compulsion.

Our first evening there we went to my first church service. The dusk was settling into the darkness of night. The interior of the church was lit by candles burning in front of the icons, and candles on stands – one large candle in the middle and many small ones around it – all reflected in the gilded frames of the icons. As usual in Russian Orthodox churches there were no pews or chairs. Everyone had to stand: the nuns in their black garb, the hermit nuns dressed in white robes with black letters on them, the girls from the orphanage in their dark dresses. The priest and his assistants wore black robes with silver brocade. The singing was slow and subdued, the church bells tolled slowly and mournfully. I was a little frightened by the whole atmosphere, and especially by what seemed to me the "living corpses" of the hermit nuns with the hoods on their heads hanging low so that one could not see their faces. Encouraged by the sight of the orphanage girls, I stood as steadily as I could through the service, but I found it quite tiring. I slept well that night.

The morning service, though longer, seemed less oppressive.

I was becoming used to standing still for a long time. After the service and the lunch that followed, I spent a quiet time looking at some picture books in my room, and then met some of the girls, so the time went fast. When an evening service was long and late, Babushka went to it alone, leaving me to have supper with the girls in the orphanage. The crude Lenten food that the girls ate so eagerly seemed quite unpalatable to me, but the whole atmosphere of quiet obedience made me force myself to eat it. I felt terribly sorry for the girls.

Finally, the evening came when I had to go to confession. I was very worried. The only thing I was told about it was that to all the questions about my bad deeds that the priest would ask me, I should answer, "I have sinned," even if I thought I had not, because I could never be sure I had not sinned.

The priest, dressed in his black robe with a wide strip of heavy brocaded cloth hanging down from his neck in front and behind him, and a golden cross on a heavy chain, sat on a chair while I stood in front of him feeling very small and quite powerless. He asked me several questions in a quiet, kind voice, trying to relieve my obvious fright. "Did you lie?" "Did you have bad thoughts?" and so on. I answered as I was supposed to. Then he asked me, "What other sin would you like to confess?" I was utterly unprepared for this. I thought about it. Finally I said, "I steal sugar lumps from the sugar bowl on the table before breakfast." The priest said, "Well, now that you know how bad this is, you won't do it again? You see, even if you think nobody sees you, God does!" He covered my head with his brocaded strip, said a prayer, and let me go. I left the church feeling saintly, cleansed of all my sins, and with my conscience clear. But it was somewhat alarming to know that whatever I did in the utmost privacy, God was always there watching me.

After having confession I was not supposed to eat anything until communion the next morning during the service. I went back to our room but I felt awfully hungry, and then faint. The only thing that Babushka could offer me was dark sweet tea. It helped, though I hated it. In the morning I took my communion, dressed in my best dress – no special dress was required. We had to stand through the service. I was getting hungrier all the time and was afraid of fainting. Finally a number of those who were taking communion, including Babushka and I, formed a line and approached the priest, who gave each of us a spoonful of tepid red wine thinned with water, with a piece of *prosvira* (a special communion bread, which looked like a two-tiered bun) afloat in it. I received my piece of this, and it felt so good to eat something – I wished I could eat the whole *prosvira*! Babushka later got one more to take home with us. The Mother Superior congratulated me and gave me a very pretty teacup and saucer as a present. The cup was of thin, almost translucent porcelain, with a little stem, decorated with pink flowers and a golden rim. I was very proud to have my own cup: it survived many miles of travel, and reached Manchuria before it was broken.

I went to the midnight Easter service with Babushka. The church was all lit up with candles. The priests were dressed in gold brocaded white robes. The church bells rang loudly; the whole atmosphere was one of overwhelming joy. It was a wonderful end to a demanding week. Though I had had a long nap before the service, I felt very tired and sleepy. I don't even remember how I got back to our room.

In the morning we returned home in a carriage sent by my parents. It felt so good to run, to speak loudly, to feel natural. The wonderful fragrance of Easter cooking permeated the house; the table was set for any guests who might arrive during Easter Sunday, as it was customary for men to pay visits to all their friends on such holidays. All the traditional Easter foods were set out: the tall cylindrical Easter breads (*kulichi*) with glazed sugar tops and paper roses stuck on them; two Easter sweet cream-cheese pyramids (*paskhas*), one white, the other a reddish color – a special Brullov recipe; a big pile of colored eggs; ham and veal roasts; several bottles of wine; and of course the samovar with charcoal glowing in it. Hot water for tea was ready at all times, and the samovar's quiet hiss made everything seem warm and inviting.

The contrast between this joyous family atmosphere and the subdued air of the orphanage struck me forcibly. I could not stop thinking of the pale faces of the girls I had met. I felt so very lucky that I told Mother about it, and she promised to invite the girls to a picnic in the spring, which she did when the weather warmed up. They had a wonderful time running and playing in the park. It was refreshing to see that they did not forget how to have fun, even under the watchful supervision of the nun who came along. I wonder what happened to those girls during the Revolution that swept the country so soon after their visit, and its long aftermath.

Summer 1915

In the summer of 1915 Mother organized a day camp in our park for the local children. With the help of a committee of residents she arranged a festival with all sorts of entertainments to raise funds for it. There were drinks, sweets, balloons, flags, and little trinkets for sale. Mother made a number of little tumbling figures, which I carried around the park, demonstrating and selling. They were cardboard tubes about half an inch in diameter and one and a half inches long, sealed on both ends, with a little lead ball inside them. A soft paper head and arms were attached to one end of the cylinder, and paper legs to the other. When you put them on an inclined surface, the ball inside caused them to tumble head over heels. I sold them for five kopeks apiece.

At one end of the park there was a puppet show and a darkened "Magic Lantern" booth, which showed slides. At the other end there was a small enclosure with "airplane rides." Airplanes were still so little known that this simple deception could impress children. A child was led into the enclosure with his eyes carefully blindfolded with a scarf. He was placed standing on a board supported by two small stools about ten inches above the ground. At the two ends of this board two people stood ready to lift it. An "assistant" stood on the ground in front of the blindfolded child, and asked him to place his hands on the assistant's head "to steady himself." The people holding the ends of the board then began to raise it slightly and shake it a little. The assistant meanwhile started slowly to lower himself until he was squatting as low as he could, and eventually brought his head practically to the ground, withdrawing it finally from the hands of the child. All this was accompanied by the shouts of the conspirators, describing how high the frightened child was flying. After the board was put down on its supports and the scarf removed from his eyes, the child could see the trick, but he would not disclose it to the other children when he went out because he would not want them to know how he had been fooled. So the "rides" remained popular.

The festival was a great success. Now the committee was able to hire a choir director and a gymnastics instructor. A successful program was developed for the whole summer, in which both Seryozha and I participated. The boys and girls from the village were quite boisterous and sometimes rough. Being smaller, I was a little afraid of playing games with them, but I joined the choir and loved it at first. But one day the choirmaster was walking with Fräulein Marie and me after our rehearsal. She asked him, "How is Mulya doing?" He looked at me and said, "It would not hurt her to practice a bit more at home." I took him to mean that I had done really badly, and after that, for the rest of my childhood and youth, I never sang in anyone's presence.

A year had passed since the outbreak of the war, and the entire country's patriotic effort was in full swing. Our young adult relatives and friends in the far-off capital were all involved in it one way or another. Ladies rolled bandages and knitted socks for the army. Young women worked as volunteer nurse helpers in the army hospitals. In Vyksa many of the local men were drafted into the army, and Father's mill was concerned mostly with war needs. Mother stayed busy with her educational projects, however, and on the whole the routine of our life remained unaffected.

The guests who now came to stay at our house were mostly painters and sculptors. For them it was an opportunity to continue their work in a new environment. I watched one of the sculptors molding Father's bust out of clay, then covering it with plaster of Paris, removing the fragile mold after it hardened, and casting a plaster copy of the head. Casting the work in metal during the war was unthinkable, since metal was needed elsewhere. I remember vividly the final removal of the mold piece by piece, which gradually revealed the perfect plaster copy of the clay head. Mother liked this head very much, and kept it with us all the way to the Urals.

One of the painters started to teach me painting. I never got any further than drawing large squares and triangles in my sketch book, which I had to fill with a light watercolor wash, making sure that the wash was put on uniformly. This technique proved useful to me later, for coloring plans as an engineering student in Manchuria. Seryozha in the meantime was making great progress in his drawing. He drew complicated battle scenes with armored knights, in all kinds of poses, and on a separate page worked out further details. I could not help but be impressed when he drew the battle banners with writing on them. And some letters were skipped because the banners were waving in the wind! He was only five years old. Everyone thought that he must have inherited the talents of the Brullov family, and would carry on their artistic tradition.

Once Mother brought home some remarkable paintings by a village boy, oils on canvas or boards. The boy painted particularly difficult still life subjects. One of them was a glass of water with a flower in it. It showed the transparency of the water, and yet one could see the water, too. Another was a lighted candle in a candlestick, with some nearby objects lit by it. There were some others that I don't remember, but they were all very impressive, especially when we learned that the boy made his paints himself. Where did he get his ideas? How did he learn to do this?

Mother felt that the boy was very talented and needed some further help. She brought him to our house, gave him oil paints and canvas, and let him make copies of some of Grandfather's paintings. Copying masters was an accepted method of instruction at that time. He came to us a number of times, and worked hard on his paintings. He was a quiet, simple country boy with blond hair, dressed like most village children in a long shirt with stand-up collar, opening on the side and hanging over his trousers, which were tied at the waist by a cord belt, and wearing bast shoes. Somewhat uncommunicative, he did not talk to us, but painted with obvious absorption. Both Seryozha and I viewed him with awe, and tried not to disturb him. Soon Mother arranged for him to be sent to an art school in a city – probably Moscow, but I am not sure. I don't know what his name was or what happened to him. Maybe he became a famous painter, or maybe he was lost in the chaos of the Revolution, like so many, many talented youths.

[1]   Every large educational institution in Russia had to have a church inside. The church of Moscow University was consecrated on January 12, which happened to be Saint Tatiana's day; thus, the church got the name of Saint Tatiana. Gradually, January 12 (January 25) became a holiday of Moscow University students, and later a holiday of all students in Russia. Therefore Saint Tatiana's day was much better known than many other name-days. January 25 is celebrated as Student Day all over Russia now.

5

Vyksa, 1916-17

In the fall of 1915 I reached the schooling age of seven. Mother had one of the rooms on the second floor furnished as a classroom, with a school desk, a table for herself, and a blackboard. One morning early in September, immediately after breakfast and seeing Father off, Seryozha and I went upstairs to our classroom for the first time.

In the classroom Mother was a teacher. Seryozha was only five, but Mother thought that he could start getting used to the routine. The tasks she gave him were quite different from mine, however. I studied reading and writing but Seryozha mostly drew, or played with educational equipment: Mother followed the Montessori method of teaching. I wrote long rows of the elements of letters in my notebook with a steel pen. I had to follow the horizontal and vertical lines carefully, learning to make thick lines on the down stroke and very thin lines on the up stroke. As Mother was also teaching me French, I used to form both Russian and French words on the flat surface of my desk with letters that Mother had cut out of paper. Each letter was a different color. Is that why each letter still has a color for me?

A loud march played by Father on the piano when he returned from work at midday was the signal to end our study period. We would run downstairs to greet him, relieved to be at liberty. Family dinner was served in the dining room around a long table. Fräulein Marie sat with us, and because it was considered impolite to speak a language that she did not understand, everyone was supposed to speak German. (However, it was all right for Father and Mother to speak French when they didn't want the children to understand.) Manya waited on table, Fräulein Marie watched our table manners, and the conversation was kept to a level that Seryozha and I could take part in. Lena was as yet too small to dine with us.

Fräulein Marie was a little upset by the fact that I was not learning to read and write German. She suggested to me that I learn to write some German Gothic script as a Christmas present for my parents. Keeping it a secret from Mother, I spent a lot of time filling a whole notebook with German words in Gothic script. I do not think Mother appreciated this present, though she thanked me profusely. She may only then have realized that I was learning three alphabets at the same time, which no doubt slowed down my progress in reading.

At one point, it may have been a year or so later, I was supposed to memorize the multiplication tables. This seemed impossible to me. I sat alone in the attic for hours, my thoughts wandering away from the numbers. They made no sense to me. I finally memorized the squares, learned how to multiply by five and by nine and how to figure all other parts of the table by adding or subtracting from these numbers. This is what I do even now. I envied Seryozha for not having to go through this trouble.

One day Mother said that I could not count to one million. It was a challenge, so I insisted that I could and started to count beads on an abacus. I did it for hours, hardly breaking for play and meals. By the end of the second day, I had reached eleven thousand. At this point I gave up. I have never forgotten how big a million is.

Mechta

The steel mill that Father managed was one of several in the district. The principal director of all the mills, Buinevich, lived in the next village. He and his wife soon became friends of my parents and often visited us. Their only son was a cadet at a military school in Moscow, which brought us closer to the events happening in the center of the country.

World War I was raging. The Germans were occupying more and more Russian territory. The large map on the wall of Father's study showed the front line with colored pins. The government was urging citizens to contribute any gold they had. Mother collected and turned in all her gold jewelry except the wedding rings and the baptismal crosses that Russians wear under their clothing. She was a Russian patriot, after all, even if she opposed the autocratic monarchy. She kept only a brooch, which I have now. It is an image of Cupid with two wings, standing on a horn of plenty full of grapes, all worked in remarkable detail. Mother's father had brought it to her from Italy, and she felt that its artistic value was greater than the value of the gold in it.

The work of the steel mill was now in large part devoted to war needs. Some special steels, previously imported from Germany, were now unavailable. Father thought he could build a new type of furnace to produce them. The two commonly used furnaces for the production of steel were the Marten furnace and the Bessemer converter. The Marten furnace used solid pig iron and large quantities of rusted metal scraps to oxidize the pig iron. The cycle of production was usually six to eight hours, and it could handle only rather large loads. The Bessemer converter was used for some special types of steel needed only in small quantities, but it had to be loaded with molten pig iron, and it had a very short cycle of production. The operator used a spectroscope to determine just the right moment for discharging the molten steel in order to get a particular kind of final product. The quality and composition of the steel depended upon the lining of this small furnace, and upon the addition of other metals in small quantities. It required a skilled operator and either a blast furnace or a special pig iron melting furnace to feed it with molten metal.

Father conceived a type of furnace that could produce small quantities of special steel, could be run on crude oil or coal, and could use solid pig iron. Its cycle of operation would be about two hours, and it would require no special skills to operate. Buinevich agreed to let Father try to build and test his idea.

Father brought home samples of the steel after various machines had tested it for strength, malleability, and hardness. He showed us how broken pieces of the different steels looked on the surface of their fractures. Everyone could feel Father's excitement at each success and his depression at each failure. He was sure there was no limit to the kind of steel he could produce. He called his invention "Mechta," which in Russian means "Daydream." Father did not want his own name attached to it. He was never interested in personal glory, but knew he had invented something very useful for mankind.

He thought particularly of the distant, small railroad workshops scattered along the enormous spaces of Russia. Usually such establishments had to wait for a long time to get those steels from somewhere else. With Father's furnace they could produce them themselves. Later, Soviet textbooks on railroad shop equipment recommended this furnace under the name "The Mechta Type Furnace."

All of this was particularly important in 1915, because the shortage of special steels was beginning to have a devastating effect on industry. One such type of steel was used for the bolts that connected the rails on all the tracks of the Russian railroads; formerly it had been imported, but now it had to be produced domestically. A test run on the Marten furnace produced a great deal of unsuitable metal. The test run on Father's furnace was successful. He brought home the first piece of that steel broken by the testing machine and we noted that in cross section the crystalline structure of the metal seemed to form a cross. "This must be God's blessing on your work!" our old Nanny said to Father. He was so touched that he recorded this remark in his notes and saved the test piece. The resulting steel turned out to be perfect. It was easy to produce, and the pig iron could be of such low quality that the Marten furnace would not even accept it, so this steel was much cheaper than that produced by other mills.

The wartime need for this product was so great that Father had to build a larger version of his invention, and a number of Mechta furnaces were constructed at another large steel mill. Mechta ended up supplying this kind of steel for the entire country. After Father started to get inquiries about his furnace from other mills he decided to take out a patent on it. On December 5, 1916 he went to Murom to apply for the patent. This was two and a half months before the Revolution broke out in Petrograd.

Family Visitors

In the winter of 1915-16 Father was working on his invention and Mother was busy teaching us at home and teaching other children at the village school. Several of our Petersburg relatives came to visit. Father's sister, our Aunt Varya Lisovskaya, with her son Sasha, a teenager, stayed with us for about a month. For me it was a new experience to have an older child in the house, someone I could look up to, but who was not an adult. I think he was not at all interested in me. He went to see the mill with Father, he rode our horse, using a saddle, which I was not yet allowed to do, and generally tried to associate with the adults. I really did not miss him when he and his mother left, but Petersburg, my parents' native city, seemed closer, and our connection with it seemed to be renewed and stronger.

Our next visitor was another of Father's sisters, Aunt Katya, whose two daughters remained in Petersburg, preoccupied with their wartime activities. She stayed two months with us. She was quite thin and graceful, with somewhat unruly curly hair, and I thought she was very beautiful. I loved her gentle ways at once, her soft voice, her lovely clothes and the jewelry she wore. She treated us all in an affectionate manner. One of the brooches she always wore was a small, golden artist's palette with different colored precious stones arranged in the order of the colors of the rainbow, as an artist would arrange his paints. It was a gift from Mother's father Pavel Brullov, a good friend of hers. Aunt Katya spent most of her time painting watercolors; she painted a portrait of three-year-old Lena that Lena still has. Aunt Katya was constantly looking for her pince-nez, which usually turned out to be on her own nose. This amused the children immensely.

In her kind and loving manner, Aunt Katya found a way to help Father during a crisis caused by his explosive temperament. In the process of testing and experimenting with the new furnace Father often had great arguments with Buinevich, on whom he was dependent for the development funds. One of these arguments resulted in a real quarrel. Father was very hot-tempered. Usually he didn't hold grudges and was totally forgiving later, but this time the quarrel lasted for several days. Peace had to be restored somehow, and Aunt Katya thought of the form that Father's apology could take. She painted a picture of two fighting roosters facing each other – one fat, with the angry head of Buinevich, the other thin, with Father's head bearing a furious expression. It was beautifully executed: the feathers were flying, the faces stern. The picture was framed and presented by my father to Buinevich. They both had a good laugh and the quarrel ended. Sadly, all I have now is a photograph of only one half of this painting – my Father's rooster.

Aunt Katya was Father's favorite sister, fourteen years older than he. She had graduated from the Petersburg Academy of Arts and studied art in Paris and in Rome, married a successful architect, Evgenii Cavos, and now lived in Petersburg, in a large house that he designed and built on Kamennoostrovsky Prospekt. The house soon became a place where painters like Repin,[1] Serov,[2] Benois,[3] Brullov, and Lancere[4] often met, as well as writers, poets, actors, composers, and musicians. Aunt Katya herself participated in numerous exhibitions, and painted portraits of well-known artists and actors, some of which are now in Russian museums. She was very public-spirited: she sketched portraits in courts during trials, in the Duma during its sessions, at concerts, and in theaters; she even visited prisons, where she painted some portraits of political prisoners. Many of these works were published in illustrated magazines. With her rather left-wing views, she was close to the Union of Artists, which sometimes met in her house. At the time of the 1905 revolution in Russia this Union supported the industrial workers' demands. In her sister's notes[5] I read that Aunt Katya once hid Rosa Luxemburg, the militant German socialist, at her dacha in Finland, and that the writer Maxim Gorky went there to visit Rosa. She supported a studio where artists without studios could paint, and where art lessons were given to people unable to enter the Academy. To help fund this endeavor she used her wide acquaintance with Russian artists to arrange numerous exhibitions, lotteries and fairs.

Aunt Katya kept in close contact with her brothers Sasha (the lawyer) and Sergey, who had been exiled to Siberia. She also remained close to my father through all their struggles with the social order. Before he was married my father often visited the Cavos house, and after Father's parents died, the house of his sister became a home for him. It was Evgenii Cavos to whom Father often appealed for help and for advice with finding new jobs, and he was never disappointed. And it was Aunt Katya who brought him to her home and nursed him after the events at Nadezhdensky Zavod. Being the youngest of eight siblings, my Father treated Aunt Katya's four children more like his younger brother and sisters than nephews and nieces. When he was in the navy he often took them onto his ship when he was in port; he had sailor suits made for them and taught them some gymnastics, and how to climb masts. He remained brotherly and protective of the Cavos' children long after they were grown up and their parents had died.

Fifty-two notebooks of Aunt Katya's diaries and family correspondence are in the archives in Pushkin's House in St. Petersburg. Her correspondence with other painters is in the archives of the Academy of Arts in St. Petersburg, which has many of her paintings.

A Trip to Moscow

During the winter of 1915-16 Seryozha became sick with tonsillitis. He spent much time in bed. Mother worried about him; he was pale and weaker than he should be at his age. The local doctor suggested that he should have his tonsils removed. There were no good facilities for such an operation in Vyksa, and Mother decided that as soon as the weather warmed up, she would take him to Moscow. Seryozha insisted that he wanted me to go along. Mother had not planned on this, and said no, while I was rather indifferent, content to stay home. But at the very last, when everything was packed, Seryozha began crying. He was so upset that Mother gave in. My things were hurriedly packed and added to their baggage, and we left in our carriage, which had to take us all the way to the Murom railroad station. Manya accompanied us to that point.

In the winter the road went over the ice of the river, since, of course, the roads were never plowed, and the river ice presented a smooth level surface. At that time, however, the ice was rather soft. At one point the horses broke through the ice and sank belly deep in the water. The ice started to break under the carriage too, and the carriage began to fill with water and sink. We were near the shore, and were able to scramble to solid ground. Our coachman, chest-deep in icy water, pulled the frightened horses by the bridle. He managed to bring the horses and carriage onto the shore, where all of us stood frightened, wet and cold. The trunk at the back of the carriage somehow did not get soaked, so Mother and Manya quickly changed our wet clothes, wrapped us in blankets, and we all climbed back into the carriage. We continued our journey along the shore. The road was not as smooth, but it was safer. This event must have made a very strong impression on me because I dreamt about it many times after that, each time reliving it in detail.

The trip was long and boring, so Mother told us stories. Sometimes she made up the stories as she told them and we loved these even more than the ones she read to us. One of these stories I still remember:

Once there lived a poor boy. His family was so poor that he had to work hard to help his father support the family. But he was very kind. He helped his little brothers and sisters to do their chores. He was always there when anyone needed comforting. He shared all he had with the others, even if he had very little.

One time after he had carried a lot of dry branches home for the fire, he sat down tired and fell asleep. When he woke up he saw a strange man standing before him. The stranger said, "How would you like to be very rich? I could give you anything you want. A big beautiful house for your family, fine clothes, delicious food, and you would not have to work for it at all." The boy was dumbfounded. He said, "Why would you do this for me? What do you want me to do for it?" "A very simple little thing," the man said. "All I want is for you to let me take your heart. I shall give you a beautiful diamond heart instead, and you will never notice the difference." The boy thought, "How many nice things I could do for all the people I know, if I had all this wealth. Think of how happy my father and mother would be, not to have to work so hard, to have all they wanted. And my little brothers and sisters – just imagine them being all dressed up in fancy clothes and eating wonderful sweets. It is not so hard for me to give this man my heart and what a joy for all the others!" So he agreed, and the man took his heart and gave him a diamond one.

All at once a beautiful house appeared before his eyes. Music was heard and servants came out to greet the boy, carrying lovely clothes and tasty food. The boy started to live a good life with everything he wanted brought to him at once. But when his father came to him asking for help, the boy refused. "Why should I do this for you, old man? I need it all for myself, and I don't want to see your dirty little urchins in my beautiful house! Go away!" And so time went by. He had everything, but he was not happy. Nobody loved him any more.

Mother's story finally came to a happy ending when the boy gave back his diamond heart to the stranger and got his own back. He lost all the fancy things he had, and returned to his poor family. He became kind again and lived happily ever after. The story left a strong impression on me.

In Murom we boarded the train with all our baggage. Mother put us to bed, and next morning Seryozha and I spent all the time glued to the window. The train rolled along the flat landscape with villages, fields, rivers and woods floating by. Then, suddenly, Mother said, "Look, there is Moscow!" And we saw in the distance the gold cupolas and crosses of the churches shining brightly in the sunlight. The buildings were not visible yet and it looked as if the city had only churches.

Very little remains in my memory of that visit. I do remember walking inside the Kremlin, and particularly the "Tsar-Kolokol" (Tsar-Bell) standing on its brick foundation with a missing piece of it leaning against the foundation below.[6] The hole in the bell looked like a window and I wondered why they did not make it into a shop or an information booth.

On the return trip our coachman met us in Murom. Spring was in full swing; the road was muddy and the carriage and its drawn curtains were so covered with splashed mud that we could not even peek outside. I was happy to be at home and feel free again, without the constraint and confinement of travel.

ങ

One morning when we were in our classroom with Mother, Manya came in, frightened, asking Mother to join her outside. When Mother returned she told us to go downstairs at once, put on our coats, and leave the house with the adults. Father was at the mill and there was no way to get in touch with him. It was thought, as we later learned, that the main river dam, some distance upstream, had been broken by the spring floods, and that the whole town would soon be inundated. Some of the older people in Vyksa still remembered the terrible flood of 1881, when the dam had collapsed, and an enormous wave of water rushed through the village, destroying all the houses and even the mill structures, with the loss of many lives.

Seryozha and I walked past the compound gates with Mother, Fräulein Marie, Manya, Nanny, who was carrying the baby Tanya, and Zuza, with a basket containing our midday meal. We continued along the village street, which led up the only hill in the vicinity. Crowds of people were climbing the hill. People around us looked grim and worried. Some were leading a lamb, sheep, or calf by a rope. Many people had their possessions with them in wheelbarrows. The children were quiet.

Noon passed, and the food was shared and eaten. There was no sign of water, not even on the horizon. People started to drift back towards the village. Finally, a messenger sent by our father came to tell us to return and stop worrying.

What had happened was this: with the frightening news of the war published in the papers, people often imagined that censorship concealed from them even worse events; thus, eavesdropping telephone operators became a very valuable additional source of information. This time an operator overheard engineers talk about checking the dam and misinterpreted the conversation. Alarmed, she passed on the news. No one checked the rumor, and it spread like wildfire.

Zoya's Birth

In that part of the country the long winters accumulate huge amounts of snow, so spring is always a time of overflowing rivers, soaked fields with rivulets flowing all around, and muddy roads. Russians call it a period of *bezdorozhie* or "roadlessness." When May comes, however, everything is in glorious bloom, especially the lilacs. On Mother's name-day, May 21, Father covered the whole table in the dining room with white lilac blossoms. For dinner we had our first crop of white asparagus, grown on Mother's instructions in cold frames covered by burlap to keep them in the darkness.

I don't know if my parents felt any anticipation of the catastrophic events that would come so soon. Mother was expecting her next child on schedule: every two years, my Father said, because less than two years was hard on Mother, and more than two was not good for the children. They hoped to have twelve children.

Mother was painfully aware of a lack of parental warmth in her own childhood and of the abundance of it in Father's. She wanted us to have what she had missed. Living here in the country, away from the strife of the city, but not too far from relatives who could visit us, she thought it was possible to create a happy childhood for her children. She hoped to take us back to the city after the war was over. Although very busy with our education, she still did not want to abandon her involvement in activities on behalf of a happier future for all the children of the country, and continued to instruct us at home and other children at the school.

So we spent another happy and busy summer in 1916, with fewer guests, because of the war, but without much change in our family routine. The adults kept their wartime concerns to themselves. In the fall Seryozha and I continued our studies with Mother, but Lena, who was now sleeping in our room and learning German from Fräulein Marie, could play all day. She was approaching four, growing well, and showed no effects of her premature birth.

Seryozha and I played chess. He was always terribly upset when he lost. I thought it was proper that I should win, since I was almost eight and he was only six, but Seryozha was very competitive. He would seize the board and throw all the pieces on the floor every time he lost, and I usually picked them up, because he refused to do so. After a while I stopped playing chess with him.

Then we started arguing about politics. I insisted that I was a socialist, and he said he was a monarchist. I could not understand how anyone could be a monarchist. It was so unfair that one person should have *all* power over the people. But to Seryozha there was glamour in it. He did not accept even a constitutional monarchy, only an absolute one!

We also invented a game that kept us occupied for some months. It was a game of joint storytelling: we each had our own hero and could tell anything we liked about him – what he did, what he thought, what he felt, what he tried to do to the other person's hero, but we were not allowed to tell what effect his actions had on the rival hero – that was for the other person to tell. For example, my hero could inflict a wound on Seryozha's man, but it was for Seryozha to tell how painful it was, and whether it was mortal. We could introduce into the story as many people as we wanted. The stories became quite complicated and lasted for days. This game ended when we learned about the existence of such small things as bacteria, viruses, and atoms, for I would make my hero so small that Seryozha's hero could not see him, and my hero now was free to do anything without any interference from Seryozha's. So the game lost its point.

In November Babushka arrived as usual to be with Mother, who had gained a lot of weight before the approaching birth of her next child. Mother was very tired and she tried to walk a lot to lose weight, but without any success. Zoya was born on November 30, 1916. Another girl! She was named after my father's mother.

The war was in its third year. The archaic system of government was cracking under the strain of it. The overburdened railroad system, servicing great distances, kept breaking down. There were riots in the country, grumbling and strikes at the mills, desertions from the front.

Why Father decided to leave Vyksa became clear to me only when I happened to read a book published in 1967 about the history of the Vyksa mills. Apparently, the mills had a number of problems. River transportation of their products, as well as the oil needed for their operation, were only available seasonally. The equipment in the mines was especially antiquated and labor troubles were continuous.

German ownership of the mills made the merchants dealing with them suspicious. Early in 1916 negotiations took place about the sale of the mills, but they were unsuccessful. Finally, in February 1917 all the mills were taken over by the Highways Division of the Ministry of Transportation.

Father was asked to assume the directorship of a large and important mill in the Ural Mountains, and he accepted it both as a challenge and as a patriotic duty in time of war. They also wanted to install one or two of Father's furnaces. He left for the Urals on February 26, 1917, the day the Revolution began.

Revolution

Defeats at the front, shortages of food in the cities, rising prices, and the dissatisfaction of the peasantry with inadequate land distribution and repeated conscriptions, all contributed to a storm of complaint and protest throughout Russia. The assassination of the unpopular *eminence grise* of the royal family, Rasputin, at the end of 1916 had solved nothing.

At the end of February 1917 (early March by the new calendar), spontaneous strikes filled the streets of St. Petersburg with protesting crowds. The vacationing Tsar, Nicholas II, attempted to dissolve the Duma, but on his way back to the capital was forced instead to abdicate, renouncing the throne for himself and his thirteen-year-old hemophiliac son, in favor of his brother – who in turn refused to accept it. A new Provisional Government, designated by the abolished Duma, took form in Petrograd, promising to call for a universally elected Constitutional Assembly that would then determine the future form of the Russian government.

Meanwhile, a "Soviet" or representative council of workers and soldiers, also at Petrograd, took upon itself the role of guardian of the Revolution. It assumed some of the administrative powers. The two groups were independent, but for a while they tried to cooperate.

Unrestrained euphoria spread through the cities. The revolution was in progress, though no one was prepared for it. All the established relations between the government and the widespread population were breaking down. Ahead lay the complete reorganization of the whole society in the midst of a devastating war, which had already sapped much of the country's blood.

In the quiet village where we lived, the February Revolution reached us as joyous news a few days later. I knew that Mother was among the speakers who went to the square where a platform had been built, covered with red cloth. She spoke as an administrator of the School for the Workers. I am sure that her sympathies were with the socialists, but not the radical ones. I have heard that she was an inspired speaker.

Although I was already eight years old, my parents seldom talked to me about politics. I knew that Mother welcomed the news of the Revolution and was full of hope for developing a more just society in Russia. I learned from my parents that there was much injustice in Russia, and Mother particularly felt that the removal of the autocratic Tsar's government would be the first step towards improving the situation. She felt that alcohol abuse among the masses was encouraged by the government itself, who produced the alcohol, and also distributed it with great profit. The drinking, she thought, was due to frustration, and it brought on apathy in the drinkers. Education was one of the ways to battle both alcoholism and apathy, and this is why she expended so much effort in organizing the workers' schools and serving on the relevant committees.

For us, the first news of the violence of the Revolution was a telegram received by the Buineviches, informing them of the death of their only son. He was killed during the armed conflict in Moscow, in which the cadets of his military school had participated. It was a shock that foretold all the future tragedies of the violent upheaval.

The news of others started to trickle down to us. There were cases in which officers in the army not only had their symbols of rank torn from their coats, but were even stoned to death. A number of estate houses were ransacked and burned. Some of their owners were killed. Different people had different ideas of what freedom meant.

The European Allies quickly recognized the Provisional Government, which promised to stay in the war and continue military operations on the Russian front. Decree after decree came out liberalizing Russian life, including one, early in March, abolishing capital punishment. I knew how strongly my parents, and especially my Uncle Sasha, felt that capital punishment must be abolished, so this was very happy news.

03

A short time later we left Vyksa for another mill town, Byeloretsk, in the Ural Mountains, where Father would be waiting for us. The students of the evening school organized by Mother gathered to say goodbye to her. They gave her a bound notebook with an engraved silver plaque on its cover, reading: "From the grateful listeners of courses in the Vyksa division of the Society for Dissemination of People's Education in the Nizhegorodskaya Gubernia."[7]

Transportation, by an increasingly overburdened system, was a problem. Mother and Father decided that traveling by boat would be the safest. On the trains and boats the crowds of deserting soldiers and sailors often helped themselves to all the places and the feeble, recently organized militia could not cope with them.

It was a big job, yet again, to pack all our belongings. Carpenters made huge crates for packing pictures, dishes, linens, and clothes, but much of the furniture had to be left behind. So one day in April of 1917 – when the Revolution was barely two months old – a short time after spring navigation on the rivers had started, we all set out on a journey. There were five children: I, aged eight and a half; Seryozha, almost seven; Lena, four and a half; Tanya, two years old, and Zoya, at only four months and in Nanny's arms, along with Mother, Manya, and Fräulein Marie. We arrived in Murom where we boarded a passenger steamer on the river Oka.

Fräulein Marie had always spoken German with us, and we were afraid that she might be arrested by the police, because all the Germans were supposed to be interned. But out concern was put to rest when we found out, to our great surprise, that she spoke Russian very well.

---

[1] Ilya Efimovich Repin (1844-1930): painter and active member of the Itinerants.

[2]   Valentin Alexandrovich Serov (1865-1911): started with the Itinerants, then worked with the association "Mir Iskusstva" (World of Art); painter of many famous portraits.

[3]   Alexander Nikolaevich Benois (1870-1960): painter, art critic and art historian; author of a well-known book of memoirs.

[4]   Evgenii Evgenievich Lancere (1875-1946): painter, member of the association "Mir Iskusstva."

[5]   The archive of Zoya Zarudnaya is in the Central State Archive of Literature and Art, Moscow.

[6]   "Tsar-Kolokol" (The Tsar-Bell): a giant bell (20 feet high, weighing 200 tons), made by Russian craftsmen in 1733-35. In the fire of 1737 it fell off the bell tower and a piece weighing eleven tons broke off. It now stands on a brick pedestal in the Moscow Kremlin.

[7]   Russia was divided into administrative regions called *gubernias.* There were 78 gubernias in 1917. Nizhegorodskaya Gubernia had Nizhni Novgorod as its capital.

6

On Our Way to the Urals

At the city of Nizhni Novgorod we changed to a larger steamer that sailed on the Volga. It was the time of year when spring waters cause the river to rise beyond its banks and inundate the adjoining fields. This was supposed to leave the fields well fertilized for the spring seeding. To us, it was an incredible sight: we could not see land on either side of the ship, but seemed to be sailing across a sea.

We stopped for a day in Kazan. Here the hills came quite close to the river. Manya and Fräulein Marie were able to go ashore and get a glimpse of the colorful city with its many resident Tartars. Aboard the ship, Manya described to us their strange costumes and the unfamiliar objects and foods they sold.

In a few days we reached the mouth of the Kama, another Volga tributary, and sailed upstream. The shores now came closer and we could see hills, trees, and occasional villages. From the Kama, our steamer turned into the river Belaya and soon reached the city of Ufa, where Father met us. Our way now was by rail into the Ural Mountain Range. Half the cars in the train were small Russian freight cars, of a type with which we would later become so well acquainted. The rest were normal passenger cars, and we boarded one of these.

The mountains appeared very soon. We had never seen mountains before and were fascinated by the views from the windows. We soon reached the little station of Vyasovaya, where we had to climb off in a great hurry, because the train stopped there for only a few minutes. It was a very small station on a narrow-gauge line leading to Byeloretsk. The next train was much smaller, and with much rattling and shaking we traveled another 150 versts[1] (100 miles) to Byeloretsk.

Byeloretsk

Byeloretsk was a town centered on a steel mill that used the ore mined in a nearby mountain called Magnitnaya (or "Magnetic"), famous for its rich iron ore. The legend was that if you climbed the mountain, your watch would stop because of the mountain's strong magnetic field. A larger industrial city, Magnitogorsk, has now arisen near there, but in 1916 the mills in Byeloretsk already had 13,000 workers.

The house where we were going to live was smaller than the one in Vyksa. It stood on a steep bank of the river Belaya, on the lower part of which we had sailed to Ufa. Here the river was narrower and shallower, permitting only rowboat navigation. Its shores and bottom were covered with small stones, which we could see from the top of the riverbank. There was no easy access to the river from our house. One of the first things that Father undertook was the construction of an addition to the house, extending the living room towards the river, with a big window providing a view. It was fun to go into the unfinished room during the construction, to smell the new wood, and look through the big plate glass window down at the river where the town boys fished for crayfish. Before we came, they used to do it for fun, but when they found out that we *ate* them, they would sell us big pails full of crayfish, laughing because they considered the creatures inedible.

Life settled into a sort of routine, but it seemed not nearly as easygoing and comfortable as in Vyksa. Mother again involved herself with the local evening school, but at home we did not have a special classroom, and the garden was not nearly as inviting. Also Manya and Nanny were busier here, until Zuza arrived with her husband, whom Father managed to transfer to Byeloretsk. They settled nearby, but now Zuza was expecting a child, and did not spend quite so much time in our house. Our cousin Zhenia Cavos had moved with us to Byeloretsk, and he and his wife Verochka now had a boy called Boom. They lived in a house very near ours and I often walked over to visit them.

One day some workers were filling the ditch around the foundation of the new addition to our house. One of them touched the wire that was attached to the rain-pipe on the stable with his shovel, and it sparked. What had happened was this: the wire from the nearby electric pole was touching the metal roof of the stable, so that the roof, the drainpipe, and the wire attached to it, its end hanging in the air, had all been electrified. When I came out of the house to watch the men working, they warned me not to touch the wire. I was sure that I knew all about electricity, so I told them that I could touch it if I wanted; all I needed to do was to put on a pair of galoshes. I knew that the rubber in the galoshes would insulate my feet from the ground and not permit the current to pass through me. The men laughed, not believing me. I was challenged. I went to the house, put on my galoshes, and came out. Confidently, I seized the wire with my hand, and to the amazement of the men, nothing happened. Emboldened by this success, I did the same with my other hand. The shock I got I shall never forget. With the laughter of the men in my ears, I ran home crying. It taught me never to brag of having superior knowledge.

The mood in the town was unsettled. There were about a hundred Bolsheviks among the workers, opposed to the Provisional Government, to which Father was loyal. There were frequent evening meetings where the workers came up with demands that the administration could not satisfy.

In July more disturbing news arrived from the capital. The efforts of the Provisional Government to continue the war with Germany were up against the public weariness with the war, and the further erosion of discipline in the army. Influenced by Bolshevik anti-war propaganda, many soldiers were deserting; transportation was in disarray, and food shortages in the cities had become acute. There were mass pro-Bolshevik demonstrations on the streets of Petrograd, arrests of some of the Bolshevik leaders, and changes in the composition of the government. Alexander Kerensky[2] became Prime Minister and Alexander Zarudny, our Uncle Sasha, became Minister of Justice.

The echoes of these events reached the Urals. I remember that once Mother said something that showed her critical attitude towards Kerensky. I was startled. I had assumed that the people in the new revolutionary government were great heroes. "And you think you could have done better than Kerensky?" I asked my mother. She thought a little and then, quite seriously, answered, "Yes, I think I could!" I was terribly impressed.

In America the Russian Revolution of February 1917 was greeted enthusiastically as a sign of the democratization of one of the largest autocracies in the world. The war "to make the world safe for democracy" against autocratic Germany began to make more sense. The United States declared war on Germany in April 1917.

In the hope of keeping Russia in the war, President Wilson sent a commission to Petrograd in June, by way of Vladivostok and the Trans-Siberian Railroad. Their published report was optimistic, except for the opinion of one member, who stayed in Russia longer and came to the conclusion that the political disposition of Russia was "beyond redemption." This man was an American lifelong Russophile named Charles R. Crane; he was an industrialist, a political liberal, and a personal friend of Robert La Follette, Louis Brandeis, and Woodrow Wilson. It was he who later played such an important role in the life of our family.

The election for the Constitutional Assembly, set for November, was approaching. Mother took an active part in the election campaign, agitating for the full participation of workers in the coming elections. The SR Party, with which Mother sympathized but to which she no longer belonged, had strong support among the peasants because of its land distribution policy. The slogans of this party were "Land to those who work on it," and "Universal, equal, direct, and confidential suffrage." Here in Byeloretsk, however, the majority of the population consisted of industrial workers, who mostly favored the Bolsheviks. They were for state ownership of land and the "dictatorship of the proletariat." It seems that my parents were effectively in enemy territory.

One morning when we got up, we found the whole household in a tense and worried state. Father returned in the middle of the morning, looking tired and sad. He said that he had been called in the middle of the night for an emergency at the mill. There had been a terrible explosion of the blast furnace, and a number of the workers had been killed. The foreman of that department had been badly beaten by the workers and Father had just returned from visiting him in hospital.

We learned later that there was a strike of the workers servicing the blast furnace. The foremen tried to convince the workers that the blast furnace could not be shut down at once, but had to be extinguished very gradually. But the urging of the foremen was to no avail, and the furnace exploded. The striking workers, both shifts of six workers each, were all around it, demonstratively idle. All twelve of them were hit by red-hot bricks and the molten contents of the furnace. All of them were either killed instantly or died a very short time afterwards.

The whole town was in mourning. A mass funeral followed, with memorial services at the church. Father attended them all. The workers were still not convinced that an explosion was inevitable if the furnace was shut down suddenly. Again, there were meetings and discussions with the workers, and Father was hardly ever home. The workers' mood was increasingly rebellious, and the Bolsheviks, who were trying to rouse them against the administration, continued agitating for strikes. Even though the blast furnace producing the pig iron, on which the entire production of the mill depended, was repaired and working again, another strike seemed imminent.

One day, in the early afternoon, we heard the sudden wailing of the mill's emergency whistles. We knew that something terrible had happened. People were running past our house towards the mill. We stood on the porch, trying to get some news. Mother stood there worried and pale, terribly worried about Father, who was also at the mill.

It was already dusk when our exhausted father returned home. He told us that the furnace had exploded again and again all the workers of that shift – six of them – had been killed. The workers of the other departments, again encouraged by the agitators, attacked the administration offices and beat up the top engineer. He was in hospital now.

Another series of funerals took place. The mood was grim and ominous. Attempting to pacify the workers, committees were formed and meetings held. The furnace was repaired again and gradually became functional.

October Revolution

The October Revolution, when the Bolsheviks took power in Petrograd, occurred on October 25, 1917. At first the hope remained that the Constitutional Assembly would still produce a constitution, and be followed by a universally elected government.

From Petrograd too came the news of the death of our Aunt Katya, on November 15. Evidently disturbed by rumors of famine, she had starved herself, refusing to take any food. I remember a memorial service in the church, pale Zhenia, and the sad faces of Mother and Father. Shortly after that Zhenia became ill. They said it was typhus, but it may have been polio. He recovered, but lost much of the use of his legs. For the rest of his life he always had to use crutches, or at best two canes.

My ninth birthday and Christmas passed with hardly any festive atmosphere, though Mother and Father tried to make it fun for the children, and decorated and lighted the Christmas tree for us. I remember this time as one of continued tension. Something terrible was expected all the time, but nobody knew what.

Most vividly, I remember the awful piercing sound of the mill's siren for the third time. The furnace had exploded again. There was a desperate feeling that this was the end. Panic filled the town again, and this time it would have been Father's turn to be beaten up. Fortunately, after the experience of the previous explosions, no workers were near the furnace, so no one was killed, though some men were severely burned. But even the relief of finding that no fatalities had occurred could not reduce the sense of doom. Later that day I saw a man running down the street, with bandages covering almost all of his body. Apparently, being in intolerable pain, he had fled from the hospital. It was an unforgettable sight: as he ran, the bandages were unrolling behind him.

Elections to the Constitutional Assembly were conducted in December. The Constitutional Assembly opened in Petrograd on January 5, 1918. Because the majority were representatives of the SR and other non-Bolshevik parties, Lenin disbanded the Assembly the next day. Upon returning to their regions, the duly elected members formed centers of opposition in different parts of the country.

In Byeloretsk the Bolsheviks now had the support of the government and began to take over the administration of the town and the mill under the leadership of an old revolutionary, P. V. Tochissky. Soon the town was under their control, and on the night of February 17, 1918 several men came to our house. They searched all the rooms, pulling out drawers, looking into cupboards, turning over papers. We frightened children, awakened by the noise, watched them arrest Mother and Father and take them away.

The next day Manya found out that both Mother and Father had been sent to a prison in the city of Ufa. Thus the responsibility for the whole household was thrust upon her. She was only twenty-three years old and had never before been in charge, and Nanny, though helpful in managing the kitchen and taking care of the little children, was of no real assistance in more complex situations. Fräulein Marie had earlier married a Czech officer and left Byeloretsk. Zuza, the cook, had just given birth to a son, and had a bad infection following childbirth. Zhenia and Verochka did their best, but Zhenia was now partly paralyzed, and Verochka, who was not very efficient at coping with things, had a baby of her own and a helpless husband on her hands. To top it all, the younger children came down with whooping cough, and Nanny had her hands more than full.

We continued to live in the same house for the following two months, with Manya and Nanny trying to maintain the same everyday routine, and some of Father and Mother's friends trying to help with advice. The Soviet Government was officially established in the town on March 18, 1918.

Manya did not know what we should do next. Communication with the capital was at a minimum. I am sure that she tried to write to our uncles and aunts, all of whom were quite helpless in Petrograd, which at that time was in a turmoil of arrests, food shortages, and political change. The new Soviet Government concluded a unilateral peace with Germany at Brest-Litovsk on March 3, 1918, which cost Russia a large part of its territory: all the Ukraine with its fertile fields, rich coal and iron mines, and access to the Black Sea. Also lost were the territories along the coast of the Baltic Sea – Poland, Lithuania, Latvia, Estonia, and Finland. Meanwhile, some of the army units, released from the German front, were unwilling to accept the new regime, and civil war began on several fronts. However, the communists controlled all the cities along the Trans-Siberian Railroad, which essentially meant all of Siberia, in spite of the fact that the Socialists and other parties opposing the Bolsheviks were in the majority there.

We were cut off in a small town, connected to the main railroad only by a narrow-gauge track that operated sporadically and was administered by the mill town officials. On March 30, 1918 news came that Zhenia's father, Evgenii Cavos, had died suddenly in Petrograd. Another memorial service took place, this time without Mother and Father. Zhenia stood there on his crutches with tears rolling down his face. I was overwhelmed: I never knew that men could cry. I was so taken by Zhenia's sorrow that I could not think of anything else. I wrote notes to him a number of times. With Mother, Father, and even Fräulein Marie all gone, I felt quite abandoned, and let my feelings about Zhenia take over completely. I would steal out to go to Zhenia's house and, unseen by anybody, hide behind a door to listen to him playing his violin for an hour at a time. It was the nearest thing to being in love that a nine-year-old could experience.

Zhenia also must have been in bad state: in one year he had lost his mother and father, while my parents – his protectors and advisers – had been taken away; he himself was incapacitated, and could not help his wife and small child. Now he also learned that his three older sisters had had to flee Petrograd, and were living as helpless refugees in the city of Revel, Estonia.

The arrests in the town continued unabated. There were rumors that Tochissky, who had assumed despotic power over the lives of the people, now preferred to interrogate those he arrested personally, after which he would shoot some of them in his cellar, rather than ship them to Ufa. It seemed fortunate that Mother and Father had been arrested earlier. Later, when Tochissky himself was killed in an uprising in July, it was rumored that his wife and daughter refused to accept his body for the funeral.

Mother and Father at Ufa

It took from February 18 to March 3 for Mother and Father to reach the prison in Ufa. Later Father described their arrival in his diary:

When at seven in the evening nine of us were brought into prison cell number 6, all twenty-two cots in it were occupied. Someone let me have a folding cot near the table; all the other newcomers slept on the floor. We were treated to tea with snacks, and everyone listened to our stories. At eleven we were told to stop talking and go to sleep. Our cell had a very interesting and varied group of cultured people, all in shirts with unbuttoned collars, because it was very hot. We drank tea, which we heated on the iron stove; this added to the heat of the cell. At night it became quite cold. At first, covering myself with a warm blanket, I felt cold from below, through the thin canvas of the folding bed. I had to get up and put my trousers and other things under the sheet to protect myself a little from the cold below.

I was first greeted by Alexander Gavrilov, who was secretary of the Commercial and Industrial Union of the city and an electrical engineer. He introduced me to the other inhabitants of the cell.

Father listed the names of some of the people in the cell, all of them people of some stature in local society. There were engineers, a bank president, the secretary of a union, a bank clerk, two admitted saboteurs, and a well-to-do peasant, Aleksei Prokopiev (whose daughter, the "Madonna of the Revolution," had been defended by Father's brother Sasha in 1906).

Father continued:

There was another cell, number 7, filled with those from Ufa. Later they were moved to our cell number 6. Among them was a young gymnasium student, Mallo, the son of very rich parents. There were merchants, Kuznetsov and the Vydineevs. Then there was Dudorov, the very pleasant owner of a match factory, who greatly helped those from Byeloretsk by procuring food for them. Our cell changed its composition constantly. One day Count Peter Tolstoy was brought to our cell. He was the editor of the "Ufimskaya Zhisn" (Ufa Life), later called "Day." He had previously been a member of the first Duma from the Constitutional Democratic party,[3] a very nice and intelligent person. We also met his wife.

Both Father and Mother were seniors among their cellmates by their position, if not by age; it was often their role to offer moral and financial assistance. Father doesn't mention that in the diary, but it is clear from some notes on the photographs of their cellmates given to them later. Father drew pictures of the cell, the yard, the plan of the prison, noting: "I am recording this because I think it will be of some interest to posterity." But his record is very sporadic. He read a lot, all in French and all about the French Revolution. He copied into the diary long passages from his reading, which obviously struck him as relevant to his own experience: French poems and monologues of executed victims of the revolution, with their noble thoughts.

Father and Mother were released from the prison on April 1, 1918, earlier than many. Most of the other prisoners were released after a short trial in the middle of May. They sat for a group photograph in the studio of an Ufa photographer. By sheer chance Father met in Ufa a man named Joseph Rotman, whose family he had once helped to escape from a pogrom in Nadezhdensky Zavod. The grateful Rotman offered to rent three rooms in his apartment to us. Because of the change in administration, there was no question of Father's returning to Byeloretsk. My parents wrote to Manya to bring the family and its possessions to Ufa.

This must have been a very hard task for young Manya. The chances of our returning to Byeloretsk were infinitesimal, and she had to decide what was to be taken and what was to be left. The furniture, of course, stayed behind. Small possessions were packed into the trunks. But the pictures, the heavy frames? She could not bring herself to cut them out of their frames, as Mother often said she would do if she had to flee. So they were all left behind. I have

Ufa, 1918
Mother and Father are seated in the front row

often wondered what happened to them: did they find their way to a museum, were they destroyed, or were they simply appropriated by townspeople, and still hang on the walls of houses there?

There remained one problem: how to get the necessary permission to leave Byeloretsk. This was solved by arranging the day of departure for a time when the dreaded Tochissky was out of town. So on May 1, 1918, the Thursday of Holy Week, Manya, Nanny, the five children, and a mountain of luggage boarded a small passenger car of the narrow-gauge railroad. We were seen off by Zhenia, Verochka, and a number of Father's and Mother's friends. Several hours later we reached the station on the main Trans-Siberian Railroad, where we disembarked and waited for the train going to Ufa.

Transportation on the railroads was badly disrupted. There were no passenger trains or cars. Manya finally got permission to load all of us into a boxcar just emptied of coal. She had all the trunks piled in the middle of the car. She urged the children to sit on the luggage, and not to budge, because the walls, the floor, and even the ceiling of the car were black with coal dust. Nanny watched the little ones, and held baby Zoya in her arms.

Thus we traveled for most of the day. It was a blackened crowd of children that Mother and Father met at the station in Ufa, but there was great joy at the end of a long and frightening separation.

[1]   *Versta* is an old Russian measure of distance, equal to 0.66 mile.

[2]   Alexander Fedorovich Kerensky (1881-1970): defense lawyer and member of the SR party in 1917. He became the first Minister of Justice in the Provisional Government in March 1917, then Minister of War in May, and Prime Minister from July 1917 until the Bolshevik overthrow in October. He fled to Finland, then to England, and came to the United States in 1940, where he resided until his death.

[3]   The Constitutional Democratic Party was a party with liberal monarchist tendencies, consisting largely of rich landowners and bourgeoisie.

7

Moving with the Front

One of the consequences of the unilateral peace with Germany was the Czech problem. Their native country was part of the old Austrian Empire, now allied with Germany. Some of the Czechs conscripted by the German Army to fight on the Russian front preferred to surrender to the Russians and become prisoners of war. The Provisional Government formed these prisoners into an army of their own, to fight against the Germans. They were well-motivated and well-armed; when the Russian Army began to disintegrate they were the most disciplined corps remaining. Since they wanted to continue fighting on the Allied side for the liberation of their homeland, they managed to become classified as an Allied division and be placed under French control. The Soviets offered them passage by way of the Siberian Railroad to Vladivostok, where Allied ships could pick them up and take them to the European front. Their command realized what an enormous distance they had to cover, but there was no other way to get home. Some of the Czechs did reach Vladivostok, but the rest, about 40,000 of them, were left scattered along the way. Struggling to unite themselves, together with Russian anti-Bolshevik units they engaged in many conflicts with the Red Army. With Allied military intervention in Russia (the United States sent a force of about 10,000 men), the so-called Czech Legion wound up fighting on the White side in the Civil War.

On April 28, 1918 Father wrote in his diary: "The situation becomes more ominous in connection with the Czechoslovaks: last night at one-thirty a.m. all the officers and Czechs arrested lately were led out of the prison. One in a white cap – Tolstoy[1] – walked briskly, the others were in pairs, holding each other by the arm. This was reported by one of the wives, who took turns watching the prison all night in expectation that the prisoners would be taken away. They say there were 120 of them. No one knows where they were taken. They are considered hostages."

Apparently, the Bolsheviks were getting ready to leave Ufa, and wished to use the prisoners as hostages in their boat, as they retreated along the river. News of this sort was never discussed with the children, and rarely even mentioned in front of us. I was so used to the adults speaking French or otherwise cutting us out of their conversations that I did not even try to find out what was going on. But Manya and Nanny were another matter, and some of their anxiety passed on to us.

The town was quiet, and expectation was in the air. A day or two later we heard loud brass music coming from the street. Running out, we saw a marching band, followed by a formation of uniformed men. The shouts of the crowd greeting the troops let us know that this was a detachment of the Czech Legion. Their arrival in Ufa was the beginning of the "White" or anti-Bolshevik occupation of the whole region. So it happened that now, in Ufa, we were on the White side of the Civil War front.

One day I heard that one of the hostages mentioned by Father had escaped, and the story he told was appalling. They were all kept in the hold of the ship. Then one of them was called on deck; after a while another was called, and then another. It became clear to the rest of them that they were being executed one by one. The man telling the story said that he came up very fast as soon as he was called, and immediately jumped overboard. The soldiers shot at him from the boat, but they missed and he escaped. He thought that the rest of the prisoners must have perished.

Through all this turmoil we children lived in our own world with our own problems and joys, which, however, reflected the strife of the adults. The brick apartment house where we lived stood in the middle of a large interior court. A shop that manufactured and sold leather products occupied the front buildings on the street. Our apartment was located on the third floor, off an entrance hall with a wide stone stairway that had smooth wooden banisters. I had never seen such banisters. We were sure that they were intended for sliding down, of course, and greatly enjoyed doing so.

There were a number of children in the house, and Seryozha and I immediately found friends. The yard outside was paved with asphalt, which I hadn't seen since Libava; it was good for bouncing a ball or playing hopscotch, but it was so easy to be bruised when falling on it. I missed the plain soft earth that one could dig, or in which one could plant something. I thought it absolutely necessary that children be in touch with the earth, and since I was the oldest among them, I felt responsible for the welfare of the rest. The middle of the interior court was not paved, but we were told that we children must stay out of it. Freshly tanned leather was hung there on lines strung from one end to the other, covering more than half the space. On the rest of it a great quantity of firewood was stacked in neat, closely packed rows, forming a huge cube. A small fence surrounded the area.

It annoyed me that this place, so suitable for children to play in, was instead occupied by things that could easily be put somewhere else. I was sure that the children's needs were much more important. After all, I was thinking of the others: the "little ones." So without hesitation I went to the leather shop and asked them please to find another place for hanging their leather. Some adults must have supported me in my request, because in a short time the leather lines disappeared and the children were allowed to use the yard. Many a knee skinned on hard asphalt began to heal.

One of our activities was to rub bricks: Manya used brick dust for cleaning the steel knives. She dipped a wet bottle cork into this powder, and rubbed the tarnished steel knives with it till they shone. I thought brick dust was an important staple to have in the house. We made it by rubbing together brick fragments that were scattered around the yard. One day it occurred to me that we could make shapes out of these fragments. I suggested that all the children might work together making miniature bricks and get a lot of brick dust at the same time. My idea was to make so many little bricks that we would be able to build a small model house. All the children got involved. We had a good time rubbing the bricks, playing games, and even digging and planting some seeds in the ground. I was pretty much the leader.

All went well until some of the children started to tease a small boy who was rather weak and could not stand up for himself. He

may have been a son of our hosts, the Rotmans. Because he was
Jewish, they called him offensive names, and he was very unhappy.
When we came home we told Mother that he was called "Yid" and
that it seemed to upset him.

"Never use that word," said Mother, "it is a bad word, and it
is very offensive!" "Why?" I asked. Father was close and heard us.
"I shall tell you a story," he said. "When I was a young man, I got
onto a streetcar one day. It was very crowded. An old woman, who
entered the car with me, tried to occupy the only seat that was left.
A young, strong-looking man rushed ahead of her, pushed her aside
and occupied the place. Someone in the car said, 'How impolite!'
and reproached him, to which the young man replied with some
crude remark. I got mad. The young man looked very Jewish and
I shouted out at him, 'Yid!' At that moment a very distinguished
older man sitting not far from me raised himself slightly, lifting his
hat as if in greeting and said, 'And so am I!' I could never forget the
shame I felt. By using this insulting word in my anger at the impolite
young man I offended not just him, but every Jewish person who
had nothing to do with it. I never used it again."

Seryozha and I were duly impressed.

Back in the yard, the children continued to taunt the little boy.
They sang offensive ditties and called him names. I was upset. I had
never seen anything like this, but I could not stop them. It went
on for several days, with the poor boy returning home in tears. I
argued and fought with the children, and Seryozha joined me, but
the situation was out of control.

Then Seryozha and I had a bright idea: we would break with
the whole crowd, and do something much more interesting. We
would dig a cave on top of the woodpile, and make it into our own
den. And so we did. Besides Seryozha and me, only the Jewish boy
was allowed in it. It was a gorgeous den. We lined it with blankets
and pillows brought from the house. We covered it with branches,
leaving a small hole for the entrance; we brought cookies and
milk and were the envy of every child in the yard. Father and
Mother looked into our cave, but of course they were too big to get
inside. So it was our own "very secret" den. The children's games
deteriorated without Seryozha and me. I think that in time they

Mulya, Sergey, Elena, Tanya, and Zoya
Ufa, Summer 1918

made peace with us – perhaps because of some interference by the adults – because I remember finally trying to construct the house with all the bricks we had produced and, thinking myself an expert, mixing cement and water for mortar and building it with properly staggered bricks. We let it stand to dry, but the next day it fell apart. Thus ended my first attempts at leadership and construction.

Father managed to sell two of his furnaces for installation in nearby mills. This supported the family for the time being, but Father had no job. He was at home a great deal, and on rainy days was very inventive in trying to entertain us. I remember his sitting with us around a table, cutting out parts of models from printed cardboard. They were very complicated models: one of a castle, one of a battleship, and some others. We learned how and where the flaps for gluing had to be left, how the cutout pieces must be carefully bent and glued. The models were works of art. Years later, after my father died, I saw the sketches for these models in his diary. He also had us write and draw in his diary, and added his own remarks: "Mulya writes poetry. Seryozha paints scenes of war, Mulya landscapes, and Lena portraits. Mulya is memorizing the Bronze Horseman now."

I was indeed memorizing *The Bronze Horseman*, a long poem by Pushkin. I decided to do it because Mother told me that when the students in her gymnasium (high school) studied Pushkin's longest poem, *Evgenii Onegin*, they were assigned to memorize only the beginning of the poem. Mother asked the teacher whether anyone could memorize the whole poem, and the teacher said that it was too long. That was a challenge, so Mother set out to memorize all of it, and she did. As for me, I thought that while *Evgenii Onegin* really was too long, I could be second best and memorize *The Bronze Horseman*, with its more than 500 lines. It took some time, but I finally did it.

Asha

In July 1918 Father was appointed a member of the temporary Board of Directors of the Simsky District Steel Mills. The other two members were the chairman Alexei Umov, a mining engineer, and Alexander Gavrilov, one of Father's old cellmates at Ufa.

The Board was in charge of the steel mills for the absentee owners. Either through the Bolshevik take-over or because the stockholders and top managers had fled the country, most of the mills in the Ural region had lost their administration. On the White side of the civil war front these mills were temporarily nationalized to keep them going, with management appointed by the local government. In July 1918 a conference was held in Ufa. It divided authority for all the nationalized mills and plants in the Urals among the various territorial districts. The Simsky District included a mill at Asha, a short distance from Ufa on the Trans-Siberian Railroad, and Father and Alexei Umov were transferred there.

As usual, Father went to Asha ahead of the family to make preparations, and the rest of the family followed some days later. It was late in the evening when we arrived. After a quick snack prepared by Manya and Nanny we were tucked into our beds, which had already been made up for us. The adults settled down to exchange their impressions and news of the days spent in separation. Suddenly one of the children started to cry, then another, and another. Soon all the children were crying. Our worried parents turned on the lights in our bedrooms, and discovered that all of us children, our nightgowns, and our beds were covered with crawling bedbugs. We were taken outside, the nightgowns shaken out, the mattresses thrown out into the garden, and we were put to sleep on benches, on the floor, or just on blankets spread over the boards of the beds. Cleaning and spraying went on all the next day.

It was summer. Seryozha and I spent most of our time outside, walking barefoot on the soft dust of the country roads, or along the rapidly flowing mountain river. Its banks were reinforced with slag from the mill's blast furnace. We took great delight in collecting beautiful large pieces of this slag; we admired their light blue and blue-green shades and their surfaces smooth as glass, but unlike glass, opaque. We also found white pieces of slag foam, which could be shaped by rubbing them against a harder stone, and which would float when we threw them into the river. The slag pieces were very sharp, and we were quite proud when our feet toughened enough so that we could walk on them barefoot, like the other village children.

They, of course, were quite used to the slag and paid no attention to its beauty; they found our excitement rather amusing. What they looked for were pieces of iron, which occasionally could be found among the slag and sold back to the mill. We started collecting the iron too, but never got to the point of selling it.

We were taken on several trips into the mountains. I remember beautiful open mines of kaolin (china clay). We could walk at the bottom of the mines. They looked like a roofless palace, with white and delicate pink walls rising vertically around us.

Climbing on the mountain cliffs was much more fun than the tedious uphill walking we had to do in order to reach the cliffs. Numerous unusual stones were easy to find there. I became interested in stones, and started a collection. Among my stones I had big pieces of asbestos rock – that lovely greenish, almost translucent rock which was so easy to pull apart, fiber by fiber. Its color reminded me of the sea, which I had seen a long time ago, in Libava. Some stones that looked like small boulders could be broken and revealed a beautiful structure of large quartz crystals.

A few weeks after our arrival, we moved to a much better house on Lipovaya Gora (Linden Mountain). I remember it as rather gloomy, however, perhaps because it was shaded by tall trees close by. We had a horse barn, two horses, and a coachman who took care of them. Every morning the coachman took Father to the mill in a carriage. I was given a chance to hold the reins and drive the horse a couple of times. After a while Father allowed me to take him to the mill alone. I was very proud, especially on the return home, driving the horse all by myself. It really was not so much of an accomplishment, because the horse knew the road so well that it did not need any direction at all.

Seryozha and I did some riding too. Now we were allowed to use saddles – the thick padded saddles customary in the region. Once our horses were frightened by something and raced into the woods, taking the bits in their teeth, out of control. The branches of the trees hung low, and we were riding without saddles that time, just on blankets attached to the horses by straps around their bellies. I managed to stay on the horse by leaning forward and pressing my head against the horse's neck, but Seryozha clutched the strap holding the blanket and slid under the horse's belly, hanging there by the strap, absolutely terrified. I never forgot that sight; I teased him about it, but indeed I felt very guilty, because I was supposed to watch over Seryozha when we went riding alone.

Although Manya and Nanny were very inventive about using what was available to feed us, food shortages began to affect the family. One thing we children knew was that the adults denied themselves sugar, which was in short supply. All the sugar they were able to get went to the children. It was then that I conceived of a present we could give to our parents for the approaching Christmas. We could save sugar, given to us for tea or porridge, a little at a time; if we all did this, we could accumulate quite a bit of it, and give it to our parents at Christmas.

On the top of a box I constructed a scene: it had a stage with pine trees on three sides of it and Father Frost with a bag on his shoulders walking in the middle. In front of him there was a small trap door opening to the inside of the little box where we were supposed to deposit the spoonfuls of our sugar. It was kept secret from the adults, of course, as a present should be. The three older children participated in this venture. I don't know how I managed to convince Seryozha and Lena to give up the only sweet thing we had at that time. We accumulated almost a full bowl of sugar by Christmas time, and ceremoniously gave it to our parents, who were touched, but also dismayed at our self-denial of what they considered an important dietary supplement.

With the beginning of fall our studies with Mother resumed, but not for long. The White army, which a short while before had advanced from its Siberian positions beyond the Urals into the European part of Russia, was now in retreat. The Communists, who had been in control of the mills before we came to Asha, were now in hiding or had joined the partisans. A number of acts of sabotage were attributed to them.

One morning some terrible news reached us: Alexei Umov, the chairman of the Board of Directors, had been shot and killed at night. He was sitting at the desk in his study reading the Bible;

the shot came from the garden through the dark window in front of him and killed him instantly. It was obviously the work of the Communist partisans. Living in a house in the midst of the woods, all of us, even the children, felt very uneasy. Father's position, after all, was not so much different from Umov's. But Father never gave way to panic, and we continued living as before.

CB

At this time most of Siberia along the Trans-Siberian Railroad, all the way to Vladivostok at the extreme east of it on the shores of the Sea of Japan, was in the hands of different leaders opposing the Bolsheviks for many different reasons. The Czechs, Japanese, Americans, French, and English supported such anti-Bolshevik policies. The English and French were worried by the Soviets' peace treaty with the Germans, which eliminated their eastern front, but the overall political picture in Siberia was taking a most disorganized shape. In the struggle for power, intrigue and crime became rampant.

In Omsk, a Siberian city about a thousand miles east of Asha, a government composed mostly of Socialists and former members of the Constitutional Assembly was organized. It was supposed to unite various forces opposed to the Communist government in Moscow, some of them commanded by different Cossack chiefs, some by former officers of the Tsarist army. That task was almost impossible.

On October 29 (November 11), 1918 an Armistice was signed in Europe. The devastating war ended, leaving Europe in shambles. But its conclusion was not even noticed in the small mill town surrounded by the unleashed chaos of the Civil War. The Reds were now advancing and threatening Ufa. Father told us he was preparing a small freight car for our travel and we understood that the time was approaching for us to leave.

On November 18 the new Government in Omsk elected Admiral Alexander Kolchak "Supreme Ruler of Russia," which effectively meant only the portions under the control of the White Army. Father had known Kolchak at the Naval Academy and remembered him as an honest, upright officer totally loyal to the government he served.

Kolchak was a brave Arctic explorer, a heroic leader of the Russian fleet in the Black Sea, a great patriot, and an ardent anti-Bolshevik who proclaimed his advocacy of a democratic government for Russia. He was, however, primarily a military leader, a man who by his character was ready to serve his country, not to lead it. Father sympathized with him, though feeling a little doubtful about his role as "Ruler." Mother was convinced that without a political program he might lead the army, but could not lead the population of so large and spread-out a country. His regime later proved to be disastrous, but at the time, the area of Russia under his command was the only place where my parents could feel relatively safe.

On Our Way Again

So, one day early in December 1918 our things were packed and the whole family filled several carriages, which took us to the station and to "our" car, or *teplushka*, as such adapted freight cars were called, meaning literally "a warm or heated place." It was a wonderful *teplushka*. The central part functioned as a kitchen-living-dining room. On the sides there were sleeping compartments with hinged beds that folded to the wall. There were windows built into the walls of the car, so that we could see the passing landscape. There was room enough to put down all our things and even to spread out our books or drawing papers and pencils, and we wondered if Mother would insist on us resuming our studies. We were dressed very warmly for the winter. The small iron stove kept us quite warm, and served for cooking as well. Manya and Nanny knew at once how to use it.

We understood that the reason for our moving was that the Bolshevik army was approaching, and that it was expected to capture Asha; we were going east into Siberia. Our car was attached to a freight train. The journey was slow and the freight trains often changed. But inside it was comfortable, warm, and really quite pleasant, except for the little sisters fussing from boredom, and demanding that someone read or tell stories to them.

The mountain landscape soon changed to flat, spreading plains, with scattered woods, sometimes in the distance, sometimes quite close. It was good to fall asleep to the monotonous sound of the train wheels, feeling surrounded by the whole family, confident that they would take care of me and that the next day would be equally familiar, with the same rhythmical sound of the wheels, the same stretching woods beyond the window, the same landscape covered with snow, level, monotonous, and the same feeling of going… going… going… somewhere. The past was behind us, and nothing of it mattered; there was only the future, and that could not be frightening, because all those who mattered were together and safe.

Christmas was coming. I was worried that the children would not have a Christmas tree. I begged the adults to try to cut a tree at one of the frequent stops. After all, everything was so home-like, why not a tree? But the adults could not be persuaded.

We arrived in Cheliabinsk, some 250 miles east of Ufa, several days after Christmas. While the family stayed in the car on one of the sidetracks at the station, Father looked for a place to stay. It turned out to be quite a problem: the city was so full of refugees that no space could be found. Father had to go out into the country and find, in a Cossack village about fourteen miles from Cheliabinsk, a family willing to rent him two rooms in their house by moving all their own family into their kitchen.

To get to that village, Smolino, we had to hire horse-driven sleighs. Mother at that time was seven months pregnant. Father put all of us on a couple of sleighs, together with all our possessions, and sent us to Smolino. He himself had to stay in the city to continue to conduct the affairs of the evacuated mills, and to keep in touch with the political situation. I gather his job now had to do with the financial affairs of the Simsky District and the payment of salaries to those members of the staff who had left and were on our side of the front. From the Bolsheviks' point of view this was in itself a criminal act.

Smolino

The small Siberian horses, with shaggier coats than any I had seen before, were pulling our open sleighs at a gentle trot on the packed snow of the road. Tightly wrapped in our winter coats and blankets, our faces covered with scarves so that only our eyes showed, we watched the snow-covered fields and woods in the distance. As dusk approached, all the children fell asleep. When we arrived at our destination, it was already quite dark. There were no streetlights, of course. Some windows in the huts showed the faint light of kerosene lamps. Beyond the two rows of houses forming the only street, the space was covered by snow. In daylight we discovered that a large lake was there, frozen and snow-covered now, on the far shores of which stood some summerhouses, barely accessible in winter. One of these cottages turned out to be a lifesaver for us later.

The sky was brilliant with a myriad of stars, brighter than I had ever seen. Probably I had never been outside so late at night. We walked into the hut through a completely dark shed. The little ones were carried in still asleep. A well-padded door opened and we saw a rather big kitchen, a quarter of which was occupied by a brick stove about four feet high, with a chimney at the outer corner. The oven was open, with a few pots visible inside near some glowing coals. Several children were already asleep on top of the stove, and on the wall above them were wide shelves that served as beds for the rest of their family. We were warmly greeted and unwrapped from all our coats and shawls. Those of us who were awake enough were seated on the benches along the table and offered hot soup, kasha, and wonderfully fresh bread. We found out later that our hostess baked bread once a week and froze it immediately on the shelves of the shed through which we just passed. Every day a loaf or two was brought in and thawed out.

Our hosts were rather prosperous Cossacks. Their house had two rooms, which they rented to us, and a kitchen. Manya, Nanny, and the three younger children settled in the larger room, using as beds the benches that were there, and our suitcases and trunks. Mother, Seryozha, and I slept in one bed in the smaller room. Tired, we were all soon asleep.

This was the first time I had slept so close to my mother. I knew that her enlarged stomach held a child, our future brother or sister. I heard Mother once saying to my father that "It must be a boy, it is so active!" It puzzled me: how would it come out of there? When I asked her, she told me that there was an opening in her body, as well as in mine and in all girls', and that some time later I might bleed through it, but that I should never touch it. I knew, of course, how girls and boys differed – when I was little I often bathed with my brother in the same bathtub – but it had never occurred to me that it had anything to do with having children. That talk with my mother was the only talk I ever had with her about sex. No other talk at all, in fact, until I was almost twenty.

In the morning, after a hearty breakfast of porridge and bread and milk given to us by our hostess, we put on our coats, shawls, and felt boots and went out. I don't remember the children of our hosts at all; they must have been very shy as children usually are with strangers. We amused ourselves just by walking in the deep snow along the edge of the road. This snow was so hard in some places that we could walk on it without breaking the crust. When, occasionally, we did break through it, we sank to above our knees. The day was frosty and still, the sky a beautiful deep blue, the sun bright but without warmth. It was great fun to walk on the frozen lake. The untrodden snow was hardened into the form of waves, so there were small ridges and gullies which added to the feeling of adventure in what seemed to us an infinite expanse of space, with no living creatures in sight.

Recently on television I saw pictures of this same landscape, with the familiar villages, lakes, and woods near Smolino, an area that is now the site of the worst pollution by radioactive materials in the world.[2] Low fences with signs now prohibit access to the rivers, but these measures do not stop children from swimming and fishing, or women from washing their clothes in these rivers. It appears that the effect of exposure to radioactive waste in that area is devastating, causing early deaths from all sorts of cancer. Many children are born sick or deformed. Watching the broadcast, I remembered the pristine beauty of the snowy winter landscape and our happy childish exploration of it in 1919.

We discovered that the neighboring house accommodated another family of refugees from Asha, the Titovs. They were mother, father, two girls and a boy of approximately our ages. The father was an engineer, like our father. One of the girls, who was my age, was blind. We soon became fast friends. I admired her being able to keep a diary in Braille, and to play with cards marked in Braille, even solitaire. Her brother, sister, and parents read Braille too, not by feeling it but by looking at it. I could not understand how she could recognize the letters by feeling them – I could not do so, however hard I tried.

But what I most admired her for was her wonderful imagination. We took long walks on the lake's hard snow, pretending we were in a jungle. I described the tropical surroundings, which she completely absorbed. Sometimes I called out in terror that a tiger or lion was ready to jump on us and we both quickly crouched, hiding from it behind the nearest snowdrift. The rest of the time we sat in the kitchen, because the bedrooms were hardly heated, if at all. When the short day was over and the long blue dusk settled in, when it was not dark enough to light the lamps, yet too dark to read, we talked and made up many stories. Manya, Nanny, and Mother were usually present – or our friends' parents, if we were in their house. When the lamps were lit, we played games, mostly cards.

After about a month, the Titovs had to move on. I often wondered what became of my little friend during their refugee journey, traveling in crowded train cars. She might so easily be lost in a crowd at a station, if the hand holding hers happened to let go. This was the first parting I felt acutely, the first of many to come, when I knew that I would never again see the one to whom I said goodbye.

Our family divided, some of us moving into the rooms vacated by the Titovs. Manya and Nanny took over the cooking in the other house, where we usually gathered for our meals. The highlight of our stay in Smolino was Maslenitsa, the Russian winter festival that takes place the last week before Lent, corresponding to Shrove Tuesday or Mardi Gras. During this week special pancakes, *bliny*, are served, usually with smoked fish, caviar, and sour cream. In our family we always had several *bliny* dinners during that week, but I never saw anything like the celebration that was traditional for Cossacks. Every horse in the village was dressed up with bright ribbons braided into its mane and tail, and every sleigh was filled with children, women, and old people. They raced back and forth along the road between the houses, their bells jingling. Older boys and young men rode the dressed-up horses, demonstrating their skills. During the competition they picked up objects from the ground while galloping past them, jumped up to stand on the saddle, and waved their whips with one hand, shouting, and holding onto the reins with the other. The sound of whoops, laughter, squeals, yelps, and sleigh bells filled the air. The blue sky, bright sun, and bright colors of the ribbons were displayed against a background of dazzling white snow. This continued the entire week, with repeated *bliny* dinners.

ଔ

Shortly after Maslenitsa, a detachment of the White Army arrived in the village, where they were to be quartered. Every house in the village had to put up some men. An arrogant young officer appeared at our house. Mother, who by then was almost ready to give birth, told him that we had no place to go, that her husband was in the city, and that the family consisted of women and small children only. He was unmoved by this. I stood in the room frightened and unbelieving, as he gave her until tomorrow to vacate the rooms in both houses or be put out on the street!

One of the summerhouses on the shore of the lake, not very far from the village, was heated and at that time occupied by the family of a woman doctor with whom Mother was in touch, anticipating the need of her help during childbirth. So Mother appealed to her for shelter, and she agreed to give us a room. The next day we moved to one room of the small summerhouse. Our trunks were arranged along the walls of the room for us to sleep on. That night, after all the excitement and commotion, Mother went into labor. Manya, Nanny, and the doctor were up, but the children did not even awaken. Mother was taken to the dining room, and there on the dining table gave birth to her fifth daughter on February 27, 1919. I heard later that Mother was quite distressed by the fact that it was another daughter and not a son, while Manya, who was present, said, "Let it be *my* little girl then!"

We stayed in that house while Mother recuperated. The doctor's son, who was about ten years old, was rather condescending towards us, which we had to accept, realizing that in a way he had a right to his attitude. His parents reprimanded him, however, and in the end we played very well together. We used the long, snow-covered steps leading to the lake for a sledding hill. It was a wonderfully long slide, after our sleds packed it down. We built a house of cut-up hard snow blocks. It had two rooms connected by a door and a ceiling of snow blocks laid on pine branches. We could creep through its "doors" on all fours, and even sat inside once eating some sandwiches brought from the house.

A week or so later Father, learning of our plight, came and took all of us with him to the city. He had found a small apartment in a brick house in the city of Cheliabinsk, where we settled for the next couple of months.

Mother was very busy with the new baby. The girl was baptized in our home, and named Ekaterina (Katya) after Father's sister Aunt Katya, who had died almost two years before. Since no close family friends or relatives were available, it was decided that I, her oldest sister, should be her godmother. I held the little baby at the christening and it was to me that the priest returned her, crying, when she was taken out of the basin. I felt very important, and took my duties quite seriously. That did not keep me, however, from continuing my tomboy behavior.

The only other thing I remember from our stay in Cheliabinsk was the crowd of Bashkir soldiers camped in the yard of our house. We could see them from our window: they were sitting on the ground and searching for lice on one another's heads and bodies. Because the typhus epidemic was beginning to spread, and was spread by lice, everyone was alarmed by this sight.

◌ঙ

In the early spring Kolchak's army advanced westward, moving beyond the Urals, and Father was sent back to Asha. We returned to our house on Lipovaya Gora, but Father would not let me drive him to the mill. It was too dangerous, he said. Zhenia with his family joined us, having been able to leave Byeloretsk after the advancing

White Army occupied it. They had two boys now: their younger son Stepan – always called Steve – was born after we left Byeloretsk. Verochka was still nursing, and as Mother did not have enough milk to satisfy little Katya, Verochka nursed her too. Zhenia was quite crippled, and walked with crutches. We were fourteen people now.

Kolchak's military skills could not overcome hopeless demoralization at the rear. Various factions of the army, often led by former Tsarist officers, antagonized the local population by their autocratic and ruthless behavior. There was rivalry among the independent Cossack leaders, called *Atamans,* who supported Kolchak, and who exhibited terrible brutality, often in the interests of their own power and personal enrichment. Some regions along the railroad were totally controlled by such Atamans, who diverted the supplies intended for the White Army for their own use and treated the locals so badly that most of them hoped for the arrival of the Bolsheviks. The intrigues and power struggles among the different political factions within the White government itself undermined the conduct of the war, and by June Kolchak's army was once more in retreat. The Reds were again approaching Ufa, and again we had to leave. Father now had no time to have a boxcar reconstructed: it was a much less comfortable *teplushka* that all of us boarded, after only about one month in Asha. There were now eight children, two of them small babies, and six adults. This time we headed further east into Siberia – to Omsk, the seat of the Kolchak government.

Omsk was terribly crowded with the foreign military units supporting Kolchak – Czechs, English, French, and Americans – and with refugees fleeing east from the advancing Red Army. Father's business headquarters had also moved to Omsk. At first Father found us a large enough house at Petukhovo, a town on the railroad line toward the city, where we were fairly comfortable living all together. We spent a month there and moved again. No houses or apartments were yet available in Omsk, so for the rest of the summer Father left us at Karachi, a resort town nearby.

Karachi was built on the shore of a salt lake and was known for its mud baths. Father found two houses there, so that we and the

Cavoses could live side by side, but separately. Zhenia could take the mud baths, in the hope that they would help his condition; the older children, with Manya, could spend time bathing in the lake. None of us knew how to swim, but we easily learned, since the lake was so salty that one simply floated like a cork. When you floated on your back you did not have to worry about keeping your nose and mouth above the water. Treading water vertically, you could not go down beyond your neck: your head was always above water. I enjoyed trying to reach for the crystallized salt on the bottom, which was supposed to be beneficial for the baths of babies who could not go into the lake themselves, but this was very hard because the water would push me up. The bottom held the famous mud, which felt smooth, almost oily, and was very black.

We stayed a month in Karachi. It was a real holiday, but it was not a place to spend the winter. Father finally found a house for us in Omsk. We moved there in late August, and Zhenia and his family joined us in October. The year was 1919.

¹   Most probably Ivan Zarudny's cellmate Peter Petrovich Tolstoy: editor of the "Ufimskaya Zhisn" (Ufa Life), chairman of the Ufa Committee of Constitutional Democrats, and chairman of the Agricultural Union of Ufa Gubernia. After October 1917 he openly claimed the Bolsheviks to be usurpers; he was taken as a hostage in May 1918 and killed.

²   Cheliabinsk was the center of Soviet nuclear arms production. In 1957 there was an explosion at a nuclear waste storage tank at the Mayak nuclear complex that polluted an enormous surrounding area with plutonium and strontium.

II

OMSK

8

Omsk, 1919

Omsk, the nineteenth-century capital of Western Siberia, was originally the city where prisoners were taken before being sent to work at various mines. It is built on the shores of the river Irtysh, a deep, wide, navigable river, made famous by a song about the early Siberian explorer Ermak.[1] The Irtysh is a tributary of the river Ob, which is one of the three great Siberian rivers emptying into the Arctic Ocean.

The city had a large prison and many well-built brick government buildings. There was also an opera house, a theater, several schools, apartment buildings, churches, stores, and beautiful private homes. The center of Omsk had paved streets. On the periphery, though, the streets at that time were unpaved and the houses were small, wooden, one-story structures. The backyards often housed chickens, horses, cows, and other barnyard animals. There were no streetcars; horse-drawn cabs could be hired at the station and at various places throughout the city. Sidewalks were wooden, made of two or three planks, under which were ditches running the length of the block on both sides of the street.

Our house stood close to the street. The street was not paved, and in the middle of it for most of the year there was a large puddle in which the houses were reflected, as in a pond. I liked the sight of this puddle. The house was built of logs with a metal roof. The thin slots between the logs were filled, as usual, with oiled jute, but by now some of it had fallen out, and the wind could blow through the cracks. Inside, the walls were covered with many layers of wallpaper, which heaved under the pressure of strong winds.

It was nevertheless a substantial house, with four large rooms, a kitchen, and a cold inside toilet built like an outhouse: it had a wooden bench with a hole in it. What dropped down could be reached from outside through a wooden bulkhead attached to the house. The contents had to be periodically removed with shovels, usually in the winter when it was frozen; and then it had to be chopped with an axe, loaded on sleds, and taken down to the river. There was no running water. We had to get water in buckets from the river and fill the large barrel in the kitchen. In the winter the top of the water in the barrel was usually frozen by morning. Bathing and washing were done in basins set on a chair or in a little metal bathtub for the small children. Adults went occasionally to the nearby bathhouse. In the summer everyone bathed in the river. The drinking water always had to be boiled.

The house was heated by several brick stoves, built into the walls between the rooms in such a way that the firebox opened into one room, while the tile-covered sides of the stove heated the adjacent rooms as well. When fuel became scarce, several small sheet-iron stoves were installed next to the brick ones. They used the brick chimney for their flues and heated one room at a time very quickly, usually for a short time and on special occasions. Outside, there was a backyard with a barn. There were heavy shutters on the windows of the house, which were usually closed at night.

The river was just a few blocks from our house. We could swim in it, fish from the landings, or simply walk along its shores. The shores were flat and sandy near the water, and there was good clay in the steeper parts of its banks. Of course there were no lifeguards, nor any supervision of the swimming children, although there were dangerous spots with whirlpools.

Father bought two cows, because he always worried that we might have a genetic predisposition to tuberculosis from our grandmother; therefore he was very cautious about the milk we drank. A short time after we settled in Omsk, our cook Zuza came to join us with her son Peter (Petya), who was by then a year and a half old. Her husband was trying to make his way to Latvia, which had just become an independent republic. He anticipated many difficulties and even dangers on his trip, so Zuza did not dare to follow him with the baby but instead came to Omsk to stay with us. She was quite lame after a postnatal infection; she was told that she could not have any more children, and doted on her son. Now we had a veritable children's colony: there were nine of us in the house.

As soon as we moved in, Mother decided that conditions would not permit her to continue her systematic teaching of me and Seryozha. We had to go to school. In Russian schools at that time instruction started at seven, so Lena, who was six, stayed at home for the time being. I was ten and Seryozha was eight, and in order to prove that we were prepared to enter at the proper levels we both had to take examinations. These were to take place immediately, because the school year had already begun.

After some investigation Mother selected a private coeducational gymnasium owned and run by a mathematics teacher named Maria Vassilievna Kaesh. She taught her subject at all levels of her school and had some progressive pedagogical ideas. The school had three preparatory classes and eight gymnasium classes. I was supposed to be ready for the second class of the gymnasium.

I was rather frightened, as I had never attended any school. However, I was not afraid of adults, even if they were teachers. The oral test of reading and arithmetic went well. But the results of my written test in Russian were not as good, because of my bad spelling, and when it came to the written French examination, I was stymied. I had to write out the conjugation of a number of verbs – some of them irregular – in *all tenses*. There was no time pressure, I was given all the time I needed, but *all tenses* – that I could not do. I filled several pages of my notebook, but was completely baffled by the subjunctives. I brought my notebook to the examining teacher in tears. They tried to calm me down, and finally I stopped sobbing, but the sense of utter failure remained with me.

Next was a sewing test, in another classroom. I was asked to sew examples of different seams, which I was supposed to know by name. I knew none of them. The teacher was kind and showed them to me; I sewed them, not very well, and she passed me. The religion exam was simple. A kind priest asked me to recite the Lord's Prayer, which I could do, and then another prayer, which I could not; but he passed me too. This calmed me enough so that I could go home and tell Mother everything without crying. I was certified as ready for the second class.

Gymnasium

I remember well entering my classroom for the first time. All the students were already sitting at their school desks, two at each desk. The middle row was occupied by the girls, the two side rows by the boys. I was told to pick my own seat. I noticed an empty seat at one of the boys' desks in the row along the outside wall of the classroom and took it. The class went on.

During the break, I found out what a *faux pas* I had made by picking that seat: girls were not supposed to sit with boys. The other girls immediately began to treat me as a pariah. This became even worse after the election of class monitors, who were supposed to air the classroom and clean the blackboards during the break between classes. The boys, who were in the majority, selected me as the chief monitor.

After that, my relationship with the girls was terrible; they would not even speak to me. I did not mind that too much because I always wanted to play with the boys, but I felt that I should do something about it. We had a ten-minute break between classes, and always returned to the same classroom. We usually just walked back and forth in the corridor, or in the large common room, while our classroom was aired. I managed to start talking to a few girls, mostly by offering to read some poetry I knew by heart – I just did not know what else I could talk with them about. So I gathered a small following that was interested in hearing the poems. I recited them during the entire break. This continued for a while, but it seemed too restrained to me. I thought of a more active way to get at least some girls on my side: I proposed that on the one day a week when our class stayed in school later than the others, we use the common room during the break before the last class for coeducational games. A few girls who went along with me would occupy one corner of the room. The boys would gather in the opposite corner. The game consisted of trying to drag the members of the opposing group into our corner. We pulled each other by whatever hold we could get, which usually meant that the girls pulled the boys' ears and the boys pulled the girls' pigtails. We would return to our last class disheveled, with red faces, the boys' ears burning, and the girls' hair in disarray. The teachers looked at us with surprise, but said nothing. I don't think this was allowed to last long, but I acquired a following among some of the girls.

In the meantime Mother and Father tried to create as normal an atmosphere at home as was possible in our difficult circumstances. One evening they decided to go to the opera and to take me along. This was the first time I had gone to a real theater. Mother always said that for my first impression she would have liked to take me to the Mariinsky Theater in Petrograd, and also to let me see Maeterlinck's *The Blue Bird*,[2] so that I would know what *good* theater was. But by now, I think, she admitted that was an unattainable goal. We went instead to see the opera *Dubrovskii* by Edward Napravnik, sung by the Omsk Opera Company. Having had a nap in order to be able to stay up late, dressed in my best dress, and alone with my parents, I felt terribly important. I could not judge how well the opera was sung, but it made a tremendous impression on me. I was overwhelmed by the scenery and the costumes – I had seen such things only in book illustrations. I was sure that being on the stage must be the greatest happiness of all. Once, in Cheliabinsk, Father had taken me to a circus, and I then thought that most of all I wanted to learn a trapeze act. Now, the stage seemed more attractive.

Father met with Kolchak. As former classmates of the Naval Academy, their visit was warm and personal, but Father was not interested in participating in Kolchak's administration, and Kolchak could be of no other assistance to him. Later that month Kolchak gave a grand banquet for his staff, to which Father and Mother were invited. Father suggested that Manya could help with it, and Kolchak agreed, so Manya worked out most of the arrangements for the banquet. Mother was very proud of her. As it turned out, this was the last of Kolchak's social events as "Supreme Ruler."

The Czech Corps, which was the most reliable part of Kolchak's army and formed his personal guard, showed signs of being tired of the struggle. There were numerous reports of atrocities committed by both armies, the Cossacks, and the peasants: crucifixions of priests and officers, murders of officials who were requisitioning food from the villages, and murders of village elders. Many personal grudges were settled under the cloak of military action. At this time the Red Army occupied Asha, while the White Army was in retreat. The fall of Omsk was inevitable.

The fleeing army and citizens, fearing Bolshevik reprisals, jammed the railroads. The various military detachments and advisers – French, British, Czechs, Japanese, and Americans – were all moving further east. While they were willing to help Kolchak, especially before the end of World War I, as they hoped that he would continue the war against Germany, they no longer relished being involved in the Russian civil war. The railway system was so overloaded that often there was not enough coal to fire the engines.

◌ȝ

Father and Gavrilov, the other surviving board member from Asha, remained in charge of the funds of the Simsky District steel mills. Mother insisted that Father must leave Omsk; otherwise his arrest by the Bolsheviks was certain, because he was a member of the administrative apparatus loyal to the Provisional Government. However it seemed impossible to try to squeeze the whole family, with six children, one of them a nine-month-old baby, into those packed boxcars, especially now that winter was coming and various epidemics were breaking out among the evacuees. Safe travel was by no means assured, with coal in short supply and partisans attacking many of the trains on their way through the vast distances of Siberian travel.

Mother did not feel that she would be in danger if she stayed in Omsk. Her former political activity had taken place in a different area of the country, and while it was not in tune with the Bolsheviks, it had always been on the side of the Revolution. There was still hope that the Socialist Revolutionary Party could be influential in Russian politics, since its policies seemed to have the backing of the majority of the Russian populace. Mother hoped to be useful in building a new society.

Father begged her to refrain from any political activity if the Bolsheviks should take over Omsk. It seemed to both of them that a mother of six small children, without a husband, should be fairly safe. They were certain that in the near future they would be re-united somehow. Mother was sure that she could find employment and support the family while Father was away.

Later, Father recorded in his dairy: "Lenochka told me at our parting 'I don't worry about you: Mechta will always supply you with enough to survive.'" And on November 6, 1919 Father boarded a *teplushka* packed with the fleeing members of his staff and others. After two days of waiting on the sidetracks, they were finally attached to a Czech train, and left on their way east. Father wrote in his diary: "For how long are we to be separated? And what will happen to them? I pray God that everything will be all right."

My eleventh birthday was hardly noticed. On November 12, Kolchak left Omsk; on November 14, Omsk fell.

On the Red Side of the Front

On the evening of November thirteenth Manya went to the east bank of the Irtysh to see if the Red Army was approaching. The river was frozen, and covered with snow. In the early dusk she could see two rows of black dots stretched along the opposite shore of the river. One was slowly but steadily retreating towards the river – another following. Occasional shots were heard. She came home to tell us this. Falling asleep, we could hear the adults still talking in low, worried voices. First thing the next morning Manya went into the street to see which uniform the passing riders wore. The Red Army was all over the city. There were only a few shots heard, and then everything was quiet.

After Father left, Mother rented one room in our house to a Doctor Pushin. It was some help financially, and particularly good to have a doctor near, with all the children subject to colds, flu, and various other common ailments. Doctor Pushin turned out to be a very nice person and he helped Mother in many ways. He lived with us most of the following year.

Father had left some money with Mother, mostly in *kerenky* – that was the nickname for the paper currency issued by the Kerensky government. We still had a few Tsarist bills too, though by that time this currency had been annulled, or declared to be of no value. Mother also had a few old gold coins, for emergency use only. Packs of money were hidden in various pillows and mattresses.

Mother immediately applied for work at our gymnasium, and was appointed a teacher of history, her specialty. In a short time the Kerensky money was also repudiated, in favor of new Soviet money, whose value at once began to drop through inflation. Mother was the only earning member of the family, which now consisted of six adults and nine children. She started to teach in two other schools as well, which often kept her occupied late into the evening.

Zhenia was still physically handicapped, and Verochka had no money-earning skills to offer. Zhenia gave a few violin lessons, and began making watercolor copies of some well-known paintings, from an album of reproductions of works in the Tretiakov Gallery at Moscow. Verochka used to take them to the market to sell, and, if successful, she sometimes secretly spent part of the money on an *izvoschik* to return home. She got off the carriage a block from the house, but Manya saw her once and disapproved of her extravagance. Manya told this to me only much later. We could not know then how bravely Verochka would manage the entire support of her own family years later, in Paris.

Nanny began to receive an old age pension. In the first month this pension was just enough to buy a needle for her sewing; later it could buy nothing at all. An outdoor market began to operate in town. With money losing its value each day, people brought their personal possessions to barter for food.

The weather continued to be extremely cold, often reaching forty degrees below zero. The snow usually fell at night, and in the morning, walking to school, we tried to step into the deep holes in the snow made by someone before us; but often the snow was even deeper than our wide-topped, knee-high felt boots, and would fall inside them. Getting to school was an adventure. Many children arrived with frostbitten noses or cheeks, in spite of the heavy scarves they wore. I pulled down my knitted cap, tied it around my neck and looked through the two small holes I had cut in it. The children teased me about my strange appearance, but I thought that I was quite ingenious, since I never got frostbite.

By the middle of the day it was wonderful to be outside. The sky was a beautiful deep blue, the sun bright, and the snow a brilliant white. In the windless air the smoke from the chimneys of the houses rose straight up like white pillars, and the crisp cold air felt pleasant against your face, if you did not try to lick your lips. As I could rarely breathe through my nose, I developed a special way of breathing so as not to let the cold air reach my throat: I closed my lips in the middle, leaving two small openings at the corners of my mouth, and directed the cold air jets against my tongue, to warm them. On the colder days my mask formed a hard crust in front of my mouth, which protected me too. Yet nobody wanted to copy my idea.

We were all encouraged to spend some time outdoors, even when it was very cold, because Mother worried about the quality of the air inside: some of the wallpaper in our rooms was covered with mold, and there was not enough fuel to heat the house through. At night it was a race to take off our clothes, and then to put on some very heavy sweaters over our nightgowns, before quickly slipping under all the blankets and winter coats we could gather, which we piled on top of our beds.

At the market stacks of frozen milk were piled up in pan-shaped pieces on open tables. One bought milk by the pound. The upper part of each frozen lump was cream, so one had to ask for more or less of the cream to be chopped off by the hatchet. The milk pieces were piled onto the scales and then dumped into the shoppers' bags. We saw Kirghiz men riding two-humped camels, wearing fur hats, wrapped in fur-lined coats, their legs so covered with layers of socks, trousers, and boots that they looked like huge stumps. They always seemed to dress almost the same way, no matter what the weather, even in summer.

We learned not to touch anything metal with our bare hands, for the fingers would stick to it so hard that part of the skin would remain frozen to the metal when one pulled the hand away. And what we learned most of all was that the winter was long, and would continue like this until spring with no change. The days were short. By three o'clock in the afternoon it was already dark.

Lena and Seryozha made great progress at home and at school. Lena had started to read some time before, and was now reading faster than I. Seryozha gobbled up book after book. As for me, it was about this time that I started to read Charskaya, a writer popular with adolescent girls. This was considered quite poor literature, full of hysterical characters, unhappy girls who always became desperately ill at critical times, often with "brain fever," but always recovered; and every bad character was punished in the end. One morning when we were getting up, I saw my Mother acting strangely. She held her hand to her forehead and said with a tragic tone: "Oh! I think I am coming down with some terrible disease! Can it be brain fever?!" All through breakfast she went on in the same vein. In the end all of us were roaring with laughter – it was so ridiculous. No one had to tell me again how absurd Charskaya's characters were.

Christmas was coming and, naturally, we had to have a Christmas tree. It was decorated with our handmade chains and toys, but we had to do it ourselves. Since Mother was too busy, I took the lead, digging out bits of colored paper left among our books and papers, and even managing to find some candles. But the mood was far from festive, because there was no news from Father.

Every day we waited for some sign, but nothing came. Was he even alive? We did not know. Rumors of terrible epidemics, and of trains stopped on their way, made us additionally anxious. Mother read the official papers, with their censored news, and this source was supplemented by "word of mouth" – not always reliable. We learned that Kolchak had been overtaken by the Reds before he reached Irkutsk; he was executed by the Bolsheviks in January 1920. We knew that Father was not with Kolchak or his army, but we had no idea where he might be.

Then, shortly after Christmas, Mother received a postcard from Harbin, a small city in Russo-Chinese Manchuria, more than 3000 miles away. It read:

HARBIN Staryi Gorod
Furazhnaya 3, M. E. Solntseva-Lanceray
Dear Lenochka, with the resumption of postal contacts
between Omsk and Harbin, where we have lived for the past

ten years, I hasten to let you know our address, asking you to write, and wishing you good holidays and a happy New Year. Your Cousin.

Mother did remember that Father had a distant cousin in the Far East. But this was unmistakably Father's handwriting!

[1] The sixteenth-century Cossack leader who started the conquest of Siberia. The main character of several folk songs and legends, Ermak is said to have drowned in the Irtysh River in full armor in a fight with the Siberian ruler Khan Kuchum.

[2] *The Blue Bird (L'Oiseau bleu)*, by the Belgian dramatist, critic, and poet Maurice Maeterlinck, was first staged at the Moscow Art Theater in 1908 by K. S. Stanislavski, who had received the play directly from the author. It was considered to be a new step in world drama. The performance was a big success and was extremely popular not only at that time but for many decades after. Soon after the Moscow triumph the same stage version was repeated in Paris by L. Sulerzhitsky and E. Vakhtangov of the Moscow Art Theater.

9

Omsk, 1920

Father was alive, and someday we would be together again! That made a great deal of difference to the family's morale. Shortages of almost everything continued to increase, and Mother was so busy with her teaching that we hardly saw her. Still, with the help of Manya and Nanny the family was able to maintain fairly much the same routine.

Seryozha became quite involved in a fantasy world. He invented all kinds of stories, which he felt compelled to share with us, always insisting on the complete attention of his audience, and becoming something of a nuisance. In a way it was a continuation of the game we had played together, when the two of us recited stories to each other; but now he made up his tales alone, very long, told with tremendous enthusiasm, with gestures, seemingly without end. First they concerned animal life, then they began to deal mostly with happenings in ancient Greece. He had absorbed all the Grecian myths that he read and now began producing countless variations on them.

After a while he had a new idea: the polytheism of the Greeks did not appeal to him, so he invented a hero, who had the inspiration to think of a single God. The name of the hero was Amzon; he had a loyal following, but was persecuted by the Greeks. Finally, he was placed on a boat with all his followers and exiled from Greece. In a long and dangerous voyage they sailed the length of the Mediterranean Sea, passed through the Pillars of Hercules, and found themselves in the open Atlantic. For days they sailed through storms and fair weather, mutinies, sickness, and death – all described in great detail and with a lot of dramatic expression – until their boat was wrecked during a storm. Amzon and a few of his most loyal followers were cast ashore on an island populated by very backward, dark-skinned natives, who of course took the new arrivals for gods, and soon subjected themselves willingly. The natives learned all the advantages of civilization. The country, now enlightened, built roads and schools and over the following centuries grew to be a powerful nation, competing with England for markets. It was called Amzonia, was populated by a beautiful race of dark-skinned people, and offered Seryozha an infinite number of subjects for his stories throughout its long and complex history of wars, struggles for power, explorations, and so on. From an absolute monarchy it developed into a constitutional monarchy, but Seryozha still resisted any reference to the merits of socialism.

Having to listen to Seryozha became more and more of a problem. Sometimes, frustrated by his unwilling listeners, he would go into an empty room, close the door and start telling his stories to himself. He dramatized them: first he pretended to shoot a gun, the next moment he was falling down as the one who was shot. Looking through the keyhole, we would think he was mad. Seryozha drew many illustrations to his stories, and when he did this we breathed a sigh of relief. One day Mother gave him a notebook, made up with lined paper like the bluebooks used for tests, but with every other leaf plain white paper for drawing. She suggested that he might write his stories, with illustrations, in the books. Seryozha took this up with great enthusiasm, and in the next year and a half, until paper became unavailable, he filled a stack of such books, three feet high, with his writing and drawings. There were detailed maps of Amzonia at different periods of its history, outlines of its constitution and educational plan, and countless scenes of fighting its different wars, from the medieval soldiers with their coats of arms to the modern airplane battles. I still regret not having saved those notebooks, which were abandoned when we left Omsk. I think they showed a remarkable talent. I remember how his handwriting changed between the earlier and later books, from carefully drawn letters between the lines of the paper to an almost adult handwriting.

School

Seryozha did not seem to make many friends in school. His studies were always too easy for him, and his classmates were not interested in his fantasies, being preoccupied instead with all sorts of physical activities – in which Seryozha took no interest at all. I, on the other hand, wanted very much to be a leader. Although my own relations with my classmates were still dominated by my desire to be with the boys, gradually I realized that I belonged with the girls, and that only among them could I find really intimate friends.

There were changes in the school. Like all schools, ours was now nationalized. The students were asked to form their own governing body and to elect a new head of the school. Most of us thought very highly of Miss Kaesh, who was a strict but kind teacher, always fair when handling students' problems. We knew that we learned a lot from her and we liked the way her school was run. So the great majority of the student body elected her. For a while the city administration left us alone.

The school was now tuition-free. We had many new students, but many of the old ones were gone. The numbering of the classes had changed, but most of the teachers stayed, and the program of studies remained the same, except that there were no more religion classes. We started German, the second foreign language for my class. Spoken German was easy for me, but in reading and writing it I was on the same level as the others. Arithmetic was very different. I hated the long calculations we had to do with big numbers. Fractions were a bit better, but what I really liked were the complex problems that required many steps. We were supposed to write in words the reason for each step; so one problem usually took up the whole hour. The problems dealt with trains meeting or passing each other, and basins being both filled and drained at the same time but at different rates. I liked that and, except for making mistakes in calculations or spelling, I did quite well. My handwriting was not the best. And sometimes I had to do extra handwriting practice – unlike Seryozha, who had a naturally good hand and an infallible memory for spelling.

At that time the old Russian spelling was still in use, which meant that there were five more letters in the alphabet than there are now. The grammatical rules for the use of those letters filled about half of our grammar books. One day we were given a dictation specifically to test us on the use of those letters. I wrote it down, terribly uncertain of myself, then crossed out most of the letters I doubted, replacing them with others, of which I was equally uncertain. In short, I made a mess of the test, and received the lowest failing mark possible. This was a terrible disgrace, since the grades were always made known to the entire class. I came home very upset. Mother consoled me, "The rules will be changed soon and these letters will be abolished," she said. "But don't tell anybody, or they will all stop doing their grammar lessons." I felt much better.[1]

But the next day at school I could hardly bear the sympathy of my classmates. By the middle of the school day I had confided to my best girl friend that my failure was not so important, since before long it would not matter, and I told her, as a secret, what Mother had said to me. At once I was terrified by what I had done: I had betrayed my mother's trust! I came home weeping. I went to the bedroom, lay on the bed and cried inconsolably for the rest of the day. Mother was completely puzzled. She tried to comfort me, seeking to find the reason for my distress. I could not bring myself to confess my guilt until the evening. Mother, of course, consoled me, and finally I was able to go to sleep. But the sense of guilt remained for a long time.

I think that a lot was expected of me because I was the oldest. I was supposed to set an example in everything, and if I did something wrong, I was reprimanded not only for what I had done, but also for "setting a bad example." I was proud of being the oldest, but resented having always to seem perfect, which I knew very well I was not. I desperately wanted Mother's love and affection, but from earliest childhood I had assumed that her love was conditional. And the first condition, which I could not possibly fulfill, was to be a boy. I tried to be brave, to be strong, to climb trees, to ride horses, to do all the things that boys do. I even wanted to be dressed as a boy, but I was never allowed to wear trousers – that was just not done.

On every possible occasion I tried to prove to Seryozha that I was a better "boy" than he was. This must have affected his character, perhaps painfully, and provoked his constant opposition to me in so many of his opinions; maybe that was the only way he could assert his young masculinity. I am sure he was very fond of me; but I, on the other hand, always worried about his feelings toward me, perhaps because I unconsciously recognized the superiority of his talents, and felt guilty about my own concealed jealousy.

At the same time, I felt that if I had the responsibilities of the oldest, I wanted the privilege of ordering the younger ones around and wanted them to obey me. This, naturally, met with a lot of resistance and resulted in fights. It upset Mother. The desperation that I felt when I "betrayed Mother's trust," I now think, had much to do with my feeling that by this act I once more proved that I could not deserve her complete love.

Like all childhood dramas, the disastrous spelling test was soon forgotten. I don't think that Mother took it very seriously; she was too busy with her teaching and too worried about Father.

೮

At this time a real life drama was unfolding in our house: little Petya, Zuza's son, became very ill. Zuza was beside herself with worry. Doctor Pushin, who lived with us at that time, examined him, and prescribed some medications, but Petya got worse; he had a very high temperature, seizures, delirium. Doctor Pushin diagnosed meningitis, which at that time was usually fatal, but was not considered contagious. Zuza would not leave the side of his bed day and night. The children clustered around, trying to do something for him, trying to get Zuza to take a few minutes for a nap. Then one day Petya began to scream. He screamed loudly and desperately; no one could do anything to stop him; he screamed for what seemed to us hours; and then the screams suddenly stopped. I remember sitting by his bedside, stroking his head, when the poor child was already unconscious. He had bitten his tongue, which showed between his lips and was getting blue. He died, never opening his mouth. I don't know what shocked me more: the fact of death or the desperate despondency of his mother. We felt so helpless.

A little wooden coffin was brought in and Petya was put into it. I cannot remember any religious services or the burial itself. It must have been too traumatic. Zuza continued to be with us for another month. She lost weight and moved like a shadow. Then she received a letter from her husband asking her to join him in Latvia, and she left soon after that.

I was eleven years old by then and the experiences of the last three years, starting with the death of my Aunt Katya and her memorial service, followed by all that happened in Byeloretsk, Ufa, Asha, and Smolino, the long travels, and now the death of little Petya, made me think of many things about which I did not talk, though they puzzled me. I had questions to which I wished someone could help me to find answers. What is death? What does the dying person feel? What happens after death? Why do people quarrel, and fight, and kill each other? Why cannot people all live in peace and be kind to one another? Why is there so much pain in the world? I did not talk about this to Mother, who was so busy that I never had a chance to have intimate times with her. The other children seemed to be far removed from such questions. The poetry of nineteenth-century Russian writers, especially Nadson's,[2] seemed to resonate with my feelings, and I memorized much of it. I confided some of my feelings to my diary, which I wrote only sporadically and kept strictly secret from everyone.

Father's Letter

After the postcard from Harbin there were no further communications from Father except a short note in January indicating that he was now in Japan. Mother tried to get in touch with him in all possible ways – through Finland, through the cousin in Harbin, through some friends in Chita – but with no success. Later we learned that Father had written a letter on February 25, 1920 from Harbin, but Mother never received it. Here are some excerpts:

> My own dear Lena, I am kept alive by the firm hope of seeing you all soon, and fear only that I might make a fatal error that would postpone our reunion or make our life together impossible. The situation is so confused that for the time being it seems that the only right course of action is for me to wait here, earning a living, which is what I am trying to do.

I live here very comfortably, if that word is appropriate to my state of mind. I love you all with all my heart and soul, but at times my love does not give me the strength to fight a waiting battle, but rather tempts me to succumb to my desire to see you sooner. But then I realize that if I went to you, my arrival might not only give you no joy, but could even cause much grief. Let us have faith that God is merciful, and that sincere and honest people can still lead useful lives on earth.

I am giving this letter to Vasilii in the hope that he will reach Omsk. If so, send a note with him on his return, to bring me up to date on your news.

Here is the current political situation. In Khabarovsk, Vladivostok, and the rest of the Far East, the Land Councils of the Provisional Government, with Medvedev as Chairman, evidently SRs, have declared that they want to negotiate peace with Moscow. Today I read in the Western newspapers that the Fifth Red Army has advanced from Irkutsk to Mysovaya, on the eastern shore of Lake Baikal. In Chita, Semenov[3] has a very bad reputation and will evidently find no support. Trans-Baikal and the Amur Region are in a state of rebellion in solidarity with the western areas, so it is clear that this area's days are also numbered. This leaves just the Chinese Eastern Railroad corridor, which is surrounded at both ends by SRs wanting to reach an agreement with Moscow. In the CER corridor the general feeling is for termination of the civil war, of course, but many people have great anxiety about future prospects for working and living here. It may be surprising, but the merchant class, especially the small proprietors, are very much in favor of an agreement. They don't seem to realize that they would probably be worse off than anyone else.

The Administration of the CER corridor manages its affairs very diplomatically and evidently will make concessions that allow it to continue operations. Therefore, the restoration of communications with Omsk is just a matter of a very short time, God willing. We can expect that order will be preserved in the CER corridor if there are no misunder-standings with the Chinese. It is then that I hope to establish regular correspondence with you so we can decide what to do next. One possibility for me is to join you in Omsk so that we could all move together to western Russia; this is what I would like best. Another option is for you to remain living in Omsk while I continue to work here. Finally, perhaps I should arrange for you to come here, to live together until the opportunity comes to travel westward. It is impossible to foresee the correct course of action right now, but perhaps we can resolve our future life together in one of these three ways. I so wish that I could see you all just for a moment, to hug and kiss you all, my dearest ones!

Be sure to detain Vasilii in Omsk. Perhaps later he can help you to come here, or you can send him to me with a letter. Of course, for you all to come here, even in the summer, would be an extremely risky journey. I don't think the railroads will be fully operational yet, and above all, there is a great danger of epidemics. May God grant that you will be able to save the kids! For now this is your one and only task, my saintly Lenochka. So the problem of your moving further eastward is very complex and dangerous. I know only one thing: I cannot live without you for very long.

In the middle of my mustache there appears a colorless hair, apparently gray. It seems to me that my eyes are less lively; the iris is less sharply delineated from the white of the eye. But this is to be expected: after all, I am almost forty-five. Today is the name-day of Zoya. I send her hugs and kisses. Whenever I think of all the dear ones who have left us forever, it seems to me good perhaps that they did not have to live through all this. But I myself don't want to go without fulfilling my obligations with respect to the children, and do not wish to pass on this entire burden to you alone, my dear Lena. It is good that it is you, and not another. Do you think that I could have stood all this without the support of your firm and kind soul? And the poor kids, what would they have done if their mother were different? My joy, my life, my saintly Lenochka. … Vasilii must come tomorrow, and maybe I shall have time to write some more. But what can I write besides that I love all of you very much and live only in hope of seeing you soon, and having the chance to live for you. I embrace you all, again and again.

Vanya

It seems that Father did not have a chance to send the letter with this unknown Vasilii. So he saved it, hoping for another chance to have someone take it, because it was too long and detailed to risk sending by mail. And then it was too late. I found it among Father's papers in an envelope marked with a cross.

Spring and Summer 1920

Spring was approaching and something new appeared outside – rats. They lived in the ditches under the wooden planks that served as sidewalks. The streets in our area were so muddy that one could not walk on them, and the rats also preferred the sidewalks. You could see the rats scurrying along the boards and then dashing under them. Formerly, the city office paid boys five kopeks for each dead rat they could bring in, since rats were known to transmit bubonic plague and other diseases. This used to be a nice source of income for some boys, but now the rule was changed and nobody paid anything for dead rats. The boys in the city were upset by this change, so they demonstrated their displeasure in an appropriate way: they brought all the rats they killed and piled them on the street in front of the new city government. I passed there once and was terrified by the view of the road covered thickly for a whole block by dead rats.

Spring brought many new activities for us children. We began to get acquainted with the other children on the street. We investigated our own backyard and the shed in it. Manya tried to teach me to milk the cow, but not very successfully, for my hands did not seem to be strong enough. I tried to learn to use a dull axe to split wood for the stove, and I remember the frustration of trying to shorten a stove log that was too long, returning day after day to my task, and finally giving it up. As soon as school was over, I started to organize the activity of my siblings and friends on the street.

I was still very much excited by the theater. We occasionally played charades, but that was not enough. Seryozha and little Lena were too few actors. So I began looking for possible actors among the children on our street. Several responded enthusiastically. Within the shed in our yard lay a pile of uncut tree trunks and an old worn-out rug. We stretched the rug over the pile of tree trunks; it made what we thought was a wonderful mountain, and I decided that a dramatization of Pushkin's *Kavkazskii Plennik* (Caucasian Captive) would be just right for this setting.

We rehearsed with great care. Everyone had to memorize his part without a hitch, and we performed for an enthusiastic audience of children and their parents. Our landlord's daughter, who was in her early twenties, promised to write an original play for our "troupe." We were becoming real actors!

As soon as the new play was written, my actors were eager to start rehearsing. But we really did not have a suitable space in which to perform. Someone must have suggested the idea to me because I cannot imagine that I could have thought of it myself: to go to the Department of Education and ask them for space. There was no children's theater in our area, and theater was considered a valuable educational tool. So off we went, empowered by all the propaganda we had heard about the "importance of the people's initiative."

At the Department of Education we were taken very seriously. An important-looking man invited us to his office and listened attentively to our statement that we had actors, a playwright, and even some experience, for which we thought our neighbors would be ready to vouch. His answer rather startled us: "Go and find a suitable place in any of the houses in your neighborhood – we will confiscate it for your use!"

So four children aged between ten and twelve began going from house to house, asking the owners to show us the house inside, with the idea that if we liked the space, we would have the city take it from the owners for our theater. We spent several days at this. Finally, in one of the houses we found a real stage and a nicely-sized hall. Perfect! The only thing it required was a large curtain, which was missing, probably used to make clothes in that time of many shortages. We could not possibly find enough material to make a new curtain, and so we gave up our search.

We performed the play our neighbor wrote for us in her family's home instead. The audience was necessarily very small – just the parents and siblings of the actors. After that we decided to suspend our theatrical activities for the time being. Besides, Manya and Nanny needed us as helpers in the garden plot that had been given to our family by the city administration, and on expeditions to the woods to gather mushrooms. These activities were essential for our survival during the next winter.

∾

The river was a great attraction for children. We went swimming and fishing in it almost every day, and because like many of our neighbors we had no bathroom in the house, we often would take a piece of soap and wash ourselves, the older children helping the younger ones. All of the laundry was done in the river too. Of course, the children wore no bathing suits or trunks. The boys ran into the water after undressing on the shore, shielding themselves with their hands. Adults swam in their underwear. But I still had my bathing suit from Libava. Even though it was bought when I was five years old and now I was almost twelve, I still could stretch it over me. It seemed so much nicer than swimming in underwear. Later there was a rumor among our neighbors that I really was a boy, and that my family only pretended that I was a girl because it was trying to change its "identity."

There were several whirlpools in the area where we had been swimming, and at times the most daring boys came close to drowning in them. Once I myself was pulled by the current towards one. It was an awful feeling. One of the boys helped me to escape the current. Another time when we went to the beach we saw the body of a drowned woman lying on the shore. Somebody had pulled it out of the river and left it there. We never learned whether it was an accident or a suicide. Several days passed before the body was removed.

During the summer there was a large increase in beggars who knocked at the door asking for a piece of bread. Manya or Nanny always had a piece of bread, and sometimes a meatball or something else ready for them, and would try to find out where they came from, and how bad things were in their home towns. The beggars would put whatever they got into their bags, say their thanks, and wander away. Most of them had traveled from the cities and villages of the European part of Russia, where, apparently, famine raged. Manya began to worry about her own family in Ivanovo, for postal service was quite inadequate, and she could not get much news of them. So it was decided that Manya should go to visit them as soon as we gathered the harvest from our garden.

Travel for personal needs was not allowed at all, so some special permit had to be obtained. Here was where Doctor Pushin could help. He procured a certificate for Manya alleging that she was being sent to an army hospital in the south of Russia as a nurse's helper. Armed with this paper, Manya packed her bags, including in them a liberal amount of table salt, which was in terribly short supply on the other side of the Urals. She left on one of the military trains late in the summer, carrying a different document with another fictitious assignment for her return. Mother hired Tonya, a local girl she knew from Asha, to help Nanny while Manya was absent, and Zhenia and his family went to Karachi for the summer. Later in the summer I was allowed to go to visit them.

This time I was supposed to try to bring home some salt crystals from the bottom of the lake, to be used in Katya's baths, as she had developed rickets. I remember dutifully collecting those crystals, which were sometimes stuck together in lumps as large as my fist, and even larger. I soon found out that what I was doing was illegal. The salt was state property and no one was allowed to transport it out of the town. That would be my first and only attempt at smuggling. I wrapped the pieces carefully in my clothes, leaving only a light dress for me to wear, and stuck them into my suitcase. I was quite cold when I arrived home, but I felt proud of bringing a possible cure to Katya.

Back at home I met Uncle Vadim, Mother's brother, and his seventeen-year-old son Pavlik, who had come to stay with us. Uncle

Vadim was an engineer, a specialist in transportation, who had been transferred to work on the Omsk railway system. Pavlik was to enter the last class of our gymnasium. He had a touch of tuberculosis, and his father hoped that the better nourishment in Siberia would help him. Pavlik was tall and pale. The hair on his face was already beginning to grow, and he seemed to me quite grown-up.

School Again

School began on September first. Lena was admitted too, and started to attend the second preparatory class. Seryozha was in the first class of gymnasium, I in the third. However, the classes were renamed now; they were called "groups," and were numbered differently.

I started algebra. The first simple algebraic exercises were very repetitious and dull. I even taught little Lena how to do them, and she did some of my assignments. I could see no point in them. To show me the usefulness of algebra, Mother once gave me a problem:

> A flock of blackbirds came to rest on a small bush. They sat two birds on each branch and found that one bird was left over – no branch for it. Then they rearranged the seating, to three birds on each branch. Now there was one branch left over – empty. How many birds were there and how many branches on the bush?

I was immediately intrigued. I sat down with a pencil and paper, working it out by trial and error. Soon I came to Mother with an answer. Then Mother showed me how to solve this problem by assigning letters to the unknown quantities, writing an equation and solving it. I was ecstatic. To think that one could perform all the arithmetic functions without numbers, with letters! It was such a revelation to me that, I feel sure, from that moment on my future career was determined. I could not wait until we could start solving problems in our algebra class. I loved every class in mathematics after that.

Mother, however, was teaching history in my class, and that presented a problem. I was never good at remembering dates and names, and this was what history required more than anything. When Mother asked questions in class, she never called on me if there was another hand up. She even told me once: "I know that you know, don't raise your hand!" But when no one could answer a question, she would call on me, and if I did not know she would tell me later at home: "How can I expect other students to know, if my own daughter does not?" I was rather afraid of history class.

In September the early Siberian fall set in. This was the rainy season: ankle-deep mud in the streets, cold pouring rains, the need to wear galoshes outside. The problem of shoes was severe. In the summer we went barefoot like all the other children; in the winter we wore felt boots, which were locally made and sold at the market. They were not waterproof; inside them, if we had no stockings, we wrapped our feet in strips of torn sheets. But in the rainy season we needed shoes. The younger children had hand-me-downs, patched and repaired. But the older children had to have new shoes, and they were very hard to get. It was the same with galoshes. Sometimes galoshes that were too large stuck in the mud and were difficult to extricate. In these conditions it was hardly a pleasure to be outside.

The evenings were dark and long. Fortunately, when darkness fell we still had books to read, and even pencils and paper to while away the time around a table with a single oil lamp. We went to bed quite early.

One stormy night the rain was beating violently on the sides of the house. Loud thunder awakened me. The window in our bedroom, which Seryozha and I shared with Mother, was not shuttered. Mother stood in front of the window, watching the flashes of lightning. I got up and came close to her; she put her arm around me, pulling me close to her warm body. "How beautiful!" she said. "Look!" We stood watching, in silence, for some time. I felt warm and comfortable against her and was amazed by the fiery display. After a while Mother said, "I wonder where Papa is now?" I felt that I had been given a chance to share her innermost anxiety and stood close to her until she told me it was time to go to sleep.

Mother's Letter

On September 21, Mother received a letter from Father. She was overjoyed. The letter itself, like all her other records of that time, did not survive the later searches of our house. But Father saved Mother's answer:

My dear, beloved, precious one, today I received your letter from Japan dated August 1st. I cannot tell you how happy it made me. I had not known anything of you since the middle of January, that is, since you left Irkutsk. Don't worry about us. We live quite well, to the extent that is possible now in Russia. The main thing is that my brother Vadim and his son Pavlik live with us now; Vadim's wife and Sonechka [their daughter] are in Petrograd. Vadim helps me very much, but more important is that I feel the support of my relative near me. I give lots of lessons in the school where Margarita, Seryozha, and Lenochka are students, and in the evening school for adults. I give lectures and, sometimes, private lessons. Altogether, I earn two or three times as much as Vadim, or what you could have earned if you were here. Sometimes I sell some things – this is very easy to do, since there is such a shortage of things. Every rag, like an old, worn, cotton blouse, costs a thousand. So far I have not had to part with anything valuable. In the summer Zhenia underwent treatment in Karachi, but with no improvement at all. Now he wants to make his way to his sisters in Revel. He can get a pass as an invalid.

The children are all well. Especially Katya, such a fatty. She grows without any supervision, and all to the good: she is so calm, happy, and strong; she does not walk yet, but stands up by herself on the smooth floor, and stands for a long time alone without holding onto anything. She has twelve teeth, eats everything, and loves me very much. All the children are nice, only sometimes they fuss and quarrel, but I believe it is not serious. Seryozha gives me a lot of joy with his drawing and knowledge of natural sciences.

My dearest, my beloved, if you knew how we live, you would not worry about us. Materially we are tolerably well, but in my heart I long for you, I miss you so. Remember, I am always with you; I think only of you. I kiss you infinitely. Be strong, wait and hope. I train myself to be infinitely patient, so your letter was an unexpected joy for me. Remember: "The night will not always darken the skies, with luck the sun will peek through soon." For the time being the most important thing we must know about each other is that we are both alive and well. I shall send this letter through Revel. You might try to do the same. Once more: do not worry. Don't think of sending me money. Here one can get nothing for money, and I have enough for what is available. I shall not drop my teaching anyway: first, because I feel needed, and second, because it gives me status, adds some meaning to my life and fills the spiritual void.

I hug and kiss you many times. Be strong, and prepare a new life for us. I have not changed my opinion about what we had to do and think that we acted quite correctly, but there are many things about which I don't feel I can write. I shall write to you also directly to Japan. Perhaps that will work. My dear, I don't want to part with you, even to finish writing this letter. I kiss you again.

Lena

Nanny and Manya are invaluable. Manya left to visit her family in the Tula District, but promised to return. I am expecting her any day now. Before Vadim came, Doctor Pushin lived with us from the first day; he helped me a lot as a doctor and as a good person. It's good we have a cow; it would be hard to live without it. In the summer we were given a plot of land for growing vegetables in the "workers' gardens" and supplied ourselves with vegetables for the entire year. In short, we manage. I kiss you one more time.

Lena

Sept. 23rd. Today Manya returned. Now things will be easier. Lately it was quite hard because of getting Zhenia ready for his trip.

Ↄ

We were awfully happy to see Manya. Her trip had been so long, and so much had happened during that time. It took days for her to tell us everything. In fact, the story was repeated for years. On her way to Ivanovo she saw people coming to the stations ready to exchange anything for salt – jewelry, clothing, linens. She exchanged a small amount of salt for a ring with a beautiful alexandrite stone. Her family was managing all right, but they had very little flour for bread. Since they had a lot of apples, they baked "apple bread." Manya brought a piece of such bread to show us. It was so hard that one could hardly bite off a piece. Manya said that even when fresh it was hard to chew, and that they even put chopped straw in it. People in Russia learned to use all kinds of substitutes, both in food and in other aspects of daily life. But, on the whole, life in the village was bearable, if one was resourceful.

On her trip back, traveling under a different identity on a hospital train, she had to be careful. But in her usual gregarious way she made herself useful looking after the wounded men, and immediately acquired suitors. At one of the stops a small boy jumped on the train; he was alone, and said he did not have any parents or relatives. He said that he was going "to the end of the Earth," and Manya's heart went out to him; she was ready to adopt him if she could – she was always so fond of children. For years later, whenever she told this story, she would say, "He was such a good boy!"

While listening to Manya's stories, Verochka did her last packing. On September 25, Zhenia, Verochka, Boom, and Steve left Omsk for Petrograd. Zhenia, barely able to move on his crutches, had an attendant, who had come with him from Karachi; without such an aide I don't think Verochka alone could have managed. With Zhenia's handicap pass, the family was able to get onto an express train, and arrived in Petrograd five days later, happy and very tired.[4]

[1]   New rules of Russian spelling were officially introduced by the Bolshevik government in October 1918. However, the preparatory work for the spelling reform was started long before the Revolution by an authoritative government commission.

[2]   Semyon Yakovlevich Nadson (1862-1887): a sentimental poet, very popular with young people because he often wrote about youthful frustration and unrequited love.

[3]   Grigorii Mikhailovich Semenov (1890-1946): Ataman (military commander) of the Cossacks, from 1919 General-Lieutenant of the White Army. In January 1920 Kolchak gave "all military and civil power" to Semenov. After 1921 Semenov lived in China.

[4]   They remained there only a few months, and were permitted to join Zhenia's sisters in Estonia. Later they all moved to Paris where Zhenia played drums with a small group and Verochka earned most of their money making hats. I visited Zhenia and his family in Paris while I was writing this book; his sons still live there today.

10

Fall / Winter, 1920

Early in October Mother asked Manya to go to Ufa and bring back or sell the things we had left behind. Mother was hoping that Manya could complete the trip before the really cold weather set in, although October in Siberia was already winter, and the temperature often dropped below zero Fahrenheit. Arranging Manya's trip took some doing, and the journey itself was full of difficulties that no one foresaw.

When Manya reached Ufa she discovered some of our possessions still on the landing of the apartment stairway; the landlords were afraid to be found with them. Much had been stolen. As she could not bring back all that was there, she sold some of what remained, which was not easily done, and being in a hurry, she often settled for less than what she felt was fair value. But she did the best she could. She managed to salvage some beautiful editions of books, and the Chinese ivory chess set, which Mother's father had brought, I believe, from Turkey. Also some winter clothing, blankets, linens, the family table silver, and what little jewelry Mother had left behind, mostly of sentimental value. She tied the small things to her body under her clothes.

Loaded with these treasures, Manya embarked on the return trip, which would take several days. The third class railway car was quite crowded and very cold. She obtained an upper bunk, a wooden shelf on which she could stretch out, which was fortunate, because she soon began to feel sick. Her temperature rose and she came down with a very high fever, becoming delirious. She lay with her head on the edge of the bunk, her hair touching the icy windowpane, barely conscious, worrying about the precious things she had hidden under her clothes. Upon waking, she found that she could not move her head – her hair was frozen fast to the window. It took a while for her fellow passengers to understand her predicament. Only at the next station was one of them able to find some boiling water in a kettle, pour it carefully on her hair, and free her head. Lying in her bunk, she spent the rest of the trip intermittently shivering from chills and burning with fever. By the time she arrived in Omsk, Manya felt a little better. After a few weeks she recovered, but she experienced recurrences of this malady for years afterward. Someone told her that it was malaria, but this seems a very unlikely disease to have contracted in the Siberian winter!

We were terribly happy to see her, and of course everybody was delighted with what she had brought. Among other things there were illustrated history books that Mother needed very much for her teaching. There were Russian translations of Shakespeare in five huge volumes and of Schiller in three volumes, with beautiful illustrations, and a two-volume *Life of Animals* by Alfred Brehm, which especially appealed to Seryozha. Seryozha, Lena, and I started reading these new books at once. We had seen them before, but now we were older and could appreciate them better. A new period in our life began – we now had much to read at home. Instead of worn-out library copies of adolescent literature, we had handsome, serious books that had to be handled carefully. The lovely illustrations made it exciting to read even difficult texts.

From the Chinese chess set the white queen, all four knights, and a white pawn had been stolen, to our dismay. The queen was an ivory statuette of exceptionally high quality carving, and the knights were prancing horses with riders; the pieces were colored white and red. The whites were on the attack: the white pawns were soldiers running with spears, while the defensive red pawns carried shields and short swords. The whites were dressed differently from the reds, the red pieces having Manchu uniforms and pigtails. The missing pieces made the set unusable for playing chess, but we saved it because of the rare quality of the carving. Only once in my life have I seen a similar kind of set, in the collection of treasures at the Sultan's summer palace in Istanbul. Years later we presented this chess set, incomplete though it was, to our American benefactor Charles R. Crane, as a remembrance.

ఴ

Around this time the school ran out of coal, and in a few days the central water heating system froze and the pipes burst. They could not be repaired without thawing out the whole system of pipes and radiators, and to thaw the pipes, the entire two-story brick building with its high ceilings, thick walls, and large stairwells somehow had to be heated. There was only one way to heat the whole building: install small iron stoves in every classroom, office, and corridor, and fire them for as long as necessary, until the ice melted and the pipes could be drained. The city promised to deliver the coal, if the school would find a way to do the rest. Otherwise the school would have to be closed for the rest of the winter, because in Siberia the cold weather does not let up until spring.

The school was now supposed to be run by the students, so it was up to them to handle this problem. A meeting was called at which it was decided that the students should collect enough iron stoves from their homes and their friends' homes for this undertaking: such stoves were at that time the principal source of heat in most homes, and all the parents promised to help. A watch was organized to fire the stoves twenty-four hours a day for several days, one student for each stove at all times.

The older students carried most of the burden, but even the younger ones, like me, came to help during the day. It took almost a week, for the temperature outside often sank to forty degrees below zero. Finally, the city sent a plumber who grudgingly repaired the burst pipes. It took him a couple of days, and the school had to be heated with the stoves day and night until he was finished. The students, young and old, and many parents helped to clean up the mess left after all this. Even the education department officials, who came on opening day to congratulate us for our devotion to education, hailed us as heroes. But that did not temper their animosity toward Miss Kaesh, the original director of the school, who still headed it – through our vote.

At that time it was announced that "illiteracy among the people must be completely eliminated in the shortest possible time." Everybody above the age of seven had to prove, if asked, that he or she could read and write. Every illiterate person had to enroll in some school or evening class. Every available teacher was recruited to teach them and all available space was occupied by the evening classes. No wonder Mother had the maximum teaching load that she could squeeze into her day. She taught history, geography, and literature at all levels, lectured, and performed administrative work. She did all this with total devotion, always believing that education would finally liberate the people.

We were worried about Nanny. We knew that she was too old to learn; we tried to teach her, but she could not even learn letters. She did not know how old she was. The only thing we knew that dated her was her remembrance that at about age seven she had worked in the fields with other children picking up little stones and putting them into the bags on their backs. "It was hard work!" she used to say. That was before the emancipation of the serfs in 1861, and if she had been born about 1854, she was at least sixty-seven now. As long as I could remember her, her face was as wrinkled as a baked apple. Fortunately, the danger of her being forced to go to school passed. No one ever approached her about it.

We heard that people who could not read or write were taught to do so in three months. After that they were designated "literate." Another month of instruction made them into *teachers!* The students in our school wondered if they would send us that kind of teacher.

☙

Of all the letters Mother wrote to Father only three reached him. Mother had received no letters from him since the one in September 1920, so in November she wrote again, not knowing the fate of her previous letters or whether this one would reach him. She realized that some of his letters could also be lost.

> My dear, my love, I wrote to you several times; I don't know what reached you. It is difficult to repeat everything, so I shall be brief. ...
>
> I teach more than fifty classes per week, which means eight or nine classes daily both in the day schools and the evening ones (for adults). I earn as much as three people, because in one school I am the president of the school committee, in the other the vice president, and in the third the secretary. I receive as much as 15 thousand [rubles per month] (Vadim receives only 3), but still it is not enough to live on. ...

Seryozha draws as before and is very keen about natural sciences. Mulya is a good student, loves to work with clay, tried to take music lessons. … It is Katya who has changed very much: she is fat, strong, begins to walk and babble – she amuses the whole house. …

My dear, I live by only one cherished dream – to be reunited with you. Sometimes I have moments of anguish and weakness, but more often my spirits are high. After all, the time must come when we shall see each other. For the time being I am not really alone: I have my brother, he does help me a lot. I have friends. … My dear, God bless you. Take from life all you can, only don't forget me. Don't stop loving me. Do not try to come here. I am absolutely sure that we acted correctly a year ago. If it is possible to use someone coming here, send me a few yen. But don't worry, I shall manage even without them. After I found out about you, I stopped worrying. If I could only continue to have news of you, I have enough spirit and strength for a long time. But for God's sake, keep your spirits up, don't worry about us, don't be depressed, and don't forget us. Trust in me, and remember that I love you infinitely, how much, probably, I understand only now.

I kiss you many times,

Lena

Friends and Visitors

One of Mother's best friends was Maria Ernestovna Shestakova, the daughter of a well-known Russian painter, Ernest Liphart. I don't know what brought her to Siberia. We knew her as Mashenka Liphart. She had two small sons, whom we very seldom saw; she herself was not well at that time. I used to go to practice the piano in her modest apartment. All I remember is a wonderful portrait of her, or perhaps of her mother, standing in a long dress, painted almost life-size, hanging there in strange contrast to its surroundings. There was not even enough room to step back in order to appreciate it. Mother visited her as often as she could, but I don't remember her in our house. She must have had some involvement with the political activities of the time, as will be seen.

The Navalikhins, longtime Omsk residents, were an older couple who had nothing to do with politics. They had one daughter, born late in their life, whom they adored. Surprisingly, they knew our old friend Yuzya, who had spent so much time with us at Vyksa. Yuzya had introduced Navalikhin to yoga philosophy, which evidently was very helpful to him later on, and which he often discussed with Mother. Later, in a long letter to Father, Navalikhin wrote:

> We often talked about this philosophy with Elena Pavlovna, and she showed great interest in this teaching. She found that it introduced some kind of emotional quality of peacefulness and reconciliation with many questions she had in the last period of her life to which she could not find answers in Kant's *Critique of Pure Reason*, on the basis of which she had structured her life's philosophy. Her sensitive and pure soul looked for reassurance on another level, outside of our strictly logical and sometimes dry and cruel Reason.

Theirs was the only home of a settled family, fairly well off, that we visited in Omsk. They had a good library and were generous in lending us books. I remember a Christmas tree party in their home, with lovely tree decorations unlike any I had seen before. They gave me a little cardboard butterfly from the tree, covered with metallic colors, which I treasured for many years. During our second year in Omsk their daughter died, and they were inconsolable. Her room was kept intact and unoccupied; they could not bring themselves to disturb it in any way. It gave me a strange, eerie feeling to glance through its door.

We also had some secret guests. One man I remember had a different name each of the two or three times he appeared. We learned never to mention his previous name. Perhaps he was one of Mother's and Father's cellmates from Ufa; at any rate, Mother seemed to know him well.

Several times Red Army soldiers came, searched the house quickly, asked questions, and left. Once that happened when the man with several names was in our house. While the adults tried to keep the soldiers busy in the other rooms, the man climbed into the root cellar through the trap door in the kitchen floor. The cellar was full of potatoes that we had just harvested from our garden plot, and he managed to hide among them.

When the soldiers came into the kitchen, I stood watching them, afraid to look at the trap door for fear of calling their attention to it, and afraid not to look, for fear they would notice that I avoided doing so. The soldiers did not find anything and left. After a while our visitor climbed out, dirty and frightened. He waited until dark, drinking the tea that Nanny brought to him. Then he left, and we never saw him again.

Mother was so busy that we rarely had a chance to discuss the events happening around us. But I felt strongly the general sense of tension. We knew of arrests in the city, of searches, and we sensed the fear that prevailed. We understood early that certain things should not be mentioned, that one did not speak to strangers, and especially not about one's family. On one occasion I remember Mother holding a small photo of the man who once hid in our cellar. She said, "I know that I should destroy it, but I have no idea what happened to him, or even whether he is alive at all," and she put the photo into her desk drawer. On another occasion I saw her hiding a folded flag – it was the forbidden Russian flag, which, as a symbol of anti-Bolshevism, was very dangerous to possess. I pretended I did not notice and tried to forget it.

Apparently Mother was among those who felt that there still was a chance that the new political situation might not be permanent. Since the SR party still remained the most popular party in the country, in terms of general sentiment, things might yet change. Mother hoped that the ideas of liberty, equality, and fairness, the prospect of which had made her so happy in February 1917, might still prevail.

Fear

In January Uncle Vadim had to travel to Chita – almost 2000 miles farther east, beyond Lake Baikal on the Trans-Siberian Railroad. He was on some assignment in connection with his job. Pavlik stayed with us, naturally, because he was still at school. No one knew when Uncle would return. Mother missed him, and we all hoped to see him by Christmas.

Christmas passed, but Uncle Vadim did not come back. Many frightening rumors were circulating, about arrests, and that those arrested were being shot, individually or in large groups. Such news never appeared in the papers but passed from mouth to mouth, and one could never be sure what part of it was true. According to some stories, the executions were held this way: the condemned people were forced to dig a deep ditch, and then were lined up at the edge of it and shot, so that they fell into the ready-made grave. We heard that the source of this story was a man who had been shot with the others but not killed, so that after falling into the ditch he managed to climb out from under the other bodies and escape, when the soldiers had left.

Children would take in these stories without panic; it was a way of life, no more frightening than Red Riding Hood's wolf, or Baba Yaga, the witch of Russian fairy tales. Fairy tales are also very real to small children. But the older children felt the difference between the world of fantasy and the real world around us. I think we reacted more to the fear that affected the adults than to the news itself. The knowledge of fear and the reality of cruelty remained in our subconscious and manifested itself years later in the form of unjustified reactions or nightmares. But at the time we children lived our own lives, with our games, friendships and quarrels, homework, school successes and failures, and our expectation of planned progress in our studies. I think involvement in their children's lives also served to distract the adults from the political events, and relieve some of their tension and worry.

Mother received one postcard from Father, which by some miracle was not taken away during the later house search, perhaps because it was written in French. Father wrote:

27 VII 20

Chère amie, je t'embrasse très tendrement aussi que nos petites et je veux te dire que je me porte très bien. Je suis à Osaka (Japon) c/o Babcock & Wilcox Ltd, 47 Kitohama 3 chome. Je *suis entré en service en qualité d'ingénieur pour leur bureau à Osaka. Je serais heureux de savoir que vous tous trouvez bien et de vous envoyer de l'argent, ou bien vous faire venir chez moi. Il y aurait moyen de vivre ici pour tout le monde. Essai de m'écrire par Finland ou autrement mais fais-le énergiquement. Je t'embrasse 10^6 fois. Bien à tous. Jean*

[My dear friend, I kiss you tenderly, and our little ones too; I want to tell you that I am very well. I am in Osaka (Japan), c/o Babcock & Wilcox Ltd, 47 Kitohama 3. I am employed as an engineer in their office in Osaka. I would be happy to know whether you are well, and also to send some money or let you come here to me. We would be able to live here all together. Try to write to me via Finland or in any other way, but do try it. I kiss you a million times. Best wishes to everyone. Jean.]

Mother kept writing letters to Father. I have one more of them, which was her last. It sounds more desperate than the first two, though she still tries to show courage and not to alarm Father:

Jan. 18, 1921

My dear, I wrote to you so many times, not knowing whether what I wrote would reach you. I don't want to repeat everything again, so I hope that you received at least one of my letters.

I live, as before, relatively well, but each day it is harder and harder to bear the separation. Good Lord! If one could at least exchange letters regularly! If I could receive an answer to at least one of my letters! The moments of weakness occur more and more often when I feel like crying out, "I cannot stand it any more!"

Materially too, life is harder and harder: food prices rise faster than do those of the things I can sell, not to speak of my earnings. Nonetheless, I can still tell you confidently that I will survive indefinitely even if I don't receive help from you, providing Manya does not leave me and Nanny does not wear out completely; they both have it so hard!

I work a lot, as before, perhaps even more. I have lost a lot of weight, and aged – you wouldn't recognize me. Our house has turned out to be frightfully cold and, even worse, very damp: all the walls are covered with mold. The children are constantly ailing.

How do you visualize our getting back together? Of course, I would like very much to join you there, but is it possible? According to the laws of the Soviet Republic, moving even inside the country, just because one wants to, is impossible, and leaving the country even more so. How could you help us with this problem from there? I still do not want you to come here: life here would be too hard on you. Even though all your friends write that you would be able to find good work you cannot imagine what an existence we are adapted to. I am afraid you would not be able to stand it.

But, we must finally reunite! Do you live only for this cherished dream, like me? If nothing develops by summer, I think there is no point in my staying on in Omsk. From everything I hear, life in Petrograd and Moscow is not as hard as here. The prices have almost equalized now, the wages here are less, the housing is worse, the climate is murderous, and most important is the loneliness, the isolation from all the family. If we cannot come to you, I shall try to go to Russia.

Aunt Dunya died. Vadim is still in Chita.

Please, darling, write more often and in greater detail. My need of news from you is simply unbearable. I received only two letters from you from Japan, one dated Aug. 1, the other dated Aug. 31, and three postcards. I need your moral support.

It would be nice to get from you a few yen (but not Soviet money). Even better would be a few things like spools of thread, yard goods, stockings. I know this won't be possible soon, and I don't expect it.

I embrace you and send a million kisses.

Lena

The procession of beggars coming by the house kept growing, but the pieces of bread that Manya and Nanny were able to give them diminished. Some of the beggars were so emaciated that Nanny, handing them a little piece of bread, would just shake her head and not ask any questions. "He is not long for this world," she would say, closing the door. On our way to school we saw one such man who had begged at our door sitting on the steps of another house, with closed eyes, thoroughly exhausted. When we returned after school, he was still there, and dead.

11

Mother's Arrest

The household was all women and children now. Even Pavlik, though he was seventeen, was considered to be a child. No wonder that the shutters were firmly closed every night and the doors bolted. There were many robbers on the streets of Omsk; it was a common joke that robbers used to say: "That fur coat is yours until ten o'clock, after ten it's ours!" and remove the coats from hapless travelers. We usually went to bed early, for there was no good light to read by, and the evenings were very long.

February 16 was a typically cold Siberian winter day. By 4 p.m. it had already grown dark. The shutters were closed and the children and Nanny sat around the table with the only kerosene lamp on it. The little ones were playing nearby while I watched the older ones doing their homework. Sometimes a quarrel or argument started at the table, but Nanny was quite used to that, so she did not stop her knitting, unless a real fight started. Manya stayed in the kitchen by the light of a candle.

We had our supper without Mother. As usual, she had left early in the morning and was not expected to return until very late, after her evening classes. Nanny put the little ones to bed; Lena was absorbed with her book, Seryozha with his drawing, and now I could start doing my own homework. When Mother came home we all rushed to meet her. She hardly had time to take off her fur coat and hat, all covered with snow. We hurried to tell her about our day: each had something to tell, or wanted to complain, to boast about good grades at school, or ask for help. Manya brought some warmed soup and kasha for her. While eating, Mother was listening, answering questions, comforting or encouraging as needed.

Finally she got us to go to bed and began preparing her lessons for the next day. I knew that she did not have time to talk with me, but a good thing was that my bed was next to her desk, so I could watch her working on her papers there.

Mother was still working on her papers when a loud knock at the door woke Manya. A late-night knock on the door – everyone

151

knew what that meant. Two men in heavy coats and boots walked in, followed by three uniformed soldiers wearing pointed hats with red stars in front. They marched through the rooms with their flashlights, waking up the children, pushing the furniture, looking into all the corners. Someone lit a kerosene lamp. The frightened children, wrapped in blankets, were comforted by Manya and Nanny, and looked on silently. Mother was calm. She answered the men's questions and pointed to the things they demanded. Their interest focused on Mother's desk, near which I slept. Sitting up in bed, I watched a man emptying all the drawers, piling up letters, photographs, and some of Mother's working papers on the top of the desk. Others tore apart the old photograph albums with padded covers, removing portraits of grandfathers, grandmothers, uncles, and aunts from their oval cutouts, and throwing them onto the pile, together with all the snapshots of children, cousins, friends, and acquaintances.

Terrified, I looked at the heap of photographs and saw the photo of the man who had once hidden in our cellar. Mother had kept that in her drawer, and there it was, lying on top of the pile! One of the soldiers stood near my bed with his back to me, guarding the confiscated evidence. The others went with Mother to the other room, continuing the search. The photo was within my reach. Should I try to remove it? If the soldier saw me do it, I would have brought their attention to it. If I did nothing perhaps the photo would not be noticed among such a quantity. I was immobilized by indecision and fear.

Another man came into the room and started to sweep all the things from the desk into a bag; the decision had been made for me. Mother walked into the room dressed in her coat. "I have to go with them," she said, "I want to say goodbye." She kissed me. I jumped out of bed and followed her to the front door. All the children, Nanny, and Manya stood there. Mother kissed each of us and, turning to Manya, said, "I don't know when I'll be back. Take care of the children and try to get in touch with their father." Then, turning to me, "Be good to your brother and sisters. Remember, you are the oldest!" The men opened the door and left, taking Mother with them.

Without Mother

The next morning Manya decided to keep Lena at home for the time being and warned Sergey and me not to talk in school about what had happened the night before. However, I was to tell one of the teachers, who was Mother's friend, that she had been arrested. It was strange to go to school without Mother. It was hard to say nothing to my friends and to behave as if nothing had happened; it was hard to keep my mind on schoolwork. Seryozha and I left school immediately after the last class and walked home as fast as we could, hoping that Mother would be back. She was not.

That morning after we left, Manya hurried to see Maria Ernestovna Shestakova to tell her about Mother. There she found a soldier guarding the apartment: Maria Ernestovna had also been arrested the night before. Manya decided to go to the Navalikhins, to let them know what had happened, and ask their advice. They lived some distance from us, so it was a long walk. Mr. Navalikhin told Manya that she must go to the Cheka (the "Extraordinary Commission" of the secret political police) to inquire about Mother. They had a special building in the center of town. Another long walk. All this took most of the day.

When Manya came to the Cheka she saw a number of people, mostly women, inquiring about their relatives. Manya did not readily enter into conversations with strangers, and she was always quite careful about saying anything concerning the family. She did, however, overhear many remarks in the waiting crowd and gathered that there had been many arrests the night before, probably more than a hundred.

I still have a little scrap of paper on which Manya wrote:

Request for information
Is Zarudnaya, Elena Pavlovna here?

On the bottom of it an answer is written:

Here. In care of the Omsk District Cheka.

The next day Manya prepared a small bundle of food to take to Mother. She was unable to see her but was allowed to leave the food.

An exact list of all that she brought had to be submitted. Someone must have written it for her, since the handwriting is unfamiliar: "2 pounds of bread, 1/4 arshin [about 6 inches] of sausage, one bottle of milk, 3 meatballs."

The list came back to Manya. On the reverse side of it there was a message in Mother's handwriting:

> Thank you! Send me 2 tin mugs, 2 soup spoons, a soup bowl, teapot or sauce boat. Stockings, shoes, underwear. A book to read. Lena.

At home everyone was subdued. The little children played in their usual way, occasionally asking, "When will Mama come back?" The answer usually was, "She had to go away. She will be back soon." We were all waiting for Uncle Vadim to return from his trip to Chita. He reappeared late on the very next day, and in the morning went to the Cheka to inquire about Mother. The result of his inquiry was his own arrest.

Uncle Vadim had never been involved in any political activities. He was a faithful and much valued employee of the railway system; the only reason for his arrest must have been the fact that he was Mother's brother. His son Pavlik and all the rest of us were stunned by this new calamity.

The family tried to maintain its usual routine. Nanny was very gloomy; we could hear her constantly grumble to herself. With mother gone it was Manya who now had to make the decisions about what to sell or exchange for food or hay for the cows. Then she had to go to the market and bargain with the farmers. Once a week or so she took a package to the Cheka for Mother.

Manya managed to save the scraps of paper with the lists of things she took to Mother. Pavlik wrote the lists in his neat, schoolboy handwriting. They would come back with short notes from Mother with specific requests, and always with thanks and statements that she was well. Later, Manya gave them to our father in Harbin, and he kept them, rereading them many times. He never showed these notes to us; Lena found them among Father's papers after he died.

About March 1, while Uncle Vadim was still held by the Cheka,

Mother managed to smuggle a note to him. After reading it he destroyed it, but after his release he wrote her words down from memory:

> I am well. The conditions are better than I expected. But the accusations are very serious. If I don't succeed in exonerating myself – death. I myself can bear it, but my soul is aching for you and the children.

಩

At the time, of course, we knew nothing about what was happening in the Cheka. Lena, Seryozha, and I went to school, where by now it was well known what had happened to us. But no one talked about it, and I felt estranged from most of the children. At home I felt the weight of the responsibility for the education of the children. No one had assigned such a task to me, but that was how I understood Mother's role, and I thought it was mine now. I was used to the fact that Manya and Nanny took care of all our physical needs; they fed us, washed us, took care of the home, yard, cows, and shopping, stopped our quarrels, and put the children to bed. But education, schoolwork – that was always Mother's province and could not be taken over by them.

Lena, whose reading was far ahead of her class, had as much trouble with the multiplication tables as I once had. I racked my brain, trying to find ways to help her. I finally hit upon a game. We sat on a springy bed in the dark, bouncing up and down to make it more fun. I would ask her, "six times three?" and then answer it, "eighteen," pulling her left ear. Then "six times five?" This time I pulled her right ear, answering, "thirty." Next time I would pull her right ear and expect her to answer, "thirty." For each combination of numbers, I tried to touch another part of her body, and always the same for the same answer. We laughed a lot, and I think she remembered a few answers, at least for a short time. In the long run I don't think it was very successful. It was my first attempt to devise a new pedagogical method.

Even though I felt quite overwhelmed by this self-imposed role, I did not realize how inadequate I was for it, or that no one else expected this of me. I ordered the younger children around, demanded their obedience, and was constantly frustrated by them, especially by Seryozha. Having no real authority, I fought with him, to the dismay and exasperation of Manya, who looked upon me as just an older child and expected me to behave as one.

But I felt different from the others; after all, I was already twelve. The "ultimate" questions now worried me worse than before. The discrepancy between the teachings in my former religion class and the course in physical geography I was now taking bothered me because it was obvious that one of our teachers lied to us – they could not both be telling the truth. First, the idea that the teachers might be lying was devastating; second, I felt that somehow I must know where the truth was, and I did not know how to go about finding it. Mother was not here to ask, and even before her arrest I never could bring myself to talk with her about what really troubled me. Pride or shyness kept me from talking to Pavlik – he treated me so much as a child. I was afraid that if I began talking about my inner feelings, I might start crying, and that would be terrible. At night I could not fall asleep, worrying about these questions, feeling restless and full of incomprehensible anxiety and longing. One night I climbed out the window, managed to get up on the roof and walked near the edge of it to frighten myself, so that the feeling of this fright might overpower my other anxieties. It worked: I climbed back into my bed somewhat calmed down and slept. When day came, I was able to act as if nothing had happened.

ೞ

On March 8, Mother's message, written in a large uneven hand, read:

Everything received. Thank you. My comrades are reading the books. I am well. Think of me tonight. Lena

The last remark was puzzling and ominous.
On March 10, she wrote:

Received everything. Thank you all very much. Manya, please wash M. E.'s laundry – she has no one to do it. Today is Katya's birthday. I am well. Prison is a good sign.

Zarudnaya

So Maria Ernestovna was with Mother! It meant at least that Mother had a friend there. As for the last sentence, it was only later that we understood it.

On March 13, Vadim, still in the Cheka, received the following message from Mother, which he again recorded from memory later.

> Forgive me, for the sake of Christ. You were taken only as a way of torturing me. You don't know the answers to what they demand of me. I confessed to everything. You don't know the answers to the other things they are trying to learn from me. Therefore you may speak about everything you know. For myself, I consider death unavoidable.

On March 16, Mother wrote at the end of her note:

> Did you get my salary for the first half of February and the second half, altogether about 20,000 rubles? Has the cow calved?

The cow had indeed calved, but the censors would not pass this information, either because they thought it to be a code or because they did not want her to have "good" news from home. Manya finally wrote some answers to Mother's questions on a piece of paper that she baked into the bread she sent to Mother. I think that Mother found the note, for she no longer asked the same questions.

On April 2 Manya was told that Mother was no longer in the Cheka but had been transferred to prison. Remembering Mother's remark in her note of March 10, "Prison is a good sign," we took heart from this news. Soon after that Uncle Vadim was released from the Cheka. He came home looking much thinner but still his usual self. He went back to work and to playing cello in the symphony, which kept him away from home most of the time. But for Manya and Nanny, it must have been a real relief to be able to consult with him, and rely on his judgment.

Mother's notes to Uncle Vadim, which he wrote down from memory after his release by the Cheka, were a tremendous shock to Manya and Nanny, but they did not share their worries with us.

By then Mother had been transferred to prison, and that gave them hope that her fears might be exaggerated.

Mother's first note from prison:

April 3, Sunday, Prison.

Send me some work: stockings to darn, some linen to make napkins, and some thread. On Saturday I sent you my things (including my blouse, etc.) from the Cheka to launder, and also the poems by Yakubovich.[1] Did you receive all that? Now I am sending some more dirty linen (I am wearing someone else's) and my plaid blouse, which I ask you to wash and return as soon as possible. Nothing is better for prison wear. I kiss all of you many times. Where is Tonya?

E. Zarudnaya

This was the first reference to Tonya, the girl whom Mother had hired to help Manya and Nanny with housework. She often went out with Red Army men, and Manya suspected that she might have talked too much about our family. She left us shortly before Mother's arrest.

For the moment it looked as if Mother might expect a long stay in prison, and we had to adjust to living without her. To reassure her that the children were together and well, Manya brought all of us to the front of the prison, hoping that Mother could steal a glance through the prison window at the six of us lined up.

For me this was a devastating experience. The huge edifice, built at the beginning of the eighteenth century as a fortress, had been turned into a military prison soon after. It was surrounded by a moat and ramparts, on one of which we stood. In the 1850s Dostoyevsky spent some time in this prison and described it in his book *The House of the Dead*. The high wall of the prison was long and gray and had narrow slits for windows, each protected by a heavy grate. Judging by the windows, it had two or three stories. Clearly it would be difficult for the prisoners to reach the windows from inside their cells.

Omsk Prison, 1921

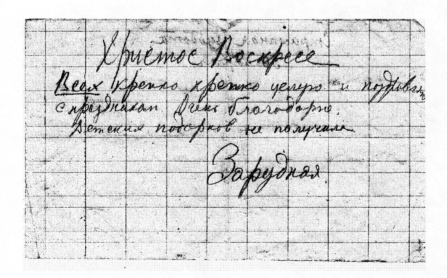

Mother's Easter greeting from prison

Moreover, it was evidently forbidden; a guard stationed in an outside observation tower, between the place where we were allowed to stand and the prison itself, shot his rifle in the direction of the prison window whenever he spotted a face appearing there. The gray wall around the windows was peppered with the marks made by these shots.

We stood in a row, too far away to distinguish any faces in the windows. Manya, who was very farsighted, seemed to think that she knew which window was Mother's, though I could not imagine how. But that Mother would try to see us from the window and might be shot at because of that seemed appalling. I tried hard to imagine how Mother's cell looked, how she lived in it, how she was taken out for interrogations. I could think of nothing else while standing there trying to keep the other children from moving. We would line up by age in the "staircase" order that Father liked to have in our yearly photographs.

We repeated this trip several times. Once when we came, instead of shooting, the guard used a mirror to send a warning spot of reflected sunlight to the windows where faces appeared, and this playful gesture seemed such a mockery that it offended me even more than shots.

About this time I developed a phobia: I could not enter a dark room without having a panic attack. As soon as I was in bed and under a blanket, I did not mind the darkness; but being on foot in the dark was unbearable. I was ashamed of this weakness. After all, I was the oldest, and was responsible for the younger children's behavior. How could I admit to them that I was afraid of the dark? I knew it was absurd, that there was no one there who could harm me. I did not believe in ghosts or fairy tales, and yet I could not stifle my fear.

I decided that I had to overcome this foolishness. I would enter the dark bedroom, close the door behind me and stand there as long as I could bear it, with my heart pounding and my hands growing cold, and then dash out of the room. I did this repeatedly, two or more times a night, night after night, gradually becoming able to stand there for longer periods, until at last I could enter a dark room without fear.

ော

Mother continued to send messages asking for material to work with, for embroidery thread, and sending back darned children's stockings. In one undated note she wrote:

Why do you send me cooked chicken? Let the children eat more. How is Vadim's and Pavlik's health? I kiss Manya.

On April 6 Mother wrote that she received "everything except the note." Evidently we had to be even more careful about what we wrote. If anything in the note displeased the prison authorities, Mother would not receive it.

On April 24, which was Palm Sunday, she sent the following message:

Please send me for the holiday two light colored silk blouses and two light colored skirts (for me and M[aria] E[rnestovna]). A full change of underwear. A pillowslip. A tablecloth. A child's sheet. Celebrate the holiday properly, and send me something, too. I kiss you. I am sending 3 pairs of stockings. Received everything.

E. Zarudnaya

Manya and Nanny did their best to prepare all the special holiday food since we did have cows and chickens, and therefore milk and eggs, which are the most important ingredients of Easter foods. The flour necessary for the traditional Easter bread was one thing Manya usually managed to get; this time she succeeded in getting fine white flour, and Nanny baked the Easter bread. On April 30, the Saturday before Easter, Manya took some things to the prison. Mother's answer was:

CHRIST HAS RISEN!
    I kiss all of you and congratulate you on the Holiday. Thank you very much. I did not receive the children's presents.

I don't remember what the presents were that we sent her. It must have been some things we made, probably our best colored eggs and Seryozha's drawings. But she never got them! It was so disappointing.

That night at eleven o'clock Manya and Nanny went to the midnight Easter service at a nearby church and took me along. Nanny carried a bundle containing the Easter foods to be blessed after the service. The church was crowded, even packed. It did not occur to me then, but as I think of it now, I wonder how many of these believers sought solace in this festive service symbolizing the ultimate hope, how many of them were downcast by all the anti-religious propaganda, and how many were grieving for relatives and friends lost in the wars and the wave of terror, or worried about escaped friends whose whereabouts were unknown, or those who were hiding or in prison?

The doors of the church stood open and people thronged on the steps. We made our way in. Manya bought thin beeswax candles for the three of us at the stand in the entry and we lit them from the candle of a man standing nearby. It was so crowded that some people had to hold their lit candles high over their heads, while others shielded them with their hands in the narrow space between the back of the person standing in front and their own chest. A lit candle seemed to be too dangerous for me, who was much shorter than most of the people around me, so Manya suggested that I blow it out. This was a great disappointment, for holding a lit candle was an essential part of enjoying the service for me. The pressure of the crowd kept increasing; sometimes a person would try to push through to the front and then the whole crowd swayed. I felt squeezed on all sides. It was hard to hear the priests' voices and I heard only one or the other choir singing on the inside balcony above our heads.

When the time came to go outside for the traditional procession around the church, a passage was formed through the middle of the church by forcing the crowd to each side. The press of people around me was so great that I was able to raise my feet and hang in the air without touching the ground. The procession went out: priests and deacons in their holiday white and gold vestments, carrying the censers with glowing incense; altar boys, men carrying raised banners, and finally one of the two choirs. Soon the pressure lessened as people started filing out of the church behind the procession. We stayed behind with the remaining worshippers and one of the two choirs. The church doors were closed and it became very quiet inside. We could hear the procession circle the church three times, with their choir singing softly until they stopped in front of the closed church door and we could hear three hard knocks. Then the priest loudly intoned, "Christ has Risen!" and the choir in the church now sang the response, "Indeed He has Risen!" The doors of the church were flung open and the whole procession proceeded through the church to the altar. Now the singing of both choirs together was thunderous: "Christ has risen from the dead trampling down death by death and bestowing life upon those in the tombs!"

The church bells rang joyously and people greeted each other with the traditional three kisses on the cheeks. Manya kissed me and told me that she would take me home while Nanny waited for the blessing of the food. We walked into the frosty night. Overhead the stars were bright; the sound of the church bells filled the air. Thin ice had formed over puddles and crunched under my feet. The painful thought that Mother was not there was mingled with the joyous mood left by the service, and the anticipation of the Easter foods waiting for us at home.

CЗ

There was a note on May 4:

> I am sending back dirty laundry – silk blouse, white skirt, empty form for paskha, cup, empty bottle, 2 napkins. … Please send me some paper for writing (you can send little sheets). Green thread for embroidery; try to find even just a few threads – I did not have enough to finish my piece. I kiss you, thank you. We had a good Easter celebration.

Next Sunday, May 8, Manya collected some more holiday delicacies to take to the prison. Pavlik wrote at the bottom of the list:

> At home everything is O.K. The children are well. Papa and I are planning to go to Petersburg for vacation. We shall return early in June. After that we shall go to Turkestan. Let us know

what you think about it. Maybe we should wait a little? Write. Kisses.

On the reverse of this note is written:

Transferred to the Cheka on May 5.

Manya went to the Cheka. Waiting in line with many others who also came to inquire about their relatives, she saw them leave the information window in tears, one after another. Some said that two hundred people had been executed the previous night. Someone said that he had seen a large group marched through the city to the outskirts where the shooting was usually done, and that among them were two women. Manya approached the window with a heavy sense of foreboding. The answer to her inquiry was short: "Shot!"

When Manya came home, her tear-stained face said everything. I ran into the bedroom. I wanted to be alone. There was no one whose shoulder I could cry on. With my siblings I always played the role of an older sister, and did not expect them ever to give *me* comfort, or want even to let them see me cry. With Pavlik, Uncle Vadim, and even Manya, I was polite, and never shared my innermost thoughts. I felt thoroughly alone now, like being left on an uninhabited island in the middle of an empty sea. There were so many questions I had not yet asked. Mother always had all the answers. Who would have them now? The sense of responsibility I had been feeling ever since Mother's arrest grew now to unbearable proportions. I felt physical pain: never to see her again. Never again to go to the prison in the hope of having a glimpse of her face in the grated window, never to read new notes written by her hand. I tried to comprehend the word "never," and I could not.

I tried to imagine how Mother must have felt when she was told that she must face death. How she walked, what she thought. What did she feel standing there, facing the cocked guns? I did not see her dead; I had no tangible proof of her death, just the Cheka statement. I remembered the story of the man who climbed out from under the corpses, and began to convince myself that the same thing might have happened to her. I could not believe that she was no more.

Mother's last photograph, 1921

And secretly I started waiting for her. This feeling that she might be alive somewhere remained with me all through my adolescence. It affected my attitude toward death in general. I never wanted to see the bodies of dead people. I wanted to keep thinking of them as if they were alive.

I don't know if I cried. I concentrated on understanding what had happened, and felt it completely beyond me. Later, when the first shock and pain subsided, I thought of Mother as a hero, a sacrifice for a great cause. The words of the revolutionary funeral march, "You fell as a sacrifice in the fateful struggle, with your selfless love for the people, for motherland, honor, and freedom," never failed to give me a feeling of pain when I heard them sung. For years afterward I had a repeated dream: I was in a prison cell waiting for my execution. I knew the hour it was to be – two o'clock. I watched the minute hand of the clock and tried to understand how it felt to be killed. I also accepted its inevitability, totally, and that too was terrifying.

I don't remember how the other children reacted to the news, except that Seryozha was angry and bitter. Lena remembers more: that I lay flat on my bed, with my head propped against a world atlas and my feet on the pillow, and sent her to tell them. Seryozha exploded and threw a chair at her, while Tanya tried to explain to Zoya that Mother being "shot" meant that she would not be coming home – ever. But the younger children still did not quite understand.

Uncle Vadim went to the Cheka. He was allowed to see the verdict and wrote down the following when he came home:

> The sentence of the Gubcheka (District Extraordinary Commission), March 14, 1921 (Written down by V. Brullov from memory):
>
> The citizen Zarudnaya is accused of participating in a White Guard organization of 1920 aimed at the overthrow of the Soviet Government, and in the SR uprising in 1921. The accusation having been well proved, the highest form of punishment is to be applied – execution by shooting.
>
> The sentence was approved by V. Cheka (Supreme

Extraordinary Commission) at the beginning of May 1921 and carried out on the night of 7/8 May 1921.

The body and things were not returned to me in spite of my urgent request.

V. Brullov, May 10, 1921

Vadim sent a telegram to Father in Harbin:

LENA DIED. DO NOT COME YOURSELF. SEND A RESPONSIBLE PERSON TO DECIDE ABOUT THE CHILDREN, AS I MUST GO AWAY. VADIM.

[1] Peter Filippovich Yakubovich (1860-1911): Russian revolutionary poet. Some of his poems were written in prison.

12

Father's Journey

We had said goodbye to Father on November 6, 1919, although his freight car did not start on its way until the Czechs agreed to attach it to their train two days later. The car was packed with people from the Asha and other mills of the Simsky District. Among them was Gavrilov, the other member of the Board of Directors. He had the cash funds and the documents certifying the bank deposits belonging to the mills. For the time being he paid the salaries of those traveling with him.

Progress toward the east was slow. At that time much of the Trans-Siberian Railroad had only one track in operation, so that two trains going in opposite directions could pass each other only at stations. The train arriving first at the station was usually shunted to a siding, where it waited until the other train had passed. Coal for the engines was in short supply, and there were many breakdowns. Sometimes trains were rearranged at the station. A train would take on another car or even a set of cars waiting there, or it would disengage a car picked up earlier and leave it on the siding for some other train to pick up. In such a case there were usually negotiations with the next train and the next one, and several days might pass before the released car was again on its way.

Kolchak and his associates left Omsk on November 12. Father and his companions were lucky to be traveling a few days ahead of Kolchak, whose train was making even slower progress. The front behind them was actually moving faster than they were. On November 17, the Czechs in Vladivostok revolted against Kolchak.

It took Father's party about twenty days to cover the roughly 1500 miles to the city of Irkutsk, where they arrived late in November. At first it seemed that they could stay there for a while, but on December 24 the anti-Kolchak revolt reached Irkutsk. A new government called "The Political Center," composed of Mensheviks and SRs, was established there by January 5 and immediately proclaimed peace with the Bolsheviks.

On January 12, 1920, after sporadic gunfire in Irkutsk, Father and several other passengers who had traveled with him earlier journeyed on in the same freight car, now flying an English flag, and attached to a Japanese train. Their passage to the city of Chita, covering about 500 miles, took several days. In Chita they learned that Kolchak had been overtaken and arrested on January 15, signaling the end of all organized resistance to the Bolsheviks.

Father's party then left Chita and headed for the city of Harbin on the Chinese Eastern Railroad, which was in Chinese territory and out of reach of the Red Army. They reached Harbin late in January 1920. No communication with Omsk had been possible since his departure, so Father's anxiety about us was very great.

A brief account of the Chinese Eastern Railroad and the city of Harbin is necessary here, to explain the political and ethnic situation Father encountered on his arrival.

The Chinese Eastern Railroad

The boundary between Russia and China beyond the city of Chita runs first along the Amur River, which flows north, then east and southeast, and finally turns northeast into the Sea of Okhotsk. At the point where it turns northeast, its tributary the Ussury joins it from the south. The Russian-Chinese border runs south along the Ussury all the way to the city and naval port of Vladivostok on the shore of the Sea of Japan. Russia urgently needed a railroad connecting Vladivostok to the Trans-Siberian track because of the threat of attacks from Japan, but a railroad built entirely on Russian soil would have had to make a giant loop.

The part of China south of the Amur and west of the Ussury was called Manchuria, a country of wide rivers, thick forests, and rich mineral resources. In the seventeenth century the Manchus conquered China and established the Manchu dynasty in Peking. To preserve the purity of the Manchu nation, migration of Chinese to Manchuria was prohibited, in spite of the comparative overcrowding of the Chinese provinces just south of Manchuria. At the same time the migration of Manchus to China for service in the army and government, and for other purposes, continued, and as a result Manchuria was relatively depopulated by the end of the nineteenth century.

The shortest and easiest route for a railroad to Vladivostok was through Manchuria. Negotiations with a reluctant China took place from 1891 onward, but only after the defeat of China by Japan in 1895 was Russia able to convince China that a railroad through Manchuria would be strategically advantageous for China as well. In 1898 an agreement was finally reached between the two governments, through which a strip of land across Manchuria was leased to a Russian company for laying down the tracks. The company had to be private, to allay China's fear of Russian expansionist ambitions. The Chinese Eastern Railroad Company (CER) was established in St. Petersburg, and the Russo-Chinese Bank was created there to finance it. CER's charter stipulated that only Russians and Chinese could be financially or administratively involved, rather to the displeasure of other countries having trade interests in China, and particularly Japan, who despite winning the Sino-Japanese War easily, had failed to assimilate Port Arthur and the Liaotung peninsula in the south of Manchuria. The lease was to run eighty years, after which ownership of the railroad passed to China. Or China could buy the railroad at an agreed price in thirty-six years.

Just after construction began, the Russian government also succeeded in acquiring a lease to Port Arthur from China. Russia fortified the town and built a railroad connecting it to the CER. The two track systems met at the point where the CER crossed a large tributary of the Amur, the Sungary River, approximately midway between the two Russian borders, and here the administrative center of the entire railroad, the city of Harbin, was built. In the early stages of construction the wide, navigable Sungary offered easy water transportation for the construction crews and materials.

Having primarily strategic significance for Russia, the CER was built without any regard for existing Chinese towns in the sparsely populated countryside. The stations along the railroad were built on the leased territory, as was Harbin. This territory, forming a narrow ribbon that widened to accommodate stations and the city of Harbin, was called "The Zone." It was administered by the Russians, and formed an essentially Russian colony, where the official and unofficial language was Russian. Besides personnel needed for the operation of the railroad, who were brought in from Russia, a number of Russian settlers arrived, looking for new opportunities. Unlike most colonies, the Zone was populated mostly by the colonists, since Chinese could settle there only if they owned property or a business.

In 1904, however, Russian territorial aggression, as perceived by the Japanese, precipitated a new war, in which Russia lost Port Arthur as well as part of the southern branch of the railroad, and a major part of her fleet. After this, Russian power in Manchuria was considerably diminished. Restrictions on Chinese migration to Manchuria were modified, and finally eliminated in 1912, when the Chinese revolution overthrew the Manchu dynasty. A steady stream of Chinese started to move up the Russian-built railroad and to settle around it. But this did not harm the original investors: in a short time the CER, heavily subsidized before that by the Russian government, became profitable.

At first Harbin was a frontier town far removed from Russian centers of art, learning, and commerce, embedded in a distant and underdeveloped province of a foreign country, looked toward as a "capital" only by the small Russian settlements along the railroad. A colonial atmosphere was established there for the relatively well-paid railroad staff who relied on cheap Chinese labor for all menial tasks, yet both the Russians and the more educated Chinese depended on cities distant from Harbin for all cultural links.

But in the two decades during which the population of Manchuria and the traffic on the CER increased rapidly, Harbin became an industrial center of real significance. Foreign banks opened branches there, many commercial enterprises were initiated, several European consulates were established, and various import/ export companies opened offices. Being many hundreds of miles from other big cities, Harbin had to develop its own educational and cultural resources. New schools were opened, a permanent opera and a symphony orchestra were organized, theaters sprang up, and several newspapers began to be published; an English tennis club and a YMCA were established, and even an institution of higher learning – Harbin Polytechnic Institute, founded to train engineers for the Railroad.

After the October Revolution of 1917, however, the Russo-Chinese Bank (now renamed Russo-Asiatic) was nationalized, like all banks in Russia, thus making the Zone in effect a Russian governmental enterprise – to the not-unjustified alarm of the Chinese. Lenin tried to have his men assume administrative power in the Zone, through his own Bolshevik representatives, and the Chief Manager of CER, General D. L. Khorvat,[1] appealed to the Chinese. After consultation with the Russian ambassadors in Peking and Japan, at that time still loyal to the previous government of Russia, the Chinese appointed their own (Chinese) President of the Zone, pending renegotiation of the agreement with the new Russian government. The Russo-Asiatic Bank was rechartered in Paris, and the operation of the CER and the administration of the Zone were left in Khorvat's hands. A border guard of Chinese was installed at both ends of the Zone, which thus became an enclave of pre-Communist Russia, and remained so until China recognized the Soviet Union in 1924, and renegotiated the conditions of the concession.

Throughout 1918, 1919, and 1920 the Russian population of the Zone was divided by rivalry between refugees and Bolshevik sympathizers, and by the activity of anti-Red military groups, some of them bordering on bandit gangs. The Japanese supported some of the latter, and also sent in troops of their own, who at one time even occupied Harbin – to the dismay of the Chinese, and of the English, French, and Americans involved in the Allied intervention, ostensibly helping to evacuate the Czechs. In short, the CER and the Zone were of concern to a number of countries. There was even a suggestion to internationalize it.

During the years 1918 to 1922 Harbin swelled under the influx of Russian refugees, immigrants, army units, and their families. Unlike other magnets of Russian emigration, such as Paris, Berlin, and Prague, there was no need for the refugees to deal with new languages and civil traditions: they were coming to a place with no history to speak of, where existing cultural resources were in their infancy. Among the new arrivals were many well-educated people, with established professional status, some of whom, like my father, could find ready employment with the Railroad and in other allied commerce. Many joined the expanding educational institutions, others started new businesses. While this Russian island in the middle of a remote Chinese province could ultimately offer them only limited possibilities for professional advancement, the Russian population of the city of Harbin grew steadily in the years 1918-31, and the Chinese population in and around it kept pace.

cȝ

When Father reached Harbin in late January 1920 the city was packed with Russian refugees. He rented a room in the apartment of a Colonel Varaksin, at 72 Bulvarnyi Prospekt. Varaskin's wife Varvara was a teacher in a local school. In his usual congenial way, Father met many new people and made some friends. It did not take long for him to find his distant cousins Maria Lanceray Solntseva and her sister Sonya, and the wife of General Khorvat, Camilla Benois Khorvat, whom he mentioned in his letter to Mother. Khorvat himself, a military engineer and the manager of the CER, was temporarily in Siberia, attempting to organize resistance to the Bolsheviks there. Both the Lanceray sisters and Camilla were related to Father through the Cavoses; Camilla's father, the well-known painter Albert Benois, was the cousin of Zhenia Cavos' father. These relatives received Father warmly and he visited them often.

For a while the Simsky Metallurgical District maintained an office in Harbin, and Father was still on its board of directors, although it was impossible to transact any business from there, or even to communicate with the mills, which had been nationalized by the new Soviet government. Father had no personal funds. For the time being he could borrow a little from the Simsky District, but he had to find some means of supporting himself. His hope rested on the furnace he had invented, the Mechta, and he began negotiations with the CER about building one, which could now be particularly useful, since it was impossible to obtain the necessary steel from Russia. However, no other chance of sales for Mechta existed in that area, and in March 1920 he traveled to Japan, hoping to activate his international patent on Mechta and obtain some orders for its installation.

His route lay first along the Southern Chinese Railroad, part of which had been lost by the Russians in the Russian-Japanese War, and then through Korea. From Korea he proceeded by sea, crossing the Tsushima strait to Japan. During the crossing the painful memory came to him of his many classmates and friends who had perished there during the Japanese war. He arrived at Yokohama on March 30.

Japan

Japan loomed on the horizon as a new and mysterious fairyland – an impression Father remembered to the end of his days. The hustle and bustle of the Yokohama port, with the strange native costumes, pointed straw hats, laborers carrying heavy loads on both sides of bamboo shoulder rods, rickshaw drivers on the trot pulling one-man carriages behind them, women in kimonos moving with little fast steps, wearing straw *zori* or even wooden ones that looked like little step-stools. Father was immediately charmed by it all, and decided he must learn some Japanese.

Until now he had survived on what he was able to borrow from the funds left in Gavrilov's hands, but after his arrival in Japan he had received only one further loan, and no answers to his letters. These funds were still the property of the stockholders of the Simsky District, the administration of which had now emigrated, mostly to Germany. An attempt to transfer money to them was only partially successful, because deposits in a Vladivostok bank could not be withdrawn in time before the accounts were frozen by the Soviet government. Some funds remained in the bank in Harbin, but Gavrilov was increasingly reluctant to touch them. From correspondence Father also learned that General Khorvat had been removed from his administrative post in Harbin in April, and had moved to Peking as an adviser to the Chinese Ministry of Communications. Boris Ostroumov was appointed in his place.

After long investigation Father was able to locate the patent agent W. A. Haviland, in Tokyo. It turned out that his office had received all that was necessary from Petersburg early in 1917 when the patent was originally applied for. What they required now to activate the patent was a copy of the official Russian document stating that the patent had been applied for, but when the Revolution began, correspondence with Russia had stopped, and even in 1920 no such copy could be obtained.

After many complications, Father received a preliminary document, on the basis of which he could begin organizing a company for the construction and sales of the Mechta. But in June 1920 Haviland found that Father's patent could not be finalized, because of similarities between Mechta and other patented furnaces, and the plans for a company had to be abandoned. Father was certain that the rival designs, which were patented after his original application, had taken their idea from his incomplete application; he appealed the decision of the Japanese patent office, but to no avail. It was a great disappointment to him. He could still sell his own drawings, but without any protection from imitators.

Now Father felt almost lost: his anxiety about the family gnawed at him, his life lacked direction, and he missed the intellectual stimulus for which he had depended so much on Mother and their friends and relatives. Now he had to provide it himself, while nothing was settled, and the future remained completely uncertain. His education, experience, and former positions seemed of little relevance, as he began to seek other employment.

During his attempts to organize a Mechta company, Father met the manager of the Zemma Works, Ltd., of the Babcock & Wilcox Company in Yokohama, an Englishman named Thompson. B&W decided to construct a Mechta at their works and paid Father 1000 yen, or about 2000 U.S. dollars. These were his first earnings in Japan. After further interviews, Father was offered a position at the B&W office in Osaka, which processed all orders, estimates, and proposals. In his diary Father adds, "All in English." He moved to Osaka on June 24, 1920. Fortunately the man he was to replace, a Mr. Vaughan, turned out to be an understanding person, who stayed on in the office with Father for over two months to help him familiarize himself with the work, before transferring to Tokyo.

By August 7, 1920 Father had moved into an apartment in Kobe. He writes in his diary, "I think I am beginning to gather my wits. I hope to start a more sensible existence. I am trying." Commuting by train in the morning and after a long day at the office left him with rather short evenings. Three times a week he had lessons at home from an English tutor, Mrs. Price. His Mechta for the CER was being completed in Harbin and he sent additional instructions and drawings to the engineer supervising the construction. He maintained correspondence with people in Harbin and with the Khorvats, who by now were settled in Peking.

His manner of living was quite Japanese: he changed into a kimono at home, and sat on the floor in front of a low Japanese table for his meals, which were served by his Japanese landlady. He surrounded himself with Japanese writing, which he practiced on the days when Mrs. Price was not coming. He occasionally called in a passing blind Japanese masseur, who, with a boy guide, usually appeared on the streets at dusk, playing a distinct tune on the flute to let people know that he was available. To the end of his life Father recalled with a sense of nostalgia those peaceful surroundings, the polite chatter of his landlady, that total immersion in the quiet atmosphere, so aesthetically pleasing, and so foreign, that assuaged his inner anxiety. He always remained partial to the Japanese language and especially to the gentle ways of Japanese women.

Communicating with Relatives

Father's attempts at communicating with his own family were still frustrated, however. He had received two letters from Mother, dated September 21 and November 10, and was not at all sure that any of his letters had reached her. He tried repeatedly to send news and parcels with travelers headed through Russia, but without any success. He wrote to relatives in Petrograd and Latvia, to friends in France, Germany, and England. The letters had to go the long way around China and through Europe, but at least some were answered.

Father had always had active family ties, and now he tried to keep them up by correspondence from Japan. In the past, even when we were far from St. Petersburg, our relatives often came to visit us, and the correspondence was always quite lively, so that all the members of Father's and Mother's extended families were usually accounted for, and Mother and Father felt as if they were part of the political and social life of the great cities they had left. It was much harder to do that now. The three daughters of his sister Ekaterina Cavos were in Estonia, and Father, who felt responsible for them, hoped that their brother Zhenia and his family could join them. Father's surviving four sisters were all still in Russia, Anastasia in a nursing home somewhere in the Ukraine, while Zoya, whom Father was always trying to help, had moved to a country village to escape the food and lodging crises of the big city. The oldest sister, Maria Grevs, lived in a university dormitory in Petrograd where her husband was a professor. The youngest, Varya Lisovskaya, who worked in a school, lived with her children in the Petrograd apartment of their brother Alexander (our Uncle Sasha), who was apparently at that time in Paris. There were also Mother's brothers and sisters: Vadim, as far as Father knew, remained at Omsk, while his wife and daughter were in Petrograd. Boris Brullov too continued to live in Petrograd, as did their two sisters, Lyubov, a physician, and Lydia. Lydia was married now, while Lyubov's husband had died.

Father corresponded actively with Varya, and especially with her daughter Galya, to whom later he would even send copies of his letters to us. Through this correspondence he was able to learn where the family was dispersed and how it was managing to survive. In a letter dated October 4, 1920 Varya wrote to Father about their brother, Alexander:

> Sasha left Petrograd in August 1918 and was in Kharkov until January of this year. ... We did not know for a long time where he went while the Reds advanced and retreated. Recently we found out that he was in Kremenchug until he left for France. I don't know his address, and know nothing of his wife.
>
> Her son (also Sasha) works for the railway near Pskov, her daughter Natasha is a performing ballerina. Transport in Petrograd is erratic, food and fuel are scarce, and many close

friends have perished. The Vernadskys[2] and Shchedrinskys have left the country for good. We are so happy that we found you.

From his friend and relative Feodor Rodichev Father received a long and informative letter from Lausanne, Switzerland. Rodichev was a member of the First Russian Duma, active in Russian politics before and after the end of the civil war in the South of Russia and his emigration to Europe. He was then surviving on the gradually diminishing income from his literary writings. He wrote:

I was arrested on September 1, 1918 in Petrograd under a false name, but was released when they went to our home looking for [the real] me. We left Petrograd posing as refugees and managed to get to Pskov, occupied then by the Germans. Then to Dvinsk and from there through Polotsk and Gomel to Kiev, ruled by the Hetman.[3] We stayed in Kiev from October 15 until December 23. Kiev was occupied by the Petliurovtsy, and it became clear that the Bolsheviks would take it. We left for Odessa. After some mishaps we arrived in Odessa, occupied by the French. We stayed there till February 15, 1919, when I went to Rostov. On my way I left my wife in Crimea with the Petrunkeviches. I intended to return to Crimea, when it was suddenly taken by the Bolsheviks, and my wife was moved first to Sevastopol and from there to Athens. It took me I think more than a month to catch up with her in Athens. … Mitrofanovich [Father's cousin] is in Petersburg; in September of 1918 he was taken hostage, then released, and now he works at the Hermitage and is very much afraid to be compromised. That's it. How are things in Russia now? Very bad: all thoughts are about nourishment – nothing else. Everybody has sunk into poverty and slavery. They have managed to get themselves into bondage.

How do the émigrés live? Badly. They don't adjust to working, don't settle down, live in hopes that it will all pass. But what is it that will pass? We ourselves will pass. I advise everyone to behave as if he will spend his entire life in exile, then return to the homeland will be an unexpected victory.

Keep writing to us, Ivan Sergeyevich. We are, after all, nearer each other than we were in Russia. Now it takes two months to get a reply to a letter sent to Moscow. For the time being the correspondence seems to be regular. Be well, keep your spirits up, and give my best to your wife.

Rodichev

But Father still hoped that as an engineer he could be useful to humanity even in exile, and that someday he would be able to return home.

The fall and winter passed and the spring of 1921 arrived. One more letter came from Mother. Father did not yet know that it would be the last.

Charles R. Crane

In the spring of 1921 the American Ambassador in Peking, Charles R. Crane, was being recalled to the USA. Mr. Crane was the son of a well-known plumbing manufacturer in Chicago and at one time himself headed the firm, the Crane Plumbing Company. Politically active as a Democrat, and an avid traveler, he had a long-standing interest in Russia. He had visited many times before the Revolution, met Tsar Nicholas II, and even lunched with him in the Winter Palace. In 1902 he sponsored Thomas G. Masaryk, who later became the first president of Czechoslovakia, to lecture on Russia at the University of Chicago; in 1904 he brought Pavel N. Milyukov to lecture on Russia at the University of Chicago and at Harvard. Like many American liberals he was sympathetic to the first Russian Revolution in February 1917, and hoped for truly democratic reforms in Russia. In 1917 he served on a commission visiting Petrograd to support the Provisional Government's war effort, but was the only member whose view of the prospects for post-Tsarist Russia was frankly pessimistic.

Now that the Bolshevik government seemed to be firmly established, Crane was curious to see the country again. He decided to return home not by crossing the Pacific, but by way of Siberia, Russia, Europe, and the Atlantic. He planned to take the train to

Harbin and then travel along the Chinese Eastern Railroad and the entire Trans-Siberian Railroad to Moscow, taking his son John, aged 22, with him. This was an adventurous undertaking for that time. Railroad transportation was just becoming reregulated. They would have to pass several borders – Manchuria to the buffer zone centered in Chita, then the buffer zone to the new Soviet Union, and then on to Europe.

While in Peking John Crane had met the children of General and Mrs. Khorvat, who at that time lived in Peking under the protection of the Chinese government, for whom the General acted as a consultant: I am sure that the General, with his long gray beard, and his beautiful, elegant wife Camilla, were a striking pair in the diplomatic circles of Peking. When Camilla learned of the intended journey, she spoke to Charles Crane about Father and his attempts to reach his family, and wrote to Father about Crane. Father went to Peking to meet Crane and ask him if he would help find out whether Mother and the family still were at Omsk. Father also asked Mr. Crane to take a parcel of food and clothing to them, and Crane generously agreed.

When Father returned to Kobe he learned of Mother's death from Uncle Vadim's telegram, but not how she had died. Mr. Crane and his son were already on their way. Soon afterwards Father decided to leave his employment at B&W and return to Harbin. The only reference in his papers to leaving Japan is a note scribbled on a short letter from his predecessor at the Osaka office, Mr. Vaughan, dated from Tokyo, July 2:

> Dear Zarudny
>
> If you would care to come stay with me until you leave please do so. Leave the hotel & come to my place. If you have to go to Zemma you could go down by train. With kind regards and sincere condolences …

On the corner of this letter Father wrote in pencil: "Example of a kind comrade's attitude after I told him of my sorrow."

He received many affectionate letters from friends and relatives, some not believing what they called "rumors," some suggesting various solutions to the problem of the children. Relatives in Russia offered to take the children, urging him not to come back, but to try to support them from abroad. Some suggested moving them to Latvia, which had become an independent country after the end of the war. Some friends urged him to try to get the family to Harbin.

Father's sister Varya wrote:

> Vadim arrived here the day before yesterday and told us everything. I still cannot come to my senses and cannot understand – could this possibly be true? All I can say is be brave and ask God to help you. ... Vadim is in a terrible state – quite sick and nervously exhausted. Today he was admitted to the hospital where he might undergo an operation. As soon as he is well again, he and his wife plan to go to Omsk to pick up the children and bring them here. Each of us here is ready to take care of one or two of them pending reunion with you. Each of them is dear to us herself and as your child and now even more so, as a reflection of Lenochka's beautiful nature. We have before us the image of her pure and wonderful life, dedicated to service to mankind, to the love of one's fellow man, and to faith in the truth. Her dear image stands before us so that we, who are weak, bad, cowardly, and silent, could see what we should be – how never to compromise one's conscience, how to be sure that one's word never differs from one's deed. This is the example that we must follow, and if anyone would have the luck to support and direct one of her children along her difficult, but glorious path, which was crowned by her heroic deed, one would experience the greatest happiness one could achieve on this earth. And this will be your and our obligation. But remember we shall for sure meet with her. Don't be weak-hearted, don't lose hope, don't offend her pure memory by not believing.

From his brother Alexander he received a telegram:

I KNOW ALL, I UNDERSTAND ALL, I GRIEVE FOR RUSSIA.

Vadim Pavlovich Brullov
(Uncle Vadim)

Alexander Sergeyevich Zarudny
(Uncle Sasha)

Back in Harbin

In August 1921 Father left his position with B&W and went back to Harbin, where he felt nearer to his family. Some things had changed: the Chinese had taken over the municipal administration; the Khorvats were in Peking; the Russian police had been disarmed and replaced by the Chinese police; and the Railroad guards and the courts were now also Chinese. Japanese were still in evidence but were no longer in charge. The Russian population of Harbin was calmer, reconciled to waiting for further political developments.

For several months Father received a salary in connection with the installation of Mechta in the CER railroad works. After that he was again unemployed. Although he knew that he could not safely return to Russia, he still hoped that eventually it would be possible for the whole family to live and work there. But now, without funds or even work, he had to make a momentous decision about the children.

Father read a lot of fiction and poetry and often copied out passages that seemed to express his moods; he used either his Russian or his English typewriter and sometimes sent or gave copies to his friends, finding it easier to use another man's words to express his feelings, always leaving a carbon copy in his files. His anguish, loneliness, sadness, his fear of a lonely old age, and his need for love permeate these pages. Here is a prayer that he copied from somewhere:

The Prayer of the Lonely Heart

Teach me, O Lord, the beautiful significance of solitude. Show me that the lonely day was given me in order that I may think quietly and feel deeply, in order that I may not continually try to escape myself, but may study to be friendly with myself.

Direct me that I may intelligently develop all the resources within myself; that I may practice the art of meditation; that I may exercise my imagination, so that it will lift me up to the beautiful meaning of the day; that I may learn the value of books – those comforters of the lonely – to read and mark and love them; that I may have some hobby which will call me each day to the hour of solitude and make it beautiful every day.

Help me to learn the courage and patience and self-sufficiency that will temper my loneliness!

Our lives are too much surrounded by the hurrying feet and fevered voices of the self-seeking. Grant that I may find my happiness not in what I have, but in what I am: not in possessing much, but in hoping and loving much!

May those hours of solitude give me strength to make real my ideals of human worthiness!

Amen!

He copied this prayer several times, and later translated it into Russian. At the end of the translation he added by hand: "I urgently ask all those who love me to memorize this prayer." Other extracts were taken from Goethe, Wordsworth, and the Russian version of Oscar Wilde's *De Profundis*. I know that copying these quotations was not an idle occupation for him, for he felt that they expressed his own feelings – he read and reread them and was much affected by them.

During this time he also contacted the International Hunger Relief Committee and various consulates in Chita about getting permission for the family to leave Omsk for Harbin, and at the same time applied for a Belgian and then for a Latvian visa, just to be on the safe side. He wrote numerous letters seeking jobs, not only in Harbin, but also in Japan and China, and corresponded actively with the Khorvats in Peking and other relatives in Petrograd, Latvia, and Europe. After he reestablished contact with us, he carefully preserved all our letters as well as copies of his own letters to us. He assembled packages to send to us whenever the opportunity for their transport arose; he began to look for a place for us to live and started to think of how to furnish it with help from his friends and relatives.

Father learned *how* Mother died from letters that were sent in a roundabout way through Europe and even by way of America. On February 9, 1922 he filled the two last pages in his diary:

SAD
MOURNFUL
Days
On May 7 - 8 in Omsk
in the year of 1921
My dear Lenochka was shot
after suffering in prison since
February 16, 1921.
Her last letter was dated January 18, 1921.
Everlasting memory to my dear, priceless one.
February 9, 1922. Harbin

On the very last page he speaks of Mother's encouraging him when he was leaving Omsk, and telling him that Mechta would support him. He adds up what he has earned from Mechta.

After this he closed and sealed his diary. It was opened by my sister Elena many years later, after his death.

[1]   Dmitri Leonidovich Khorvat (1858-1937): Lieutenant-General, manager of the CER in 1902-20. In 1918 he declared himself "temporary supreme ruler of Russia"; in 1918-19 he was the Kolchak administration's main representative in the Russian Far East.

[2]   George [Georgii Vladimirovich] Vernadsky, 1887-1973: historian. Son of the prominent Russian scientist, Vladimir Ivanovich Vernadsky (1863-1945), who remained in Russia, George Vernadsky and his wife Nina emigrated after the Bolshevik Revolution, first to Prague, and in 1927 to the United States. He served as Research Associate and then Professor of Russian History at Yale University from 1927 to 1956; author of many books on Russian and Ukrainian history, including the five volume *History of Russia* (1943-69).

[3]   On April 29, 1918 Pavlo Skoropadsky (1873-1945) was declared *Hetman*, or leader, of the Ukrainian State; he was removed from power in November 1918 following an uprising led by Simon Petlieura (1879-1926).

13

Omsk, 1921

A few days after Uncle Vadim sent his telegram to Father, Nanny went to a nearby church to arrange for a memorial service. So one morning all six children, Manya, Nanny, Uncle Vadim, and Pavlik started from our house for the church – a somber procession. Mother's death was the kind one could not speak about, and only our closest friends knew of it.

When we arrived the Navalikhins and one of Mother's colleagues, a teacher, were already there. Nanny bought the candles and gave one to each person. Little Katya was not quite sure how to hold it, so I helped her. We stood in the empty church with our lit candles, watching the priest and the deacon walking about with the smoking censer, and smelling the familiar incense.

The service seemed extremely long, especially for the little ones who had to be admonished all the time to be quiet, to stand still and keep their candles straight. Manya and Nanny were completely absorbed, crossing themselves, bowing, with tears running down their faces, while I watched Katya and Zoya. Tanya and Lena understood the seriousness of what was going on and stood quietly, but Tanya kept shifting her weight from one foot to the other, it was really hard on her. Seryozha stood straight and somber, fully appreciating the solemnity of the occasion.

When it came to the final singing of "Let her rest with the Saints and keep her in eternal memory," every one knelt and I could hear Manya's sobs. All I felt was sharp pain and a tremendous desire for all of it to be over. I felt that our grief was something so private that this demonstration of it was inappropriate. Manya and Nanny might do it, but not we. The awful thing had happened. One had to live on. Most of all I did not want to be pitied, to be called a "poor orphan." The candles were snuffed out, the priest stood while we approached him in turn to kiss the heavy cross he held in his hand, and we walked out into the bright light of the street.

൫

The daily routine continued. There were a few more weeks of school left, but school had become almost a farce: new teachers trying new methods of teaching, unruly students for whom getting a free lunch was the most important thing about school. Nobody seemed interested in learning anything. Manya and Uncle Vadim decided that there was no point in sending Lena to school, so she stayed home and spent her time reading, which they felt was more educational than what the school offered.

I became very concerned about Tanya's education. She still did not even know her letters, and she was already six years old. I decided that I should teach her but it was difficult to get such an active girl to sit still and listen. She really did not want to be taught. I would assign her written exercises but she would not do them. I was exasperated. One day I really lost my temper and locked her in the wardrobe full of our clothes. Tanya screamed and cried, but I turned the key, put it into my pocket, and went to the other room. Nanny was busy in the kitchen and Manya was out.

Soon Manya returned and asked after Tanya. By then only pathetic whimpering could be heard from the wardrobe. Manya dashed to the wardrobe and tried to open it, found it locked, and angrily demanded the key. I gave it to her reluctantly. "How could you do this?" she asked, after releasing Tanya, and I said that Tanya did not obey me and would not do the assignment I gave her. Manya was furious; I never saw her so angry before or since. She called in Pavlik, and together they put me down on the bed, lifted my skirt, pulled down my bloomers, and spanked me. I cannot even describe what an affront to my dignity it was. None of us had ever been spanked; and now I, the eldest, had been, and by my older cousin to boot! It took me months to get over it and I never forgot the experience. At the same time I realized that I had done something very bad and I really tried not to lose my temper again.

Soon after this Uncle Vadim and Pavlik left Omsk. Vadim promised to try to do something for us with the help of other relatives, and hoped one day to return. I still felt a little resentful towards Pavlik, so I did not mind his going, but for Manya an important source of moral support was now gone. Only the Navalikhins remained in that capacity.

Our supply of stored vegetables was dwindling. It was Manya now who had to make decisions about buying food for us or hay for the cow, so that we could have milk. The money left from Mother's earnings was gone. Our table silver – forks and knives – began their trek to the market. Manya thought of trading Mother's silver medal for a load of hay that some farmer was offering, but decided against that sacrifice. The beggars knocking at the door many times a day now rarely got anything from Nanny; usually she would just say "The Lord be with you!" We ourselves usually had only one piece of bread a day each.

It was then that Nanny decided to contribute all her own savings to the common survival. She had always felt herself separate from our family, however much she was devoted to Mother and the children, but now she dug into her own trunk, which she always kept locked, and brought out a bag of the old imperial Russian bank notes. She presented them to Manya and Manya gasped. "But Nastasia Pavlovna," she exclaimed, "these are old bills, they are annulled, you cannot buy anything with them, they have no value!" Nanny was thunderstruck. She suddenly understood, and covering her face with her apron sat on her bed. She was soon weak from sobbing. All her savings "for a rainy day" were *nothing!*

Manya managed to rent Uncle Vadim's room to a group of Red Army officers. They treated us well, but we tried to keep clear of them. They liked Manya; one of them was especially fond of her. He could not understand her devotion to this "bourgeois" family. She knew how to counter his questions and advances with jokes.

A typhus epidemic was now raging all over the country, and many thousands died from it. One of the officers became ill, and again it was Manya who looked after him, bringing him water and soup while his companions were away during the day. Manya and Nanny were seriously alarmed by this new danger: typhus was carried by lice, and we all had lice at one time or another. With no hot water except what could be heated on the kitchen stove, and only manure to fire the stove, we rarely had a chance to wash our hair. Using a special comb we just combed the lice out of our hair, bending our heads over a piece of paper, and then squashed the fallen lice with a fingernail. It was a tedious procedure, so Manya decided to cut all the children's hair short with clippers, except mine. Being more responsible, I was supposed to comb out my hair every day, and to wear a kerchief or hat all the time.

Summer 1921

Manya realized that no matter what the future held for us, we must eat. Vegetables had to be planted on time. Because there were no more earning members in the family, she petitioned the city officials to give her more land to cultivate, on the outskirts of the city where we already had been allotted two plots. Their response was an offer to place the children in various orphanages. "I already have an orphanage," Manya replied. "Give me more children, and I'll take care of them, but I will not give these away." Baffled or impressed, the official assigned her more land.

We now had three plots, one of which extended over a dirt road, and had to be broken up with a pick before it could be spaded and planted with potatoes. Manya worked on spading and seeding, while Nanny looked after the little ones at home and prepared all our meals. Every day as soon as school ended, we older children would go to the gardens on the outskirts of the city. We learned to weed, to pinch the tomatoes, to hill the potatoes. Sometimes Nanny came too, with the younger children, who helped by standing in the line at the well from which water was carried in pails: this way Manya did not have to waste time waiting for her turn to get the water.

To increase our food supply Seryozha and I, and even Lena, tried to fish in the river. We had no fishing rods, no lines, and no hooks. We simply tied a bent nail or a bent pin to a string, baited it with an earthworm, tied a small stone about a foot from the "hook," and threw it as far as we could from a wooden dock. Most of the time the fish slipped off the hook before we could grab it; but we still caught some, mostly tiny fish three or four inches long. Once in a while we got something bigger, sometimes even small sterlets. We brought them all home, where Manya and Nanny cleaned them and cooked them for us. It must have been more trouble for them than it was worth, but they never complained and even praised us for providing an important dietary supplement.

The summer days were long. Tired from our daytime activities we would settle down to reading after supper. Seryozha continued with his fantasies and his drawing, but the lack of available paper became critical. All the notebooks prepared by Mother were filled long ago, and Seryozha used every blank margin in them for further sketches, but he never drew in our books. Once we ran some errands for one of our neighbors, a composer, who gave us a stack of his compositions printed with wide margins, and at least these gave Seryozha new opportunities.

⋘

Sometime in June, I asked Manya if I might go with some children I knew to a village about ten or twelve miles from Omsk. One of the boys had an uncle there. Obviously we thought that we might get some food, if not to bring home, at least to eat there. Manya let me go.

It was probably the longest walk I ever undertook. The day was beautifully warm, with not a cloud in the sky. We walked on the country road, along fields of tall grass, full of wild flowers which we could not resist picking. The girls made flower wreaths to wear on their heads. The road led us through woody areas of lovely birch groves, so airy and light, with white birch trunks as far as one could see into the wood, and with tempting mushrooms that we did not pick, being too far from home. The boys picked up broken tree branches, sharpening them with their penknives to make spears, and competed with one another hitting various spots on the way. It was a happy, unhurried trip.

We arrived at the village when it was already dusk. We could not find the boy's uncle: he was either away for a while or perhaps had moved on for good. Nobody would tell us. The local people, afraid of city-dwellers inundating villages in search of food, were extremely hostile to us, and all told us to go home, but it was really too late: some of our companions had turned back earlier, but by now we were afraid to be caught by darkness on the way. We were terribly hungry, and no one would give us any food.

When the village had quieted down and most people had gone to sleep, we crawled into a garden that we had noticed earlier, when a girl had been thinning out the carrot bed. A pile of tiny carrots was left in the garden, probably to be collected later to feed yard animals. We ate enough of them to blunt our hunger somewhat, and then we curled up and went to sleep between the vegetable beds. We woke up very early, and quickly left the garden before the owners could discover us. Most of the children were anxious to get back to the city, but four of us, three boys and I, wanted to explore more of the area.

The village stood on the shore of a small river, crossed by a large ferry for horses, wagons, and passengers. The boy whose uncle was supposed to live here thought that he might have a hut by a field of potatoes on the other side of the river. We slipped unnoticed onto the ferry and rode across.

We were still very hungry, and the hut and the potatoes seemed quite far away. We decided to catch fish and eat them before walking on, but we had no fishing rods, string, or hooks. One of the boys had an inspiration: he removed his shirt and tied the sleeves and neck to create a bag. Two of us then dragged the shirt-bag against the current, wading waist deep in the river. We caught several small pikes this way. I don't think that they were cleaned very well before we cooked them, piercing each with a stick and toasting them over a campfire we built. Even the campfire required some ingenuity, for we had no matches. The sticks holding the fish burned and broke before the fish were quite finished, so we ate them half-raw, but how tasty they seemed!

When we reached the hut no one was there, nor in the field. The day was half gone. We picked some small potatoes at the edge of the field and brought them to the hut. There was a hearth with a hole in the roof above it, but we did not dare start a fire, for fear that someone nearby would see the smoke: we knew that we were intruders. We ate the potatoes raw. By then it was dusk, and we fell asleep on the benches in the hut. It was better than sleeping in the garden.

Early in the morning we left the hut and found several workers already in the fields; a man saw us, and came towards us threateningly.

We started to run, and went on running all the way to the ferry landing, where we hid in the bushes to wait for the ferry. Our pursuer did not see us. When the ferry came and was unloading, we slipped onto it, hiding behind the wagons. The man who had followed us came aboard too, but still did not see us. We managed to get off unnoticed on the other side of the river, and set off for home. Before long we were out of the village and out of danger.

Hunger really troubled us, however, and I felt quite weak. We found some berries in the woods, though they were pretty much picked over. We ate a few raw mushrooms. By the time I saw the buildings of the city on the horizon, I was so faint that I could not imagine reaching them. The boys, who seemed still energetic, encouraged me and for a while even had to support me as I walked. I was barely upright as I dragged myself into our house. Alarmed and anxious, Manya and Nanny sat me down at the table to eat. Needless to say, I was quite proud of my adventure.

Unexpected Visitors

In the middle of July days were long; daylight lasted until ten o'clock in the evening, and the dry dust on the road felt soft and warm against our bare feet. The big puddle in front of our house was completely dry. One day we did not go to the gardens; everything was growing well and it was too early to harvest anything. As usual, the small children were playing near the house; Nanny wanted them not to wander far from it. I was playing with some friends near the neighboring house, Sergey was at home drawing, and Manya was busy with something in the house.

An open carriage with two well-dressed strangers stopped in front of our house. The driver called out to the children asking if the Zarudny family lived here. "Yes," said Tanya, and ran into the house to call Manya. Manya came out. The driver said that these two foreign gentlemen wanted to see Madam Zarudny. Manya was stunned. The two men got out of the car, but there was no way of communicating with them; they spoke no Russian. With gestures, Manya invited them in, and asked Tanya to go and call me. I came running. The strangers tried English on me. I tried German, but they did not speak it. We settled on French, though none of us could speak it well. I understood that these men were two Americans, Mr. Charles R. Crane and his son John. They knew our Father and had a package for us from him.

Years later, in the Columbia University Library, I read in John Crane's diary an account of this meeting: "We asked for the mother, and were told that she was taken off to prison last May as a counter-revolutionist. We asked if we could see her in prison, and with reluctance they said, 'No, she was executed six weeks ago.'" The guests took a large bundle from the carriage and gave it to us. Then they left, saying that they would come back, as Manya promised to find someone who spoke English. She went to the Navalikhins immediately, while we started opening the package. Nanny watched us as we pulled out food, clothes, and a big square package, which we thought was paper, to our great delight, since paper was so scarce. We soon discovered that this was not paper, but *money*. Money in uncut sheets of twenty 1000-ruble notes, sheets upon sheets of them. By then 1000-ruble bills had so little value that at church the priest asked people not to put them into the collection baskets, and at the market some peasants would accept such uncut sheets only in order to paper the insides of bridal dowry trunks. Still, this large parcel amounted to a great deal of money, and Manya and Nanny were very happy and grateful.

When Mr. Crane and his son came back, Navalikhin was with us and he explained our situation clearly. Mr. Crane promised to let Father know all he had learned, and to do what he could to help. Before leaving he took a photograph of us, to give to Father. I lined up the children in our usual way, in order of age, but Mr. Crane asked me to stand in the middle.

In his memoirs, now in the archives of the Hoover Institution at Stanford University, Mr. Crane – who seems to have misunderstood our situation somewhat, as concerned my role and Manya's – wrote this:

My first experience with the terror was in connection with a fine Russian engineer Zaroodny, who had escaped to Japan.

Photograph taken by Charles Crane
Omsk, July 1921

… When he learned that I was going to Russia he asked me to take some provisions and money to his wife and children at Omsk, from whom he had not heard for more than a year. When I reached Omsk, my first move was to hop off the train before anybody knew that I was there, and start in search of the family. The town is seven miles from the railroad station, and it was difficult to find anyone. When at last I located the family, I found that the mother was taken out and shot the week before, leaving six children, the oldest a daughter of 12, the youngest a baby of two. The little girl, a charming creature who seemed to find me the only friendly person she had seen, was doing her best to manage the family. I should like to have adopted the whole family, but of course I could not take them along with me. I found two old Russian women in the same house, who, although having a hard time themselves, were willing to watch after the children. I gave them the materials and money their father sent, bought them a supply of wood, and left them 10 million rubles with instructions that the existence of the money was to be kept secret, and that their supplies were to be bought quietly.

Mr. Crane's visit, and the the food, money, and clothes that Father had sent, made all the difference in our life. Most important, we felt that the link with Father had been reestablished. It seemed now that it was no longer a question of *whether* we would join Father, but *when*. The only thing that we were afraid of was that Father might decide to come for us himself. Everyone thought that would end in his arrest.

On July 18 I wrote to Father on a small piece of paper using red beet juice and a chicken quill, because paper was scarce and neither pencil nor pen nor ink was available. There were no envelopes, of course. The letter was enclosed in a homemade envelope about 2 by 3½ inches, tied with a string for the lack of glue. At the top right corner in small letters I wrote "Mama died":

Dearest papa, all of us can't wait to join you. We received your parcel, and we thank you very much. I shall be in the fourth class of the gymnasium this fall, Seryozha is in the second and Lena in the middle preparatory. I cannot write to you much about our sorrow, you shall find out everything when we meet. I warn you that under no circumstance should you come to Russia. This could end very badly. I cannot write much about it now, but try your best to bring us over to you. Many, many kisses.

Mulya

Manya's Letters

From the conversation with the Cranes we understood that Father still did not know about Mother's death at the time that Mr. Crane left China. We did not know if he had received the telegram that Uncle Vadim had sent him. We began to wonder whether any letters or even telegrams from us could reach either Harbin or Japan. Manya decided to write to our cousin, the sister of Zhenia Cavos, in Estonia, and ask her to forward a letter to Father. It must have taken a great effort for her to write these two letters. I shall try to translate them, but I cannot convey the full flavor of Manya's faulty grammar and profound warmth. The letters are dated July 29, 1921:

Dear Maria Evgeniievna! Excuse me for writing to you. You don't know me, but probably heard about me from Ivan Sergeyevich. I have lived with his family for ten years and now am with the children. We have this sad situation with Elena Pavlovna. She was shot the night of May 7. Vadim Pavlovich sent you a telegram to notify Ivan Sergeyevich, but until now we had had no answer. Is it possible that you did not receive the telegram? The accusations against Elena Pavlovna were very serious and everything possible was done, but to no avail.

Dear Maria Evgeniievna, together with this letter for you I am sending a letter to Ivan Sergeyevich, but I am afraid to write to him that E. P. was shot, I wrote that she died. I am very afraid for him – how he will take it. It is a hard and painful moment here for us, but it will be even harder for him. I have told him that all the children thank God, are well and healthy. Vadim Pavlovich went to Petrograd on business and took sick there, and we have been living two months now without him, myself and Nanny, Nastasia Pavlovna Pavlova. As for provisions and feeding the children, we are still not badly off. We received a package from Iv. Serg. that Mr. Crane brought and that was a big help. As for our life, the relatives wanted to take the children to Petersburg or Moscow, but it is worse there than how we are living, so we have decided to stay here and wait to be joined with Ivan Sergeyevich. Maybe, God willing, we will see each other soon. Ask Iv. Serg. how will he move the children, but tell him better not to come himself, I am afraid for him. Please forward this letter to him.

Maria Kuzminichna Yourkina

Dear Ivan Sergeyevich,

I apologize that I did not write to you for a long time about our sad situation in connection with the death of Elena Pavlovna. I wrote to M. E. Cavos in Revel. Dear Ivan Sergeyevich, I fear for you and pray for you to keep your health for the sake of the children. We ourselves are pained and grieving, but Nanny and I are trying to look after our health in order to help the children. Let the Lord keep you for years to come, to bring up the children, all the hope now is laid on you. Thank God the children are alive and all are healthy. So far we haven't had privation; and if we are to stay here for the winter we have enough to take care of ourselves. We have received your parcel, which was a great help. Dear Ivan Sergeyevich, don't worry about us. Although there are only a few of your friends here now, but still there are some to advise us. In the sense of material help they are feeble, but it is good that they care to help us with advice. Valentin Pavlovich Navalikhin has been very kind to us, and the acquaintances of E. P. also. Vadim Pavlovich has left on an assignment in Petrograd. Your relatives wanted to take the children to Petrograd or Moscow; but right now they don't want to move us, since so far we have managed to keep going. We have kept the cows. The children have all grown a great deal. Katya talks and runs, and is quite plump. Your decision before was that it would be simpler to reunite with you from here. Dear Ivan Sergeyevich, do not worry about the children, Nanny and I will not abandon the children. I am ready to face the most difficult minutes, all for the sake of the children until we connect with you. I shall not abandon the children; they are dear to me like my own, as I have watched them all grow, and on top of that I am awfully fond of children. Even though there is much trouble, we have to put up a struggle with life. We have three vegetable gardens 50 square sazhen [about 270 square yards] each. 110 for potatoes, 50 square sazhen for carrots, beets, tomatoes, cucumbers and other. We shall have enough vegetables for the winter. Dear Ivan Sergeyevich I shall not forget your request not to leave E. P.'s children. I am with them all the time, and now more than ever they need looking after, being so young. We all love you and embrace you, Nanny, Manya, and all the children.

Dear Ivan Sergeyevich, when do you think we shall reunite with you? It would be better for you not to come here, but send either documents for the right to exit, or else an authorized person. Hope to God that we shall see each other soon. I fear your coming here.

May the Lord keep you. I implore you to keep in good health for the sake of the children. We all want to see you. Be well.

Your loving Manya

Navalikhin wrote a long letter to Father too. He admonished Father to look into the yoga teaching, since that helped him so much when his own daughter died. He also wrote:

We think that the children ought to stay in Omsk for the time being, though Vadim Pavlovich, having been transferred to Petrograd, asked Manya to bring all the children there. They plan to distribute them among different relatives' families.

Your good friends in Moscow also ask to bring the children there. But knowing how hard life is for those who want to take them, and also taking into account that the children would be separated from each other, we came to the conclusion that in many respects it is better for them to stay here, in order to be reunited with you at the first possible moment.

Therefore I think that all your efforts should be spent in this direction, avoiding the intermediary sojourn of the children in Petrograd or Moscow. If for some reason you would be unable to accomplish this, then try to send them another package, which would make it possible for your family to survive better in Omsk.

14

Writing and Waiting

Even though Manya and Nanny tried to maintain the old routine, the sense of impending change was felt by everyone. We went about all our daily tasks, but as soon as any friends appeared the talk always centered on when and how we were going to join Father. We all wrote letters to him. The younger ones dictated their letters, usually to me. I was quite used to taking dictation verbatim, as I did it often for Manya and Nanny. I was heartened by the prospect that Father might soon take some responsibilities off my shoulders. In my letters to him I reported the progress each of us was making. Manya also asked me to report our finances to him – what we received, from whom, and so on.

Of course I remembered Father very well, but the two years of separation and so many different experiences made me feel somewhat estranged. I felt that I had changed a lot, and I wondered how much he had changed. I heard Manya and other friends worrying about him – what were they afraid of? I remembered the story of the strange and gloomy father of the crippled boy in Frances Hodgson Burnett's *The Secret Garden,* and other tales of people who had lost their minds after experiencing a tragedy, and it worried me. But Father's loving and tender letters soon reassured me.

I felt terribly lonely, and tried to make close friends with girls now. Among Mother's friends there was no one to whom I could talk intimately about things that were really important to me. Probably I did not really know how to put them into words. The Navalikhins were closest to our family and they visited us often, but they had to pay attention to all the children. As before with Mother, I felt left out because my needs were quite different. Everybody's main concern was that I should help Manya to manage the younger children, and be an obedient child myself. Yet I quarreled with Seryozha and often fought with him physically, to the great dismay of Manya and Nanny. With no adults close by on whom to model myself, I felt as if I was at the top of a ladder and did not know how to go any higher.

After Pavlik left I found in his desk drawer a letter written to him from his older sister Sonya in Petrograd. Sonya wrote about family news, but also about her own life and thoughts. She was studying singing, philosophy, the history of Russian social thought, and art history. She was going to lectures by famous people, such as the literary critic R. V. Ivanov-Razumnik,[1] the symbolist poet Andrei Bely,[2] and her uncle Boris Brullov. Written in a clear schoolgirl's hand, her letter had so much warmth and such concern with that inner world – which I did not think that brothers and sisters spoke to each other about. I longed for such a relationship, and I saved that letter as one of my precious relics. The famous names she mentioned meant little to me at the time. But the letter gave me a flavor of that distant life of the capital city to which both Mother and Father belonged, to which they were forever drawn, and which they had missed so much.

Yuzya's Visit

In September of that year another dear friend appeared at our doorstep – Yuzya, whom I remembered from Vyksa, where he had taught me gymnastics and talked to us about yoga. He and his family had lived for a while in Tomsk, the only Siberian city with a university, and now they were on their way back to their hometown, Staraya Russa. Yuzya was much as I remembered him, but older and with a beard. He was still absorbed in yoga philosophy. He said that he had been sick with pleurisy and cured himself by doing yoga exercises. He also had dreams about Mother and believed that her spirit was always near us and watching us. It was comforting to hear, though I did not quite believe it. I heard the same from Navalikhin, whose introduction to yoga was due to Yuzya, his old friend.

On September 17, 1921 Yuzya wrote to Father:

Dear Ivan Sergeyevich,

On September 14 we arrived, expecting if necessary to stay here or to take all the children with Nastasia Pavlovna and Manya to Staraya Russa, where we have a five-room house with a fruit orchard and piano. But after we sized up the situation it became obvious that there is no point in our staying here. Nanny and Manya are managing very well. …

You probably know that your children are fed very well. Meat is quite cheap here (2,500 rubles), and they get milk from their cows. Nanny and Manya's love creates a very good atmosphere for their life. Mulya and Seryozha are already very clever children. ... Your children are rare children, worth dedicating your life to. I am sure that they all will be remarkable people, needed by mankind. It is important that you reunite and live together. Right now they are undoubtedly being helped by invisible helpers and by Elena Pavlovna, who gives energy to Nanny and Manya that they may cope with the colossal task that confronts them. I would like so much to see you, my dear brother, but probably it will not happen soon. ... Life around us is a nightmare. Everywhere there are orphaned children. I console myself only with the thought that "Suffering is a sign of spiritual growth" and that suffering is necessary for us even though we don't know why. Perhaps for our future life when we wake up in a better world.

ᥴ୫

School was supposed to begin on September 1, but there were delays because the building was occupied during the summer by the city government for other purposes. We were busy harvesting the vegetables from our gardens. The biggest and heaviest harvest of potatoes had to be done all in one day so that the hired horse and wagon would be used to full advantage. Everyone worked all day long to pick as much as possible. The rest of the vegetables were harvested every day and each of us carried home as much as we could in bags and baskets. Manya and Nanny pickled cucumbers, made sauerkraut, and buried potatoes and other root vegetables in sand in the cellar. Finally in October school began, and so did the steady autumn rains that put an end to all our outdoor activities.

Lena, Seryozha, and I started going to the same school, which in our letters to Father we still called by its former name, *gymnasium,* though now it was officially the "57th Soviet School." There were two shifts, morning and afternoon, and the classes or grades were now called groups. I was in the fourth grade, now Group VI; Seryozha was in the second grade, now Group IV; Lena was in the second preparatory grade, now Group II. Tanya and Zoya started kindergarten. The most important thing about kindergarten was that the children were given lunch, so that a part of their daily food ration was supplied by the state.

With the help of some friends the striped green cotton flannel cloth that Father had sent became school dresses for all the girls and a shirt for Seryozha. We felt well dressed. Last year's shoes and winter coats were tried on and altered, the felt boots were checked for holes and everything was passed down the age line.

The house itself had to be prepared for the winter. Winterizing the windows was an arduous procedure. Most windows in Russia, as well as in Siberia, were of the casement variety, and had to be sealed, usually with putty, which was then covered with glued-on paper strips. After that an interior winter frame was fitted behind, like double-glazing today, and in the space between the two frames was placed a small glass half filled with concentrated sulfuric acid, to absorb any moisture between the two windows. The interior window also had to be puttied, and again covered with paper strips. For ventilation there was usually one small pane in one of the windows in each room, which could be opened, in both the interior frame and the outside one, to let in fresh air. This pane was called *fortochka*, or sometimes *was-ist-das* – the French word for "transom" being *vasistas*, supposedly originating when a German traveler pointed at one and asked what it was, which his hosts understood to be an accepted term for that (then still nameless) object. Both the inside and outside parts of it were carefully weather-stripped; the same kind of weather-stripping was added to all the outside doors.

The days became noticeably shorter, and the dusk and the dark evenings longer. We ate our supper with a single small kerosene lamp in the middle of the dining table, by the light of which we also read, did our homework, and wrote or drew. Nanny managed to ignite a small wick in a jar lid filled with some waste grease, so there was a kind of night-light in the other room. Sometimes we used alcohol lamps, which gave a steady but very weak light as well.

The hope of rejoining Father before winter was fading. No one seemed to know for sure how, where, or from whom one could obtain permission to travel and leave Russia. Besides, we were not even sure where to go. It seemed risky to undertake a long railroad trip during the winter unless the travel conditions were exceptionally good, which was unlikely. It was decided that we would spend the winter in Omsk. At least the letters from Harbin were beginning to arrive more or less regularly. Sometimes they took as little as two weeks in transit.

In their letters the children complained about the shortage of paper and pencils. Every little scrap of paper was used and was precious. The ink in our inkwells dried up. When we could not find any pencils, we became quite inventive. First we used up all the red ink Mother had for correcting students' papers. Then we shredded the lead in any indelible pencil stubs we were able to find and dissolved the shreds in water, thus making some purple ink; this could be used longer than the stubs we had broken. When we had no penholders, I made some from pieces of wood. After we ran out of steel pen points, I started making quills out of large chicken feathers. When indelible pencil stubs could not be found, I learned how to make "beet ink" from the beets that we had in abundance from our garden, by shredding the beets and squeezing the juice into a small jar. Surprisingly, the poems I wrote in my album with beet juice more than eighty years ago are still easy to read.

Manya and Nanny's requests were for some spools of thread for sewing. However, it was sugar that was greeted with the greatest pleasure whenever a parcel arrived from Father. At other times we used saccharine for sweetening our drinks. Since there was no coffee or tea, the drink we called "coffee" was made by Manya from strips of carrots and beets, toasted on the stove, then ground up and boiled in the coffeepot. Among other things Father sent us an ample supply of millet, which constituted the major part of our meals the rest of the winter. As far as I remember we ate millet porridge every day.

Seryozha felt the lack of paper more acutely than the rest of us, as drawing was his dearest occupation. Whenever he wrote to Father he illustrated his letters profusely, including (as Father encouraged him to do) some of his "Amzonia" stories. In a letter dated October 5, 1921 he began his myth-making:

Amzonians were originally Greeks, or more accurately, a mixture of Greek and Indian. Amzonia was founded by a Spartan Amzon, who was banished from his country for some religious heresy. He and twenty of his followers occupied themselves with something like piracy in the Mediterranean, then sailed to the Atlantic on their ship Argo. After long wandering, they stumbled on to the coast of South America. There they lived for two years fighting with the Indians. One day they left America and came upon two islands, which lay at 4° Eastern longitude and 2° Southern latitude.

Despite careful use, the firewood left us by Mr. Crane was running out. Manya and Nanny were using dried cow dung to fire the kitchen stove. One of the rooms was heated only once in a while, when the children had to be bathed. Seryozha and I were big enough to be taken to the public bathhouses. The rest of the time we wore our winter coats, felt boots, and mittens in the house. We took off our mittens only to eat or to write. Manya thought it more important to buy hay for the cow than wood for the stove, so long as we were warm enough in our coats and mittens.

γ

About the middle of October both Manya and the Navalikhins received letters from Yuzya in Petrograd where he was staying with our Aunt Varya Lisovskaya. Writing on her instructions, he told us to sell all our things in Omsk immediately, and come to Petrograd to stay with Aunt Varya. Shortly after that two documents arrived from Uncle Vadim. Addressed to the Bureau of Travel of the Omsk District Administration, they requested that permission be issued for all of us to travel to Petrograd.

This was a shock. We were ready to spend the winter in Omsk and hoped to travel *east* to join Father in the spring. We looked forward to a certain continuity in our family arrangements and relationships, which had changed in the four years since we last saw Aunt Varya. Manya and Nanny had become an integral part of the family; moreover, Manya's role as manager of all the family affairs, and mine as her assistant, were unquestioned. Our hopes were concentrated on joining Father as soon as possible, and the thought of postponing this indefinitely was unwelcome. Furthermore, we had not heard anything about this decision from Father.

We held an urgent conference with the Navalikhins, and decided that it would be unwise to do anything before hearing from Father. Meanwhile, in Harbin Father received a letter from Yuzya explaining Aunt Varya's offer and his own strong support of it, as expressed in his letter to us. At that time Father was jobless, and without any clear prospects. He thought of going to Belgium, where he had received his engineering education, or to Latvia, where he had worked before, and where he had hopes of building more Mechtas. It would be much easier to travel westward if he were alone, and he would be closer to us there if we were in Petrograd. He had already applied for visas to both countries in case such a program seemed best. After two days of anxious indecision, he sent us the following telegram on October 19:

SITUATION CHANGED. I APPROVE DECISION FOR ALL TO MOVE TO PETROGRAD TO LISOVSKYS.

This disturbed us, but there could be no thought of moving anywhere in the middle of winter. The children kept coming down with colds, and we were all set up to spend the winter in Omsk. So we took no immediate action on Father's telegram, and decided to wait for a letter.

Early in November another telegram, dated October 25, came from Father's friend Pickersgill in Chita, near the Chinese border on the way to Harbin. This instructed us to go there instead, which was *east*, "as per previous arrangements." That was even more confusing, and again all we could do was await Father's letter.

In November Katya caught cold. We all caught colds, but her cold developed into pneumonia, the second time this had happened to her. The house was cold and damp, and the doctor insisted that Katya should be taken outside, even though the temperature outside was near 40 degrees below zero. Manya treated us herself, reading and rereading a book Mother had, called *Letters to Mothers*. This book listed all children's diseases, with detailed descriptions of symptoms and pictures of different rashes, swellings, the general appearance of children's bodies in cases of various diseases, including bowed legs and large stomachs in the case of rickets. It gave detailed advice on various home remedies that mothers who were far away from medical help could use, though it urged them to rely on professional medical help whenever possible. Cupping was one of the methods advised for treating a lung infection, and most of us at one time or another were cupped with small glass jars, into which a few drops of alcohol were dropped and lit; as soon as the flame went out these were applied to our backs. As the air in the jars cooled, the skin was pulled into them, and this was supposed to suck out the infection. When the jars cooled, they were removed, leaving red circles all over our backs.

Late in November we received a letter from Father dated October 20.

My dear, beloved children, Anastasia Pavlovna and Manya,

Two days ago I received a letter from Yuzya, sent from Petrograd, in which he writes that, after his telling the relatives about your life in Omsk, all of them decided that you must move as soon as possible to Petrograd, where all of you, with Manya and Nanny, will live with my sister Varya. With the money that I will be sending you will have everything you need. Therefore yesterday I sent you a telegram through Pickersgill.

I am very, very sad to lose the hope of seeing you here soon, but my situation has really changed for the worse – I lost my chance of steady earnings and therefore your stay with me would involve a certain risk, while at Aunt Varya's all of you would be with your loving relatives, your educational opportunities would be better than here, and it would be easier for me to earn what you need.

This decision, which is forced on me by circumstances, and against my fervent desire to see you, evidently is destined by Fate and nothing can be done about it.

I send you many kisses and implore God to bless you. But if you have already started for Chita, then, of course, continue on your way to join me. I am awaiting a telegram from Pickersgill about the situation, and shall write to you in Petrograd. Should you need money, telegraph to Pickersgill in Chita. Once you are in Petrograd, I ask Manya, Mulya, and Seryozha to write to me regularly on Sundays and Thursdays.

My love to all of you

Papa

By this time the Siberian winter had arrived and Katya was still not quite well. We held another conference with the Navalikhins and decided to stay the winter in Omsk. This was lucky, as it turned out, because on November 14 Father wrote to us again, although we did not receive his letter until late in December:

My dear beloved children, I have changed the instructions I sent you in my letter of Oct. 20 and my telegram of Oct. 19 about your going to Petrograd. I telegraphed to Pickersgill, asking him to wire you instructions to go to Chita as we had agreed before, that is to wait in Omsk for permission to leave for Chita. I am terribly afraid that the telegram missed you and you already have left for Petrograd. Even if this happened I shall still do all I can to get you here. Unfortunately, from Petrograd it would take more time and you would have to wait till spring. It would be a great shame if this happened, so I do hope that you are still in Omsk. In this case, in a little while, maybe in a month, it should become clear whether there is a chance for you to get to Chita. If not, you yourselves should decide whether you want to go to Petrograd or stay in Omsk. I am absolutely sure of one thing: that I want to have you here with me, all of you, with Manya and Nanny, most definitely, otherwise we could not manage. I am sending this letter to Varya too, so she will know what I am writing to you. I also telegraphed her that I want you here. … I didn't send any paper to Seryozha, since I thought that you were already on your way; but apparently things don't happen that fast, and one must have patience and courage. As Mama used to say: Night won't always darken the skies, the sun must rise and end the gloom.

I send you many, many warm kisses and my love. Write more often.

Papa

A few days later we received another letter from Father, dated November 16, sending 500,000 rubles through a friend visiting Omsk. He knew that this was only a small part of what we needed to survive, but hoped to supplement it in other ways. He asked Manya to keep accounts of all the money received and spent, which she conscientiously did: I remember the long lists of figures she kept with all those endless numbers of zeros. The lowest price of anything at that time was in hundreds of thousands of rubles. This continued until new currency was introduced, and each new ruble became equivalent to 10,000 old ones.

⅓

Early in December Manya managed to obtain some firewood, so that in the mornings and when we came home from school the house was relatively warm and we could take off our coats and mittens. Some friends arranged to have electricity connected and installed an electric lamp in the dining room and in the bedroom where the little children and Manya and Nanny slept. Now we could read, write, and draw at the big dining room table without arguing about who sat closer to the kerosene lamp. The howling of winter storms at night made us feel especially cozy and secure in the house.

Lena had a great deal of free time now and she spent it reading everything she could lay her hands on. She wrote to Father:

During the last week I read Brave Life by Charskaya, Thousand and One Nights, The War of the Worlds and The Island of Doctor Moreau by H. G. Wells, From Earth to the Moon, Around the Moon, and The Lottery Ticket by Jules Verne. I got all the books except Charskaya from Alexander Lvovich Yousofer. I visited him. He took my bag, put in eleven pieces of sugar and some dried apples, and did not let me peek into it. When I came home I looked at what was in the bag. Then it was Tanya's name-day, and everybody started eating, so in a week all was gone. After that we did not see any sugar anymore. ... Today we received your parcel, Manya started to cry, and said "How hard life is!" and Katya said "Don't cry, Manya, look, we have sugar now!"

Christmas was approaching. The snow outside reached our windows, and sometimes covered a good part of them. It was the third year in Omsk for us, and we had become quite accustomed to the Siberian winter. It always seemed to snow at night; when we opened the outside door in the morning we had to shovel the fresh snow from the doorway. We usually walked to school in the middle of the road because it was difficult to guess where the wooden sidewalks were. The windless air was bitingly cold; the white vapor of our breath settled like snow on our scarves, which soon became quite stiff. It was an effort just to navigate through the unbroken snow, but we would arrive at school refreshed and full of energy. On the way back from school it was much easier to walk because by then the snow on the streets was trampled down by the horse sleds and squeaked pleasantly under our feet.

We were going to have a Christmas tree. As before, Seryozha and I tried to make Christmas tree decorations. There was no more colored paper anywhere, so Manya suggested that we use some of the Kerensky paper money, which by then no one expected ever to have value again. They were the bills that Father had left with us two years before, hidden in many strange places – inside pillows and mattresses. We dug them out: the light blue, pink, and light green bills were large enough to cut into chains, little baskets, etc. We even tried to remember how Mother used to make various polyhedrons. The tree was not very colorful, and we did not have any candles or lights: but we joked that it was a veritable "money tree."

Seryozha continued to tell his stories in his letters to Father:

Amzon died and his older son, Voika, after a long struggle among Amzon's sons took the helmet and sword that were the symbols of imperial power. Duchies remained in the possession of the brothers of Voika. This happened in the fourth century BC. Here are the drawings of the clothing in that time.

I now have changed my mind about Amzonia – it is not a militant country any more. I am becoming more and more disenchanted with war.

A New School

Shortly after Christmas the head of our school, M. V. Kaesh, was discharged. A new head was installed in the school, to the great dismay of all the old students. Many of the teachers left voluntarily or were forced out. The whole atmosphere of the school changed even more for the worse, and it seemed almost a waste of time to attend. Lena stopped going but Seryozha and I continued, quite unhappily.

Soon after that a group of our former teachers organized a private tutorial school. This was possible under the law because one of the teachers was a Polish citizen. As the teachers had known Mother personally, and knew what had happened to her, Seryozha and I were allowed to attend this school free. Lena, who was much ahead of her grade in reading, went to take arithmetic only, with Miss Kaesh. The school met in a private home, while the residents were at work. My class met in the dining room, in which there were also several beds. We sat around a big table. We missed having a blackboard, but one of the boys found an old piece of worn linoleum with a rather rough black surface. We had no chalk but found it was possible to write on the linoleum with pieces of broken plaster. We were quite proud of our inventiveness, but I don't remember the teachers using it very much.

Our classes were small, and the teaching was intense. A lot of homework was assigned, but the class schedule was very light: two or three 45-minute classes a day, usually from 9:30 to 12 or 1 p.m., and we did not have each subject every day. Both Seryozha and I studied Russian grammar and literature, French, German, and geography. In mathematics Seryozha took only arithmetic, but I had both algebra and geometry, and also Latin and physics. There was no teacher of history, which had been Mother's subject in our former school.

One day after school two boys from my class and I decided to revisit our old school to see how matters stood there. We walked into the big recreation hall: it was empty, dusty, and unkempt, and most of the classrooms were already empty. Finally we found a classroom where something was going on. We walked in and said that we wanted to visit. We were allowed to sit down. The classroom was so cold that all the students and the teacher had their winter coats on. In the front of the classroom stood a small iron stove apparently now unlit, for the teacher sat on it. It was a history class – ancient history. The teacher was telling the story of the Trojan War. To us it seemed a very primitive account, like a story for small children. We asked a few cheeky questions, got no satisfactory answers, and left. We felt very smug. There could be no comparison between the seriousness of our little school, meeting in somebody's bedroom, and this "education for the masses."

After our classes we children would make a small ice-slide in the school yard out of boards we had found. When we poured water over the slide it froze immediately with a crackling noise. The first few pails of water froze even before reaching the bottom of the slide, so it took a number of pailsfull to cover the whole of it. There was a well in the yard with a winch above it, all crusted with ice on the sides, so the lowered pail would often catch on the icy sides and spill water. Getting the water was quite an adventure, since our mittens, felt boots, and even coats were often stiff with ice. I loved to look into the dark hole of the well, trying to catch a glimpse of the water at the bottom of it, which usually one could not see at all.

For sleds to be used on the slide we found short pieces of boards, which we first covered with soft cow manure to smooth them out. When we poured water over them, it froze immediately and made the boards thick and smooth and excellent for sliding. The local children taught us this technique, which evidently was traditional. We had a lot of fun on that slide, even when the weather was extremely cold. Our younger siblings sometimes joined us. But the days were short; dusk would start about three in the afternoon and usually it would be so cold by then that even the ice slide could not keep us outside.

Lena's Story

Many years later Lena wrote out a third-person memory of this period in our life:

Tanya, Zoya, and Katya did not remember Father, but Lena thought about him quite often. He was vaguely connected in her memory with some actual person. Someone to write letters to. ... All she knew about him made her sorry for him. "Poor Papa would be worried if we didn't write to him," Mulya once said. "He would think we don't love him!" Lena thought it was awful. Whatever he was, she was sure she loved him and she never failed to write to him on Sundays. Why she loved him she could not tell. She knew that Father lived in another country and for some mysterious reason he loved them and from time to time he wrote letters to them.

He became somebody of utmost importance when she stumbled upon *King Lear* in one of the thick volumes with beautiful illustrations that Manya brought from Ufa. Lena read slowly, struggling with difficult words, eager for the story, which filled her with pity for the poor king. Wrapped in mother's big fur cape she continued reading when everybody went to sleep, for now there was no one to object when she moved the only candle they had closer to her book. It was quiet in the room except for the familiar howling of the wind in the chimney; sometimes the nurse would start to snore or the wind would suddenly rattle on the roof, and then everything would be quiet again. By and by the excitement grew. She turned the pages nervously. ... At last she let the book down and started to cry. The shock of the end was terrible. She could not stop, her sobs grew louder and louder. The fur cape fell off her shoulders and she was freezing. Her sobs woke Mulya up. "Lena, what is the matter?" she asked. "Oh, Mulya, I finished *King Lear* and they are all killed!" Lena answered through her sobs. Mulya was reassuring: "I know, but it is only in the book, it is not real, go to sleep!" Mulya blew out the candle and tucked Lena in. It was such a relief that Mulya woke up. The burden of the book was too much to bear alone.

She could not fall asleep for a long time. She lay in the bed trying to warm her feet. She thought about the steppes and the drifting snow, about the homeless children who live in haystacks, and King Lear out on the steppes, and the rain. By and by Lear turned into a boy in a haystack wrapped in newspapers and flowers. ... "Through the sharp hawthorn blows the cold wind..." Do the newspapers help? And father with a long white beard was standing on the snow saying, "Oh, my heart, my rising heart..." The wind howled in the chimney. She was falling asleep.

ɔ

In March I received a long letter from Father dated December 20, 1921:

Dear, beloved Margaritochka, ... You are now our main housewife, together with Manya and Nanny, and most important, the substitute for our dear poor Lenochka for your brother and sisters. Remember this well – now they have nowhere else to receive good and kind advice on all those things they could only consult with Mama about. This is a large and heavy responsibility on your shoulders, my dear little Mulechka. You are now a big person who must give support to all the rest. God give you the strength and goodness of spirit to fulfill this task. ...

There are after all many good people in this world. This is what makes it possible to go on living and believing that everybody will live well, and will love one another, and that those who are no longer with us did not perish in vain, but on the contrary, created the conditions of well-being for those who are left. The most important thing now is to raise your brother and sisters to be good loving people; I am sure that this is what all of you will be.

I think Father's letter, if anything, only added to my anxieties. I was still being treated as a child, I had no authority over my siblings, and yet somehow I had to "give support to all the rest" and provide good advice on matters about which it had been possible to consult only Mama. I myself needed such advice; I looked forward to our reunion with Father because of that. He hoped that I would have the strength of spirit to do what I must, but I needed much more than that. I simply did not feel up to such a task! And the prospect that bringing up my siblings was to be my life's work made me feel additionally depressed: what about all my dreams about being an actress, or of being involved in heroic deeds? But soon the everyday problems of study, play, and reading, and the prospect of seeing Father, drove such self-pitying thoughts from my head.

In this letter Father also wrote that he hoped to arrange our moving to Chita, a city east of Lake Baikal and not far from the Chinese border. From 1920 Chita was the capital of the Far Eastern Republic, a kind of "buffer state" between the new Soviet Union and Japan, governed by a coalition of Communists, Mensheviks, and SRs. There was open communication between Chita and the USSR as well as between it and China and Japan until November 1922, when the Far Eastern Republic was taken into the Soviet Union. Father had friends in Chita, and went there often himself; apparently he thought that we all might settle there for the time being. Babcock & Wilcox had invited him to work for them again, this time in Tientsin, China, but if we went to Chita he would immediately meet us there.

The winter was coming to an end and the prospect of our traveling east to join Father was now bright. Father was making arrangements in Harbin, possibly with the help of Mr. Crane, to have one of the representatives of the Hunger Relief Committee, D. S. Epishin or a Mr. Pokrovsky, pick us up on his way to Manchuria.

In 1922 Russian Orthodox Easter fell on April 16. There were no dyes for egg coloring available, so we colored the eggs with onion skins or scraps of material left over from sewing. We wrapped the fresh eggs in little pieces of cloth, covered them with onion skins, and then wrapped them tightly in pieces of old sheeting. The bundled eggs were then dropped into boiling water, and after fifteen minutes taken out and unwrapped with excitement and expectation. One never knew, until that moment, how the coloring would come out. It was much more fun than dipping the eggs in colored solutions. The whole family, with Manya and Nanny supervising, sat around the table for this traditional ritual.

Seryozha drew a vase with Easter eggs on a postcard and wrote:

Christ has risen, dear Papa!

We are celebrating Easter as we did in the old days with red paskhas, white kulichi and colored eggs (we had only 17 of those). Everybody is well. … School begins again tomorrow and probably two weeks after Pokrovsky's arrival in Harbin we will be there too, and we shall all see each other.

Leaving Omsk

In the middle of May we received a telegram telling us that D. S. Epishin had left the city of Perm, about seven hundred miles west of Omsk. He was traveling in his own *teplushka* and expected to collect us en route to Harbin. Manya had already succeeded in selling our cows; the chickens were all eaten after Easter, and Manya and Nanny had begun packing our possessions. The furniture was all sold or promised, and our landlord had found new tenants. It was already getting warm, so our winter clothing was packed away. Manya and Nanny cooked up a great deal of food for the trip.

Manya still had some gold money left, and this was a problem as it was forbidden to export gold. At that time a necessary part of a child's underwear was a short vest buttoned in front, with buttons along the bottom hem of it, to which bloomers and the garters holding up the stockings could be attached. It was almost impossible to buy any buttons, and people often made them from round pieces of wood covered with cloth, which allowed them to be sewn on to the vest. Manya used the gold coins instead of pieces of wood. When we finally got dressed for the journey, the children complained of the weight of their vests, but they never learned why the vests were so heavy. Manya worried during the entire trip that one of these buttons might fall off and reveal her secret.

On Saturday May 27 we were all ready; our trunks were at the station, the children all dressed and ready to go. Epishin's train was expected any minute, but the Navalikhins, who went out on the platform to meet the train, returned to tell us that the train had arrived, but without Epishin's *teplushka*. That meant we had to wait until the next day, which was a terrible letdown. What should we do? The house was empty; the new tenants would move in any minute. Leaving our baggage at the station in safe keeping, we spent the night at the Navalikhins, quite a distance away. All eight of us crowded into their apartment, sleeping in their living room, with the sofa and armchairs for the little ones, and with some on the floor. I was allowed to sleep in the "untouchable" room of their late daughter.

The next day we went to the station again, and again Epishin's *teplushka* was not there. Another day of waiting, of nothing to do in a strange house, where we had to keep the little children from doing any mischief and from being bored. Since all our things were left at the station, we had no books, no paper. We were totally suspended in waiting. Several telegrams came from Epishin but nothing definite. Finally, on June 3, after a week of waiting, we learned that Epishin had arrived.

In a great hurry we packed what we had with us, and took a horse cab to the station. Here another surprise awaited us: there were additional passengers in the *teplushka*. We had known that Mrs. Pokrovsky and her nine-year-old daughter Olya would be there, but there was also another lady, Zinaida Evgeniievna Gramatchikova, with two children, aged thirteen and eight. This really overloaded the car, and we could take only a small part of our baggage with us, just necessities for the trip itself. Manya did some hurried repacking and all our books and winter clothes were left behind.

The train was ready. We climbed in, Manya counting the children carefully. Even with all the delay, we were unable to say a final goodbye to many of our friends, whom we knew we would probably never again see. While this saddened us, the thought that we were at last on our way to join Father was uppermost in our minds. We waved to the Navalikhins. Three rings of the bell, and the train started slowly forward.

[1]   Ivanov-Razumnik (pseudonym of Vassilievich Ivanov Razumnik, 1878-1946): critic, writer, editor and historian, founder of the St. Petersburg Free Philosophical Association (VOLFILA).

[2]   Andrei Bely (pseudonym of Boris Nikolaevich Bugaev, 1880-1934): poet and writer, one of the leaders and theoreticians of the symbolist movement.

15

The Long Train Ride

We crowded at the open car door to watch the railroad station recede, and our friends wave goodbye. When the last small houses of Omsk began to vanish we turned to meet our fellow passengers and investigate the interior. Our *teplushka,* as before, was a small Russian freight car adapted for passengers; it was attached to the end of the freight train, with only the caboose behind it. One of its large sliding doors was closed permanently, so that there was only the one opening, and no windows. The interior was divided into three parts, the middle one with a small iron stove that served for heating as well as for cooking, and a small table for food preparation. One end of the car was separated from the rest by a partition with a door in it. This was where our guide, Epishin, had his bed and his office, and the children were not permitted to enter. The other end had three tiers of wide wooden bunks on each of three walls, where all of us had to find space for sleeping. I do not remember any toilet facilities. We had chamber pots that could be emptied out the open door while the train moved. Besides Epishin there were now thirteen passengers: nine children – three boys and six girls – and four women.

It was decided to put the older women on the lower bunks and have little Katya sleep with Nanny. Manya and the rest of us were arranged on the two upper tiers – the boys on one, the girls on the other. While we became acquainted with the other children Manya unpacked our bedding and Nanny got out the food, for by now we were hungry. It was still light when the smaller children were put to sleep, tired but protesting.

It was relatively warm and the wide sliding door remained open. While the adults were trying to stow the baggage and calm the younger children, the rest of us sat on the floor in the doorway, our feet dangling outside the car. We watched the flat landscape of marshes, grassy spaces, and a few intermittent birch groves move past: it extended as far as one could see, to the distant horizon.

219

There were few signs of human habitation. Occasionally we could see smoke in the distance from houses in unseen villages, or perhaps from a campfire, and it was tantalizing to see so many wild flowers that we could not pick. In early June the day was long. But dusk finally set in, the landscape became less and less distinguishable, and the air became cooler. We joined the others inside, as the sliding door was shut for the night, and a kerosene lamp was lit in the central common area. With the iron stove still burning it became warm and cozy. We found our places on the upper bunks, arguing over the few books we had to read, and whether we could have lighted candles to read by.

It was wonderful to go to sleep again to the rhythmic sound of the train wheels and the occasional low mournful whistle of the engine. I had a feeling that everything bad was in the past, finished, never to be returned to. Again we were all together – all that could be – with Father waiting somewhere ahead of us and no one left behind. Even the shaking of the car was not unwelcome, as we passed occasional spur tracks, or stopped at stations and maneuvered to exchange cars: it added some interesting variety, enveloped as we were in our own secure space.

Ahead of us were more than two weeks of such travel, so we had to settle down to a routine with our co-travelers and find constructive occupations for all the children. As the trip proceeded there were naturally some frictions and disputes among people who had not known each other before, and were now forced to live in such close proximity. Manya and Nanny had to struggle for space when they prepared food. Each mother looked out for her own children, especially when arguments arose. Seryozha was happy to have a new audience for his stories, but was frustrated by the lack of space and materials for his drawings.

I always tried to organize games that involved everyone, but not all were used to the kinds of games we usually played. We settled on cards and word games, particularly "Geography," in which everyone had to write as many geographic names as possible in a given time, starting with a given letter. There were more active games in which we divided into two groups, and invented codes that we had to memorize and use in speaking. At the station stopovers we had walking races on the rails or put copper pennies down under the wheels of the trains, to pick them up later squashed into thin, much larger circles. We played a game called *chizhik* with a small round piece of wood tapered on both sides, like a lemon. When you struck it with a stick at one end it flew upward, spinning, and then you tried to hit it again while it was in the air. It was our nearest approximation to a ball game, since we did not have any balls.

Whenever the train stopped at a small station during the daytime there were always village women or children who would come by, selling eggs or chickens or even home-baked pies. As our supply of food from Omsk dwindled, Manya would climb off the train and bargain with the vendors. At some stations our stay could be rather long. It was difficult to keep the children from jumping off and playing by the tracks, for it was nice to feel solid earth underfoot after being confined in a moving carriage. But we never knew when the train would start up again, or when it would be moved to a different spur track at the station. So Manya and Nanny were always terribly tense at the stations, keeping an eye on all of us all the time. It was also my responsibility to watch the younger children while we played.

Often we would go to sleep when the car was standing on a spur track at a station, and then be awakened in the middle of the night by violent bumps, realizing with excitement that we were on our way again. After a few days of travel the landscape began to change. Woods and then hills started to appear, first at a distance and then closer, sometimes obscuring the distant horizon completely.

Irkutsk and Baikal

It took almost two weeks of such travel to cover 1,800 miles and reach the city of Irkutsk, the final destination of our train. Our car was detached and maneuvered to a siding; we were not expected to resume travel for a day or more, since negotiations had to be conducted for us to be attached to another train, and Epishin had to present travel permits and other documents to the civic administration. We did not know anyone living in Irkutsk, but decided to venture into the city anyway. Manya, Seryozha, Lena, Tanya, and I set out from the station on foot.

Irkutsk is built on the Angara River, which flows from Lake Baikal, the largest fresh-water lake in all Eurasia, and the sixth largest in the world. This river is famous for the clarity of its water, and we wanted to see it. In Omsk we had lived in a quiet suburb, surrounded by unpaved streets, small one-story wooden houses, and the big brick building of our first school; only rarely had we gone into the center of the city. Irkutsk, though a smaller city than Omsk, remains in my memory as a place of tall houses, sidewalks with tall streetlights, many shop windows, and the traffic of horse carriages and even some motor trucks. But what impressed us so much that we all remembered it years later was the river. A wooden bridge crossed the Angara, which is not as wide as the Irtysh, and we stood on it, looking at the quietly flowing water below. Nothing disturbed its surface, and we could see every little round polished stone on the bottom, shining through the crystal-clear water in the light of the bright midday sun. We returned to our *teplushka* quite satisfied with our adventure.

The next day our car was attached to a freight train taking supplies to repair the numerous tunnels and galleries circling the southern tip of Lake Baikal. The heavy train moved slowly, its wheels screeching on curves. After eighty miles we caught sight of the glorious lake between the mountains. The train moved out onto a bank cut into the mountains, just above the water. On the right side was the steep slope of the mountain, which we could not see, for we had no windows on that side, but right in front of our open sliding door was a marvelous prospect: the bright sun made the snowcaps on the mountains shine, and they in turn were reflected in the green-blue waters of the lake peacefully lapping the shore below. How we yearned to leave the car and run down to the water's edge! And we soon got our wish: the train stopped before entering the first tunnel. Disregarding Manya's warning, we jumped off and scrambled down the slope. The water was terribly cold, so we resisted the temptation to wade in it. Manya, afraid that the train would start up, was frantically calling after us. We climbed back just in time.

At one of the stations we were startled by little shiny pieces of mica, which covered most of the visible ground. The station was named Slyudinaya, from the word *slyuda*, or mica. A few larger pieces could be found at the edges of the roadbed. We delighted in collecting them and then trying to split then into thin slices to see how nearly transparent they could become. We knew that mica had often been often used in windows, before glass was available, in the remote settlements of Siberia.

Loaded with stones, bricks, sand, and cement, the train moved slowly, stopping frequently, and often noisily applying its brakes. Once the brakes of one of the cars caught fire. The train stopped, and the passengers and crew climbed down the steep slope with pails for water to put out the blaze. It took us three days to travel around the tip of Lake Baikal.

A day later we arrived in the city of Chita. There another visa had to be obtained for us, and it was necessary to be photographed. Manya worried about the expense of this, as we still would need to buy train tickets when we reached the Manchurian border and changed to a CER train. So she got permission to take a group photograph of all six of us. After almost two weeks on the train, wearing the same clothes and without any chance to take a bath or wash our hair, in these photos we look exactly like the refugees that we were.

We were almost 2,000 miles from Omsk and still had nearly half that distance to go.

Manchuria

After another day of travel we finally reached the Manchurian border. The railroad station at the border was called simply that: Manchuria. By now our things were all packed and we were ready to part with our *teplushka*. Porters appeared from nowhere and offered to cart a couple of our trunks; we followed them with our suitcases, making our way across the tracks to the passenger station building of the Chinese Eastern Railroad. Manya bought tickets, our papers were examined, and we emerged onto the platform, where a passenger train was waiting. We climbed in and found places on upholstered seats. Our baggage was put into the baggage car. It was all very new to us.

As the CER train got underway a boy about my age joined us. He introduced himself as Volodya Varaksin, the son of Father's landlady in Harbin. He wore a school uniform, and made me feel shy about my rather unkempt appearance. But he was very friendly and quite talkative; his parents had allowed him to travel alone to this station to meet us. We showered him with questions about the city, the school, and Father. "Oh, he is quite crazy," said Volodya. "You should see what he did to his room: there are lots of birds flying about!" I was suddenly very alarmed. Was our father really insane? What are we doing, going to join a mad father? Did he lose his mind from the shock of Mother's death? I remembered his fits of rage in the past, when he was upset by someone, as well as some of Charskaya's stories, where people succumbed to "brain fever." I could not go to sleep that night, even though our bedding arrangements in this passenger train were so much better than what we had before.

The next day the train pushed on through Manchuria. We saw high mountains, rivers, and wide valleys, and had our first glimpse of Chinese villages. All this was accompanied by the constant chatter of Volodya, telling us of his life in Harbin. But I could think of nothing else but what kind of father awaited us at the end of our trip. It was now late in June 1922, almost three weeks since we left Omsk, and there was no way to retreat.

Finally Volodya cried "We are almost there!" The train was slowing down, our suitcases were all packed and ready, and we clung to the windows. The station platform appeared with a crowd on it. We were looking for Father ... and there he was! I recognized him instantly, his hunched figure in a dark coat and hat, his familiar cane in hand. He had a beard and long mustache whiskers, but his cheeks were now clean-shaven. There was nothing wild in his looks. He was searching for us and at once found our faces in the windows. When the train finally stopped we all clambered down from the car and ran to him. Though I kissed and embraced him, I was still very wary. I did not mention my concern to anyone else, for everyone was elated, Manya and Nanny crying for joy. Father picked up Lena and hugged her especially warmly, tears running down his face. "Lenochka!" he whispered, Mother's name.

Father had friends with him who helped Manya collect the baggage and load us into two horse cabs. With the small children sitting on the laps of the older ones and the suitcases at the back, we started towards our new home. The cabs trotted on for about half an hour, first through the city, then for a while on a country road, and finally stopped before a small one-story house in the middle of a grass-covered yard. Impatient, the children poured out of the cabs to look all around, while Father, Manya, and Nanny unloaded our baggage. Then Father led us in. The house was plainly and sparsely furnished, with makeshift beds for each of us, one or two chests, and a few chairs. The dining room had a long table, two narrow benches, and two chairs. It did not take long for Manya to unpack our samovar and we sat down for tea around the table, Father and Nanny in the two available chairs at the head and foot of the table, and the rest of us on the benches. Every one had something to tell about our trip, and we interrupted each other, until Father had to ask us to take turns. Manya and Nanny had no chance to speak until the children were let outside to examine the yard, the horse stable, and the horses. But soon the hot water in the bathroom was ready and we were taking our baths, the small ones two at a time.

It took a long time to settle all in their beds, but it felt wonderful to be clean and to lie in a separate bed, on clean sheets, and this seemed such a good end to a remarkable day. Father came to make the sign of the cross and to kiss each one of us on the forehead before we fell asleep, a ritual he would keep up for years. As I was dropping off I heard Manya, Nanny, and Father still talking in the other room. Their voices had that rhythmical cadence I remembered from falling asleep in Vyksa, where the adults talked late into the night. I tried to imagine that all the years in between were just a bad nightmare, that Mother must have been miraculously saved and would find us here, and that our life would again be as comfortable and secure as it had been long before.

III

HARBIN

16

In Harbin

For weeks before we came Father had been preparing for our arrival. He explained to his friend Vaughan:

I started this way: I leased a large piece of land surrounded by a big fence; there is a little house (three rooms and a kitchen) and some new trees planted this spring. There is also a stable with two horses and a coachman (a Russian officer) living with them. This is about four kilometers from the town of Old Harbin and about 100 meters from the road leading to the village. All this is quite off to the side and independent, and has all the advantages and disadvantages of a property standing by itself in the land of the Hunhuz, but I have it for forty dollars a month and can take care of it for a while with my cash.

Father's friends helped him prepare some clothes for us and furnish the house. Mrs. Lachinov, the wife of the acting head of the Railroad, used to say, "Just imagine, six pairs of socks, six sets of underwear, six sweaters – and each gets only one!" Camilla Khorvat found some extra furniture that she could contribute. Father refused to take anything valuable, and insisted that he would repay them for everything. He had no idea what we would be able to bring along in the way of clothes or other possessions. As always, thinking of something interesting or unusual that might amuse us, he prepared for each of us a Japanese cotton kimono (*yukata*), and Japanese straw sandals (*zoris*).

The day after our arrival he invited a photographer to take a picture of all of us, now washed and clean, dressed in these *yukatas* in front of our new home. He arranged us exactly in the same manner as we were in Mr. Crane's photo in Omsk. The contrast was striking.

In a few days I began to feel somewhat more relaxed. My worry about Father's mental stability obviously had no foundation. Father was patient, full of affection, willing to listen. Now I knew that the major problems of education were no longer mine. Manya and Nanny also felt the burden of responsibility lifted. They were busy with the new market, the new kitchen, and all the problems of housekeeping. There was no doubt that now Father was in charge, and could be appealed to in every instance. Having no job, he spent a lot of time with us. Seryozha now had a listener who was amazingly patient, and all of us had a parent to help us settle arguments and listen to our stories. Father constantly wanted us near him. As he sat in his folding chair in the yard, usually reading, he seemed to enjoy having the little ones play beside him. He immediately arranged to have some sand brought in, and he admired each new castle that we built.

Still bothered by what Volodya Varaksin had told us while we rode on the train to Harbin, I finally asked Father, "What was it that I heard about the birds in your room, where you lived before we came?" "Oh, that," Father answered. "I installed a net across my long and narrow room and filled one half of the room with various birds, mostly tropical. It was just so lonely without any friendly voices in that house, so prosaic and dull!" So that was the silly boy's reason for thinking him mad! By then I had met all of that family and knew how dull it must have been there. The story not only stopped troubling me but even helped me to understand my father better.

Some of Father's friends visited us. We went to see Mrs. Khorvat when she came to Harbin in order to close their house and move everything to Peking. It was an imposing house full of heavy, carved, uncomfortable Chinese furniture and marble Chinese statues. By that time they had not occupied it for over a year and must have removed all their personal belongings. Beautiful and charming, Camilla Khorvat met us warmly, but I felt uneasy among the imposing surroundings, especially because we tried so hard to show good manners.

It was only the middle of the summer, but the question of school had to be decided. The largest and the best-equipped school was the Commercial School, run by the Railroad. There were other schools, all with the same program of the old Russian secondary schools, differing only in emphasis: the gymnasium emphasized the classical languages, Greek and Latin; the Technical School (*Realschule*), mathematics and physics; the Commercial School taught practical subjects like commercial arithmetic, accounting, economic geography, and political economy. All these schools gave the standard secondary school diploma. At the age of seven, children started three years of preparatory (elementary) education, followed by eight years of secondary school. None of the schools was tuition-free, but the Railroad Commercial School had a sliding scale of charges, dependent on the parent's salary.

Father wanted us to have a Russian education, still hoping that eventually it would be possible for us to live and work in Russia, and he did not want to subject us to the rejection of socialist ideas prevalent among the émigrés. Besides, he realized that he was no longer young, and not in perfect health – he may not have considered his tobacco habit a factor of the latter, but he literally chain-smoked the powerful Russian cigarettes with long hollow tips, lighting one after another from the glowing ember of the last, all day long – and he felt that we needed a practical education that would permit us to earn our own living, always hoping that the older children would help the younger. He therefore chose the Railroad Commercial School for us.

We had to take entrance examinations. The list of subjects was impressive: fourteen examinations for me, eleven for Seryozha, and five for Lena. In most subjects tests were both written and oral, even in mathematics. We set to work preparing for fall exams. English was a required language in the school, so Seryozha and I also began to take private lessons during the summer to catch up with our classes.

I remember well one of the events of that summer, a frightening hailstorm. We used to love hailstorms with the small pieces of ice rolling all over the road. But this was different, this hail was enormous; some of the ice pieces were as big as pigeon eggs and capable of killing a small animal. We ran inside to hide, huddling against the walls between the window frames, while pieces of glass from the shattered windows flew around the room. Although the storm did not last long, it took hours to clean up and to cover the broken windows with whatever we could find in the house.

Commercial School

One morning in late August the Russian officer who lived in the stable where the horses were kept took Lena, Seryozha, and me to the school in the horse carriage, because it was too far to walk. The school consisted of two imposing brick buildings connected by a passageway. We were met by Mrs. Varaksin, who taught there. She introduced Lena and me to the principal of the girls' school, a small prim lady dressed in a dark blue dress with a little white collar; her hair was neatly piled up in a bun on the top of her head. The principal shook hands with us politely and expressed the hope that we would pass our tests and be good and obedient students. Mrs. Varaksin then took us to the appropriate classes and Seryozha went to the boys' school through the glassed-in passageway.

We were a little intimidated by the new surroundings. After the informal family ways of our schools in Omsk, we suddenly entered the atmosphere of the pre-Revolutionary Russian schools – the kind we had never attended. Taking their make-up exams with us were students who had failed subjects during the school year. They were all dressed in school uniforms, the girls in brown dresses with black pinafores and the boys in black long trousers and black shirts with insignia buttons and uniform caps, which they removed when inside the building. The new students, still without uniforms, stood out.

We all passed our examinations, not brilliantly but satisfactorily, and were accepted. I was enrolled in the fourth class, Seryozha in the second and Lena in the third preparatory. Tanya entered the first preparatory, which upset me because she was already able to read and write. It looked as if my teaching efforts were in vain.

Now we needed uniforms. Students were required to wear their uniforms whenever they appeared in public, and the girls also had to wear white aprons on dress occasions, unless they were in mourning. With our limited funds it was a problem for Manya to outfit us, and we picked out the cheapest available brown cotton flannel for Lena, Tanya, and me. Pleated skirts meant more material, so we settled for gathered skirts. A dressmaker was hired; assisted by Manya, Nanny, and me she sewed all our uniforms, as well as fall dresses for the two younger sisters, in about a week, using a hand-operated Singer sewing machine. Since even underwear could not be bought ready-made, this session with the dressmaker was repeated every year both spring and fall until after I left Harbin.

Finally school started, on September 1st. Dressed in our new uniforms, with bags full of textbooks, notebooks, pencils and pens, the four of us traveled to school in a horse-cab. The buildings were now full of students. Finding our classrooms was no problem for Lena and me, but Tanya was a bit shy, so I helped her find hers. Seryozha went to the boys' building. Everyone was greeting old friends but I knew no one. My uniform seemed cheap compared to the other girls' elegant woolen dresses. This was natural – the school population was made up mostly of children whose parents had lived here for many years and were well established, while we were refugees. I was determined that it would make no difference, and that I would establish my status in the class by my abilities and conscientious study. I would not repeat the mistakes I had made at my first school in Omsk.

Before classes began we were lined up in pairs, by height, in the corridor near our classroom, and marched to the church on the second floor of the girls' school. The boys from the boys' school were waiting in the corridor for their turn to march up the stairs. The school church was a large rectangular hall, well lit with a number of tall windows on one side and the altar at the end, on a slightly elevated platform. As usual, the altar was separated from the rest of the church by a screen called the *iconostas*, covered with large icon paintings. What was different in this church was its brightness and its rectangular form, reminding one of an ordinary school auditorium. I was struck by one of the paintings, an icon of the Holy Mother and Child, looking much more modern and realistic than most I had seen. Later I found out that it was a copy of a painting by the well-known Russian painter Victor Vasnetsov.[1]

The girls formed neat rows standing on one side of the church, with the boys similarly lined up on the other side. The school priest, who was also our religion teacher, conducted a fifteen-minute service. To my surprise, we were supposed to join in the singing of some of the prayers. They were familiar prayers which all knew well. During the church service the priest admonished us to sing in full voice. I had not sung since the unfortunate remark by the choir director to my governess in Vyksa, so now I was only pretending to sing, mouthing the words without making any sounds. The admonition of the priest sounded to me as if it were directed to me personally. I was distressed; I was eager to follow all the instructions in this new school, and here was the first instruction, and I could not follow it. Somehow I needed a formal excuse from singing.

I could hardly wait for the first intermission to go to see the principal, who was surprised to see me in her office. "What is the trouble?" she asked. Almost in tears, I admitted that I could not sing. The principal did not seem to be shocked; she comforted me and said that I should try, but that it was not important. I left satisfied, but still distressed by having to admit to what seemed to me a major defect; I also sensed that the principal felt my coming to her was inappropriate. My inability to sing remained for many years a really vulnerable point, making me feel as if I was some kind of cripple.

The classroom desks were each occupied by two students. Each class met for forty-five minutes in the same room for all subjects, except those taught in laboratories. Different teachers came to our classroom for different subjects. One homeroom teacher was in charge of our attendance records, behavior grades, dispatching us to different laboratories, and maintaining order. Wide and well-lit corridors ran through both floors of the school buildings. The physics and biology laboratories and the school church were in the girls' school, while the gymnasium, geography auditorium, and a large auditorium with a stage were in the boys' school. Thus the girls and the boys constantly had to march through the corridors of each other's school, always in pairs arranged by height.

During the ten-minute intermission between classes, while the classrooms were aired, we were required to walk in the corridor, which we did usually in rows, this time freely choosing our companions. I liked these sedate walks the length of the corridor, at the end of which usually stood our director, Nikolai Viktorovich Borzov, and the woman principal. The director was short and portly, with a gray mustache and a back straight as a ramrod, smiling benevolently when we approached, all the girls curtsying together. We knew that the benevolent smile could change drastically to a menacing scowl when he reprimanded a culprit. Often, to avoid curtsying, the rows of girls would turn around before reaching the end of the corridor, so that one part of the corridor remained empty, while the rest of it was overcrowded.

We had two half-hour intermissions – one for a hot lunch served in the dining hall, and one to go outside for fresh air. The school program was rigid: all subjects were compulsory, and we had no choices. We had five periods of instruction every weekday and four on Saturdays. There was a lot of assigned homework, but no self-study periods during the school day. The school clubs, such as the drama, physics, biology, and geography clubs, to which I belonged during different years at the school, met on Sundays in the laboratories or in the auditorium under the direction of the teachers. Students who failed in any subject at the end of the school year had to pass a make-up test in the fall in that subject, or repeat the whole year in all subjects. We always had a few repeaters in the class. Many parents hired private tutors for children who had trouble with any subject. This was a good source of income for young people who had graduated from the school – as it would be for me.

At home in our crowded and simply furnished little house Manya maintained the same routine of cleanliness, order, and regular meal and bed times. She and Nanny did all the housework; our only duties were to make our beds and to keep our books and clothes in order. We always felt that they and Father wanted us to live up to Mother's standards. Her socialist principle, "to each according to his needs, and from each according to his ability," was always in evidence. Fairness in equal attention, the distribution of treats, and the sharing of our few books and toys, was often a source of squabbles, however, usually to be resolved by the adults. For distribution of duties or privileges it was assumed that we were naturally paired: Mulya and Seryozha, Lena and Tanya, Zoya and Katya.

Seryozha and I were such a pair, but we constantly argued. Seryozha felt he was supposed to do something because he was a boy, I, because I was the oldest. Seryozha was particularly good at winning arguments on logical grounds. The arguments often grew into quarrels. The rest of the children were "the little ones," and there were too many of them for me to handle.

ଔ

As I look back on it now I realize how radically Father's life had changed with our arrival. He had always loved children, but in the past our upbringing had been Mother's affair. Father had always had time and space for adult associations and intellectual pursuits, and Mother with whom he could share his thoughts and problems. While living alone after he left us in Omsk he had led a bachelor's life, often visiting his friends and sometimes entertaining them. Now he lived in a house dominated by children. He took it in stride. Presiding over our meal times he was amused by the picnic aspect of it, the lack of fine service, the childish lack of manners. We were boisterous, often fighting, shouting, and interrupting each other. Father called our mealtimes "the feeding of the animals," as in the zoo. He did not seem to realize that except for me, and perhaps Seryozha, this sort of environment was all that the children knew.

Occasionally he went alone to visit his friends. Once I was invited with Father to a dinner at the home of the head of the Railroad, Mr. Lachinov. I put on my best dress, making sure it was not the pretty one that was a hand-me-down from Vera, the Lachinovs' daughter. Their house stood in the middle of a garden. Inside, the fine furniture, rugs, and paintings reminded me of Vyksa. Vera was a beautiful girl, taller than I, with two magnificent thick blond braids that reached the seat of her chair when she sat down. Friendly and relaxed, she tried to make me feel at ease, but her neat, well-furnished room full of books only intimidated me. Vera did not go to school; she had all her instruction by tutors at home, including three foreign languages. Once a year she would take examinations at our school and receive a certificate of promotion to the next class. She had two brothers, one older, one younger than she.

We were invited into the dining room with its beautifully set table. There were several other guests. Again I was reminded of Vyksa, but that was so long ago. I sat next to Vera, unsure of myself. The worst came when a maid offered me a serving dish and I had to help myself to the food on it. In Vyksa I was too small to do that myself, but now I had to act as an adult. Having watched the others, I managed this stage all right. Now I had half of a small chicken on my plate. How does one eat it – with a knife and fork? I wondered. I had always used my hands to eat chicken parts. Nobody else was doing that here. I sat for a while, perplexed. My father, sitting opposite me, noticed my hesitation and told me to watch him. With trepidation I managed to eat most of the chicken, but was distressed that I had left some part of it on my plate. My understanding of good manners was that everything on one's plate should be eaten.

All through dinner I watched my father. He was a part of this world, so gracious and lively, responding to the remarks of other adults in English, German or French with ease, and often wittily, causing others to laugh. Vera, completely relaxed, took part in some of the conversation. Father was at home in these surroundings, while I felt decidedly awkward.

After dessert the children were excused and we had to approach the hostess, Vera's mother, to thank her with a curtsy. After this we ran out into the big garden. For a long time the memory of that dinner made me feel a little shy whenever I met Vera, though eventually we became good friends. Her parents remained Father's closest friends to the end of his days.

Father understood my embarrassment, and from that day on he began to watch our table manners, so that my younger sisters never had so humiliating an experience as I did that day. What I learned about Father was that while that world of "society" was comfortable and familiar to him, in different situations he put himself on the same level as the people he was with. He could use the language of workers and know not to appear superior, and he could deal with children and servants on their own terms. Later he told me: "A real aristocrat should not *need* to appear different. The essence of good manners is in making others feel comfortable."

The City of Harbin

In late fall of that year we moved into an apartment in the new brick apartment house that the Lachinovs had just finished building in the city, and into which they themselves had just moved. Our apartment had electricity, hot water, central heating, and enough rooms so that the older children had good places for study. To my delight I now had my own desk in a corner of the bedroom I shared with Lena. From the Lachinovs' house we could walk to school, and gradually we became acquainted with the city.

The Lachinovs' building stood on Bolshoy Prospekt in the part of Harbin called Novy Gorod (New Town), built near the railroad station on a plan with wide streets, sidewalks, many administration buildings, and a large area of houses for the employees of the Railroad. Bolshoy Prospekt ran through the whole town. A wide straight avenue, well paved, it was lined with trees and sidewalks with occasional benches along it, making it inviting for promenades. The cemetery with its church was at one end and our school and the Railroad Club was at the other. Our newly-built apartment house was some sixteen blocks from our school.

About half way between home and our school Bolshoy Prospekt crossed a large square with a beautiful wooden Russian cathedral in the center, built by Russian and Chinese craftsmen without using any nails. It was surrounded by a fence with brick columns connected by elaborate wrought iron grates. A wide sidewalk allowed plenty of space for traditional processions around the church on church holidays. The cathedral was burned down by the Chinese in 1966 during the Cultural Revolution.

At a right angle to Bolshoy Prospekt, Vokzalnaya Ulitsa led from the square to the main railroad station. At the corner of these two streets stood the big department store Churin, where one could buy almost everything. There were a number of smaller shops, restaurants, apartment houses, and administrative buildings near the square. At the other end of Bolshoy Prospekt, where the twin buildings of our school were located, stood the buildings of the Railroad Club, with a large auditorium with balconies and a well-equipped stage. During the years that I lived in Harbin a resident opera company gave several performances a week all through the winter, often with visiting performers. The orchestra that played for the opera gave symphony concerts during the summer in a shell in the park surrounding the club.

The language we heard in this central area was always Russian: the few Chinese whom we knew or met on the streets spoke Russian and the laborers often spoke pidgin Russian. The only Russian I knew who spoke Chinese fluently was our teacher of oriental studies.

An older part of Harbin, which we came to know later, was called Pristan (the Russian word for a landing); it lay near the river, and had a somewhat international flavor, with both Chinese and Russian shops and businesses, a yacht club, and homes of people not directly connected with the Railroad. Here there were many more Chinese on the streets, and the prevailing language seemed to be Chinese. There was also a Chinese city, Fujiadian, which stood quite apart and was populated exclusively by Chinese, and where only Chinese was spoken. But we seldom went there and I do not remember it well.

The fields far beyond the city and Zone boundaries, except for some areas around the various stations along the railroad, were off-limits for us because that is where the Chinese outlaws called *Hunhuz* lived. These bandits terrorized unfortunate travelers, sometimes attacked Chinese villages, and occasionally kidnapped Russians, demanding an exorbitant ransom and badly mistreating their captives. The city of Harbin was at that time fairly well protected by the Chinese army, which dealt cruelly with the Hunhuz whenever they were captured.

There were a few taxis in Harbin. They usually followed a prescribed route and picked up several unrelated passengers, with a fixed price for the given route. Chinese policemen, who stood on all important street crossings, straightened up whenever such a taxi approached and pointed an outstretched arm in the direction it was to go. I never understood why this was done until I came to the United States and found that it was called "directing traffic." There were also many horse cabs, driven either by Russians or Chinese. The cheapest vehicle for hire was called a *drandulette*, a two-wheeled Chinese cart, in which two people could sit with a driver in front. Aside from an umbrella, the passengers had no protection from the weather. Little Manchurian horses pulled such carts, whose drivers were usually Chinese.

During the school year we could easily distinguish the students of the various schools by the color of their uniforms – brown, navy blue, or dark green. The girls all wore the same kind of aprons – black, or white for festive occasions. Boys had different colored bands on their caps.

Winter, 1922-23

Winter was approaching, and another clothing problem arose as the weather got colder. The Manchurian climate was a little different from that of Omsk, since we were at the latitude about 10° farther south. The summers were warm day and night; and the days were not as long as in Omsk. There was a long rainy period in the fall, and a cold, windy winter, with temperatures reaching -40° F, but there was much less snow than in Omsk. In fact, the white snow was often covered by a thin layer of fine reddish dust from the Gobi desert, carried by the winds for thousands of miles. The red dust penetrated even the sealed windows to form a thin layer on the windowsills.

Our winter outerwear had been left in Omsk along with our other possessions. The Navalikhins had tried to send us some of these things by post, but we had received nothing, so Father had eight people to dress for the winter. The only warm coat we had was a large dark-blue cape lined with gray squirrel fur, which Mother used to wear in winter when riding on an open sleigh, and which we now used as a blanket on extremely cold days. It was too precious to cut up, and besides it would be unfair for just one person to have such a luxury. As a blanket we each could have a turn with it; years later, when we were already in America, it was converted into a fur coat for Lena. For the time being we had to be satisfied with the cheapest coats that Manya could find in an out-of-the-way Chinese shop, crude looking, with gray dog or cat fur collars. The older children could hope to grow out of them fast, but the younger ones wore the hand-me-downs for years.

At the end of November, Father was appointed Secretary of the commission supervising the installation of an automatic system in the telephone office, with a salary of 250 rubles a month. He was quite proud of how up-to-date that system was; he once even took me to see the complicated set of levers and switches, which responded automatically to a call, instead of the usual row of telephone operators with their hands busily moving plugs from one hole to another. While still on that commission Father became an "assistant controller" of the Railroad with a yearly salary of 1,500 rubles plus a 325-ruble allowance for living quarters. The work was not particularly interesting and the salary, a good part of which was deducted for our tuition, not really adequate, but with no other prospects, Father accepted it. The appointment eventually gave him the right to an apartment in one of the Railroad houses, and a favorable tuition rate for the children at school. Like all office workers employed by the CER, he worked only from nine in the morning until three in the afternoon, which left him a lot of time to be with the children.

Father often read aloud to us in the evening. We would all gather in one of the bedrooms, which served as a common room too, and settle in for a quiet hour or so. Nanny would knit stockings on four thin metal needles until she started to nod and gradually fall asleep over her knitting. If Manya was not too tired to sit with us, she would do some mending or embroidery, and I too would darn or cross-stitch embroider; Seryozha drew at the table surrounded by paper and pencils, and the rest of the children sat as quietly as they could. Father would pick out some book that we were not likely to read by ourselves, for example the *Iliad* and *Odyssey* in Zhukovsky's translations. Later he read to us a number of Charles Dickens' novels, again in Russian translation. I remember how touched he sometimes was by passages that he read – his voice would start faltering and tears might appear in his eyes. At the time this was simply embarrassing to me, and only when I had the same experience, years later, reading stories to my own children, did I remember his reactions with sympathy.

That year Father became much involved in the work of the Parents-Teachers Association in our school, and was elected its president. Not being used to working with people over whom he had no control, and of whose ideas he often disapproved, he did not last long in that position. He gave it up under pressure, but with a sense of relief. While it lasted, however, he often brought reports home for me to read, and tried to share his frustration. But to me, the reports seemed dull, long, and hard to understand; I did not want to take time reading them and Father was obviously disappointed in my lack of interest. In general Father's irritability frightened me; sometimes I disagreed with him on minor matters and, being stubborn, quarreled with him. Our conflicts were often about the way the younger children should be treated – for example their bedtime, or the manner in which they studied or played. I felt I was carrying on Mother's tradition and therefore felt righteous about my opinions. These "fireworks" alarmed everybody; they usually resulted in my tears and, later, final peace-making before going to bed at night.

In the spring we all passed our final exams successfully and were promoted, but I still felt that Tanya should have been a year ahead. I suggested to Father that I should study with her all summer and prepare her for the examinations to the third preparatory class in the fall. Father agreed, as long as Tanya was willing. This was to be a test for me as a teacher, and Father promised to give me a silver wristwatch if I succeeded.

Tanya and I worked hard that summer. She had a soft, pliable character, and I tried not to overtax her. In the fall she passed her examinations and I got my watch. It was engraved: *To Mulya for Tanya, 1923*. I treasured it for many years.

[1]   Viktor Mikhailovich Vasnetsov (1848-1926): painter, initially a member of the "Itinerants" and later known for his paintings based on scenes from Russian legend and history.

17

Glavnaya Ulitsa

On the first day of school I came home hearing the excited cries of paperboys, "Earthquake in Japan! Thousands dead!" I felt my heart jolt, and panicked. I remembered the events in Byeloretsk when the wail of sirens signaled explosions in the mill, the family's anxiety as we waited for news of what had happened, frightened about Father's safety. In my mind Japan was associated with Father. I ran home and shouted: "Earthquake in Japan! Papa, lots of people died! Oh, it is terrible!" I almost wept. It seemed so close, so real – Japan, of which Father spoke so often.

Father first tried to calm me down, explaining that however terrible, it was not happening here, right now. Then he asked me to go out and buy a paper, as he was concerned for his friends; he would write to his friends and find out if any of them had suffered. Such practical considerations pacified me; later we learned that none of his friends had been hurt.

In summer of 1923 Father was finally assigned an apartment, as a part of his salary, at 35 Glavnaya Ulitsa ("Main Street"). We moved in early in September, as soon as it was cleaned and painted inside. After all the temporary quarters we had occupied during the last few years, we finally had a place we could call our own. The house was within walking distance of our school and the Railroad Club, and Father also could walk to his office. I still can see his stooping figure, in a long dark coat and fedora, jauntily swinging his cane, striding down the hill past the picket fences of our neighbors' bungalows.

Number 35 was a one-story brick structure with two apartments, each with a separate entrance at opposite sides of the house. We entered ours through an open porch. The front door opened into a long corridor, at the end of which there was a bathroom with a tall wood-fired water boiler, which we lit only when we needed hot water for baths. It was the only place in the house where I could be alone when I wanted to. Later, when I became a student in the Polytechnic Institute, I spent my first earnings on a soap dish to improve its appearance.

The first room on the right was Father's. His narrow metal bed stood along one wall, its metal springs so stretched that it resembled a hammock. I wonder now whether it made him think of the hammocks he slept in aboard ship when he was a Naval Academy student. Father often went to bed early, urging us to come to his room to read, study, talk, or just to be near him, sitting on his bed, chairs, or the floor, until he would finally fall asleep. A bookshelf along the other wall and his hobby table near the window opening onto the garden completed the furnishing.

On the other side of the corridor was a small bedroom for Manya and Tanya, with an enormous wooden trunk where our winter clothes were stored during the summer; this also served as Manya's bed. Next to that was the room I shared with Lena, which was also the common living room. It had a small fireplace in the corner with a white tiled chimney above. Lena slept on a sofa, while I had a narrow bed made from two sawhorses with three boards over them, covered by a thin horsehair mattress. I had a desk and Lena her own small table for study. The family's only armchair stood in our room. Enlargements of various family photographs hung on the walls.

Opposite our room was a dining room with a long dinner table covered in oilcloth, with wooden benches on each side, a piano, and Seryozha's bed. Over the years the oilcloth wore out and Seryozha spent his first earnings on a new covering. Beyond the dining room was a narrow and rather dark kitchen with a brick wood-stove, which had a built-in boiler at one end so that after cooking a meal, one had warm water for dish washing. A door led to the backyard through an unheated shed.

The last and the largest bedroom on our side of the corridor was for Nanny, Zoya, and Katya. There were no closets in the house so we installed plywood wardrobes, designed by Father and built by a Chinese carpenter. We had electric lights: the open wiring was fastened to the walls with little ceramic insulators. The house was heated by two brick stoves, built into the walls between rooms and fired once a day.

We lived almost seven years in this house, longer than anywhere before. It was the place where I grew from a shy schoolgirl to a senior engineering student, where little Katya turned from a baby into a schoolgirl, where we all became conscious of the political problems connected with any decisions that we made about our own lives.

At the end of our front porch a few steps led to a large garden, which extended a whole block along the side street. Surrounded by a low fence and separated from the backyard by a higher one, it was full of tall, shady trees, and had an open area in the middle with flowerbeds. The grass between the trees was seeded every year and grew tall – we had never heard of lawnmowers – and we tried not to trample it too much. Graveled walks edged in brick crisscrossed the garden, which was the center of our activities during the summer. Chinese labor was cheap, so in the spring an excellent Chinese gardener came to sow grass and plant the flower seedlings in the beds according to Father's instructions. In the summer we watered and weeded the flowers ourselves. Always trying to occupy us with something constructive and interesting, Father had an inexhaustible stock of ideas. One of them was to create a flowerbed in the shape of the African continent. It had a string of small blue flowers to mark the Nile, yellow flowers to fill the area of the Sahara Desert and tall flowers in the tropical regions. It even had a piece of glass representing Lake Chad.

To collect the water for the flowers a barrel was dug into the ground near a faucet; the small children would occasionally take a dip in it. The barrel was surrounded by rocks, piled high on one side, and a hose attached to the faucet ran between the rocks, its free end turned up and provided with a metal nozzle so that it made a small fountain. To amuse us children Father often placed a ping-pong ball in the thin stream of water shooting upwards, which would stay aloft there for hours.

Another project was to level the center part of the garden for a tennis court. With no money for a net, we learned how to weave fisherman's nets and began to save string for it. Finally we had a net, some rackets, and two balls. It became a great attraction for our many friends. The balls were always getting lost in the tall grass and the bushes surrounding our court, however, and we spent more time searching for them than playing tennis. We had a makeshift trampoline in the garden made of a long board on supports at each end. A child or even several children could jump up and down on the middle of it. Two years after we moved in, Father had a Chinese carpenter build a small play-house on one side of the tennis court, but by then only my three youngest sisters were interested in it.

In the winter the tennis court was covered over with ice, for skating. Flooding it was a problem, because at temperatures of zero to twenty below the water from one bucket froze in ridges before the next one could be poured. To make a smooth surface for skating we gathered all the possible containers in the house – buckets, pots, tubs, and jars – filled them with water, and lined them up around the court with one of us behind each one or two of them. Then at a signal we turned them over all at once. Crackling in the frost, the water ran toward the center, sometimes leaving a small spot in the center uncovered, but even then we had a good smooth surface for skating around it.

Once we had a painting project. Father proposed that we paint a landscape on a large blank wall of the porch. We had no oil paints so he suggested we mix them ourselves. We used oil, soot from the stove, bluing for laundry, crushed chalk, and ochre, but we finally had to buy a little red paint. Seryozha sketched the outlines of two pictures, a Japanese gate standing in the water of a lake with mountains in the background, and a view of the Chinese Great Wall. We all took a hand in the painting.

We kept a few chickens in the barn at the far end of our backyard. Several times they were killed by predatory animals, and once they were stolen, and my most ambitious project was a proper hen house for our chickens. Our house, the kitchen entrance shed, and the high fence offered three walls, and to close in that space I built a wall with a door in it and a sloping roof. Waterproofing the roof presented a problem, and I used many empty tin cans, which I cut apart, opened, and flattened out to make shingles. Watching the chickens hatch was very exciting. We were so afraid that the mother hen might crush the small chicks as they emerged, that we used to bring the slightly cracked eggs into the kitchen to let them hatch there, before returning the little creatures to the warmth of their mother's feathers.

From time to time a traveling Chinese puppeteer, or magician, or even a "rice dough doll-maker" would announce his presence by a specific musical sound – chimes, bells, or rapid beating on a sounding board. The whole crowd of children who were always somewhere in our house or garden would react enthusiastically, and Manya would sometimes pay the performers to entertain us. The rasping sound of metal on metal would tell us of a passing knife-and-scissors man, and we would watch him working his wheel if Manya needed something sharpened.

As we grew older the garden was used in the evenings for parties. We made lanterns of colored tissue paper, using Father's cigarette boxes for frames, put candles inside, and hung them from the tree branches all over the garden. We walked, talked, and danced to the Victrola music. The atmosphere seemed terribly romantic to us. Occasionally a candle would fall, and the lantern would flare up and drop from the tree, still burning, which added to the excitement.

At Home

As the years passed Nanny was becoming noticeably older. Gradually the responsibility for cooking the meals shifted to Manya, which along with shopping at the markets occupied most of her time – there were never fewer than nine sitting down to each meal. Manya also cleaned the house and washed the painted wooden floors every day. I still remember her small figure doubled over to the floor with her knees unbent, her hands on a large rag in front of her, moving backwards while rubbing the cloth rhythmically, left to right. Nanny mended, knitted, helped in the kitchen with preserves, and dressed and bathed the little ones.

A woman named Nadezhda Gavrilovna came once a week to do the laundry. She worked with a washboard over the tin tub in the dark end of our kitchen. Large sheets were boiled on the stove in a big kettle with wood ashes. The laundry was hung out in the yard. In winter it froze stiff and was brought in like huge pieces of cardboard, filling the kitchen and even the dining room with the fragrance of freshly washed laundry and frost. Nadezhda did the ironing in the same dark end of the kitchen with a charcoal-heated iron, which

Manya, 1925

Nanny, 1924

she preferred even though its fumes made her nauseous. She was a simple woman of no education, the refugee widow of a merchant. But she always wore her small diamond earrings as a reminder of better times, and to me it lent her a certain dignity.

Every month Father would turn his salary over to Manya, keeping the minimum for himself. The children never received any allowance; in fact we never handled money at all except for change given us to buy student tickets to concerts and plays. It was Manya who planned the budget and paid for everything. Manya's sense of priorities – food, health, education, books, and proper clothing for us – defined our day-to-day life. Nanny looked askance at all this, however, and while it was easy for us to ignore Nanny's grumbling and suspicious glances, Manya must often have felt quite uncomfortable.

Manya was the first person up in the morning, seeing to it that we too were up in time for breakfast and not late for school. She greeted us when we came home, made sure that we did our lessons, and took care of us when we were sick. Our quarrels and bickering upset her, and while tired from her own work and our incessant calls for attention, she seldom became angry. Only rarely at the end of her patience, exhausted, she would tearfully complain: "Let me be! I am not a part of your family, not your own!" Yet we felt that she was indeed, and such outbursts made us feel ashamed. I don't remember anyone of us ever being rude to Manya.

It was difficult to give anything to Manya. On some occasion, with Father's assistance, we would buy a piece of cloth as a present for her, but it would always end up being made into a dress for one of us, or for Nanny. Manya never went out except to market or to church. Her social life was confined to contact with the guests who came to see Father or us. All visitors, whether adults or children, were welcomed to our house by Manya, Nanny, and Father. Father much preferred to have our friends visit us, rather than that we go to them. Some even brought their own birthday cakes to celebrate at our house, and Manya never complained. The noisy crowd would run around our rooms with Father playing marches or waltzes on the piano, and the livelier and noisier the children were, the happier he was. Whenever one or two of us were away Father would say: "There are not enough children around. I wish I had more!"

We usually arrived home from school shortly after three in the afternoon, at the same time as Father, and immediately upon arrival we all had our main meal together. During this time we competed for a chance to report on all the events of the day, and Father saw to it that each had his or her turn. He always listened attentively, approving or reproving us as need be.

One day, as we sat down to eat, Father announced, "A strange thing happened today as I walked along our street: I saw something written in chalk on the picket of a fence. I looked closer and saw that it was a name – Elena Zarudnaya. So I took out my handkerchief, bent down and erased it. A little further there it was again – the same name on the fence. I erased that too. There was another, and then another picket with my little daughter's name on it; and old Papa worked hard to erase all of the names with his own handkerchief!" We said nothing, looking at Lena. She blushed but was silent. "This is all I wanted to tell you," said Father, pursuing it no further, and the usual conversation resumed. Years later Lena told me that she had been so impressed with herself at being called by her last name in school, and thought it sounded so good, that on that day she had stolen a piece of chalk from her classroom and written her name on all those fence-pickets on the way home. The story Father told made her feel terribly ashamed, both for writing on the fences, and for stealing the chalk.

Father did not seem to be bothered by the arguments, squabbles, fights, and screams of the children unless they were vindictive, in which case they were put down quickly. If we angered him, however, he could be quite stern. Both Seryozha and I frequently roused him – I because I was too strict and domineering with the younger children, and Seryozha because he quarreled with me. However, we always knew that Father's anger was directed at our deeds and not at ourselves. Even though we thought he sometimes misinterpreted our intentions, we never doubted his love, which he would inevitably demonstrate by hugging the penitent culprit. I remember his reaction to our progress in school and our grades:

we each got a kiss for a good report, but a bad report often resulted in two kisses – one additional to console the recipient, for he or she felt so bad about it. He assumed that we all tried to do our best.

Our day usually ended with high tea; there was a puffing samovar, and always some friends joining us. On school nights they would leave by eleven. Nanny would put the little ones to bed earlier, and Manya, exhausted, would drop off to sleep on her trunk even before the end of the animated conversation at the dining room table. We never helped her with the dishes; she claimed we were in her way in the dark and narrow kitchen. "You had better go and study, or read!" she would say, if we intruded upon her domain.

At home there was no shortage of pretexts for celebrations. Besides Christmas and Easter with all the trimmings, we celebrated both the birthdays and name-days of each member of the family. On a birthday father always played the triumphal march from *Aida* on the piano when the birthday person entered the dining room for breakfast, and a present, usually a book, lay on the table. Name-days were generally known to friends and they arrived in the evening without any invitation to congratulate the celebrant. On Father's name-day in June, the Lachinovs and several other adults would come. As she did for all such occasions, Manya baked a big *krendel* – a sweet bread, somewhat like coffee cake, in the form of a huge pretzel – and everyone sat round the table drinking tea. In the summer there was ice cream, which we made in a churn with salted ice, everyone sharing in turning the handle. The chair of the honored person was supposed to be draped in green branches – a custom we picked up in Libava – but in the end it was done only for Lena's name-day in May, maybe because she was born in Libava, or because it was easy to get small green branches in May. For Father, Lena's name-day had a special significance for it was also Mother's.

CB

Father developed an absorbing new hobby – radio, early in its world-wide development. One could buy small crystal sets and try to receive a signal through the earphones. At first one could hear only Morse code, but by 1922 live voices and music came through. Father studied articles in various magazines and soon managed to build a small vacuum tube set, which could be joined to a dynamic loudspeaker. The acquisition of the speaker was a great event: Father would gather us in his room and tune in, through the cracks of static, barely distinguishable human voices. "Listen!" Father would say. "This is an Italian opera transmission from Rome!" And the world seemed to be shrinking around us. I listened with some interest, impressed by Father's enthusiasm, but failed to get involved. I remember Father walking into our bedroom one morning with his loudspeaker, to wake us with the midnight strokes of Big Ben from London.

For a while Seryozha became interested in building receivers too, and made himself a one-tube set that allowed him to hear London. Father was proud of him. But there was not enough money to pursue this hobby on a larger scale, and Father never attempted to broadcast himself. In fact each time he wanted to try something new, he had to dismantle his old set and use its parts for a new one. But it fascinated him, and gave him a feeling of being a part of the world he had formerly known. And it was something whose results he could share with us all.

When not busy with his radio, Father read; the books he borrowed from his friends were often in French. Occasionally he went out in the evenings to visit his friends, among them the Lachinovs and the Ustrialovs. Professor Nikolai Ustrialov had been at one time in charge of political publications for Admiral Kolchak. Since he had a legal education, he lectured in the newly organized Faculty of Law and published many articles on current politics in local newspapers. A tall, imposing figure, he was an inspiring speaker, prominent among the Russian émigrés; the local press published several of his books. Politically, he was one of the leaders in a movement called *Smena Vekh*, or "Changing the Landmarks," which attempted to explain and justify what was happening in Russia without necessarily approving of everything. Their premise was this: since the government of Russia was now in Bolshevik hands, all who did not wish to sever their ties with their country entirely must recognize and accept this fact. Moreover, they thought that the Bolsheviks were committed to keeping the former Russian Empire intact, which appealed to their sense of patriotism. They argued that one could hope for a gradual evolution and improvement in the political situation, but that such improvement could and should occur with their participation. The Soviets at first welcomed their position, especially because it caused a split in the ranks of the Russian émigrés all over the world. It also influenced many émigrés to return to their homeland.

Father had great respect for Ustrialov and, while he did not quite agree with him, some of his arguments struck a common chord of sympathy. Whenever Father visited the Ustrialovs he came back invigorated by the lively discussions that took place, and by the interesting people he had met.

In 1934, when our family was no longer in Harbin, the Ustrialovs did return to Russia. Professor Ustrialov was able to work there for almost three years, but in 1937, during the purges, he was arrested, imprisoned, and eventually shot. His wife spent eight years in the labor camps, during which time their older son died from tuberculosis. After her release she was not permitted to live in Moscow. Even though their younger son was given a chance to graduate from the university, he could not find employment and finally was assigned a job in the extreme north of the country. He married and had children, but was killed by lightning at the age of forty-one, while inspecting the railroad.

Adolescence

In my adolescence our home was dominated by the young children. The adults usually paid more attention to them, so I felt somewhat isolated. I had no associations with peers other than those in school. Seryozha's friends were too young for me, and none of Father's friends had children of my age except the Lachinovs, but I never seemed to fit into their world. So school became the real center of my social life.

During the first year my favorite subject was Russian literature, mostly because of the teacher – whom I adored. She was young and enthusiastic: short, with long red hair piled up on the top of her head, which sometimes fell down her back below the waist – when she would hastily pile it up again and pin it with long bone pins. She recited poetry by heart as she walked around the class, her eyes burning, enjoying it so much that we could not help but be involved in its beauty. I memorized an enormous amount of poetry that year and practiced declaiming it in full voice, standing on our porch after dark, when no one was in the garden. I spent hours at this every night in the fall, even after it grew quite cold outside.

Mathematics, especially geometry, was so easy that I found the classes boring. I would bring the novel I was currently reading to class and read it while some girl was struggling over a problem at the blackboard, with the gentle prodding of our infinitely patient, slow-spoken teacher, Mr. Koretsky. He was famous for the pat phrase he so often repeated – "Think! Say! Write!", prescribing the order in which we must act. Observing my book, he would come to my desk and suggest a different, more difficult variation of the problem. I would go at it, solve it, and open my book again. He never sent me to the board or responded to my raised hand. I felt justified in reading, and after a while, he let me alone. I read several complete novels during his classes.

For the final test, to prevent copying, he wrote four different problems out on the board before assigning one to each of the four girls who sat at adjacent desks. While he was writing, I solved all four of them and then surreptitiously copied the solutions to pass on to those girls who needed help. If I hadn't done so, the girls would have ostracized me. The student code was that bright students should help those in need, even at the risk of being caught.

I joined every school club that I could. The first year it was the zoology club, which met on Sundays, where I performed laboratory experiments beyond those done in the regular class. Sometimes we prepared specimens for other students to use during the week. Then there was a drama club, which occupied a lot of my time. I took on some major roles in school plays and loved the excitement of appearing on stage in front of the darkened hall full of people. My voice seemed to have a natural "placement," allowing me to speak loudly without effort and to be easily heard: this may have been the result of my solitary poetry readings on our porch. We could also learn ballroom dancing in our school. I remember a violent controversy in the parent-teacher assembly about whether we should be allowed to dance the American "fox trot." The decision was a resounding NO – on "moral" grounds.

On Saturday nights and Sundays there were services in the school church, which some students attended. I went frequently, and even volunteered to sell the candles that people fitted into the candelabras near the altar. I also often carried the collection-baskets through the rows of churchgoers, as I enjoyed being helpful. Father was not sure he liked such activities on my part – they seemed to him a little sanctimonious – but he did not vigorously object and I continued to participate.

Teachers, I think, liked me, but they expected me to be a good student simply because I was a Zarudny. They recognized the name as Father's, or as my uncle Sasha's, and I resented that, because I wanted credit for my own accomplishments, not for my family's. Yet I did not want to be a "teacher's pet": once, when our prim superintendent reprimanded the girls for their frivolity – covering their ears with their hair or curling it or, God forbid, trimming the white collars of their uniforms with lace – she asked me to stand up to exhibit my own head, with two tightly braided pigtails, as a proper hair-do. I stood blushing, wishing the earth would swallow me up, and at that moment I hated the principal. It was she, too, who once returned to me my notebook of my poems, which I had lost somewhere in the school, with what I remember as condescending remarks.

Blushing was one of my problems; I blushed furiously on any provocation, almost to the point of tears. The girls teased me, for I could in effect blush to order: they would demonstrate this to the others by saying: "Blush, Mulya!" and I would blush.

I don't know how popular I was among the girls. I think I was considered too serious and too innocent. Never at the top of the class scholastically, I was usually close to the top, and was often elected to one of the class offices. In the atmosphere of a girls' school I began to feel shy with boys, whom I met only during club meetings. Somehow I could not establish any social or friendly relationship with them. The girls in my class were obsessed with boys and often gathered in small groups chatting excitedly about them, but if I approached they would say, "This should not interest you, you are too young yet!" – and obediently I would go. I felt vaguely that there were things I should know. The central question was sex, of course, though I did not know even how to name it. I thought I must learn how children were conceived because it was my responsibility to teach my younger sisters about it, but I put off finding out, not knowing how to go about it, and apparently sensing no urgency.

So on the whole, while wanting very much to belong, I felt "different," and beneath my positive exterior I often experienced depression. It was partially a feeling that my growing up lacked the glamour I thought it should have, based on the little I had heard from Mother of her own youth in Petersburg. At home I was grouped with the children when Father's friends came; they would try to have their adult conversations alone with him, either in his room or around the dining table without the children participating. Talk with Manya and Nanny was almost on a child's level; I think I was too young to appreciate Manya's quiet, worldly wisdom. Neither Seryozha nor I ever could ever quite bridge that natural gap between ourselves and those older.

I missed my mother, but I resented mothering from other women; among the adult women I knew no one seemed to approach her in judgment and intelligence. This feeling was enhanced by Father's idealization of her, and his reverence for her memory: there was a sort of cult of Mother at home, and she seemed an invisible presence. For as in Omsk, when Mother was too busy to spend much time at home, the family was governed in her name, now, when Father encountered a crisis in managing the whole brood, he would say, as if to himself, "Lenochka, help!" To him we were always *her* children.

Since I still read slowly, finding time to read was a problem. I tried to read in bed after my bedtime, but Father usually caught me at it – the door of our room was made of glass, and he could see my light from the corridor. He would be angry, for he thought my light disturbed Lena, and he also thought that I myself needed more sleep. It made for constant trouble between us. During these years Seryozha, Lena, and I read many foreign writers in Russian translations – Dumas *pere*, Hugo, Dickens, Scott, James Fenimore Cooper, and Jack London. Seryozha learned by heart the Russian translations of monologues from Rostand's *Cyrano de Bergerac*. But as we grew older the Russian writers of the nineteenth century began to occupy us most. Father started to give us collections of works of Russian classics as birthday presents, in this way building up our family library as well, and before long we had the complete works of Pushkin, Lermontov, Nekrasov, Zhukovsky, Gogol, Chekhov, Turgenev, and Tolstoy.

Some weekends or vacation nights we went to the opera at the Railroad Club. Having to wear our uniforms with white aprons for the occasion made most girls unhappy, as they thought they looked like maid-servants. But I never minded it, for it saved me from worrying about not having a nice dress to wear. We bought our student tickets for fifty so-called "Mexican" cents, which was very little, and were allowed to sit in any unoccupied place, often near the front. The resident Harbin Opera Company was not the best, but it was strengthened by the many refugees and, later, by guest singers. The accompanying orchestra was no doubt of a similar quality, but not knowing any better, we enjoyed its performances greatly. The operas were sung in Russian so that we could always understand all the words.

Almost two years had passed since we arrived in Harbin. At fifteen I was still a very innocent adolescent, friendly mostly with girls who shared my own interests. My closest friend was Margarita Sechkina, my namesake, the youngest daughter of the Registrar of the Polytechnic Institute. Margarita read more than I, loved poetry as much, had incredibly good handwriting, and made the same or better grades than I in all subjects except mathematics. Her one sister was much older than she, and we spent a lot of time together.

At school dances the girls and boys arrived separately, and girls often danced with each other. Margarita was bolder than I and helped me to meet boys. At each dance the orchestra would at some point play the Caucasian *Lezginka*. Few knew how to perform it, and the middle of the dance floor usually remained empty. Margarita was very skilled at the difficult male part of the *Lezginka*, and would urge me to join her, taking the easier female part. The rapid-fire, almost wild exercise would occupy most of the floor, with everyone watching us. She, of course, was the hero.

Spring

The approaching spring brought Lenten church services, and my evening walks along Bolshoy Prospekt – romantically alone – were accompanied by the slow, mournful toll of church bells calling worshippers to vespers. On the night of Holy Thursday, after the long "Twelve Gospels" service, when each person in church holds a lighted candle, many carried their candles home, still lit, to ignite those under their own icons. In darkness the whole town seemed alive with lightning-bugs. If your candle went out, you would relight it from somebody else's.

On the anniversary of Mother's death Nanny, who always attended to religious matters, ordered a memorial service in the cathedral. This was the only occasion during the year when Father went to church. All of us walked silently together to the square and into the dark, empty church. The long service ended with the singing of "Let her rest with the saints," during which we all knelt, even Father, for whom it was difficult. As usual, I felt emotionally frozen during this service, and wanted it to be over as soon as possible. During Lent, the same prayer was sung in the school church on Saturday morning before classes began, and each time at least one of the girls would faint or burst out sobbing because a loved one had died recently. I always anticipated such reactions with dread, determined to show no emotion. It was painful.

We usually made our confession and took communion during the Holy Week before Easter. Prior to confession we were expected to rid ourselves of all feelings of resentment or guilt, and ask forgiveness of everyone we knew, especially anyone with whom we might have quarreled. It took some courage. But then everyone was asking forgiveness of you too, and you had to take it with grace and really forgive. A remarkable feeling of self-cleansing followed confession.

"Stairsteps," 1924

Father's favorite photo of us, 1924

One spring, however, I had a special problem, which I brought to the priest during confession: I could not believe in all the words of the prayers I heard in church. I did not know whether I believed in saints, paradise, eternal life, or in Someone above who arranged everything. All I knew was that it was comfortable to pray. The priest, who was also our teacher of religion, resolved my doubts: he told me that all the ritual and all the traditional prayers are created to put one in the mood, in the state of mind that allows one to pray, and this is all that matters. I was relieved and happy to hear this, feeling that I could simply enjoy the services for their beauty. This defined my attitude to the Russian church for many years.

At home in 1924 the general spring cleaning took place. All the furniture was moved, brushed, turned over; every corner was dusted and washed. Both Manya and Nanny worked to the point of exhaustion, and then the Easter food preparation began. They prepared *paskha,* colored the Easter eggs, baked the *kulichi.* Yet neither Manya nor Nanny ever missed the daily church services.

Finally on Easter night, with the older children dressed in their best clothes, Manya and Nanny set out for the midnight service, after laying the table with flowers and all the Easter dishes: ham, roast leg of veal decorated with paper frills, *paskhas,* colored eggs, *kulichi,* and several bottles of wine. Father stayed home. The church was full of excited celebrants with lighted candles. We stood through the midnight part of the service, which ended with joyful singing and the overpowering peals of the bells. People kissed each other on the cheeks three times, the boys happily searching out the girls they liked. We walked home where Father awaited us, ready to kiss each of us, and sat down together for a festive meal at the table – where, during our absence, Father had placed Mother's photograph prominently among the flowers and food.

Summer 1924

The Civil War was now in the past. The Union of Soviet Socialist Republics came into being at the end of 1922, and Russia, devastated by years of fighting, starvation, executions, epidemics, and economic failure, began the process of recuperation. A key to this was the New Economic Policy, or NEP, introduced in 1921.

Early in 1924 Lenin died, and a new Soviet constitution was adopted. The Russian ruble was stabilized, and England, Italy, Norway, Austria, Greece, Sweden, and Denmark established diplomatic relations with the USSR. It looked as if the Soviet Government was more or less firmly established in Russia and that a period of relative stability had begun; in the minds of some Russian expatriates hope arose that conditions in Russia might yet evolve into something they could accept.

Correspondence with relatives in Petrograd – now renamed Leningrad – was still difficult, as diplomatic relations between the USSR and China were not yet established. The fate of the Chinese Eastern Railroad was one of the stumbling blocks. Intense negotiations between the USSR and China continued, but so far without a final resolution of the differences. The Railroad was operating now under a new head, Ostroumov, but it was obvious that there would be many more changes when an agreement between the two nations was concluded.

Father believed that the children had already experienced too many upheavals, and tried to keep the atmosphere at home as calm and normal as he could. We did not discuss political topics at home, and they were not mentioned at school. Father read the newspapers, of course, but he talked about current political events and issues only with his adult friends.

Father liked us to have plans for the summer vacation. Seryozha and I proposed our own program of "constructive activities," mostly reading and some sports, and Father readily approved of it. Besides working on projects in the garden, we went occasionally to swim in the river Sungary, sometimes taking a boat to the other shore to swim there. To amuse the younger children during that summer I put on a play, a fairy tale that we dramatized. The characters were under a spell for some misdeed, and they involuntarily added a nonsensical phrase (*"tilly-boom-boom"*) to each word they pronounced. When the characters properly repented the spell was lifted, but the children laughed so much from having to speak in this manner that it was hard to make them act their parts. It took us several weeks, with our primitive facilities, to create the costumes and decorations, and then our play was performed on the porch by the younger sisters for an audience of all the neighborhood children.

I must admit that there were times when I yearned to get away from the house and garden, so full of the young ones' activity. One way to be alone was to take long walks along the streets of the city. In the evenings there were symphony concerts in the park of the Railroad Club. There were always empty chairs among those arranged in front of the brightly-lit music shell, and the music was absorbing. On many evenings I stayed in the park long after the concert was over, walking on the sandy paths and talking with friends, with the scent of flowers in the cool air.

Lena and Tanya went to a summer camp situated at one of the stations along the railroad, in a place that served as a resort for many of the Railroad employees' families. Father paid for a certain number of bottles of *kumys,* which they were supposed to consume before returning home. *Kumys* is fermented mare's milk and is supposed to be good for one's health. They did not like it, but they drank it dutifully.

That summer I started menstruating. Father took me to a performance of Shakespeare's *Hamlet* in an outdoor summer theater. It was the only time I remember that he went to the theater with me. I had a white dress … and it started … I had no idea what was happening to me. Then I recalled that evening in the snow-bound Siberian village six years ago, when my pregnant mother told me that some day I would bleed, and I understood. How many other questions remained unanswered! I tried desperately not to let Father notice my stained dress. "Let others see it, those whom I don't know and will never meet again, but not my father," I thought. I hardly remember the play and I think Father decided that I was too young to appreciate the fine performance of the famous visiting actor.

18

The Final School Years

During the spring and summer of 1924 the USSR and China continued to work on establishing diplomatic relations between the two countries. The management of the Chinese Eastern Railroad was a key part of these negotiations. An agreement was signed in Peking on May 31, but it still had to be accepted and signed in Mukden by Marshal Chang Tso-lin, the warlord of the northeast provinces. On September 20 the final agreement, with minor changes, between China and the USSR was signed. Parts of it affected us directly:

1. The Railroad would be managed by a board of directors consisting of five Russians and five Chinese, to be named by their respective governments, one of the Chinese members serving as the president of the board.

2. A Soviet manager and a Soviet assistant manager would be appointed by the board of directors, who would also define their duties.

3. The municipal Government of the city of Harbin, as well as other stations along the Chinese Eastern Railroad, would be Chinese. This included the police, courts, and the Department of Education.

4. Old Russian passports issued by the Russian Imperial government would be invalid.

5. In Harbin the Soviet Government would be represented by a consulate. The consulate staff would have diplomatic immunity, but would not engage in Communist propaganda, since the Railroad was strictly a commercial enterprise.

6. The Soviet consulate in Harbin would, at its discretion, issue Soviet passports to persons requesting them. Persons not having Soviet passports would be under the protection of their own consulates or of the Chinese authorities.

7. All employees of the Railroad must be either Soviet or Chinese citizens, their positions assigned according to the principle of equal representation of both nations.

These points had a radical effect on the life of Russians in China, and especially the employees of the Railroad, including our own family. In order to keep their jobs, émigrés had to apply for either Soviet or Chinese citizenship, or face being discharged. Their former Russian passports became invalid, so that unless they acquired Soviet or Chinese citizenship, they remained passportless, and unprotected in any conflict with the local police or the administrative functionaries in the corrupt Chinese local government. The Soviet Consulate would certify those who applied for Soviet passports as applicants, which would allow them to keep their positions until they either received Soviet passports or were refused citizenship. In the latter case they would be automatically sacked and replaced by a newly arrived Soviet citizen from the USSR.

Now Father had to make the momentous decision of which citizenship to apply for. The most important question was whether he was ready to abandon all hope that he and his children would return to Russia. In the past, many Russians spent years abroad, either voluntarily (as my father had done, for educational purposes), or as self-exiles, permanent or temporary, chiefly for political reasons. They always maintained their Russian passports, and most of them intended to return home one day. They stayed in close touch with events at home and with their friends and relatives. But now it was different: without a Soviet passport one's ties with Russia were severed, and in the eyes of the Soviet Government, one became an enemy. There was little chance of reconciliation and re-entry, and even contact with relatives would be difficult.

It was clear to Father that at present he himself could not hope to return to Russia and survive. But what about his children, in the future at least? Without either Chinese or USSR citizenship Father would automatically lose his job, and finding another one in Harbin was unlikely. Moreover, we had no money to move elsewhere with such a large family, even if Father could collect his pension from the Railroad. Going anywhere from Harbin other than China or Japan meant a long trip into the unknown. Losing the job would also mean that the children would have to find other schools, which would probably be much more expensive. Where else but in Harbin could he give his children a Russian education that would permit them not to be outsiders, should they ever return to their homeland?

Father
Harbin, 1924

This was a period of intense soul-searching for Father. Late into the night we heard his shuffling steps as he paced his room from one end to the other. He always seemed to think better when he walked. He knew very well the excesses of the political regime in Russia; the people now in power were the ones who had murdered his wife. Could they change? Yet, whatever the government, Russia was Father's native country, the land of his forefathers, his long-suffering motherland, to whose welfare he and his whole family had once dedicated their lives. It was still home to most of his relatives, and he hoped that some day it would be possible for his children to live, to work, and to be useful citizens there. He did not want his children to become enemies of the land of their birth.

Many of Father's acquaintances chose to apply for Chinese citizenship. But Father could not imagine bringing up his children as Chinese, accepting China as a "homeland," or living there as permanent refugees. He wrote to his brother Alexander, the lawyer, in Leningrad. The consensus of the Zarudny and Brullov relatives was that he should apply for Soviet citizenship, even though he would probably be refused it eventually, but possibly with the understanding that he could stay in Harbin under the protection of the Chinese for the indefinite future. For the time being, however, he would have applicant status, which permitted him to hold onto his job, and the children would be allowed to attend the same school, now run by the Soviets, getting the same education as children in Russia. When we came of age we could apply for Soviet citizenship on our own, if we chose to do so. Father agreed, and applied for USSR citizenship.

The Russian community of Harbin, with all its range of political persuasions, was experiencing a traumatic split. There were the old settlers who had no direct experience of the revolution and the civil war. For them the question of passports was very simple: they had always been Russian, no matter what government Russia had, and it was simply a matter of exchanging their passports one more time. But there were also refugees, from many different political parties or no party at all, some of whom had suffered in the convulsions of the revolution, while others had come here simply by choice.

For everyone, however, the unsettling experiences of recent years remained fixed in their minds, so it was no wonder that openly declaring their relationship to the present USSR was an act of major importance. For many of the Russians it was not only a political decision, but a moral one.

Former friends stopped greeting each other; mere acquaintances wanted to know which passport you had applied for, before entering into a conversation. Those who applied for Soviet passports felt that they were being watched, and that what they said, or whom they associated with, could mean rejection. Nonetheless we managed to retain our own friends, regardless of which passport they sought, or even if they chose to remain stateless.

Changes at School

In 1924 the school year began on September 1, as usual. At first it seemed to be the regular routine: excitement about new courses, new teachers, and renewing old friendships. There was no real inkling of upheaval, but by the end of September some of us knew that the administration of the Railroad would soon change, and that our parents were in the process of making some serious decisions. Still, it did not seem to concern us.

One day early in October we sensed an air of excitement among the teachers. We marched to church as usual, but this time all students, even those of other faiths, were told to attend. The Director, the principals of both schools, and all the teachers were there. Instead of the usual fifteen-minute service, the Director addressed us from the pulpit. He said that he must say goodbye to us because a new director had been appointed. There would be other changes, he said: some of the teachers would leave, some subjects would be changed. There would be no more church services before classes. The church would remain in the school until the spring, when it would be relocated. He hoped that we would all continue to be good and obedient students as we had been before.

For most of the older students this was not altogether unexpected. They knew that some radical revisions to the program were bound to occur, though they did not know when. For the younger ones, however, usually shielded by their parents from such concerns, it was more of a shock. We marched silently to our classrooms. We did not know what the new order would bring. In the lower classes many of the little girls, frightened by the impending changes, burst out in sobs. In the upper classes there was a flood of questions: how will the curriculum be affected? Which teachers will leave, which will stay? It was hard for the teachers to conduct their classes as usual, but somehow the day passed and we all hurried home to share the news with our families.

The new school director appointed by the Railroad board of directors was Father's old friend Professor Ustrialov. His writings in the local papers, as well as in the wider émigré press, were well known by then. His political position on the reconciliation of opposition parties with the present regime had met with approval in the official Soviet press. Yet he was by no means a typical Soviet official, and his appointment was acceptable to much of the remaining staff and student body. Nevertheless some teachers left, as did a good number of students, many of whom were our friends.

Religion classes were abolished and a new subject, political economy, was introduced for the upper classes; in the lower classes the new subject was "anti-religious propaganda." There was now a Student Committee, composed mostly of students who had just arrived from Soviet Russia, which served as an advisory body to the faculty. One day we saw some carefully arranged sheets of writing on the corridor wall that resembled the page of a newspaper. This turned out to be the "wall newspaper" introduced in Soviet schools. It contained criticism of some teachers and students, and its flavor was distinctly communist. Instead of the old Russian anthem we now had to learn the "International" and some students saluted while singing it. They obviously had belonged to a communist organization.

At home Father tried to calm us. He said that we had to learn what children in Russia learn. He knew that he now had a new task, to counterbalance the hard line of the school by showing us the possibility of other points of view, but without polarizing us against the new administration.

Uncle Sasha

Now that mail and rail communication with Russia was restored and Soviet citizens could travel to the Zone, a number of artists, lecturers, and musicians began to arrive on tours from the USSR. Alexander Zarudny, our Uncle Sasha, decided to visit us. By that time he had given up legal work, and made his living by giving lectures throughout the Soviet Union on his courtroom experiences – defending political victims, investigating anti-Jewish pogroms, the Beilis case, and so on. He obtained permission to deliver a series of lectures in Harbin in January 1925.

Uncle Sasha was born in 1863, twelve years my father's senior. He was educated as a lawyer and became a prosecutor at first. He did not last long as such, and it was said that if he was unconvinced of the guilt of the accused, his speeches in court sounded more like arguments for the defense. He served as a judge for some time, but that did not satisfy him, and he resigned to become a defense attorney. Regarding this latest career change the principal judge of his district remarked: "I am happy that I was able to convince Zarudny to stop being a judge; this service obviously depressed him. How could he, with his saintliness and painfully sensitive nervous system, do our stern duty? He was born to be a defense counsel and his place is in their ranks."

At that time the Association of Defense Lawyers attracted a lot of idealists. Uncle Sasha confined his work to political cases, or those involving miscarriage of justice, press censorship, or mistreatment of ethnic minorities. One of his colleagues, Oskar Grusenberg, said of him that "he dashed about in the trackless and slushy mud of the political justice system like a one-man rescue squad." Grusenberg recounts that Uncle Sasha once compiled a list of 157 cases he handled all over Russia, from Eastern Siberia to the Caucasus and Moldavia, in the period 1885 through 1917, and then added, "there were also 265 other cases."

In early 1917 Uncle Sasha was Deputy Minister of Justice in the Provisional Government, but he resigned in May in disagreement with some policies. In July 1917 he was appointed Minister of Justice by Kerensky but in August he resigned again. During the Soviet regime he was saved by the fact that former political convicts of the pre-Revolutionary period, who now organized a prestigious Association of Political Convicts, elected him an honorary member. For a while he had a chance to do some defense work in the Soviet courts but soon abandoned it in frustration. He was married early but soon divorced. He adored his only son, Sergey, who shared his apartment in Leningrad, as did his sister Zoya. She did some secretarial work for him, and he supported her too.

Uncle Sasha arrived in Harbin in January 1925 and we met him at the station. He was no taller than Father and had a round, well-clipped gray beard, friendly black eyes, and a wonderful warm smile that charmed us immediately. We knew he was "a celebrity," and we were at first a little in awe of him, but that didn't last long. He had a way with children, becoming almost a child himself when he was with them.

For us he was a source of continuous fun. Alexander Benois writes that in the Petersburg of the 1890s Uncle Sasha was known as "Zarudny Furioso," always the life of the party, rousing even the most apathetic guests. Now, aging and gray-haired, he still knew how to make even the most ordinary things exciting. He was a magician, with a great store of card and sleight-of-hand tricks. Every day there were little surprises put on the table for each of us. During meals he told us interesting stories, never losing anyone's attention.

Once he announced that the presents he brought would be distributed by chance. All the presents were wrapped, numbered, and placed on a shelf in Father's room. In Uncle Sasha's hat there were tickets with numbers for each present. As each of us drew a ticket Uncle Sasha would bring the present with the corresponding number and every time it was just the right present for that child. Tanya really worried about this at first: she knew that she did not want to draw a ticket for one of the remaining presents, because it seemed to be damp and smelly. She drew a ticket and got a doll, just the kind she wanted. Father got the smelly package, which turned out to be a lobster! How did Uncle Sasha do it? Tanya pondered, and the next time Uncle Sasha proposed to give out his presents the same way, she slyly clutched two tickets and found out: they both had the same number! Now she realized that Uncle Sasha changed the tickets each time and they all had the same number – right for each person. With remarkable restraint, she kept her discovery a secret from the rest of us for a long time.

Katya had just learned to read, and Uncle Sasha professed to be so amazed at her achievement that she volunteered to teach him to read too. He was all attention – an eager student. Poor Katya – when we let on that she was making a fool of herself, she hid in a closet and could hardly be consoled.

The local papers announced Uncle Sasha's lectures, one about the Beilis trial of 1913, others about the investigation of the Jewish pogroms, and on the political trials he had defended – all pre-Revolutionary events. This concentration on the past aroused criticism in some of the papers. Father, Seryozha, and I attended all of the lectures. I was very much impressed by the big hall packed with people and the loud applause when he emerged on the stage dressed formally in a tailcoat. He lectured in a simple and intimate manner as if he were in a small room with us, talking to friends. And yet even at the very back of the auditorium his voice could easily be heard. He spoke of the unfairness and prejudices of the old regime, of people unjustly accused, and about those who rebelled against such abuses, disregarding their own safety – idealists who fought for the rights and equality of the oppressed, and who believed in the ultimate triumph of truth and justice. He spoke also of his own struggles to defend these idealists. The crowd was electrified, and the applause at the end was thunderous. I was so proud to be his niece. It was an event in the life of Harbin.

Father and Uncle had many arguments late at night. Father could not reconcile himself to the harshness of the regime in present-day Russia. I remember him shouting from his bed to his brother, in bed in the next room, "All that goes on in Russia today revolts me!", followed by my uncle's conciliatory response. Yet they had strong fraternal feelings; they belonged to each other, and we belonged to Uncle Sasha as well.

All too soon he departed for the rest of his lecture tour, leaving an indelible impression on all of us. His kindness, his constant willingness to listen to the other side of the story, his belief that justice and truth would ultimately prevail, even when the situation seemed so gloomy, inspired me. And the knowledge that there was in that distant Russia a person we knew, a person who loved us – "our own" – brought Russia closer to us.

On his way from Harbin to Vladivostok Uncle's suitcase, with his formal clothes in it, was stolen. "Somebody needed my tails more than I," he wrote Father. Later, when his son Sergey married, Uncle Sasha moved out of his own apartment, leaving his room to the newlyweds, rather than ask his sister Zoya to vacate hers. After this, Uncle Sasha lived until his death in a building devoted to housing former political prisoners. He died in 1934 and was buried on the same day as Sergey Mironovich Kirov, the head of the Communist party in Leningrad. Kirov's assassination began a wave of terror that developed into the Great Purge by Stalin in which most of the "Political Convicts" perished; Uncle Sasha, had he been alive, would most likely have been one of the victims.

Spring 1925

After the new agreement between the USSR and China, the political situation in Manchuria became more complicated, as it was clear that the two countries interpreted its terms differently. In April 1925 the Soviet manager of the Railroad, A. N. Ivanov, ordered the dismissal of all non-Soviet Russians. Among them were Russians who had applied for Chinese citizenship, and a protest demonstration by Russians and Chinese was protected by the Chinese police. Ivanov was forced to revoke his order, but the situation was more precarious than anyone had expected. A sense of uncertainty was in the air.

School days, however, went on without any obvious problems. The major part of the program remained the same, and we were unaware of any more impending revisions. The drama club and poetry recitation absorbed much of my time and energy. Poetry readings on the stage continued to be popular. A new performer appeared in Harbin, Leonid Yeshchin, who read poetry professionally. He was an accomplished actor and had his own, quite peculiar technique – he almost sang – and I was fascinated by his style. I met him, and when I told him how I had worked on my own recitation, he invited me to read some poems to him. He approved of my manner, but he wanted to teach me his way. I tried, and he liked it. One day he came to visit us and told us that he planned to open a drama school in Harbin. It would be a full-time school. I was very excited, for I longed to become an actress.

So I cautiously approached my father. "What would you think if I transferred to a drama school?" He thought for a while, and trying not to dash my enthusiasm, he replied: "Of course, to be an actress one needs a talent, and maybe you have enough of one. But it is worthwhile to be an actress only if you are a *great* actress. Can you promise me that you will be as great an actress as Komisarzhevskaya?[1] If not, I don't advise you to drop out of your school." I did not have that much confidence in myself and decided not to press it; the theater remained, for some time, my unfulfilled dream.

Spring came, with the familiar pealing of Easter church bells. Many of the students attended the Easter service in our school church, knowing it was the last Easter before the church would be moved. And after all, how could the boys and girls pass up the chance to kiss after the service? I still helped with the candles. To our great surprise we saw our new Director Ustrialov enter the church, so tall that his head could be seen above all others from any part of it. No one expected the head of a Soviet school to come to church, and it was a daring act on his part. I developed a new respect for him.

Already subjected to systematic anti-religious propaganda, we knew that going to church was not the "correct" thing to do, nor was wearing the baptismal cross on a chain, even though it could not be seen under our uniforms. I resented this psychological pressure, however – not that I felt especially devoted to the church, but I felt that religion was such a personal matter that no one should tell me how to observe it. Of course I would not take off my cross; I attended church even more frequently and continued to assist in it. Now that the Church was persecuted I had to support it, if only in principle, and as a protest. This sense of resistance guided my attitude toward religion until I came to the United States, where I found there was no need to campaign in defense of religious freedom.

At the end of the spring term we were told that the number of school years would henceforth be reduced. Instead of three elementary and eight secondary years, the program would consist of ten years altogether, and thus, my class learned, the next year would be our last. The change seemed of minor concern to the younger classes, but ours had just one year instead of two to complete the entire secondary school program. It hardly seemed possible. Many of the boys who planned to apply to the Polytechnic Institute, the only technical institution of higher learning in Harbin, were at once delighted that they could enter sooner, and alarmed by the amount of work ahead of them. I realized that a decision about my further education would have to be made a year sooner, and yet so much was up in the air. Father still hoped that he would be able to send me to a Belgian university, but I knew that this was something of a fantasy. For the time being I took things as they came, month by month.

On one of his trips Father apparently spoke with an old woman friend about our life at home. His friend chided him about taking Manya for granted. After this conversation, he wrote a letter to me, reminding me of how much we all depended on Manya, and remarking that his friend had advised him to marry her. Terrified, I wrote back:

> Dearest Papa, … What you wrote to me at the end was something I have thought about for a long time and terribly feared. I am extremely conscious of what Manya has done for us. We are all terribly grateful to her for that. We all love her, and I am sure that she loves us too. In a sense we have taken this love from her and forced this attachment to us on her by taking away her independence. I understand that very well and sense that you have been thinking and tormenting yourself about this for a long time. I saw this before, I sensed it was coming, and was very afraid of it; therefore I always avoided talking to you about it. I think it is easier for both of us to write about it.

Manya shall always remain for us wonderful, dear and kind Manya; but what you write about should never happen! Please understand how hard it would be for all of us. Maybe only Zoya and Katya don't understand this yet, but all the rest – I can't even tell you what this would be for us. After all, we are growing up, I shall finish school soon, and then I'll be of more help at home. One can forget about my going to Europe and all the other beautiful fantasies, if the children are a burden to her; and maybe our life may change for the better? If not, I can stay. After all, Manya cannot give the children what they need. I can make her life easier and by and by the others will grow up and we will be taking care of all of you, our dear caretakers. If what you speak about happened, I would think of nothing but how to get away as far as I can. When I read those lines in your letter, I froze; I could not read any further; I could not believe it. Papa, we shall be able to prove our love to her, we shall make her feel part of the family. Don't be angry if now I don't help her enough. You know, because it may happen that I shall not be able to continue my education (it is awfully hard for me to contemplate that), I try to get as much as I can from the present school, and later I can devote all my time to helping her. Now it is most important not to be in her way, to understand how tired she is. ... I remember once when I was with Nanny and you called Manya, Nanny said "Listen to him, he can live without your mama, and lives without her, but he cannot live without Manya!" I know, Nanny always grumbles, and especially at Manya, always unfairly accuses her, but think what a tense atmosphere would be created if Nanny and the others found out that her fears were justified! Nanny would set the little ones against her, would instill in them a sense of bitterness and maybe would even leave for good. No, Papa, don't even talk about it. If we need to do something for Manya, even if it causes some deprivation for us, we should do it, we must do it, but only not this.

I meant every word I wrote. Father never again spoke of this, but he saved my letter.

A Concession at Echo Station

Manya and the younger children were going to spend the summer at Hingan, a town on the railroad line far up in the mountains, where some Japanese people Father knew had a concession, and where a Russian family he knew from his Ural days worked for these Japanese. I had thought that my own summer would pass quietly with tennis, symphony concerts in the Railroad Club park, and reading. Only Seryozha and I would be home and Nanny would cook for us, and I hoped we would not quarrel too much.

But early in the summer I received an unexpected offer from a friend, Mrs. Il'yin. Her brother, Alexander Voyeikov, an agronomist who was experimenting with new types of corn and rice suitable for the Manchurian climate, lived and worked in a concession near the railroad station Echo, where his experimental fields were located. Mrs. Il'yin wanted to send her daughters Natalia and Olga, aged twelve and nine, to spend the summer with her brother. He was a bachelor, and she felt that the girls were too young to be there alone with no other woman. She asked me if I would accompany them. It sounded like an adventure, and Father let me go.

It proved to be quite an interesting summer. There was no one of my age there, only the little girls and grown-up men. The settlement consisted of a large house, in which we lived, with various out-buildings and servants' quarters, surrounded by the experimental fields. Mr. Voyeikov had hired Chinese from a nearby village to work there, and there was also a small company of Chinese soldiers, with one officer and a cannon. They were quartered in the village and were supposed to guard the whole settlement from the Hunhuz.

The Hunhuz outlaws continued to terrorize the Russian population of Harbin. The most shocking case recently was that of a talented young pianist who came back from studying abroad to visit his parents, and gave several brilliant concerts. He was kidnapped by Hunhuz, who demanded an exorbitant ransom, which his parents could not raise. One by one his severed fingers were delivered to his parents, before he was finally murdered.

A Chinese cook, whom Mr. Voyeikov had taught to cook Russian food, prepared our meals. A young assistant, about 35 years old, began to pay much attention to me, confiding his hopes and aspirations. It was the first time that something had begun to stir in me, something very personal toward this man, much older than I, who seemed to like me. He was always quite proper and polite; he took me for rowboat rides on the river and spent many hours talking with me. I was flattered and began to feel almost grown up.

The girls were no problem. Natalia and I rode horses that belonged to the concession. We often went swimming in the wide river with tall sandy banks. The water was so clear that we could watch fish moving and crayfish crawling on the bottom. Mr. Voyeikov was busy with his work. The rest of the time he read and paid little attention to us, and so I had much time to myself. Once, after walking along the river shore I decided to take a short-cut home and climb the steep sandy bank. It was almost vertical and some thirty to forty feet high, sparsely covered with occasional small shrubs and clumps of grass: a challenge. I started and easily got about half-way up, holding on to a few feeble shrubs as I climbed. At this point there were no shrubs and a clump of grass I grabbed at gave way. The sand was slipping out from under my feet. There was no way I could climb down; another moment and I would fall all the way down onto the rocks below. No one would hear me if I called. I stretched out and clutched another clump of grass, knowing full well I would pull it out too. But before it gave way I managed to reach one above it, and so on. I was doing something that seemed to me quite impossible. When I reached the top I could not believe that I had, but it gave me a strange feeling of confidence that remained with me the rest of my life. It was the knowledge that in extreme situations, when one's life is at stake, one does develop an unexpected strength. For many months after I would relive this experience in my dreams.

One morning when we came to the breakfast table Mr. Voyeikov quietly told us not to venture beyond a very small area around the house. It turned out that our Chinese "defenders" had abandoned us the night before, together with their officer and the cannon, to join the Hunhuz. Even though the adults tried to seem calm to keep us from worrying, it was obviously disconcerting. Shortly after that Mrs. Il'yin came to fetch us home.

Several years later the Il'yins left Harbin for Shanghai, where Natalia worked as a journalist and eventually returned to Moscow. There, after finishing the university and marrying a professor, a well-known literary scholar, she herself became a recognized writer. Her mother joined her in Moscow, while her sister married a Frenchman and eventually settled in France. Natalia came several times to Boston and once gave a lecture in my house. She died in 1994.

Voyeikov continued working on his experiments, but finally was kidnapped by the Hunhuz and held for ransom. They treated him roughly, as they did all their victims, but he was finally released. He could no longer continue his work, however. I heard that after his release he once saw one of his tormentors in the streets of Harbin.

The Last Year of School

When we returned to school, we found that the boys' and girls' schools were now united: the school had become coeducational. Our class, however, remained segregated. It seemed clear to me that our doubled-up program was overloaded and that it would be impossible to cover all that was required, especially in mathematics and science.

About this time I became more interested in science. I knew that with my slow reading I could not easily specialize in the humanities, although I loved literature – I hardly had time to read all that I wanted to read. In natural and physical science and mathematics my slow reading was not such a handicap. I loved writing essays, and was praised for them by my teachers, but I still made many mistakes in spelling. I decided to specialize in science.

Many girls in my class did not plan on any further education, but as Mother and my aunts and female cousins had all been university graduates, I could not imagine my future without attending some university. But I did not know which or where. For the time being it was still too far ahead, and much could happen before the end of the school year.

Physics and physical geography fascinated me. The logical explanation of natural phenomena seemed constantly to offer new ways of understanding the world. What struck me most forcibly was that not all is already known, that there seemed to be an inexhaustible opportunity for future discoveries. To me it seemed highly romantic that somewhere, at that very moment, those wonderful people – scientists, who had expanded the limits of our knowledge – were living and working. In Harbin I did not know anyone involved in scientific research, but the very existence of such people elsewhere excited me. One day I read a short article about Albert Einstein, and although I understood nothing about the Theory of Relativity, the idea of a man developing a new theory that explained the most fundamental facts about our universe obsessed me. I clipped from somewhere a small portrait of young Einstein and hung it over my desk. I liked the way he looked and felt personally inspired by him.

cs

Outside school the strain between the Chinese and the Russians was showing again. On January 16, 1926 the Railroad manager Ivanov precipitated another conflict. The Chinese Railroad guards were supposed to pay a reduced rate for transportation on the Railroad, but when three thousand of them attempted to board certain trains Ivanov demanded cash payments in advance, claiming that part of their load had a commercial purpose. They refused to pay; he refused to let them board. The Chinese authorities then arrested Ivanov, charging that parity was not being observed by the Soviets, that the profits from the Railroad were not deposited in the proper banks, and that the Soviets had engaged in communist propaganda, contrary to their agreement. For the time being, however, a new Soviet manager came in, some operational details were more definitely spelled out, and life went on more or less as before.

As a graduating class we made an excursion to the Chinese city of Tsitsikar, involving an overnight trip on the train. Tsitsikar was a busy provincial city with no European residents, where only Chinese was spoken. Our bearded Oriental history teacher spoke fluent Chinese and marched us easily through the curious crowds.

We stopped to admire various products sold in the market and in the shops; I bought a small bamboo cage with a singing cricket in it. When we finally came to the main square, we were shocked to see, hanging on a pole in the center, a larger cage with a human head in it. Our guide explained that this was the head of a Hunhuz who had been captured the previous week.

I was elected president of the physics club. The members were students from both the boys' and girls' schools, still quite distant and awkward in personal relations. Now I had the key to the laboratory where we met on Sundays, taking turns delivering papers on subjects going a little beyond our class program. We tried to perform experiments, too, usually well-described in our texts and with known results. There was a primitive shop connected to the physics laboratory, used for the repair of the equipment. Here I learned to use a small foot-operated lathe and made tiny candlesticks from some brass rods I was permitted to turn.

Coming to an almost empty school and having access to tools, a telescope, and other physics apparatus was exhilarating, but what excited me most of all was the chance to examine carefully the statue of a horse in the upstairs hall of our school. I had never been to a museum, and had seen only photographs of sculptures. This lovely figure fired my imagination. I wrote poetry dedicated to it, secretly, never to show to anyone. I was photographed with it. It spoke to me of the freedom of endless plains, which I had never seen, but about which I had read so much. And it inspired in me a kind of homesickness, love for my homeland somewhere far away now, and a desire for sacrifice. I dreamed of dedicating myself to the "holy" profession of teaching, of being a quiet, unknown hero.

I took many photographs with my box camera and everyone asked me for copies. I printed them myself, but to do this for everybody seemed too much for me. Then I had an idea: we should all have an album with photographs of our last year at school. We would order from a printer a small album with our school insignia for each girl, each of us would paste in pictures of all the teachers, and of the girls we wanted to remember, and there would be enough space left to have a note written by each of them. I would take the pictures and we would all order prints. The idea was taken up with enthusiasm. I collected the money, ordered the albums, and started taking the pictures.

It kept me so busy that I collected only a few signatures for my own album. My literature teacher, Mr. Godnev, wrote in my album: "You are carried away by science, but don't forget that by nature you are first of all a humanist; thus art, and therefore also literature, must occupy the first place in your life." On the next page my mathematics teacher, Mr. Petrov, wrote: "I would gladly add my signature to the signature of N. G. if the words 'literature' were replaced by the word 'science' (and its derivatives)." The director of our school, Ustrialov, photographed at his director's desk, wrote: "*Levis haustus philosophiae ducit ad atheismum, plenus ad Deum* (Bacon)" – Superficial study of philosophy leads to atheism, profound study to God. Latin was not taught in the school, but I understood that much, and was amazed that the director of a *Soviet* school would write this. I still have the album and regret that I cannot now remember the names of many of the faces I photographed.

In the spring I fell in love with a boy whose name I also no longer remember. He was a member of the physics club and I often met him in the empty corridors of the school. He was my age, but a class behind me. My heart trembled when I saw him; I felt very shy. At the height of this romance I would pass him my favorite book of collected verses in which I would mark some not too obvious lines. He would reply in the same manner. Once he carried my books all the way to my house and quickly gave me a kiss on the cheek. I was overwhelmed.

ᛊ

At the end of the school year the administration decided not to give us the final examinations taken by all the school graduates in Harbin. We certainly could not have passed them, since we had not covered the material required. We had our graduation party, for which we were allowed to wear white dresses. The excitement of the event, however, was dampened by the news that the Department of Education had refused to grant us diplomas, on the grounds that we had not taken the final examinations. The boys who planned to apply for admission to the Harbin Polytechnic Institute would first have to pass examinations to get their high school diplomas, and then take the competitive tests in mathematics, physics, and chemistry usually required for entrance. These were the subjects that we did not complete during our compressed school year. Diploma examinations, administered by the Department of Education, would be offered in the fall, and anyone wishing to gain a high school diploma could take them. Several of my girlfriends, including Margarita Sechkina, decided to do so, and began to study.

I had a long discussion with Father about registering for the private courses being offered to those who wished to pursue the diploma. Father did not see any sense in it. He could not imagine my entering the engineering school, which among other things required that students obtain a license for driving a train before graduating, involving a summer's work as a coal stoker on a steam engine. He still hoped eventually to send me abroad, even though he could not afford it just then. We even corresponded with Uncle Sasha about the possibility of my entering Leningrad University. Uncle Sasha was all for it, and even sent me some notes so that I could study "dialectical materialism" for the entrance examination; our relatives decided that I would live there with Aunt Lyubov, Mother's sister. But Father was still reluctant to let me go back to Russia, and we finally decided to postpone the decision for another year, agreeing that I should register for a postgraduate year at my school, which would give me the right to teach in the elementary grades. Secretly, I thought of the boy I liked. He would still be in the school, for he was a year behind me, and we would have a chance to become better acquainted.

The summer of 1926 started quietly, as we relaxed after the strenuous year of study. I began earning a little money by tutoring, and when Father asked me what I planned to do with my earnings, I decided that I should pay for violin lessons for Tanya. Spending the money on my own pleasure seemed shameful to me, yet I wanted to retain control over it. Playing the violin was my own secret dream, which could be partly fulfilled by hearing Tanya do it.

Father was concerned about our foreign language skills. The language lessons at school gave us no experience in speaking. He often helped us with French pronunciation, having us read to him aloud, but he was not so sure of his own English. One day he came home and announced that a young woman would be coming to our home to speak with all of us in English. She turned out to be a very pleasant young Russian, brought up in an English convent in China, but I don't know how much her lessons helped us. She visited once a week for about two hours, and all six of us would gather around her. I was seventeen; Katya was eight and the others in between, so one could not really carry on a single conversation. We learned some songs, we talked, and took our turn saying a few things of interest to all of us, and I suppose it overcame our natural reluctance to express ourselves in a foreign language. I became very fond of her, really my first older friend. After less than a year, however, she left Harbin for Shanghai.

Father's work continued as before, but there was still no news about his citizenship application. There were rumors that several Soviet citizens had been arrested for "communist propaganda"; I did not know any of them and I don't think Father knew them either, so that did not really disturb us. Still, the feeling of being suspected by the Chinese police persisted, and there were more and more Chinese soldiers on the street. We became used to being careful when speaking to others, always bearing in mind their citizenship. Being of age now, I applied for and received a Soviet passport. Going to the USSR for my further education now seemed a real possibility. Margarita Sechkina was studying French and Esperanto, preparing for the diploma examinations, and getting ready to travel to Brussels, where she had been accepted by the University: my dream, fulfilled by her. I still thought that I might join her a year or two later.

ও

In August Father left for an extended business trip and I looked forward to the beginning of school, anticipating with a tremor again seeing my "beloved" of last spring. I had not seen him all summer. The first day arrived and, to my dismay, he paid no attention whatever to me. During recess he walked with another girl, whom

I did not know. I endured this for two days, during which I began to reason that Father would never have enough funds to send me anywhere, and I had better apply at once to the Polytechnic Institute. That was my only choice. I called Margarita Sechkina's father, who was registrar at the Institute, about my decision. He said that it was still not too late to apply, but that I had to take all the exams just like the other students who had been studying all summer for them.

I consulted with Mr. Petrov, my mathematics teacher. My class had not even begun trigonometry, and had not finished the full course of algebra or solid geometry, all of which would be included in the competitive examinations; and the electro-mechanical department, which I hoped to join, required higher grades in these. But even to be admitted to the competition one must have passed the diploma examinations, which were to start in two weeks, with ten or twelve of them in the course of ten days, both written and oral. The competitive exams were offered just one week later, so I had about three weeks to cover all the additional mathematics for the latter, while simultaneously taking the first.

Never in my life, before or after, did I work so hard or sleep so little. Mr. Petrov volunteered to help me. He spent hours teaching me the subjects I had not yet started. When the diploma examinations began, I read and made notes all night, and wrote my papers all day for ten days, trying to squeeze in some study of mathematics. We now learned that we were to be examined according to the program of the old Russian schools, which meant, for example, that one test had questions on old Russian laws regarding the ownership of real estate, which had not been in effect for six years, since the revolution. Political Economy, too, was not at all what had been taught to us in the last two years. The examiners were quite lenient on these points, mercifully, as can be seen from my own experience with Political Economy: I had had no time to read the recommended book, but Margarita had read it thoroughly, and on the day before the exam, in the course of an hour or so, she summarized it for me. I passed with flying colors, getting a better grade than she did.

All through these trying weeks Manya was an enormous help:

she sat with me to keep me company and help me stay awake late into the night. She would bring me tea and sandwiches without my asking for them as I concentrated at the dining room table, strewn with papers and books.

By the first of October it was all over. I had passed all the exams and was admitted to the electro-mechanical department of the Institute. Father returned to find out what I had done. He was amazed and proud of me. I was now a college student.

[1]   Vera Fedorovna Komisarzhevskaya (1864-1910): a great Russian actress.

19

Student Years

While I was completely absorbed by my examinations, more ominous events were occurring in Harbin. In September 1926 the Chinese seized the Russian river fleet and its offices on the river Sungary. A Russian protest had no effect. Then the Chinese took over the education department of the Railroad, claiming that it was used for communist propaganda. Political tension increased, and many Russians, including some of our friends who did not have Soviet passports, began to leave Harbin for various cities in China, mostly Shanghai.

Soon after the diploma examinations Margarita Sechkina left for Belgium, promising, as I did, to write often. I was left without any really close friends. I felt that Harbin was a dead end, and that someday I must escape from it, but this seemed impossible for the time being, and the Polytechnic Institute was my last resort. It was not the sort of institution I would have chosen, but at least it allowed me to continue my education without loss of time. The memory of my unsuccessful romance of last winter still hurt, but I looked forward to making new associations at the Institute.

The lectures began on October first. The solid, gray Institute building, with its high ceilings and large windows, was full of male students, many of them in their uniform jackets – black with golden buttons and green piping for the civil engineering students, and blue piping for our electro-mechanical department. This made it easy to see at once who were one's "colleagues," as we called each other. I envied the boys for their uniforms, though they were not obligatory, and wished I could have one of those jackets. There was only one other girl in my class of sixty, named Yulia Kruglova. In the five years I spent at the Institute I never became intimate with her, though we were always quite friendly, and she often visited our home.

I felt quite comfortable in this almost exclusively male company, and was able to share common academic interests with the boys. The fact that I had passed my exams with good grades and experienced no more difficulty than most of them in following the lectures, solving mathematics problems, and designing and drafting projects put me on a par with them, and they treated me as an equal.

All the lectures were given in Russian except for a one-semester Chinese language course. Chinese students undertook a two-year preparatory course in Russian, mathematics, and mechanical drawing. The program of studies was heavy: twelve courses in the first year, all of them quite technical. All of these were required – we had no electives. We were not provided with textbooks, except for a few in the library, which could not be taken home, so we were dependent on our lecture notes. There were no homework assignments, except for mathematics, in which we had problem-solving sessions.

Attendance at classes was not obligatory, but there were final exams in each course. Students signed up for these whenever they felt prepared. They were oral, and each student was examined individually, being called to a blackboard to write out the required mathematical derivations, or draw sketches and describe them to the examining professor. All the exams took place in our lecture rooms in the presence of any other students who wanted to listen.

The examination periods were at the end of each semester and in the fall, and a student could postpone taking any exam to another period. To graduate, however, a passing grade in all subjects was required, and failing any exam only meant that one had to take it again. As a result, many students took five years or more to complete the four-year program of courses, after which one more year was spent working on a large design project. A diploma in engineering was granted only after the student successfully defended his final design project in public before a committee of Railroad engineers and professors. Each summer, too, had to be spent on assigned work intended to give us "practical experience."

Most of our time, often late into the night, was spent in the library or in the drafting room, working on the detailed drawings for each semester's design project, using India ink and watercolors. These projects had no direct connection to our coursework and had to be defended before a panel of professors. They required a great

Mulya, 1925

Lena in her name-day chair
Harbin, ca. 1926

deal of independent effort, as well as drafting expertise. Drawings were made on large sheets of drawing paper, moistened and glued by the edges to the drafting table, where it dried tight as a drum. After months of work the finished drawings were washed, dried, and then cut off the table, clean and shining. They were supposed to represent the working drawings from which a machinist could produce a finished construct in all its necessary detail. I really enjoyed that part of my schoolwork. In my pocket I always carried a small plastic triangle, a ruler, and even a protractor. One of the other students once told me that looking down from the balcony during an opera performance, he saw my head with such a straight part in my hair that he wondered if I used my ruler to make it.

ଓଃ

In spite of my heavy load of studies I also had to earn some money. I resumed tutoring high school students who had failed mathematics. I was becoming quite experienced at that; my earnings were supposed to cover the cost of my school supplies and, as before, Tanya's violin lessons. With all six of us in school, tuition took a considerable bite out of Father's salary. As if sensing that his time was short, he concentrated on giving the children everything he could to prepare them for life on their own. Our future was unpredictable, at best. Most of all Father tried to keep us close to each other, so we could rely on each other's help. "It is more important to love than to be loved" was his constant refrain.

My sisters were growing up: Lena was now almost fourteen. She had close friends among girls, and even boys, now that the school was coeducational; they visited our house often, enlivening the conversation around the supper table. In the spring, summer, and fall the tennis court in our yard was seldom empty. Lena read constantly, and showed signs of being educated in a Soviet school, learning things (I felt) that I did not know. She read the new literature coming from Russia, learned poems of new poets I had not even heard of. The distinctly Soviet aspect of our school influenced the younger children more than their immediate elders, a process that Father partly accepted as historically inevitable, while at the same time trying to counterbalance its effects.

Seryozha was in his next to last class in school and was definitely bored, and often depressed. He seemed to have few friends, and was resisting the Soviet influence. The rough language of his schoolmates, which he could never repeat at home, upset him very much. Father had always demanded that he behave as a gentleman with his sisters; Seryozha detested fighting, and yet he sometimes fought with his classmates, "defending the honor of his sisters" when he believed that a reference to us was disrespectful. We girls were so completely shielded from bad language that Seryozha once told me that I simply did not know "real" Russian at all. Indeed, when I was already in America I had to buy the *Dictionary of Russian Obscenities* published by Harvard students in Cambridge, in order to learn the meaning of such words.

Seryozha was an excellent student, especially fond of history and romantic literature. Rostand's *Cyrano de Bergerac* was one of his favorites: he knew several of the long monologues by heart, in Russian verse translation. But I felt that his approach to life was unrealistic. We both loved our father, for instance, but with different aspects of his character in mind. While I was most drawn to Father's sensitivity, his liberalism, and his nobility of spirit, Seryozha saw in him a proud aristocrat, a former naval officer, and an affectionate but sternly demanding parent.

I remember once when Father, particularly upset by our fighting, wanted to punish Seryozha and said: "Now, take this book, go to my room and don't come out until you memorize the whole of the first act of *Woe from Wit*" (a verse play by A. S. Griboedov, which all of us had read many times). Seryozha took the book angrily, went to Father's room, and slammed the door. The mood in the house was subdued, for it was not often that we were punished, and two hours later Seryozha was still inside – this was rather a long absence. One more hour passed and we began to wonder whether he planned to stay away forever. In another hour, however, Seryozha triumphantly emerged, handing the book back to Father and announcing: "I memorized all four acts!"

cs

After the novelty of being an Institute student wore off, I began to realize that all I was getting there was training, and not what I thought an intellectually demanding person should have, a true "education." The Institute was going to make me an *engineer,* which to me meant someone concerned only with the technical solution of any problem, not the broader view.

The Law Department met in the evenings in the Institute building, and soon after the beginning of the school year I tried to attend lectures by Professor Ustrialov on the general theory of law. These were famous, for he was a remarkable speaker. I was aroused by his delivery, which was eloquent and full of poetic quotations. But I had no time to do the reading that should have accompanied his lectures, which made me feel inadequate and frustrated, and I soon stopped attending. More and more I sensed that I was falling behind in my overall education.

Appearing on stage still was exhilarating for me, so I joined the drama club where there were students with interests apart from engineering. Among them I tried to find others in my class who regretted, as I did, the absence of the humanities in our program. I began inviting them home, hoping that they could contribute to a kind of seminar in which we would take turns delivering papers on all kinds of untaught subjects – literature, psychology, music, etc. I thought that Lena's younger friends could listen to what we might say, and even participate. For the students from predominately male schools the attraction of a house full of young people, mostly girls, was obvious.

The first "seminar" in our living room took place soon after my first examination session in January 1927. Among the participants I remember were Yura Aingorn, a year ahead of me, who later went to Moscow and perished during the repression years; Vasilii Prianishnikov, who later emigrated to the USA, received a doctorate from the University of Michigan and became a professor at Stanford; Nikolai Oglesnev, who ended up in Germany; Evgenii Shmatov, who eventually returned to the USSR and died in the Soviet Gulag in Kolyma; Konstantin Koltover, who probably also died in the Gulag; Mikhail Bakich, an architecture student, who later emigrated to Australia where he practiced his art; and George Shakuta, a poet and actor, also a year ahead of me at the Institute, who went back to the

USSR and whose fate is unknown. We were joined later by several of
Lena's classmates: Lera Soloviova, Tanya Gustova with her brother
Lev Gustov, a young poet, Lev Barsov, and Tanya Ablova who later
married Mikhail Bakich and emigrated with him to Australia. All of
them except Tanya Ablova eventually ended up in the USSR.[1]

The room was packed to capacity on that first evening as on
many succeeding ones. The given topic was the psychology of
dreams. We finished around the dining table with Manya serving
us tea, jam, and sandwiches, and Father participating in a lively
discussion. Over the years these friends formed a close circle, some
of them visiting us almost daily, and on every weekend. They were
our extended family, warmly accepted by Father and Manya, and for
some of them Father became an important lifetime influence.

☙

Father followed the news from Russia closely: the rise of Stalin to
one-man rule in 1926, his conflict with Trotsky and other members
of the Politburo, the tightening of censorship, the end of the NEP,
the peasant resistance in the autumn of 1927. Appalled by what was
happening, Father hoped that he could keep his children as long as
possible from what they would face should they return to Russia.
In his own time many members of our family had struggled against
a despotic and cruel government, so that opposition was nothing
new for him. But now resistance seemed to be so hopeless that he
dreaded to see his children involved in it.

Indeed Father had received a few job offers in the Soviet Union
from his former colleagues, although I now wonder if they could
have been prompted by the Soviet secret police, in order to test him,
or even lure him back to the USSR. But since he was not yet a Soviet
citizen he did not pursue these invitations. He probably knew that he
could not safely return to Russia at that time. From Leningrad, Uncle
Sasha wrote that he was almost certain that Father's application for
citizenship had already been denied, and that the authorities were
merely waiting for a convenient time to say so.

I don't know exactly what Father did at that time to plan for
the future. I know that he wrote to Charles Crane, describing the
family's progress and mentioning that he would welcome any

prospect of work anywhere on the globe. I am sure he contacted all the prospective employers he could, during his infrequent business trips. There was absolutely nothing he could do in Harbin.

To us, Father seemed old. Even though his enthusiasm was undiminished, his stooped figure seemed more hunched over, and his shortness of breath more acute. We all worried when his flashes of anger, often provoked by some very minor disagreement with Seryozha or myself, would cause him to go to his room and pace the floor, trying to catch his breath. He would always get over it, and eventually would conduct a reasonable conversation with the culprit, but we knew that he had a bad heart. Such episodes were frightening.

One day in April 1927 Father brought home a paper with the startling news that Marshal Chiang Kai-shek had ordered a search of the Soviet Embassy in Peking, and also the offices of the CER. A sense of foreboding hung in the air. During the summer the Soviet government recalled its entire embassy staff from Peking; the USSR consulate in Harbin remained open for the time being, but one could sense the mounting antagonism of the Chinese toward Soviet citizens.

1927

My concern over Seryozha's psychological condition reached the point of alarm. He kept saying that the world was in a terrible state, that every one was wicked, and that nothing at all was worth living for. I argued with him to no avail. I myself often felt discouraged by the lack of opportunities to build a good future, but even in the gloomiest of times I never lost hope that somewhere, somehow, I would find a way to apply my energy constructively. I felt that at present I must prepare myself for such a future as best I could.

I could think of only one solution to Seryozha's problem: he should leave the school in which he was so unhappy. He had only one more year left and could skip it. We all felt that an art school or a good university would be the place for him, but there was no art school in Harbin, and in his present state of mind he was unlikely to pursue anything else. He was not yet old enough to obtain a Soviet passport, and anyway Father thought he was still too young, at seventeen, to be away from the family. The Polytechnic seemed to me the only reasonable alternative, since it was the one institution that gave a legitimate degree, offering the probability of a job. Seryozha was extremely capable in the required disciplines: mathematics, physics, and mechanical drawing presented no problem for him. He could study during the summer, and take both the examinations for the high school diploma and the competitive entrance exams in the fall. Having done this myself with much less preparation, I was sure it would be easy for him. Seryozha readily agreed and set out to prepare by himself. He worked hard that summer, did well in his exams, and was admitted to the electro-mechanical department of the Institute, like me.

In the break between the end of the Institute year and the beginning of the fieldwork assigned to us for the summer, the dramatic club planned a trip to the various stations along the Railroad, where we would stage a play for local audiences at each stop. The Railroad was to assign us a sleeper car, which would serve as our sleeping quarters, and we would perform in the available theater halls. I was excited by the prospect. Father, on the other hand, was cautious. "Will there be chaperons?" he inquired. I did not know, and asked my colleagues. The question amused them: "We are adults! Why should we have chaperons?" Father consulted some women friends, and finally urged me not to go. "I am afraid that it would give you a bad reputation," he said.

I was dismayed. For me to worry about "reputation" was nonsense. I felt that what mattered was what I *was*, not what someone thought of me: it seemed that Father did not trust me enough, and that hurt me. I remembered his saying that I should not close the door to my room when my friends from the Institute visited me, and my objecting – because, after all, how else could I keep the little children away when I wanted to talk with my friends? We were just talking; he should know that I would not behave improperly.

In the end, however, I obeyed, and missed the excursion with my dramatic club. The practical work assigned to me that first summer at the Institute was at geodesic camp, where we took profiles of all kinds of small hills in the open fields near Harbin, drawing them up at home. The final problem was a profile of the bed of a small river, which meant wading into the river up to our necks. We had not been told to bring our swimming suits, and in any case there was no place to change: professionally, we were supposed to be ready to do anything required, without special warning. It was simple for the boys: they took off their shirts, but not their trousers, the presence of just two girls rather cramping their style. We girls, on the other hand, had to prove that we were not intimidated, and walked into the river fully clothed. We felt embarrassed when we had to walk out with our dresses clinging to our bodies, but tried to act as if it was all part of the game.

In the autumn Sergey and I started the new school year together, Sergey much happier than he had been in his old school. Since the Railroad sponsored the Institute, all students were required to be citizens either of the USSR or China. I had my passport already, but Sergey was still too young to have his. He nevertheless came under the Soviet quota because Father had applied for Soviet citizenship, although a long time had passed without either a positive or a negative answer, so refusal seemed increasingly likely. But for the time being Father held his job under the Soviet employees' quota, and each month that he was still working meant that the children could go on attending the Soviet schools.

ଔ

The Institute's Soviet students organized an evening school for Soviet workers, to help them earn high school diplomas, which reduced the number of years of obligatory military service in the USSR. All members of the group active in this school seemed to be communists. I say seemed, as I did not know for sure: membership in the party was kept secret from those outside it. I felt that this group was part of something bigger than our limited Harbin émigré society; their horizons stretched over all the vastness of Russia, while mine were limited to colonial, or foreign, Manchuria. Yet to me they were strangers, in some way that was hard to explain. I wished to be like them, yet I knew that I never could be. My appearance, my manners, and even my accent and my use of our common language, were different from theirs.

I was offered a job, nonetheless, teaching in this evening school, instead of continuing with my tutorials, and I gladly accepted: it paid the same and was much more interesting. Two other members of our home seminar circle taught there – George Shakuta and Evgenii Shmatov – but I was the only female teacher. I taught the workers algebra, geometry, trigonometry, and physical geography.

At the very beginning we were told that we would follow the Soviet program, although we knew that if we ever were asked by the city educational authorities what textbooks we used, we should not admit to the Soviet ones. We carried the old approved texts in our briefcases, even though we never touched them. Being admitted into this conspiratorial atmosphere still did not quite make me a full-fledged member of the group of young teachers, however. I knew that I had so much experience that I could do a better job than almost any other student-teacher, but I was still an outsider. The few times that we gathered socially I felt quite alone, even though everyone was pleasant and polite. Except for the two teaching students who were already often at our house, I never asked my new colleagues home. They just would not have fitted in.

I liked my students: most of them were my age or older, and worked very hard. Their workday at the Railroad ended quite late, and many came to the classes directly from that. Some were so tired that they fell asleep at their desks, so I had to teach in a very lively manner simply to keep them awake. Most started their work at seven in the morning, and with two or three classes each evening, their day ended at nine or ten. And they still had homework to do.

Often after an evening of teaching I would go back to the Institute to do more drawing in the drafting room: by then there were very few students about, and I could work without distractions. If one of my friends was still there, however, our conversations could last beyond midnight. If a boy then offered to accompany me home, I always declined, since I felt I should not require special treatment. But on such lonely late walks I sometimes had to worry about Chinese soldiers. They inevitably would shout out some Russian obscenities, which I did not understand, or even try to touch me in passing. I never saw any more aggressive action than that on their part, but it was still frightening. The Chinese saying seemed true: "One does not use good iron to make nails, and a good man would not become a soldier." I tried to dress and walk like a man, though in those days it was unthinkable for a girl to wear trousers, but I did wear a long, plain coat and a masculine hat with my hair tucked under it. Coming home when everyone was already asleep, I would find my evening meal, prepared by Manya, on the dining table.

There were now noticeably more Chinese soldiers in Harbin. By the end of the school year the political situation in the Zone had become tense indeed. There seemed to be Chinese troop movements on the Railroad toward the Soviet borders, and a few incidents occurred. There was talk of a strike by Soviet employees.

The second summer my class was supposed to work in the Railroad machine shop as mechanics or mechanics' helpers. At this time the shop workers were preparing to strike and it was obvious that the Railroad would wish to use the students as strikebreakers. And if that happened we knew that the Soviet students would be pressured to support the workers by refusing assignments to the machine shop practice. But this did not directly affect me, as I will explain.

Dairen, Summer 1928

For a long time Father had wanted his children to spend a summer at the seashore. He would have liked us to see Japan, but that was much too expensive, so he explored the possibility of sending us to Dairen. The Russians had built Dairen on the Pacific shore of the southern Manchurian peninsula, at the tip of which Port Arthur is located. After the Russo-Japanese war, when the Russians lost Port Arthur and the South Manchurian Railroad, Dairen and the whole area around it became completely Japanese.

The future seemed menacing, the political situation in Harbin was tense, and money was short, but Father decided to wait no longer. Mr. Kono (Kono-san), one of Father's Japanese friends who had moved to Dairen, promised to find a place for us. Father and Manya had a long discussion about the budget. Manya would go with us and keep house; Father would stay in Harbin and continue working, with Nanny cooking for him. I worried about missing my required summer apprenticeship at the machine shop, but Father insisted on my going and I gave in. Perhaps Father also wanted to keep me out of the growing political controversy, and he may even have thought that working as a shop mechanic was not appropriate for a girl.

Father took a short leave from his office and on June 16, 1928 we all boarded a train for the South. Kono-san met us in Dairen and took us to a small Japanese fishing village, where he had rented two rooms for us on the second floor of a Japanese house, close to the sandy shore of a bay filled with moored fishing boats.

An exterior wooden stairway led to a landing in front of the door to our rooms. The landing was used for cooking with a *hibachi,* an arrangement which rather intimidated Manya at first, but she soon mastered it. There was no running water in the rooms: we had to draw it from the well in the yard, where there was also an outdoor toilet. The rooms were separated by a sliding bamboo partition, called a *shoji,* covered with rice paper. The floor was covered with straw matting called *tatami.* The only furniture was a small table on which we could serve food or write, while sitting on the floor. For sleeping we had *futons,* which in the daytime we rolled up and placed along the walls. We were expected not to wear shoes in the house; Japanese straw sandals were usually lined up at the entrance door while we were inside. In short, we were supposed to sample the real Japanese country way of living.

Father could not remain long, but in his short stay he used his Japanese to speak with the landlord and with some local fishermen, arranging the renting of rowboats and gathering information for us about shopping and transportation. He returned to Harbin on June 26, urging us to become acquainted with the village and the city of Dairen, to rest, to learn to swim, to study, to read, not to quarrel, to obey Manya and help her, and above all, to write to him often.

Each of us had a task to accomplish during the summer. I had a program of reading, Sergey wanted to study Japanese and Morse code, Lena was to teach Zoya Russian grammar. Tanya had to practice her violin, and Katya had reading and letter writing to do.

Since we were seven, I made a schedule according to which each of us had one day of the week to write to Father, so that Father would receive a letter from one of us every day. He wrote to us, too, and he saved our letters, all forty-eight of them, but sadly we saved none of his.

It did not take long for us to meet some other vacationing Harbinians whom we knew. Kono-san visited us often, and a Chinese friend took us on a train to Port Arthur, where we visited the museum commemorating the Russian-Japanese war and ate the best Chinese dinner I had ever had.

We tried to share all our experiences with Father, whom we very much missed. Lena wrote in one of her letters that "Sergey and Tanya are studying Morse code and Japanese language, Sergey also lectures us on the effect of ultra-violet light. ... Mulya is dismayed that she forever must explain things to us: to one, that one must not sing the International, to another that one must not write when there is not enough light, to the third that one must not eat condensed milk, to the fourth that one must not tease Katya, to the fifth that one must not eat a lot of bananas when one has stomach trouble, and so forth." Apparently I took my responsibility for the younger children very seriously.

One day Manya and I went to the bathhouse, looking forward to washing the salt of the sea-air from our bodies, and out of our hair. We took a bus to the village and easily found it, a long one-floor structure with a receptionist at the entrance, to whom we paid our fee. My Japanese was just good enough to ask the price. We were conducted into a large room with a pool in the middle, where a number of naked Japanese women soaped and washed themselves, using small buckets to scoop the water from the pool, into which they then waded to rinse. The room was separated by a flimsy partition from a similar men's room.

Manya was appalled. She did not want to take off her clothes in front of such strangers. She said to me, "There must be private rooms here with bathing facilities. Go, ask the receptionist!" I had with me a small phrase dictionary with Japanese phrases spelled in Russian letters. There was no phrase for "private bathing." I tried to find something else. "One room?" No response. "Alone?" Blank look. "Not many people, two only?" Suddenly, recognition on the bewildered face. "Come, come!" in Japanese. I followed her down a long corridor with closed doors on both sides. Finally she opened a door to a small room with a bed shelf, on which a Japanese man was reclining; a smoking device stood next to him, and he held the tube in his mouth. The receptionist spoke to him in rapid Japanese. I asked him "*Wakarimasu-ka ruski?*" thinking that he might be able to translate my request, but at this point the receptionist left the room, closing the door behind her. Terrified, I seized the door handle to reopen it, while she held it shut. I managed to prise it open enough to squeeze out, and ran down the corridor into the arms of Manya, who was waiting anxiously. We settled for the common bathing – we needed it badly!

The summer passed with swimming, hikes, and meeting new Russian friends, all described in minute detail in our letters to Father. Kono-san took Sergey to a small Japanese temple and Sergey wrote:

> Beyond the milk farm we found a lovely Japanese temple. It is especially wonderful to go there during twilight. A zigzagging path, little bridges, some tori [traditional Japanese gateways] among the trees, the mountains on the near horizon, pine woods. We went there with Kono-san. He clapped his hands and prayed that all of us would be well and happy. I could not imagine before that such a beautiful place could also have a religious meaning besides its aesthetic qualities.

We really did have a taste of Japan, although my holiday was less enjoyable that Sergey's or the girls', because I was worrying about the approaching fall session of exams, and about missing the summer practice and work on the current design project. I missed my friends and did not make any new ones. What I remember best was a rowboat ride alone on a clear dark night over the fluorescent sea. Every splash of water looked like fireworks, and the oars of my boat moving through the water seemed like torches with glowing traces following them. The dark cliffs of the shore were outlined against a sky swarming with brilliant stars. The natural beauty filled me with a wonderful sense of peace that I never had experienced before.

Another scene remains with me: I am standing at the edge of a cliff high above the churning waters of the bay in the aftermath of a typhoon. The sky is deep blue, the wind has already died down, but the spray of the waves crashing against the vertical walls of the cliffs covers my dress and everything around me, displaying the power and fury of nature. The day before the whole village had been in a panic over the fishing vessels that had gone to sea in the previous week, and the whipping rain and the roar of the boiling sea with its towering waves had kept us always indoors. And now I am able to stand at the top of this cliff and take it all in – but while I am out of danger today, I can see that even the spent rage of the sea is an overwhelming force.

1928 - 1929

In August 1928 there were rumbles of distant troubles, in a part of Outer Mongolia east of Manchuria. Mongolian troops occupied some stations on the CER, and although the Chinese Railroad Guards soon forced them to withdraw, Chinese concern about activities on their borders, and by extension Soviet meddling in the internal policy of China, increased yet again.

Yet the school year started more or less uneventfully. I was busier than ever with teaching in the evening workers' school, and with my own design projects. My term project was to design a boiler that used powdered coal, and one day, while reading the *General Electric Review* in search of information about powdered coal furnaces, I stumbled on an article about research in progress at the Massachusetts Institute of Technology. I knew nothing of any university in the United States, but this one sounded exciting. A lot of research seemed to be done there, with some wonderful facilities for it. I hoped that some day I might work at a place like that.

For me this was a period of intense self-searching, a quest for "identity"; I was sorting out my feelings and aspirations, and despairing about my ability to control them, alternating between periods of energetic activity and boundless depression. My notebooks contain my own poems, and copies of others, extolling heroism, dedication to great ideals, and the search for true love.

As to the last, by the spring of 1929 I was in love – with a member of our group, Kostya Koltover, who was suffering from similar turmoil, and apparently in need of some kind of support. We talked or walked on the darkened streets, not even holding hands, but finding solace in each other's company. But Kostya then fell in love, not with me, but with Lena, and I was heartbroken. To add pain to injury, Father was displeased with the obvious flirtation between Lena and Kostya, whom I had brought to the house, and blamed me for "passing him on" to my younger sister. I was supposed to do something about it, but how could I? Father told Lena that if she wanted to marry Kostya and "wash his socks" then she should do so, or else stop flirting with him. Lena cried all night, thinking Father a brute, but by morning she felt that she did not want to see Kostya any more and told him so. We had very little contact with him after that. This was the second time that I had been rejected by a boy, and my confidence in my own attractiveness plummeted.

I derived a little solace, however, from the attention of another friend, Yura Aingorn. Yura was a small, dark-haired, gentle and sensitive boy with beautiful brown eyes and a rather sad face. He was one year ahead of me at the Institute and considered one of the brightest students in his class; the only son of a doctor, who had died some years before, he lived with his mother. He read a great deal outside of the required technical literature, and loved music and poetry, but he was lonely at home and enjoyed the busy family life of our house. He played the cello, which he brought along with him. As the months passed he told me that he was in love with me and wanted to marry me, but I was not yet ready for this: there was still much too much to accomplish before I could think of marriage, and even the idea of it alarmed me. I enjoyed his company, however, and welcomed his moral support. I did not exclude the possibility that someday I might marry him.

The workers' school held its first graduation. The students were given certificates that would be recognized in the USSR, as most of them planned to go there. We had a goodbye party, as much for the teachers as for the graduating students, since it had been decided that the school could not go on operating in the unsettled political environment.

∞

On May 27, 1929 we were shocked by the news that the Chinese police had raided the Soviet Consulate in Harbin and seized a number of documents that were apparently being burned at the time of the raid. The Chinese insisted that they had proof of a planned communist revolt in China. On June 1 the Soviets recalled their diplomats from Harbin, and on July 10 the Chinese arrested several of the CER administrators and effectively took over control of the Railroad.

On July 16 the Chinese rejected an ultimatum by the USSR, and the Soviets severed their relations with China. Russian and Chinese armies were massing on the border; news of military clashes and the bombarding of border towns was reaching us in Harbin. The Soviet Army occupied some railroad stations near the border, and from the White Russian Guards who still remained in the Zone a regiment was organized, which clashed with the Soviet troops. Since Chinese war equipment was being moved on the Railroad, the Soviets urged Soviet employees of the Railroad to strike, and threatened them with loss of their citizenship if they refused to do so. The strike was supposed to include teachers and students as well, and the Chinese police reacted by arresting some strikers, who were sent to a prison camp on the other side of the river, where living conditions were said to be unbearable.

Father now had another decision to make: to strike or not to strike. Knowing that his application for a Soviet passport had probably already been rejected, he decided against joining the call. No one could tell how long this situation might last, but if he continued to work, the children would at least have a few more months of schooling. For the time being some teachers continued to teach, and the schools tried to maintain their programs with only minor modifications.

I had a Soviet passport. My examination session was over and the summer apprenticeship lay just ahead. Working on the Railroad would be equivalent to strike-breaking. How could a Soviet citizen help Russia's enemies transport their war equipment and troops? I could not do this. Father argued with me, but in his own liberal pro-labor way he accepted my position, even though it was strange to find himself and his daughter on different sides of a political fence.

The fall examination session at the Institute arrived, and the Soviet students, naturally, did not sign up for any. Some of the professors did not offer to examine us, while others, who were Chinese citizens, did. Sergey had no problems: he took his exams and Father was satisfied, but I felt I could not. After a vigorous argument with Father I stood firm and took none. Father was distraught. He was afraid that I might be arrested by the Chinese and sent to a prison camp. I did not think that could happen. Our arguments were emotional and painful. I did not want to upset my father; I worried about his heart. Walking alone on the streets of Harbin I mulled over my position until late into the night.

I was sure that I was right for the time being at least, but the near future was more difficult: Father was certain to lose his position on the Railroad. What then? What possible job could he find in Harbin? Or anywhere else? He was old, I thought, and ill, and I had no confidence in his being able to begin a new occupation. We would surely have to leave our house, which belonged to the Railroad and was a part of Father's salary, and where could we go, all nine of us? Even while Father was employed we had had a hard time paying for the summer in Dairen, where we lived in a small summer shack.

I knew that Father would receive as severance pay all his pension fund, in a lump sum, but that would not be very much – at most it might pay for the rental of an apartment for a couple of years. The children would still be quite small then, and Father even older. What then? I realized that I was the only one old enough to get a job, but I knew that my earnings would do no more than help the family survive. And there would be no way out for years, until the young children grew up, and I would then be too old to build a career or get married. The prospect was grim, and I struggled to think of some alternative.

Gradually I decided that the only solution would be to spend Father's pension fund at once, before any of it was used up on rent, on building our own house. We would then at least have a roof over our heads, and everything else could be managed somehow, or so I hoped. The idea took hold of me, and from then on during my walks I would imagine the plan of the house, and how we should all live in it. Such thoughts calmed my anxiety, so that I could concentrate on my tutoring work and on reading and preparing for the beginning of the term. I said nothing to anyone else about my house plans.

At the beginning of the new term all of the Soviet students were instructed by members of the communist party to attend the first lecture. After our professor entered the auditorium we were all supposed to rise, at which time our student leader would announce that because of the present situation in Harbin we could not participate in our normal studies. We would then all march out of the auditorium.

When Father heard about these plans he was adamant. He knew that such a protest would give me an unfavorable record with the Chinese police, and that any further relations with the local authorities would be permanently affected. He also pointed out that now was hardly the best time to interrupt my studies and delay my degree, since this was my last year of classes, and in a short time the family might desperately depend upon my having graduated.

I gave in. I promised not to participate in the Soviet students' demonstration, simply by missing the first day. On the second day, when there were no Soviets left, I went in to attend lectures, and continued my studies for the rest of the year, conscious of the fact that as far as my Soviet colleagues were concerned, I was a traitor.

The struggle over the CER attracted international attention, but in spite of everything our own family life went on as before, little changed by these events. The future, however, seemed more uncertain than ever. Father insisted that his other daughters must stay in school. Lena, who was in her next to last year at school, attended somewhat reluctantly, but she never dug in her heels against Father. She began to teach privately a group of children whose parents were on strike, and who did not go to school. Tanya became fascinated with sports. She was good at all of them, and they offered her the best escape from political worry. Zoya and Katya were still too young to be concerned with such matters.

The USSR and China finally reached a new agreement over the Zone and the CER in late December 1929, essentially preserving the previous arrangements with a few concessions to the USSR, among them the removal of the White Russian Guards from the territory. A final conference was planned for May.

೫

In February 1930 Father received the official rejection of his application for a Soviet passport, as he had long expected. It would now be only a matter of weeks before he was sacked by the CER. Late one afternoon in March, when I came home from the Institute, I found the whole family around the dining table in a subdued mood. As I sat down, Manya explained to me, "Father was given notice at his job today!"

I looked around at the gloomy faces; no one else said a word. But I had already thought it all through, and I had found a solution. I now had to cheer them all up.

"Then we shall build our own house!" I exclaimed.

"What?!" Father, Manya, Sergey, Lena, all seemed shocked and indignant. "How can you be so flippant? What a thoughtless remark!"

I tried to be logical. I said that I had thought about it for a long time, and felt that this was the only solution that would give us any sense of security. "There are so many of us," I said. "Where could we live? If we don't need to worry about where to live, we can always earn enough to eat, we remember that from Omsk!"

Manya seemed thoughtful. Father said he would think it over. "Let us not discuss it any more. It is time to do your lessons, or whatever each one must do." Father rose, walked to his room, and closed the door. Manya went to the kitchen and Nanny resumed her knitting. Lena and Sergey were angry. They told me that I was always too sure of myself, and too bossy. I had to return to the Institute, so Manya gave me a quick supper and I left.

¹   Georgii Mikhailovich Aingorn (1907-38): moved to the USSR, worked as an engineer in Moscow. Arrested and shot in 1938.

Evgenii Lukich Shmatov (1906-38): married Lera Soloviova, moved to the USSR; arrested, died in the camps.

Kaleria (Lera) Anatolievna Soloviova (1912-2000): married Evgenii Shmatov. Moved to the USSR, arrested, spent eight years in the camps. After her release she graduated from the Medical Institute in Arkhangelsk and worked as a doctor in Ukhta, Russia.

Lev Dmitrievich Gustov: moved to Shanghai, worked as an engineer and college professor. In 1947 he moved to the USSR; he worked as an engineer in Sverdlovsk and designed several power stations.

Tatiana Dmitrievna Gustova (1913-95): moved to Shanghai with her parents and brother. In 1947 she moved to the USSR where she worked as a teacher of Russian and English.

The fate of Konstantin Koltover, George Shakuta, and Lev Barsov is unknown. (The above information received from Margarita Shkarlat, Ukhta, Russia, a daughter of my classmate. She collected much data about the fate of Russian repatriates from Harbin, most of whom died in Soviet prison camps.)

20

The House

I still believed I was right. I knew the family had no other way to proceed, so they would inevitably come to the same conclusion. But I realized that the way I had presented my idea was rather tactless, since I had never discussed it with anyone before.

Father spent some time finding out about his pension fund. It would be a considerable sum after all, but it was unclear when it would be paid, for all the financial arrangements of the CER had to be settled at a meeting in Moscow. The meeting was planned for May, although no one really knew when it would actually take place. For two months or so we could stay in our present house.

All the Soviet citizens arrested by the Chinese were released, and the strikers went back to their positions. The schools resumed their pre-conflict state, the striking teachers and students returned. In the Railroad Commercial School the Soviet flavor was restored, stronger than ever. Those who had not gone on strike knew how they were regarded.

Still, life went on. Several days after my abrupt proposal Father talked with me about it. He agreed that it was a possibility; the trouble was that we had no reserves, no more salary, and the disbursement of the pension fund was held up. What to do? We could live on credit for a while, but we could not move away: Father had to stay put to do what he could about getting some advance on his pension fund. Anyway, we must at least look for a piece of land.

In two weeks we found one, out in the suburbs. Land in Harbin was almost never for sale, but we could purchase a long-term lease, which was just as good for our purposes. A street leading there was marked on the city plan, but in reality it was just an unpaved track across an open field, with no other houses near our plot. There was no electric transmission line in the immediate vicinity, and it was clear that we would have to pay for one or two poles to bring power to our house.

We began to work on the plan of the house, Father seeing to it that everyone was involved. Each member of the family had his or her wishes: we all agreed that there should be separate rooms for Father, Sergey, and me, and I insisted that Nanny have a room of her own, for she habitually used strong-smelling ointments that permeated the air, which I thought was bad for the children. I also wanted a place for theatrical performances, which would require two rooms to be joined by a large sliding door. Sergey called for the house to be well-insulated for heating efficiency, and to be cube shaped, to provide maximum interior space for the surface of the exterior walls. Father pointed out that two stories would give us twice as much floor space for one foundation and one roof. "We must have space in the yard to have some chickens and maybe a pig," Manya added, "and we can get vegetables from the Chinese farmer who has a garden and lives in a dug-out nearby."

We could hire a Chinese contractor who would wait to be paid for the work until the CER administration released Father's pension. However, no one would let us have construction materials on credit. So Father had an idea: we could try the Railroad's own stockyards, charging the cost of whatever we took against the forthcoming pension. He made inquiries and found that the stockyards had bricks, with which we could lay the foundation, and logs used for making railroad ties or telegraph poles. We decided that we could have the logs cut by hand into lumber at the building site. Our budget was drawn up, and the decision was made: we would build a house! Father said it would be my project and that I would be the supervisor. I was properly awed and proud, and took my responsibility quite earnestly. Of course I knew that Father would always be there to advise and approve.

I had to postpone some of my examinations again, but they could easily be made up in the fall. In the meantime I needed to find some more tutoring work, for my earnings had now become an important part of our family income. So I applied for the position of mathematics teacher at the Railroad Commercial School in the summer session, which was organized for students who had failed subjects during the year. There were an unusual number of failures at that time, because so many students had missed part of the year while their parents were on strike. It would be a marvelous opportunity for me, and I was a qualified candidate.

I had a good interview with the head of the school, but received no response for some time. One of my friends at the Institute told me that some of my Soviet colleagues had protested my appointment on the grounds that I had not participated in the strike. This was discouraging, and I began to realize that I might have trouble finding jobs in the future.

One day early in June we had a heavy downpour, typical of Manchurian summers. At about nine in the morning a messenger came to our house from the school: would I come right away and start teaching at ten? I had no raincoat, and no umbrella, but I put on my best white dress and set off right away. By the time I arrived my hair was soaked, and my wet dress clung to my body – I was a ridiculous sight, hardly the authority figure of a teacher. I entered a class of unruly students, many of whom were taller and larger than I, and began. Some students were disrespectful, but I dispatched them immediately to the principal of the school, after which I had no trouble at all, for the rest of the summer. The material was so familiar to me, I could teach it (I thought) blindfolded, and I was sure of my ability to make it clear even to the slowest of listeners.

At home the house project absorbed everyone. Once the draft plan was completed and agreed to by all, we gave it to our friend Mikhail Bakich to make a drawing of the exterior. Mikhail, a future architect, was now a third year student in the civil engineering department of my Institute, and this was his first design to be actually built. It was essential that the house be finished before winter set in. No construction could be done in the coldest months, and if we were to rent an apartment for that period we would not have enough money left to proceed. The spring air was still quite cold when the first materials were brought to the lot. Nanny insisted on blessing the spot by sprinkling holy water on it. We all gathered for the occasion.

The work started. The foundation had to be laid deep, because the frost line in Harbin is very low. The ditch for the foundation was dug by hand. When the first bricks were ready to be laid, we were all present again: Father placed a gold coin under the first, and then each of us was allowed to place down one brick apiece, as the mason spread the cement.

The house was to have outside and inside walls built of wood. For insulation between the two we would use dust from the sawing of logs at the site. For fire retardation the sawdust was mixed with a good deal of railroad slag, which we obtained free. Provisions were made for adding fill after the insulation had settled. The house would be plastered both outside and inside.

࿇

At home the atmosphere was one of imminent departure. The flowerbeds were abandoned, although the tennis court was still an attraction for our friends. To help the family finances Lena began tutoring in Russian grammar and in beginning English, and Sergey too tried to give lessons. He was never as successful at this as Lena and I were, but he was able to earn some money by making mechanical drawings for his classmates. Tanya spent most of her time, when she could, at the Yacht Club on the river, while Manya, Zoya, and Katya stayed for part of the summer in Maoershan, a station in the mountains along the CER. Father thought that necessary for the two younger sisters: Katya was too small for her age, and Zoya had always had a hint of lung trouble.

Father typed out innumerable letters seeking some kind of work. Among those he wrote at the end of August was one in English to Charles R. Crane:

Dear Mr. Crane,

Some years ago I had the honor to be introduced to you in the home of my friends General and Mrs. Khorvat in Peking. At that time you planned to journey through Russia and promised to see my family in Omsk. You saw my children in June 1921, shortly after the tragic death of my wife. The assistance you gave proved greatly helpful to bring my children to me in Harbin one year later.

Since then, aiming at the best possible Russian education for my children, I severed my connection with Babcock & Wilcox, Ltd., and joined the Chinese Eastern Railroad in

Harbin. I worked with the Railroad until this month when I was dismissed for the reason that Moscow refused my application for USSR citizenship, made in 1925.

I am now confronting the difficult matter of looking for another business, and take the liberty to remind you of myself. I shall be deeply grateful if you will bear in mind my circumstances and qualifications in case you or your friends should have any commission to entrust to a reliable person in the Far East. I would be ready to devote myself entirely to any work of a commercial or technical nature giving me the minimum possibility of keeping up my family, and am ready for this to leave Harbin for any place on the globe. I would also accept any other position in Harbin that with a small emolument would let me have leisure for additional earnings. …

I enclose the photograph made by yourself in Omsk and another to show the progress the children have made: the eldest daughter 22 years old, and the son, 20 years old, are on the eve of their engineering diploma and both would be glad to work in America. The little girl has reached her eleventh year. …

I want to thank you once more for the assistance you kindly gave to my family, and would be happy to hear from you or your friends on any prospect that would better my fate.

On October 8 Father received an answer (dated September 30) from D. M. Brodie, Mr. Crane's personal assistant, telling him that Crane was just now en route to Peking, where Father's letter had been forwarded. Father immediately sent off another copy of it, through the American consul in Tientsin, but on the very next day, October 9, he received a most exciting telegram from Mr. Crane himself:

SENDING FIVE HUNDRED DOLLARS. HOPE ELDEST DAUGHTER AND SON CAN VISIT ME AT YENCHING UNIVERSITY SOON PEIPING. FAMILY GREETINGS

This was followed a day later by a letter:

Dear Mr. Zaroodny

It is very good to have a message from you and the children – I wish that I might see them, but I fear that Harbin is too far off my route – I enclose you a check for their education and wish that I might hear from them now and then. If it would be possible for your eldest daughter, or for her and her brother to come to see me at Peiping, I should be happy to arrange the journey. … I hope to be in Peiping about ten days.

Father telegraphed back:

I THANK YOU. HAPPY SENDING DAUGHTER AND SON, VISIT YOU NEXT WEEK. ZAROODNY

A Trip to Peking

It was not easy to arrange our trip to Peking on short notice. In order to receive a visa for China, travelers needed a recommendation as being reliable people, not criminals, and not disseminators of communist propaganda. The Chinese authorities were lukewarm about citizens of the Soviet Union, which I of course was, so Father found someone at the British Far Eastern Company to provide that assurance. And Manya worried about our clothing – we must not appear shabby before Mr. Crane and the Khorvats, with whom we would stay.

It was already mid-October and cold weather was setting in. We needed to buy roofing material for the house, which we could not obtain from the Railroad stockyards. Without the roof we could not finish the house before winter set in, and our available funds were exhausted, so it was tempting indeed to use Mr. Crane's money toward that. We decided not to buy first class tickets to Peking. Sergey and I would travel third class and we would use the balance for the roof. The decision was somewhat risky, for no Europeans traveled third class in China.

All this had to be considered, arranged, and completed in a week. Manya bought some fabric, and got a dressmaker to come sew a dress for me. Meanwhile, I tried to make the many urgent decisions about the house construction, such as where to find sheet metal roofing, and how much we needed. Sergey helped with the calculations. Father dashed about getting the tickets, the recommendations, and the visas.

On October 14 the whole family saw us off at Harbin railroad station. The third class cars were full of Chinese workers, their families, children, and even animals. Our car was dirty and smelly, with hard wooden seats, and no place to sleep. We knew that we must be very careful with our baggage and our money. No one else spoke Russian, and any communication we tried had to be in sign language.

The next morning we were exhausted, after trying to sleep sitting up on hard benches, squeezed between other passengers with whom we could not exchange a word. We got off the train at Mukden, in the hope of seeing the Ming Dynasty burial grounds before boarding the next train to Peking, as Father had told us that it would be a shame to miss them. Using a mixture of signs, Russian, and English, we managed to find a tourist bus to the historical tombs.

After eight years of living in Chinese Manchuria, we saw old Chinese architecture for the first time: solid red brick structures, with several layers of tiled roofs. Smaller buildings surrounded the burial area, which was paved with large square stones with long straight courses of different, smaller, stones. Dry leaves rustled on the ground, blown about by a gentle wind. It gave us a glimpse into the Chinese past, and a sense of her ancient grandeur, stretching much farther back than the history of our own country. Tall pine trees surrounded the buildings, shedding their needles and cones on the calm emptiness of the cemetery. There were no grave markers and no individual monuments, except for the occasional statue. A few Chinese walked quietly among the buildings, led by a Chinese guide, but since we could not understand him, we walked alone.

It was hard to break away from this, but we had to catch the next train to Peking. The return bus was nowhere in sight and there were no taxis, so Sergey and I hired rickshaws, in which I had never ridden before. It was a strange feeling to sit on the rather comfortable seat of the carriage and be pulled by another human being: I was afraid to relax in my chair, somehow trying to make myself lighter, while all the way I watched the sweating back of the lanky rickshaw driver, feeling guilty.

When we arrived at the station, I climbed down with a great feeling of relief. I knew just enough Chinese to ask how much we owed, and paid the man exactly what he asked. The response was indignation. The driver spoke in rapid Chinese, gesturing more and more excitedly, and before long the other drivers standing nearby began to shout too. We were surrounded by a loud threatening crowd and could not understand what they wanted of us – I tried to offer a little more money, but this only increased their anger. We moved toward the station building where we had left our luggage, but the crowd blocked our path. We were both now quite frightened, when fortunately a Chinese policeman saw our plight and approached. In a mixture of Russian and the few words of Chinese I knew, I tried to explain what had happened. He understood, and quickly ordered the crowd to disperse, explaining to us what the trouble was: we should have bargained with the rickshaw driver about the price! By then our train was already approaching the station and we barely had time to collect our luggage and board it.

ଓଃ

We arrived in Peking so late at night that we were afraid to disturb the Khorvats and decided to go for one night to a hotel. We did not of course know of any such place in Peking, so we asked the rickshaw driver simply for a European hotel. He took us to a fine building on a very quiet square. At night we could not see its surroundings, but when we entered we realized that it must be very expensive. We had never stayed at, or even visited any hotel at all, and the luxury of this one – with a doorman, an opulent lobby, and uniformed attendants – intimidated us completely. The desk clerk looked quizzically at us, considering our appearance and our youth, but handed the valet the key to our room and asked us to follow him there. Our bags were so light we did not think we needed any help with them. We certainly knew nothing about tipping.

The luxurious room with two enormous beds, huge windows, high ceilings, and private bath made us feel even more sheepish and guilty for spending so much. But we each had a pleasant bath and a wonderfully sound sleep after the dirty ride and the upright night on the train from Harbin. I remember waking in the morning and looking out the window at the beautiful square, and being amazed by the quiet, gentle traffic of the rubber-tired rickshaws, drawn over the smooth asphalt by running men with soft shoes on their feet. At the earliest acceptable time of day we took rickshaws to the Khorvats' home.

The Chinese Government had allowed General Khorvat the use of the old Austrian Embassy's unoccupied residence. That huge structure was surrounded by a park which had been neglected for years, as maintaining it was certainly beyond the occupants' means, and at the time we arrived the General and his wife occupied only a small part of the house.

Camilla Albertovna (as we called Mrs. Khorvat in formal Russian style) welcomed us warmly, and chided us for not coming to them at once. She led us to a comfortably furnished living room to meet the General, of whom I had heard so much. He greeted us graciously. His appearance was imposing: a tall, rather heavy-set man, with a long gray beard that reached half-way down his chest. He wore a military-style coat without any medals, but there was an aura of obvious importance about him, and I was deeply impressed. We answered all their questions about our family and school, and then sat down to a tasty lunch, prepared by their French-speaking Chinese servant.

Camilla Albertovna called Mr. Crane to tell him of our arrival and in the afternoon we went to his hotel to meet him. He did not seem to me very different from nine years before, when he had appeared at our lodgings in Omsk so unexpectedly. A rather stout man with gray hair, a small goatee, and kind eyes, he met us with a warm smile that put me immediately at ease. Sergey was extremely respectful and formal. I tried to carry on a conversation in my halting English, talking about my sisters, my studies, and Father, and Mr. Crane's compassionate interest in everything won my heart. In spite of my difficulty in expressing what I wanted to say, I felt that he really cared. As I struggled, I promised myself to work hard to improve my English. Mr. Crane said that he wanted to see us again and show us the city, and we left him, agreeing to meet the next day.

In the evening, while the General talked with Sergey, Camilla Albertovna took me around the great house to show me the reception rooms. The entire building was too expensive for them to maintain, so they heated only the three rooms that they used, with their one servant, a combination cook, butler, and housekeeper. The General received very little if any pay from the Chinese government for his consultancy. Camilla Albertovna made designs for a Chinese rug manufacturer, but kept quiet about this, as she thought it should not be generally known that she needed the money.

She told me about a large reception for some important persons that she had had to give one day in Peking. Under her direction, her skillful cook-butler managed to prepare a great variety of appetizing foods from the one butchered calf she had bought. She told me how she made her own dress for the reception and, with no time to finish it, wore it basted in places that did not show. This tour of the mansion, her talk about financial problems and practical difficulties, made me feel quite at ease with her. I admired her dignified bearing, her classical beauty, and not least her resourcefulness.

The following day Mr. Crane collected us in a chauffeured car and took us to the Temple of Heaven. On our way he told us that it was the sight he most admired in Peking. Leaving the car and approaching the first building of the compound, I could not understand at first what was so beautiful about it. The buildings stood directly behind one another, lined up so precisely that through the archway of one you saw the arch of the next one, and then the next one. But their rather plain tiled roofs became more elaborate as we walked on, and finally we saw the temple itself. I gasped. I had never seen anything more simple and more beautiful. The round building with its blue-tiled conical roof, crowned by a simple golden sphere, stood on a pedestal of concentric circular terraces, each surrounded with lacy white banisters. Where the banisters were interrupted, the terraces formed stairs. I could not imagine a more perfect representation of heaven than this, but finally, beyond all

Charles R. Crane
Peking, 1930

the arches was the ultimate image of heaven's temple – the same concentric terraces, but without anything built upon them: the sky itself was the roof. It was the first time in my life that I understood that architecture could express an idea, and from then on I looked with different eyes on such creations.

On the walk out I took a photograph of Mr. Crane. As I look back at the overwhelming impression that the Temple of Heaven made on me, I realize how important was my empathy with this kindly man who showed me it. Years later I realized that when looking at something together with a person close or dear to me, I would see it through his or her eyes. Things that might move me if I were alone might not at all if my companion were unimpressed, and the opposite could also be true.

Back at his hotel Mr. Crane asked me if I would like to go to the United States to study. I was genuinely startled: I did not expect such an offer. Of course I had secretly hoped that he would do something for Father or for the family as a whole, but he had singled me out! The memory of the article I had read in the *General Electric Review,* about research at the Massachusetts Institute of Technology, flashed through my mind. Did this offer mean that I could go there and be in the place where "science grows"? For so long a time I had hoped to go somewhere with a real future in prospect, but now the situation was changed: how could I leave my family at so critical a time? I was the only member of the family who might hope to find work at this moment. And another problem concerned Sergey: his frequent quarrels with Father disturbed all the family, while his capacity for earning seemed uncertain, since he usually refused to adjust to conditions he disliked.

After a few moments of stunned silence, I told Mr. Crane that it would be more important for Sergey to have the opportunity to go to America. Mr. Crane seemed surprised, but at once he suggested that both of us go together. I thanked him, but said that I myself could not give him an answer before I consulted with Father, and in any case both Sergey and I had one more year to complete at the Polytechnic. We left it at that, I promising to write to him with my decision as soon as I had discussed it with Father.

When I told Camilla Albertovna about Mr. Crane's offer, which I somehow could not quite believe, she assured me that, coming from him, it must be taken seriously, and that this was a remarkable opportunity. I was still in doubt, though, and worried about my responsibility to the rest of the family.

Mr. Crane's assistant showed us many beautiful sights in Peking the next day, but nothing seemed to me as beautiful as the Temple of Heaven – or perhaps I was too agitated by Mr. Crane's proposal to appreciate them. I was anxious to return to Harbin and talk with Father. Besides, I was waiting for a reply to my application for work as a controller on the Railroad, and was afraid of being late if they wanted me to start right away. Two or three days later we left Peking.

21

The Last Year in Harbin

The family was already settled in the new house when Sergey and I returned to Harbin on October 20, 1930. The newly plastered walls were still damp and their strong smell was everywhere. On the ground floor, the large dining room was the center of the house. It was connected by a wide arch with sliding doors to the fireplaced living room, which also served as Lena and Tanya's bedroom. If ever the living room were used as a stage, it was equipped with a convenient small side door, leading to a tiny hallway off which lay the bathroom, the kitchen, and the room shared by Manya, Zoya, and Katya. On the opposite side of the dining room, doors led to Father's room and to the front hall, with the stairs to the second floor. Sergey and I each had a room of our own there, and Nanny had a small bedroom off the stairs.

Manya and Father and our sisters showed us all that had been added to the household while we were away, including a large piglet, several hens and a handsome rooster, and a new dog – a big shaggy mongrel called Pirate, with a dog house of his own in the yard. Manya prepared a wonderful meal, and as the whole family sat around the dining-room table we made our report. Sergey gave a sparkling and detailed description of Mukden, Peking, General Khorvat, and Mr. Crane. Finally I explained Mr. Crane's offer, and as I had expected, everyone was excited and happy for us, especially for Sergey, but at the same time concerned. If it went through, the family would be divided for the first time, and quite naturally we all understood that my earnings were important to the family budget. I don't think, however, that Father ever doubted that we should accept. Even though his own unsuccessful efforts to find work were frustrating and worrisome, he was sure that Sergey and I would be able to help the family from America after we had completed our education there. But it was too early to make any final decisions, as it would be at least a year before we two could depart, and much could happen in that interval.

I was still waiting for an answer to my job application, but two days later I learned that I had been turned down for work on the Railroad. It was unlikely that I could find any other work in Harbin or elsewhere in China, with my Soviet citizenship and passport. Going to Russia would not only separate me forever from the family but would give me no chance to help them. Some of our friends were trying to emigrate to Japan, New Zealand, Australia, or South America, for obtaining a regular visa to the United States, especially for a Soviet citizen, was next to impossible. An application for such a visa had been made on Yura Aingorn's behalf when he was a child and there was still no real hope that he would receive one. Going anywhere for any one of us would cost money we did not possess. And with all these dead ends in prospect, I had Mr. Crane's offer!

Both Father and I wrote to him in Peking that Sergey and I would be happy to accept, and go to the USA. Our letters enumerated the hopes and plans of the other sisters. Sergey tried to write one of his own, but gave it up, instead adding a postscript to mine: "I have nothing to add to my sister's letter but my happiness and great thanks. Sergey Zaroodny." Yet I still have a draft of what Sergey wrote and did not send to Mr. Crane. After listing all the work he had to complete at the Institute he wrote, in Russian:

> The most brilliant thing that I can visualize for myself, of course, would be to go to America. ... Like all Russians now, my plans for the future are very much complicated by the political situation, so painful at present. I determined not to break with my motherland, but so far I have not received a Soviet passport, and they look at me askance. The Soviets demand that a person must join them body and soul – "who is not with us, is against us." But this is very hard to accept – not to speak of the material side. Papa says that with my character I would find Soviet citizenship impossible, but for me this cursed question is not yet resolved. This is a question of choice between oneself and service to one's native land.

Sergey apparently decided not to continue. Perhaps he thought that this was not what one writes to a sponsor, but Father was sufficiently impressed by his sentiments that he saved this scrap of notepaper.

Having accepted Mr. Crane's offer, I began to dream of the future. I told Sergey about the *General Electric Review* article and he felt as enthusiastic as I did about the possibility of doing research. The Massachusetts Institute of Technology became the focus of both our hopes.

Surviving and Waiting

Autumn's pelting rains transformed the road to our house into a river of mud. At night the surface froze into sharp peaks and ruts, hard to walk upon, but in daytime the sticky mud seeped past the tops of our galoshes, and often sucked them off our feet. Yet this did not seem to discourage our friends, who came to visit us almost every evening, and virtually filled our house on Sundays.

Sergey and I concentrated on completing our programs of study. I had to make up many missed examinations and finish several delayed design projects, and I was overwhelmed with work. Lena, after tutoring in the summer, continued to give lessons in Russian literature: she really enjoyed this subject and felt that she was learning more by having to teach it. She also worked on her French and English, and was enrolled in the tenth and last post-graduate class, in which Chinese language was the only subject offered. Tanya was busy with sports programs, and all the girls now had quite a distance to walk to their school.

Father found some translation work and spent all day at his typewriter. It paid very badly, but at least it was something; our situation was precarious indeed, and once more our survival depended on Manya's ingenuity. We all gave her every penny we earned, and she managed somehow to make ends meet. All our future hopes were now fixed on the answer we would receive from Mr. Crane.

My professor of electrical engineering, Alexander Ivanovich Drozhin, offered me some interesting work. He wished to compose a textbook for his course, but was too busy to write it himself. Yura Aingorn was Drozhin's assistant, but Yura was at work on his final diploma project, and had no time to devote himself to such a task. So Drozhin proposed that he would occasionally meet me for an hour in his office and give me a short lecture, in which he would describe in general terms the proofs and sketches that he wanted. I would then write this up, filling in the omitted details. I now think he may simply have been trying to find some excuse for helping me earn a little money, since he was aware of our difficulties, but at the time this thought did not cross my mind, and I performed the work enthusiastically until leaving Harbin. I was quite proud of helping Professor Drozhin to write a book.

As before, Father would visit his friends some evenings, which now meant he walked to the nearest bus stop, and then took a bus to the city. I remember his stooped figure moving along the muddy street with his cane. His black Persian fur hat had lost its original shape, and now resembled a bell-shaped cap. Because the cold wind was so penetrating in the open field, he wore an old, long jacket of brown wide-wale corduroy that had survived from his student days in Belgium. It was lined with reddish muskrat fur.

Once, before going out, he sat in his armchair with his feet on another chair, and thoughtfully pushed the sole of his shoe away from the rest of it, with his toes, making the shoe look like the open jaws of an animal. "Do you think one can visit people wearing such shoes?" he asked Sergey.

"It depends who you visit," Sergey replied. "If they are clever people, they would pay no attention to such trifles."

"I am visiting the Ustrialovs," said Father.

"Oh, that would be perfectly all right!" exclaimed Sergey.

That evening when Father returned he said, "Sergey was right: I sat there and kept opening my shoe all evening as we talked, and no one took any notice."

Manchurian winters were long, without periods of thaw. There was very little snow, but strong freezing winds. That year an exceptionally cold winter set in, with the temperature outside sometimes below -40°. I tried to avoid walking hunched over and shivering on the open road from our house, and discovered that if I straightened up, raised my head and relaxed my body, I would stop shivering, and the cold would not seem so bad.

But the brick stoves built into the walls between the rooms could not keep the humid air of the house above 50° Fahrenheit, so we had to add, temporarily, some small iron stoves. The hallway with its stairs was so cold that we kept the door to it closed. To avoid frequent use of the hall, Father installed a metal pipe between the two floors, so that if one needed to speak to someone a floor away, one knocked on the pipe and then conversed through it – a primitive intercom.

Our many windows froze over so completely that one could not see through the glass. The drying plaster supplied an endless amount of moisture toward this. We put towels on all the window-sills, their ends stuck into bottles suspended at the side of each window, which had to be emptied several times each day.

The water required pumping by hand every day to a tank in the attic, thus supplying the necessary pressure to the water lines below. A hired Chinese man performed this task every morning. The tank lay in a large wooden box, surrounded by sawdust to keep the water from freezing; its cover was not welded shut, so there was always a danger that the water could overflow, soak the sawdust, and freeze, thus reducing its insulation value even further. To prevent this, we installed a float on the surface of the water in the tank, with a string attached to it, leading up over a pulley and down through a hole in the floor. A small weight at the end of the string hung close to the kitchen wall, with a scale showing the level of the water in the tank. We proudly showed each new technical improvement to our friends, welcoming their suggestions.

❧

During the long magic hours of winter dusk, blue light filled our house, with its many windows looking on surrounding snow-covered fields. It was the time when the lights are not yet turned on, and one has quiet time to contemplate, without reading or writing.

Usually we had lively company around the table in the evenings: the house was always full of young people – my colleagues from the Institute and Lena's friends from school – and Father, Manya, and Nanny always joined in. Now that Father was at home almost all of the time he became even closer to our young circle. Yura

Aingorn visited constantly, and his lovelorn appearance was for me a source of both comfort and guilt. He would sit beside me and even quietly kiss me on the cheek, but I still felt traumatized by my failed romance with Kostya, and I did not want to inflict the same sort of pain on Yura. I knew all too well how it felt.

But I was increasingly concerned that there seemed to be something very important, involving human relations, that I knew nothing about. Clues were everywhere – in literature, movies, people's remarks – and they all seemed to point to the problem of conceiving children, about which I was still entirely ignorant. My thinking went thus: people usually fall in love, and when in love they feel something special towards each other, something like an electric current passing between them. They want to see each other all the time, to share each other's thoughts and feelings. The other person becomes the one and only in the world. While they are young it is just a pleasure, if it is reciprocated, but when they are old enough to settle down to a permanent way of living they want to get married. To marry, one must love a person very much, have much in common with him, want to spend the rest of one's life and to share everything, every thought, with him. To marry without love is terrible. When people love each other they like to be close, they want to embrace, maybe even kiss each other. When people marry they want to have children. They must do something to conceive them. What, I did not know.

That any of this had anything to do with "sex" never occurred to me. I did not even know what the word really meant. The grown-ups usually referred to it as something dirty or funny. Maybe it was all right to know nothing about it? I had never had much of a chance to observe my parents together – I never saw them kissing, or sharing a bed. I knew they loved each other and loved us, but most of my life they were apart and yearning to be together. It did not seem to diminish their love for each other, even when one of them was no longer alive, or their love for the rest of us.

It was some time during that winter that I had a conversation with my sister Zoya. I don't know how it started or how it was that Zoya, to her surprise, realized that I knew nothing about sex: she was only fourteen and I was twenty-two. She told me what the male organ was and how it can change from what I knew only as a pissing faucet. I could hardly conceal my amazement and shock. For days afterward I walked about in a fog of dismay. The creation of children, which I accepted as the inevitable function of women, and which I firmly expected to assume for myself, involved what I thought of as the dirtiest parts of our bodies! That was incredible! The thought that such things had anything to do with love had never once occurred to me.

Shortly after, as I passed a narrow side street in the city, I happened to notice a man who had stopped behind a building to relieve himself. He saw me as I passed, and I observed his strangely expanded organ. It filled me with such disgust that for a while I could not even think about men. After a while I recovered and almost forgot the whole matter, but I still could not quite believe what Zoya had told me, and being ashamed of my ignorance, never dared ask anyone else. The information lay dormant in the back of my mind for a long time, but it was more comfortable, in my imagination, to return to my innocently romantic notions about human love.

Departure

Early in February 1931 the American consul in Harbin, Mr. Thomas, informed Father that Mr. Crane had written to him about his invitation. On the thirteenth Father, Sergey, and I saw Mr. Thomas, who explained that visa regulations at the moment seemed favorable, but that they could change at any time. He promised to wire Crane, and Father wrote to him too. It began to look as if we might really go.

But on March 7 a disturbing telegram arrived:

NECESSARY TO DEFER ACTION ON ZAROODNY CASE. FATHER TRAVELING
ARABIA. JOHN CRANE

When further exchanges did little to clarify matters, we were left in suspense and uncertainty, stymied for the moment, and with no other prospects in view.

In March I suffered my usual bout with bronchitis, and spent two weeks in my bed on the second floor. In spite of visits from numerous friends, and having the rest of the family around my bed every day, my inability to see out the ice-covered windows began to suggest that the rest of the world had ceased to exist. I was full of anxiety, worrying about the hopelessness of our family situation, about Father's inability to find a job, and about hearing nothing from Mr. Crane. I had a recurrent nightmare in which I stood all alone in the middle of an enormous dark plain, the horizon like a circle around me separating the earth and the gloomy sky, and not a soul within reach of my sight or voice. I would wake up in terror. I realized then what anxieties prisoners must experience when unable to look through the high, shuttered windows of their cells. Clearly, memories of Mother's last days remained fixed in my mind.

In April Father finally received a letter from Donald Brodie, Mr. Crane's personal assistant. He wrote that John Crane was sailing to Europe and would speak there with his father about us, but that "there are certain difficulties in the way of arranging for your son and daughter in this country and it is necessary that everything be arranged before the final word is given." Two years later, when Sergey and I were already in California, Manya heard from a friend that we were lucky to have obtained an American visa at all, because the Consul knew that we were considered "red." Perhaps this was the problem: if so, my cherished Soviet passport almost cost me my future.

Finally the winter neared its end. The frozen road turned muddy again, the spring air became warmer, the windows in the house regained their transparency – and again Father was full of ideas. The house was now surrounded by a fence, giving us a chance to plant flowerbeds and to put out benches in the yard. Since the house itself was so tall, Father knew that we would want to climb up on the roof for the view, so he installed a plank with crosspieces leading up the incline, and a platform at the very top, which became quite popular. He also had a large swing built by the side of the house.

Summer approached, with the usual prospect of excursions to the river, relaxed reading in the front yard, and intensive work on

The house, 1931

On the roof

projects for me and Sergey. But there was still no word from Mr. Crane. Had he changed his mind? Even if the invitation did come, should I really give up the idea of one day returning to Russia? Lena, whose study of French was advancing rapidly, dreamed of going to Paris. I was sure that America would not be like I imagined Paris to be, where the Russian emigrants inhabited a sort of national island, never blending with the native French, or adopting French customs. To my mind, they were simply cut off from Russia and now subsisting on nostalgia, which seemed to me unacceptable. If I did not go back to Russia, I needed to find a new homeland, which I could love for itself, and to which I could feel entirely loyal. What bothered me most of all, however, was the thought that in America I would forever be "a foreigner": I would never lose my Russian accent, I would never quite belong. But I did not seem to belong, either, with the Soviet students in Harbin – how then would I feel *in Russia?*

One night I had a dream: I was in the midst of a huge crowd in a large square surrounded by skyscrapers. Around me were strangers; I knew no one. Suddenly I caught a glimpse of a face, a familiar face – it was Mother! I lost sight of her at once, and started desperately to search for her in the crowd, with no success. Dejected, I left the crowded square and found myself on a narrow street with tall buildings on both sides. It was getting dark. Then, right in front of me, coming toward me, I saw her again. She came close, put both her hands on my shoulders and turned me around. "Don't go there, they won't accept you!" she said – and by "there" she meant Russia. I awoke, with my mind completely made up: I wanted to go to America.

It was not until May that Mr. Crane's letter from Europe arrived, confirming his invitation. On June 19 Father received a telegraph transfer of $1500, toward the long voyage. It took several visits to the consulate before a visa was issued, but Mr. Thomas solved the problem of my Soviet citizenship by providing me with a letter certifying that I was a citizen of a country "with which the USA has no diplomatic relations." I was not to use my Soviet passport henceforth.

On June 30 Lena wrote in her diary:

> Mulya and Sergey are leaving. I shall be the eldest in the house. I hope that I shall be able to reconstruct that tenderness and intimacy of the family environment, which is always so dear to all the family members. I hope to be the directing force for Tanya, Zoya, and Katya. To be the eldest one must not only be able to approach the youngsters, one must have a certain tact, be able to sort out many things for oneself, and also have some rather weighty knowledge.

The least expensive passage across the Pacific turned out to be by the *Hikawa Maru*, a Japanese ship sailing from Yokohama to Seattle on the third of August. Father thought that we should travel in tourist class, but only steerage turned out to be available. He wanted us to spend a week in Japan and to have Lena accompany us there, so that in this way she could at least share part of our luck. She would spend another week or two with Father's friends there, before returning to Harbin. There were a lot of letters to write, and the last-minute arrangements and preparations took most of July.

Father had always felt rather awkward about my studying to be an engineer and thus competing with boys. He thought that I could probably take up mathematics in graduate school and then teach it. He wanted me to be more feminine, as his parting gift made clear, symbolically: with little money to spend on it, he bought me a hand mirror, with a simple white enameled frame and handle. I had never owned anything like that and was terribly touched. Seventy-five years later I still keep it on my dressing table.

Manya planned our wardrobes, repeating to me the Russian proverb "how they greet you depends on your looks, how they part with you depends on your wisdom" each time I objected to trying on the new dresses sewn by our dressmaker. Manya herself worked along with her, while I was busy assembling my school records and recommendations, and saying goodbye to my friends. Lena was really excited by the prospect of her trip to Japan: she was working hard on her English, and trying on the clothes that I would leave behind.

The night before our departure Father had a last talk with Sergey and me. "I know," he said, "that you are good and honest persons. I have full confidence in you. Do not forget that this is most important. Study hard, work honestly, and be grateful to those who help you. Keep in close touch with friends and relatives, whose addresses I gave you, but don't feel that you should make a friend of anyone just because he is a Russian. Don't become a part of the 'Russian ghetto.' In fact, should you see another Russian you don't know on your side of the street, cross to the other side. You will be in America – learn everything you can about Americans and their way of life. And don't forget your family. Write often and much, and try to help your younger sisters in any way you can. May God bless you."

A very large crowd of friends saw us off at the station. Manya and Nanny were crying. Father blessed me with a small Russian icon and gave it to me. He had tears in his eyes – he did not know whether he would ever see us again. A young Japanese girl, Sitya, who was staying with us at that time, put that thought into words: "Oh, this is very sad! It is like dying – parting, and knowing that we shall not meet anymore."

I always remembered this. Ahead was a new adventure, frightening, but exciting. And no, we never saw Father again.

IV

AMERICA

22

To America

Lena, Sergey, and I had a compartment of our own on the railroad car from Harbin. Manya had supplied us with plenty of food to eat on the way; soft beds were made up for us at night, and it was pleasant to fall asleep once more to the clicking wheels of a train. But it was so different from our earlier travels, when the whole family was together. And as ever the sense of responsibility for me, as the eldest, seemed daunting – not only during the trip, but especially in America. I needed to concentrate on helping the family, which meant that I had to arrange my program of studies so that I could begin earning as soon as possible. And my personal life, too, would have to be managed carefully: I thought that soon I would be old enough to get married, and have children of my own, and that I should not postpone that for too long. But natural curiosity, amid all the new impressions, soon took over my thoughts, and for the time being I stopped worrying.

We traveled south through Korea. There, at a station stop, I saw a scene that I have never forgotten: a poor old Korean man, maybe a beggar, stood on the platform with a bag at his side. A Japanese policeman ordered him to move on. The old man hesitated, and the policeman slapped him in the face so hard that he reeled, clutching his cheek. When he took his hand away, I could see the red imprint of the policeman's hand on it. The old man left the station, obediently. I had heard that Koreans hated the occupying Japanese, and now I thought I saw why.

From Korea we sailed on a Japanese ship to Japan, a short hop. The Japanese coast loomed up on the horizon in a strange, jagged line, just as Father had described it, and soon we docked. We were met on the pier by an employee of Father's friend and former colleague Britton.

Mr. Britton, a manager of Babcock & Wilcox Company's Zemma Works, was a rather formal but friendly Englishman with an American wife and a thoroughly English home, where we stayed at first. Impressed by our ambition to attend MIT in America, he took us to look over his factory. He also took us to the American Consulate, where the cheerful young consul checked our documents. Mr. Britton told him that although we had applied for Soviet passports, we were not "Soviets," and the consul acknowledged that if Mr. Crane had made the arrangements, "everything must be okay." Sergey wrote to Father that "he certainly behaved democratically – Hooray for America!" But Sergey was not starry-eyed about everything, and not without a trace of Soviet influence still. Telling Father that at first he did not like Mr. Britton, he explained: "He is rich, almost like a caricature; on his wall there hangs a photo of a group of his co-workers – all capitalist sharks. Perfect order at the Works, mass production and exploitation; while going through the shop he bumped into a working Japanese girl and did not even apologize."

We tried to communicate in English, I perhaps with somewhat more success than Sergey, and I began to believe that I could deal with "foreigners" without being cowed. In a couple of days we were passed on to another former colleague of Father's, Mr. Munro, for as Sergey wrote in one of his letters, Father's "magic wand" accompanied us all through Japan. Munro was married to a Russian woman, and lived in a little house more informal and more Japanese than Britton's. This put us much more at ease.

We had detailed instructions from Father about what we should see in Japan, and having heard so much about the country from him, and received so many postcards when he visited it, we thought we knew it already. We were prepared to love Japan, and we did – the brightly colored kimonos on the street, the paper parasols of the women moving with short steps in their narrow dresses on the wooden *zoris,* the bookstores with crowds of children reading at open counters, the vendors on the streets with their different cries, the packed streetcars with their polite conductors watching out for the children and making sure that they found the right stop, and the strange paper objects, so decorative and so fragile, sold so cheaply in all the stores. My immediate impulse was to buy presents for all the family in Harbin. Everything was so pretty: delicate cups without handles, rice bowls, teapots, exotic fabric, and much else.

The night before our ship sailed we had a long talk with Lena, who would stay a week or so longer with the Munros. As in all such final conversations, we could never say all that we wanted. And just before boarding we learned that we could be accommodated in tourist class after all. We had to pay a little more, but the Munros strongly advised us to do so. Steerage is quite rough, they explained.

On August 3 Lena, Mrs. Munro, and Mr. Britton's representative saw us onto the Yokohama pier and onto the *Hikawa Maru*. The last sentimental touch was the traditional throwing of paper ribbons from the decks to the shore. Those on the pier caught the other ends, linking us until they were stretched and torn by the receding ship. Sergey and I watched the small figure of Lena on the pier as long as we could still distinguish her in the crowd. For the first time in our lives we had no family awaiting us. There were just the two of us now.

Crossing the Pacific

We had a nice interior cabin with two bunk beds, one above the other, and we found a telegram there that read "EMBRACING WISHING YOU HAPPINESS. FATHER." We unpacked our things and I set out to connect the flat iron, for to be economical on the ship we needed to do our own ironing. To my dismay the adaptor I had just bought did not fit the lamp socket: the ship had a different system of sockets. But my engineering training paid off. I found an old lightbulb, broke it, and connected the wire of the flat iron to the two terminals inside the broken bulb. It served well the rest of the trip, but I was lucky that I did not start a fire.

Dinner was served in the second class dining room, where our table companions were two rather formal young women, both of them American teachers. We could not understand their American accent at all, and they paid little attention to us. The dinner was quite adequate and we wondered what we should do with the food Manya had packed into our trunks – all kinds of Easter delicacies, the fanciest she could think of preparing: *kulich*, ham, cheese, and even a bottle of champagne.

Afterwards we went out on the deck. A dark cloud covered part of the sky, promising rough weather tomorrow. We could see a narrow line of lights on the distant Japanese shore, and ahead of us, far away, the lights of two ships that had sailed earlier; behind us, the endless dark waves were streaked with the white foam of the ship's wake. The *Hikawa Maru* was rather small for ocean travel and its sway was quite noticeable, which made both of us a little uncomfortable for a while, but we soon got used to it.

Our Japanese attendant asked each of us to pick a time for our daily bath: he would call us at this time each day to say that it was drawn. Sergey picked seven in the morning, and I nine at night. As it turned out his choice was better, for when we met the young people with whom we would talk all evening long, it was a nuisance to be called for a bath in the midst of it all. That night, however, we went to bed early and slept soundly.

The next day we discovered the steerage deck, with its mixture of American students, teachers, and families with children returning from summer trips to the Orient. They were not very happy with their accommodations, which were dormitory cabins with six or eight beds in each, and little privacy. Their food was Japanese poor man's food.

But the atmosphere in steerage was animated, informal, and friendly, and from then on we spent our days on that deck. The attendant from tourist class would come to tell us that "a bath is drawn," or that one of the meals was being served, and for as short a time as possible we would return to the more luxurious but much duller environment of that class. We were happy, however, to eat and sleep there, and we wrote home every day on the colorful dinner menus we were given in tourist class.

Before long we made many friends in steerage. We brought out all our Easter treats and hosted a delicious picnic on the deck. I was amazed when some of the Americans refused to drink our champagne "because there was prohibition in America." We danced to the music of a record player, and stayed up late into the night watching the fluorescent foam in the wake of the ship, and the glowing medusas floating like lanterns. We talked, talked, and talked. Time and again our noisy conversations and music were interrupted by the long-suffering attendant, who would politely ask us to quiet down, for

On board the Hikawa Maru
Mulya (top) and Sergey (center)

other passengers were trying to sleep, and as a last resort would lock the smoking room and send us to our cabins.

The fact that we were Russians provoked a multitude of questions. The Americans we met seemed to know very little about Russia and their opinions seemed naive to us. The first question was always the same – "Are you Red or White Russians?" – which disconcerted us, for the answer was far too complicated to be put in such simple terms. We wanted to avoid talking politics, but that was almost impossible.

Our tentative English was met with an enthusiastic desire to help and to correct us. When our new friends heard that we wanted to go to the Massachusetts Institute of Technology, they told us that it was indeed the best technical school in America, but hard to get into. I began to worry again: would I be admitted?

The trip ended for me with the "inevitable" shipboard romance and a marriage proposal. Malcolm Proudfoot was a graduate student in political economy at the University of Chicago. Wearing a Russian embroidered shirt and a Tartar skullcap, he loved to talk about his extensive travels, including three months in Russia, where his sister lived with her German husband, an engineer. He thought that the organization of work in Russia was terrible, and his tales of inefficiency, bad planning, and bad standards of construction shocked me. Malcolm found the practice of state price fixing economically absurd and abhorrent, and unfair to the general population. He had gone to the USSR after working in Germany for a year and studying Russian economics, in the hope of learning something new from the "grandiose" construction projects in Russia, but the overall impression he received during his stay was one of grandiose confusion. "All the construction projects will have to be rebuilt or abandoned, or they may become useful only decades from now," he said.

I was mortified. After all, my friends and I had all wanted, at one time or other, to return and participate in the grand plan of building a future for our native country. Malcolm also felt that all those working on the projects were afraid to speak out when they recognized what was wrong with the plans or the work being done.

"Nobody wants to sign anything – they are afraid of being accused of sabotage later," he said. Yet, as if consoling me, he told me "still, to remain proud of your country," but only after admitting that he was happy not to have been born there. I made a mental note to write about this to Tanya, because Tanya was so enthusiastic about everything Soviet. I, on the other hand, felt reassured that my decision to come to America was the right one after all.

Everything about Malcolm was new and different for me – the stories of his travels, and his independence, which made him seem older than the boys of the same age I knew in Harbin. His American speech was also rather easy to understand. Having studied foreign languages himself, he understood my difficulties and made an effort to speak clearly, explaining that he did so because he was "more educated than all these Americans" on the ship.

He did not mix quite as enthusiastically with the rest of our crowd, and he and I often left their company to play chess in the smoking room. One evening we were leaning over the rails of the ship watching the fluorescent effect of medusas floating by. Malcolm offered me his jacket, and put his arms around me, holding me close. Suddenly he asked me, "Would you marry me? I will graduate soon and have a good job." It startled me and even frightened me a little, but I liked him so much that I was very happy. I told him that I had to finish my education first and help my younger sisters finish theirs, and only then could I think of marriage. Yet, to myself, I was thinking that I was already almost twenty-three, and my twenty-fourth year – when I should think about getting married – was rapidly approaching. This romance was my first sexual awakening, the first time I enjoyed kissing, and had my first feelings of desire, still very tentative. I decided that I might marry this man, someday. The memory of Yura Aingorn began to fade.

Uncertainty Again

On the fourteenth of August, still at sea, we received a telegram from Mr. Crane:

MAILING LETTER CARE OF HIKAWA SEATTLE PLEASE REMAIN SEATTLE UNTIL MESSAGE RECEIVED ON ACCOUNT CHANGED PLANS AND

TELEGRAPH YOUR ADDRESS TO CHARLES CRANE 522 FIFTH AVENUE NEW
YORK CORDIAL GREETINGS CRANE

What did this mean, we both wondered. That our hopes to go
to the Massachusetts Institute of Technology would be dashed? Or
even that there would be no schooling at all? Did Mr. Crane want
to send us back without even seeing us? There were four more days
before we would reach Seattle, but it was hard to enjoy the rest of the
voyage. Sergey was less concerned, however, because he trusted that
somehow all would turn out right in the end. Now the sea became
rough and Sergey was very seasick. I myself did not feel bad if I lay
down on my cot, and I could even walk on the deck for a while, and
take my meals in the dining room. But Sergey really suffered.

On August 17, after two weeks at sea with no sight of land, we
glimpsed the outline of the Canadian shore near Vancouver. Later
the same day Sergey wrote home:

In Vancouver our passports were checked, and permits to go
ashore were issued. A kindly smiling official hesitated when
he saw that we were Russians, but our new American friends
vouched for us, and we were given one. We liked Vancouver
even more than Japan. We liked the flowers, grass, asphalt,
and the architecture of the cottages. Lots of trees, and no
one uses car horns. It seemed as if we were already seeing
America from the window of the car. All Americans seem to
love their country.

I court the girls like crazy. They seem to like it – they are
not spoiled. However they all seem to have bad teeth. We are
sailing from Vancouver to Seattle among islands. Now I have
fallen in love with an American girl – a very tall, beautiful,
brunette gymnastics teacher – and, to be polite, also with her
companion, a sweet girl who looks like a boy. In general all of
them are miserable because of their teeth. [Sergey and I had
never seen teeth braces before, which so many of the young
American girls wore.]

I act as a knight in white armor and they like it. ... I did
not realize at first how much the Americans resemble the

Russians. ... The simplicity of manners is wonderful: it is, for example, permissible for a girl to sit on a boy's lap, or for a boy to be present in a girl's cabin when a girl is lying in bed! (Mulya says that even kissing is allowed.) ...

I wrote to you about the telegram. Mulya worries, and this is noticed by others. Crane's letter will probably arrive tomorrow morning. I feel very well and have full confidence in Crane, though

1) I don't like "on account of changed plans", and
2) when, finally, shall our situation become clear?

It feels a little empty on the ship after some passengers left at Vancouver. We noticed that Russian fellows who have lived in Canada for a little more than a year are much democratized. They say that there is great unemployment in Canada, and that it is even worse in the US. But generally everything is excellent.

The *Hikawa Maru* was now approaching Seattle, and it was already quite dark when Sergey, Malcolm, and I, standing on the deck, spied the lights of our first American city. Malcolm said: "I hope that this country will become your home and you will be happy here!"

When we awoke on the morning of August 18th, the ship was already moored. We were given a letter:

Dear Friends,

At Mr. Crane's direction we are sending a radiogram to the Hikawa Maru asking you to wait in Seattle instead of leaving at once for New York.

Mr. Crane thinks that you both had better remain for one year on the Pacific coast. He is suggesting that Sergey attend Pomona College and that his sister attend Scripps College. Both are located in Claremont, California – a few miles from Los Angeles.

The colleges open Sept. 18th and it would be best for you to arrive at Claremont about Sept. 10th. On this account Mr. Crane thinks that you had better not make the long trip to New York and back.

Instead he suggests that you remain several days in Seattle, visiting one day the University of Washington, and possibly also going to Spokane for a day. He may send word to the Crane Co. manager in Seattle to look you up.

Then after Seattle he suggests that you spend a week or so in San Francisco, visiting while there Stanford University at Palo Alto and the University of California in Berkeley.

In the radiogram we asked you to telegraph your address in Seattle to New York.

If you have not enough money for expenses to Claremont please let us know by telegraph.

Very sincerely
Donald M. Brodie

So our fears were unfounded. But the plan was so different from what we had expected that we had to become used to it. Sergey's first reaction was that his freedom of choice was being restricted, while I was concerned that the time when I would finish my professional education and could start helping the family would be delayed. We knew nothing about the colleges mentioned in the letter, and it was lucky that we now had American friends, especially Malcolm, who might know all about them. We rushed back to the steerage deck.

Our friends there were happy for us; they said these were good liberal arts colleges and a year in Claremont would be the best thing we could do to improve our English and learn more about America. Even Malcolm, who hoped to persuade me to come to the University of Chicago, had to admit that Mr. Crane's idea was a good one, and he was willing to wait a year before we could get together again.

Before we disembarked we all exchanged addresses. Our correspondence with some of our friends of the voyage lasted for years.

23

In America

Malcolm Proudfoot took charge of us. He helped us through customs, he found a hotel for us, and he took us there in a taxi, promising to show us the city. Everything seemed wonderful: our room on the eighth floor with a marvelous view, the first breakfast of cornflakes – which I liked so much that I continued with cornflakes every morning for the next twenty years – Malcolm's thoughtful guidance, and the beautiful city of Seattle, where we immediately felt we had no need to be wary of passers-by, or afraid of policemen. A gentleman from the Crane Company called on us and was relieved to find that we could manage without his help. In Seattle we saw all we were supposed to see, and even went to a party given by one of our fellow-voyagers. On Malcolm's advice we chose the cheapest way to San Francisco, by Greyhound bus, which would allow us to see the famous redwoods; Malcolm would accompany us, and from San Francisco take a train back to Chicago.

The bus was very large and comfortable; not long ago it would have astonished us, but by now we both were becoming more experienced, and such luxury no longer surprised us. In northern California the bus stopped to let passengers walk among the enormous tree trunks in Redwood National Park. The trees were so wonderfully straight and so high – it made me dizzy to keep looking up, trying to make out their tops.

In San Francisco we rented two rooms from the Lebedevs, a Russian family who had emigrated from Harbin several years earlier, and whom we knew of through mutual friends. Despite all the excitement of our arrival, and our initial optimism, it must be remembered that in 1931 America was in the depths of its Great Depression. In the Lebedevs' household we had a chance to hear stories that showed a clear picture both of the slump and the problems of immigrant life. The Lebedev brothers worked, and owned a car, but the family had to supplement their income by renting out rooms. Several members of the family had recently been

345

in an automobile accident, and some of them were still bedridden. Yet they were all hospitable and helpful, and we liked them very much. Their friends in San Francisco were mostly Russians, who ate Russian food and followed Russian traditions. That reminded me of Father's instructions about avoiding the "Russian ghetto," and made me anxious to join into American life as soon as possible. I wrote to Father: "Apparently the colleges to which we are being sent have practically no foreigners, and no Russians, which is just as well."

We met several other Russians, among them an aspiring musician who worked as a house-helper for an American family to support his continuing education. He managed to buy himself a piano, but found that after a day's work he was too tired to study music. Nonetheless what he could earn by playing occasionally for dance groups could not justify dropping his full-time job.

Two Russian girls boarding with the Lebedevs had come from the countryside to earn some money in San Francisco. They wanted to help their family expand their chicken farm, which even with 2,000 hens was not large enough to support them all. The older girl wanted to further her education, but had to work instead. She had found a job as a cleaner in a hospital; the younger was still unemployed. On the whole, people we met felt that education would not help them make a living.

We looked up several American friends from the *Hikawa Maru* and they helped show us the city, the University of California at Berkeley, and even took us to Palo Alto to visit Stanford University, where my teacher at the Polytechnic Institute, Alexander Drozhin, had taken his degree.

The Lebedev brothers drove us to Los Angeles. On this 400-mile trip we could not stop admiring the broad highways, the frequent service stations, the full and polite service our car received on the way, the simple, inexpensive eating places, and the sunny mid-Californian landscape. The Lebedevs dropped Sergey at the YMCA and me at the Women's Hotel, where we would stay until the college dormitories in Claremont were opened to students. Not being allowed to visit one another's rooms was also a new experience for us.

℃

In Claremont we met with the presidents of both colleges and were admitted with no problems. Sergey was assigned a dormitory room at Pomona that he shared with a boy named Robert Taylor, who later became a famous Hollywood movie star. Because he would be given credit for the science courses he had taken at Harbin Polytechnic, Sergey could probably obtain a bachelor's degree at the end of the year; he decided to study English, American history, psychology, and art. Examining the Scripps College catalogue, I thought that the year there would be extremely easy for me, and I planned on taking a great number of courses. I began at once to dream of getting a Ph.D. and embarking on a career of research.

At that time Scripps, a small women's college, took only 200 students. Pomona College was older and coeducational, with a football team, a good concert hall, many laboratories, and a small observatory. Scripps, on the other hand, had only recently been organized, and had graduated its first class the previous year. Within its intimate compass, it aimed at establishing a high scholastic reputation.

Scripps' dormitories, in Spanish architectural style, housed only fifty girls each, in single rooms. No boys were allowed beyond the living rooms, but there were small individual sitting rooms where I could meet with Sergey. Each dormitory had a common room, separate kitchens, and a dining room; shaggy rugs, comfortable soft furniture, and a relaxed, home-like atmosphere of genteel living prevailed. One had to be on time for each meal, and girls were supposed to be in the dormitory every night by 10 p.m., although they could have several permits each semester to stay out until midnight, and just one extension to 2 a.m. It seemed demeaning to me to be treated this way, and I determined never to ask for such a permit.

On the first day after I moved in a girl met me in the corridor, threw her arms around me, and exclaimed, "I am so glad you are in our hall! You are the first foreigner I have ever met!" Other girls were also wonderfully friendly, and tried to help me with my English. They wanted to learn about my past, which I tried to talk about, but

I soon realized that it was all too strange for them. They were all so young, and yet to me they looked older and more sophisticated, with their American clothes, curled hair, costume jewelry, and make-up – which I had still never used.

An essential part of the Scripps program was the history of civilization, required of all students during their first two years. A different aspect of the same historical period was taught in each of the courses offered, and at the end of the second year a comprehensive examination was given. But since my English was still elementary, and I expected to be there just one year, I could not participate in this program: I was still worried about delaying the completion of my technical education and tried to find courses that would help me professionally. I could take natural science courses at Pomona, and I signed up for astronomy, but they offered nothing else beyond what I had already had in Harbin.

The courses offered at Scripps to third and fourth year students seemed so interesting to me, however, that I wished I could take them all. I found out, however, that five was the limit, and registered only for those I thought would be useful later in my technical studies – freshman English, French, German, and American history. For the physical education requirement I chose horseback riding, but even then I had to adjust to something new, for I had learned to ride on something like a Western saddle in Russia, quite different from those in use here.

My choice of courses made it even harder for me to learn English, however. It also resulted in my being considered a foreign literature major, and since my language courses were not sufficiently advanced, and my own English was below any freshman level, I could not get a degree at the end of the year. As a humanities college, Scripps would not grant me credit for my engineering courses in Harbin.

On October 12 I wrote to Father:

> In history we have just been given a book of 400 pages and told to read it as soon as possible. I don't know when I can do it. In English I had to read and submit a paper on Aristotle's On the Art of Poetry. Terribly hard reading. I just finished reading it and sketched the plan for the paper. Now I must

read several plays by Shakespeare, Bernard Shaw's Saint Joan, Meredith's The Egoist, Sophocles' Antigone, and Molière's Misanthrope. I shall try to read the last in French. All this in two weeks! Of course I won't be able to finish. ... I signed up each week for "German Table" and "French Table" – we meet at lunch and speak the language.

In the first few weeks I realized that keeping up with the history reading was too much for me, so I dropped the course. I was not allowed to become just an auditor in French since a four-course load was the minimum allowed for full-time students. My old problems of slow reading and bad spelling increased here manyfold: I could not get credit even in freshman English. I felt that I lacked fundamentals and was not getting what I needed. I was terribly frustrated, while working harder than I had ever done before. I felt that talking with the girls and listening to lectures was what I needed most, but my adviser did not agree.

One of the assignments in English was to write a one-act play. I based mine on an event that had occurred in Omsk, when a man hid in our cellar during a search by the secret police. I worked very hard at it, but when my teacher read it her only remark was "Do you think people in real life make such long speeches?" Well, *I* thought that they did.

೮෫

With his fast reading, exceptional memory, and perfect spelling in any language, Sergey had a much easier time. To graduate he had to take a foreign language exam. Russian was not accepted, so he picked German, even though he had never studied it formally. He prepared for the exam in two weeks all by himself, and passed.

Sergey's enthusiasm about everything American made me look for evidence to contradict him. Our arguments were often long and passionate, and he was so much better at arguing! He was utterly happy here, and generally more comfortable in our new environment than I, and even admired football and its rah-rah atmosphere, which rather bored me. Being accustomed in Harbin to the company of mostly male students, of my own age or older, I felt strange in an exclusively girls' school, while Pomona had no graduate program and most of the students were no older than twenty-two. The boys in my astronomy class, or those who were Sergey's classmates, were far too young to be interesting to me.

All this I described in detail in my letters. I enclosed small items I could buy in a local five-and-ten-cent store, like a kerchief for Lena, a pair of nylon panties for Tanya, a vegetable peeler for Manya, a celluloid stencil for drawing shapes of chemical vessels for Zoya, or even just a dime for Katya. As Father used to do on his business trips, I wrote to each member of the family separately, knowing that each of them would read to the others all the parts of their letters that were not strictly personal. I wrote my impressions of college to Father: "Life here is carefree both in a good and bad sense. In a good sense, because it is so calm and easy-going; in a bad sense because it is so remote from real life. They live in their own special small world that has nothing to do with what happens outside it." Sergey, who wrote almost as much as I did, usually addressed his letters to all at once, avoiding intimacies altogether. Father carefully preserved all our letters, and these thick folders were later brought to America by Lena, so I now have both sides of the correspondence.

The Spanish style of the architecture at Scripps, the palms and the eucalyptus trees around it, the orange groves on the foothills beyond, the ever changing hues of the snow-capped mountains in the distance – all these left me with an unreal feeling of being either in paradise or in an art gallery. One could not help but admire the landscape all the time, but I was becoming almost tired of it, for it would not subside and allow me to relax. Everything was strange, too: the grass did not grow naturally, with wild flowers and trodden paths, but was either mown and irrigated by water piped underground, or else burned by the sun. It was nice to see no fences, and to have the houses open to view, but everything seemed to me too exposed. The palm trees were exotic as well, and there were no birches, no soft-leafed and vulnerable-looking trees. But the weather was always warm and my letters home swelled with superlatives.

Father's letters were long, loving, and encouraging. He typed them single-spaced, without margins or dividing paragraphs, on thin paper, so that he could send each of us a copy and keep one for himself. He responded to each letter from Sergey and me, reported details of family life in Harbin, and wrote about the translations he made and how much he earned. He insisted that each member of the family should write separately and often, and urged our friends, during their visits to our house, to add something to his own letters. He even sent us copies of his letters to other relatives, in order to encourage us to keep in contact with them.

I learned that Lena had had a difficult time returning from Japan to Harbin, as the strain of Japanese-Chinese relations had made a return visa hard to obtain. As a result she spent almost a month in Japan, rested and improved her English greatly while with the hospitable Munros, and was even invited to come back again next year. She was now the principal earner in the family, and Father remarked several times that it was time for her to be at a University, and that we should try to arrange for her to come to America too, perhaps with Tanya as well. "Could you write about it to Crane?" he asked.

I simply could not. After all that Mr. Crane had done for us already, how could I ask him for more? And living here in this beautiful college, locked up in it like in a boarding school and overloaded with studies, how could I find any other way for them to come? I thought of many ways in which, once here, they might pursue an education, but not how to bring them. Depressed by the contrast between the luxurious atmosphere in which I was now placed, and my family's needs, I dreamed about the problem. Meanwhile, the telegraph reports appearing in the papers were alarming: Japanese-Chinese relations were deteriorating further, and a Japanese occupation of Harbin seemed quite possible. Should that happen we had no idea how the family would be affected. I knew they had no money with which to escape, and the thought that they might be deported to the USSR made me panic. I could not study. We sent telegrams home, "WORRYING TELEGRAPH US," but received no answer. Finally Sergey sent one with a paid reply and word came back that everything was well. Evidently they were not concerned; they may not even have known what we read in the American papers.

෪

On October 28, 1931 I wrote to Father "and all":

For some reason there's been no word from you for a long time, and since there are more of you than us, we hope to have letters at least once a week! ... It seems that the Manchurian situation is settling down, at least the newspapers here are not so excited anymore. It is possible that each new event causes them to write a lot about it at first, but then they get used to it and write less. ... Here everything is as before – peaceful and quiet. "Sunny California" is indeed marvelous. Today it is too warm even in a blouse with short sleeves, and on the coldest day so far a suit jacket was all one needed.

I went to a symphony concert in Los Angeles – 35 miles from here – by car. Can you imagine driving that far to hear a concert? I was invited by one of the girls here, the charming Anne Hopkins. Her grandmother helps the college a lot – she is terribly rich. We stopped at her house for lunch on the way, and after the concert stopped at her cousin's house for dinner. So I have had an inside look at how American millionaires live, and I ate an American home-cooked lunch for the first time.

Everything was beautifully served, and simple, without any special pretensions, but their life is quite barren. It seems they have no other interests besides their own entertainment. Isn't it strange: we talk of freedom, we strive for it, and here it is achieved, at least for those who have some money – complete freedom of speech, of action, of movement. But what is most important is that these freedoms are "individualized." What I am trying to say is that such privileges separate people from each other too much, nothing seems to link them together. Therefore it is easy to understand their extreme politeness and attentiveness, for there is nothing binding in that. All their social organizations, clubs, and so on, somehow do not form one cohesive whole, but consist of separate units unrelated to each other. Thinking people, who are interested in community spirit and public life, feel this, and are troubled by it. There is no public social life: today you are in a club, tomorrow you take your car and go to spend the winter in Chicago, or the summer in Europe, and you do not care about what is happening in the club, just as the club does not care what is happening to you. Some people treasure this freedom, but some are oppressed by it. It seems that America has already achieved what so many strove for, but the result does not seem quite so wonderful. I speak, of course, about the effects of this "American freedom" as experienced by people who have money, or who at least have work.

For the unemployed, naturally, it is different. But the question remains whether the American "ideal" is really that, after all? In any case, it is pleasant to rest in a sort of freedom from overdependence. But it is characteristic for a man to desire dependence, and to feel himself connected with others, perhaps as part of one active crowd.

Before long I tried to organize teas in our living room and suggested some poetry readings. No one wanted to do that. "Why don't you read us some Russian poems?" they asked, and I readily agreed. I have never forgotten that evening, when I tried to recite my favorite poems. The absurdity of reading aloud before a group who did not understand a word I was saying! And their polite applause, their praise afterwards! I promised myself never to do that again, and I put away my collection of Russian poetry so it would not remind me that I had no one to share it with.

I now immersed myself completely in my courses. My language studies were complicated by the fact that I had no Russian-French or Russian-German dictionaries. I used my French-English dictionary and found either exactly the same word (only with a different pronunciation) or several other words I did not know, then looked these up in an English-Russian dictionary, sometimes ending up with a dozen words to chose between. The vocabulary of both French and German was so much easier for English speakers than for me, and I was amazed at the progress my classmates were making. Luckily, one of the teachers volunteered to give me lessons in English pronunciation. And another student was helping me with English grammar.

All our old friends were leaving Harbin. Lena and Tanya seemed more and more inclined to go to the Soviet Union. The family's financial situation was very bleak: Lena was giving a few private lessons, Tanya remained in school, and Father slaved at some badly paid translations. By cutting our expenses Sergey and I each managed to send them $10 every month. I was called occasionally to wait on tables and earned a few additional dollars to send home.

Early in December 1931 Lena sent me a long letter written over several days, which reflected her own new role in the Harbin household, and her conflicted intentions:

> It seems to me there are now two alternatives – the Soviet Union or America. We must choose between them. You have chosen America. ... I understand what you want, and what makes you feel dissatisfied in America. I think about it myself all the time. Right now, you must find interesting things in America: it is impossible to think that in that huge and cultured country you could not find interesting studies, work, and interesting people. You only need to learn to read – a lot. Then you will probably reach partial satisfaction with yourself, because even if complete satisfaction leads to mediocrity, some partial kind is necessary for happiness. ...
>
> Father says that life is interesting everywhere, and that one can only find satisfaction in one's personal life and in work. He is probably right. ...
>
> I am tortured all the time by the problem of the USSR and America. I begin to think that I should not go to America. Perhaps it is better for me to finish the courses here and go to the USSR, where with this much education I shall always find work. While in America it is so problematic, with all the unemployment, and the cost of going there is so high. ... I am also worried that both Father and you want to send Tanya to the USA, not taking into account her own wishes, perhaps still rather confused, but developing in her mind. ... Considering all this as I begin a new stage of my life, I must think it over thoroughly, and then seek the advice of friends – also a long process. I know what Father writes about my

going to the USA, and if this happens, so much the better. But in any case one must wait and think. ...

Don't even think of bringing us to America for at least four years. ... This will give me a chance for four years to be with the family. You know that I am now replacing you and I cannot leave here within a year simply because without all three older children the family cannot function, and Father would sink completely into depression – whereas now everything is calm and nobody quarrels. I have great influence on Father. Besides, I feel that it would be easier for me to live, if I select my life's path now and go along it honestly, without counting on outside assistance or influence. ...

I shall devote my year to intensive work educating myself, developing spiritual depth and general growth of mind, and go to America only when I have a definite self-image and would not need to choose my path, only to continue that process. ...

I know, that if I go to Russia instead I must enter the Soviet organizations sincerely and completely and that it is connected with struggle. So I shall struggle. I have friends who can help me. ...

Each one walks his own path, but life must have some sparkle. I am sure yours will have much, and I hope mine will too, perhaps not as much, but I am sure there will be sunlight in it.

I was amazed by how much Lena had matured since I left, but I worried about her shifting plans for the future.

Christmas 1931

Christmas vacation started on December 18. At Pomona Sergey was allowed to stay in his dormitory, but I had to evacuate mine. Fortunately I had several invitations for the holidays and accepted one from Nina Brownrigg, who was helping me with my English. A number of traditional Christmas events in the college took place before then, and for the first time I heard Christmas carols, saw the American decorations, exchanged Christmas notes, and heard

Christmas convocations. There was not even time to write letters.

Nina's family lived eight miles from the city of Pomona, in a large house in the midst of orange and lemon groves. There was a huge living room with a great fireplace always burning, lots of rugs, soft furniture and low lamps, and enough bedrooms, each with its separate bathroom, to put up several guests.

Charming Mrs. Brownrigg welcomed me warmly. We had wonderful dinners, to some of which Sergey was invited. We went Christmas shopping in Pomona, and on Christmas day, after opening presents at breakfast and eating a wonderful Christmas dinner, we visited relatives of the Brownriggs in Los Angeles.

I was also taken to the California Institute of Technology in Pasadena, and introduced to some of the researchers there. To my dismay I found out that while "Cal Tech" was considered as good as MIT, I could not study there because women were not admitted. I was shocked. I did not know that there could be a university with such restrictions. Was MIT open to women? No one seemed to know.

I was deeply touched by the friendliness and kindness of the Brownriggs, although since coming to California I had encountered so much effusive friendliness, often from complete strangers, that at times it did seem superficial to me: I felt that my concerns and anxieties were quite alien to them, and they might really not want to know about them. But I learned to accept this. and tried to respond in the same friendly manner.

24

California Spring

On returning to college we had our examinations, which were painful for me because of my usual spelling problems. How happy I had been with oral exams in Harbin!

In February Donald Brodie, Mr. Crane's personal assistant, was in California, and took Sergey and me out to lunch, to talk about our future plans. It was decided that Sergey would try to enter MIT. For me Mr. Brodie suggested Radcliffe or Columbia, as everyone seemed doubtful about my going to MIT as well. Both Dr. Edwards, the President of Scripps, and Mr. Brodie wrote so to Father. I still much preferred MIT, but I did not like to protest too much.

Meanwhile Father kept repeating in almost every letter how important it was for Lena and if possible Tanya to come to America to continue their education. Letters from him and my sisters were often in conflict with each other, and I sensed that the influence of the Soviet school and of their friends, many of whom planned to return to the USSR, made Lena and Tanya reluctant to come here, while Father seemed to insist on it more and more.

A disturbing letter came from Manya. Tanya, who was deeply involved in the local ice skating competitions – she would later win first place in the 100-meter dash with a record time of 13.5 seconds – had invited a group of her teammates home for tea. Fearing that the icons in our house would shock them, and alienate her from the group (symbols of a religious nature were derided by Soviet teaching), she took down the icons and hid them. Manya was highly indignant: the mere possibility that Tanya could be ashamed of her family's religion, and dare to remove the icons so dear to the other family members, was shocking. Tanya was severely reprimanded, but Manya could not get over it. She was seriously hurt. I tried to pacify her, tried to explain that there is no better way to learn something than by making a mistake, and then realizing how wrong it was. I don't know if my letter did any good.

Tanya's team won the competition, mostly because of her performance, but Tanya herself, who was already coming down with a cold, became ill with rheumatic fever soon afterward, and none of her teammates went to visit her. In spite of her efforts to conform, and her success in sports, Tanya apparently could not be a part of their crowd. Lena considered this an example of the lack of consideration and disregard of personal feelings by "sovietized" youth.

೦३

The problem of how to approach Mr. Crane about bringing Lena and Tanya to the United States continued to worry me, so I wrote for advice to our only relative in America, my older cousin George Vernadsky, who was then a lecturer (and later a distinguished professor) at Yale. In reply I received a very friendly letter from his wife Nina, advising us to settle in the Boston area if possible, because of the excellence of the educational institutions and cultural opportunities there. But they suggested that we seek admittance to Yale as well, as an alternative, and warmly invited us to share their house with them.

It was wonderful to know that the Vernadskys really felt like family towards us. We had never met them, and had only heard about them, a little, from our parents. But the letter did not really help, for their suggestions simply introduced new options, and we were in no position to make such decisions ourselves, without knowing what Mr. Crane had planned for us, or now expected of us. I sent a copy of Nina's letter to Father.

In the meantime I wrote to my former teacher, Professor Drozhin, who had become a frequent guest at our Harbin house after Sergey and I left. He had recently visited the USSR. I wanted to know what he thought about it, and I asked him whether one could live there, adding that America seemed to me somehow too self-satisfied to be challenging, even if it offered more possibilities.

The answer I received startled me. I had always treated Drozhin with a certain deference, as my teacher. He had hired me to help him with his book, but I never had any personal conversations with him, and I knew nothing about his life. This was a very personal letter, with a professional photograph of himself enclosed, in which after recounting his trip to Russia, he suggested that I come back to Harbin in the summer, finish my thesis, and get my engineering degree. He offered to help me, both academically and financially, and even to meet me in Japan.

He wrote, "I am sorry that America stole you while I was in Europe." During the few past years he had been unhappy, and buried himself in his work; his trip to Europe had been for personal reasons. Now he wanted to share the joy of what he felt was restored to him, his own personal freedom: "I want to live, I shall live!" Since 1923 he had been living abroad, and yet he felt at home in the USSR. He thought that he understood the Soviet people, although they understood less of him; he knew he was watched by the secret police while revisiting, and that it was still too early to return permanently, but he felt that the dawn of a new era was near. Labor ennobles mankind, and many young and intelligent people who had spent time abroad, and who wanted to build a new life, were reappearing in Russia. The idea of global revolution was fading. It was becoming possible to talk with people again – education, even in its primitive form, softens their rough edges. All this influenced him to stay on the good side of the Soviets, and to believe that he would find a use for his abilities in the homeland, and a job that would make living there possible. He asked me to show some daring and "take up his challenge," for "daring enriches your life."

I was dazed: this was just what I wanted to hear! The idea of going back to Harbin, even for a short time, to see my family and friends was like a fairy tale, impossible but enchanting. But when I shared these feelings with Sergey he was incensed. He could not see how I could help but admire everything in the United States. We quarreled bitterly, which upset me even more.

On March 11 I wrote a long and personal letter to Father about Professor Drozhin's offer. I told him about my growing doubts concerning my tentative engagement to Malcolm, and also the general American attitude towards marriage. I expressed my fear that I would never feel quite at home in America, and that after bringing my sisters here for education (which I understood as a non-negotiable obligation on my part), I might wish to go back:

I may still want to return to Russia if, as is possible, I cannot find a soulmate in America. I have all this ability to work, love, sacrifice, but there is nothing here to sacrifice for, nor is it needed or desired by anybody, unless it is to work with some destitute people which would mean working for a revolution, which I think is neither possible nor necessary here.

I wrote that in the USA the depression was raging, bootlegging was flourishing, money was everything and that only people who had money were respected. I had met a movie actress who told me that things just couldn't go on that way, and who wanted to go to the USSR and spend a year there, to see if the Russians had a solution. Everything that I respected in myself was unneeded here, and what I thought unimportant was overvalued. In spite of my improving English, more than ever I missed the richness and power of my native tongue – its poetry, sonorous and beautiful. If I should have children here, I thought that bringing them up in the Russian culture and the Russian language would make them unhappy and estranged from their environment, yet that bringing them up entirely American would estrange them from me and make me unhappy instead.

I thought that finishing my thesis at Harbin Polytechnic in two months would be quite impossible for me, since I had been away from any technical studies for a whole year. Even under the best of circumstances it would take a year. I wrote:

> There just may be a chance that I could manage to ask Crane to bring Lena and Tanya here. Maybe then I could take them back with me, if I visited Harbin this summer? ... Dear papa, what should I do? Please advise!

I had to wait six weeks for an answer.

News about Manchuria was infrequent in the American papers, but the few reports I read were ominous: war between Japan and China was in progress, and on March 16 the newspapers had a note about the occupation of Harbin by the Japanese. Knowing the city very well I was sure that their troops must have marched right past our house. I was now so upset that coming to my adviser

I burst out sobbing. No telegrams could be sent to Harbin, and letters took three weeks in transit, but at last we received one dated March 8, with the news that everything was all right. On the night the Japanese entered, my sisters stayed overnight with friends in another part of the town, while Father, Manya, and Nanny remained in the house with the doors deliberately unlocked, as the troops marched by. Nothing happened to them. Manchuria was now called Manchukuo, under a puppet government in Mukden and a Japanese administration in Harbin. The situation had begun to stabilize, and for the time being our family's way of life did not seem to be affected. Many of our Russian friends had already left, however, or were planning to leave.

After the good family news, so much of a relief to us both, Father came to a more general point:

> There is now no communism in Russia, only Stalin's despotism. The good that your mama and I hoped for exists also in a democracy, if only it is a little inclined towards socialism. ...
>
> Now here is a very important question – about my way of bringing you up. I always advise caution, consideration of others' opinions, and modesty. But is this right? Was I myself a good example of these qualities in my own stormy youth, with my marks of 3 on a scale of 12 for behavior? Is it not better to live life to the full – youth, courage, even death, if necessary. Is not this more beautiful? To express one's good, right, and honest thoughts boldly without worrying about the opinion of others? All this seems to me in my own character, and just the sort of advice I should be giving my children – yet it appears I am doing quite the opposite. What then is the matter? Am I committing a mistake – really a crime – pushing them into a direction opposite from the one I always esteemed?
>
> I think that I instilled in you long ago these "good" qualities of courage, independence, and honesty. You yourselves had them already, by nature, especially from your mother; I even fear for Mulya's tendency to "sacrifice." Well

then, if all these good qualities already exist, maybe it is right to warn you a little, and remind you, now and then, about caution. Those brave acts were good in their time and place – in one's homeland where one knew for sure that people would sympathize with you, would appreciate you, and in no case banish you from your country, unless as a political exile, temporarily only. Such an exile could even flatter one's ego – "how lucky you are to have been imprisoned two times!" But all this was in quite different times, in a bygone age, and nowadays gestures of that sort are not so appreciated, and may even be condemned for their obsolete chivalry, or their stupidity. What is needed now are the willingness and ability to work, physical health, and the necessary skills. These skills are what you should be acquiring in America. ...

None of this diminishes the importance of the poetic and sentimental side of life, and there is no life without love. Love is necessary and good, as is altruism. Even from an egoistic viewpoint: it is pleasant to do the kind of good that pleases others, but especially because it pleases oneself. In short, you will sort out all the other details for yourselves.

Your old Father

I don't remember exactly how Sergey and I reacted to this letter, though I suspect it was something like "we have heard all this before!" But at the same time I think it must have moved us, and reconfirmed what we had absorbed from him earlier.

ദ

My ability to speak English better did not seem to improve my chances of making close friends or being better understood by those I knew; the novelty of luxury and the heavenly climate was wearing off. Malcolm's letters, passionate and expressing his impatience to get married, began to seem trivial. When in one of them he said that he was "ripe" for married life, I was almost offended. He wanted a wife for *himself*, not to help me with my struggles. I did not want to go to the University of Chicago, whose catalogue he sent to me, and which did not seem to me very inviting. I wanted to study science, to do research, to be socially useful, but before that I had to ensure that all my sisters were on their feet, and now I had to help them in Harbin.

Malcolm sent me some photos he took when he was in Russia. It only made me more homesick, especially his remark about a photo of a bad Russian road with terrible potholes in it. I thought that the country needed so much more than eliminating potholes; my heart ached for it. I wrote to Malcolm that he should not consider himself engaged to me – my plans were too uncertain.

During this period I developed a great friendship with one of the girls in my hall, Barbara Loomis. She was a sophomore, four or five years younger than I, but she seemed to be more mature than the others. A very shy girl, she impressed me first by the fact that she always slept in a sleeping bag under the open sky. At Scripps she would sleep on the roof in her sleeping bag instead of using the bed in her room. She said that a ceiling above her head was too oppressive. She was a studious girl, not very talkative, but a very good listener. She liked to come to my room with her work. The two of us spent many evenings together, each doing her own assignment with Barbara occasionally helping me with spelling or with English expressions. She seemed to sense when I was disturbed by letters from home, or worrying when there were no letters, and she was thoughtful without prying.

Two years later I met her again in the East, on Martha's Vineyard, where her parents had a summer house. At one critical moment in my life, when I was despairing of my inability to send any money to Harbin, the Loomis family sent fifty dollars to them; I was touched and grateful. I eventually lost track of Barbara. I know only that she went to graduate school, got married, and became a scholar – I am not sure in what field.

Early in April, during the spring recess, I went to Pasadena to have a better look at Cal Tech. One of the students helped me find a room there. I could spend mornings in the library working on my assignments from Scripps, and most of the afternoons at the University. I met the only woman researcher there, and spent a whole day helping her freshen up and paint her equipment. I was also introduced to the only woman engineering graduate from MIT.

She said that to be employed I would have to be better than any man in my field, "otherwise they always prefer men," and that much depended on connections established during one's student years there. It all sounded difficult, but not impossible.

In the physics department I met a graduate student, John Blackburn ("Blackie" to everyone), who had a research project in progress in a laboratory. I offered to help by recording the readings of the meters on his installation, and he readily agreed. I spent a happy week there: the environment was so familiar to me that I felt quite at home. And I was quite impressed by Blackie's "inexhaustible reserve of knowledge," as I wrote to Lena. He took me in his Model A Ford to show me the desert in bloom, a whole day's trip of about 120 miles each way. We arrived there at about three in the afternoon, and I was overwhelmed by the beauty of it: innumerable varieties of blooming cactuses, the light blue and purple mountains in the distance, some of them snow-capped, and huge yuccas with blooms reaching far over my head. We walked, we sat on the stones; he read some poems by Kipling to me, and I showed him some postcard reproductions of pictures by Russian painters that I had taken along. Blackie took a photograph of me standing by one of the yuccas. He was the first American, except perhaps for my silent friend Barbara Loomis, who seemed to have the same values as me.

Blackie was a real California enthusiast and state patriot, and I began to understand how one could really love its natural scenery, which was mostly so lush, and yet in places so barren. And I started to appreciate the beauty of the desert myself. Blackie spoke of exploration for oil, about applications of mathematics to seismology, and I began to think that it might be an interesting field in which to specialize, that there were things to be done here. My homesickness began to abate. On the way back Blackie even let me drive his car, and for the first time in my life I really flirted, as I admitted in a letter to Lena. I felt that I was liked and it flattered me; yet I felt a little guilty, too, for I knew I was not really ready to become more interested in Blackie.

It was the California spring that I felt in my bones, although in this country of eternal spring and continuous blooming one could hardly see any difference between the seasons, except in the desert. Gradually my yearning for the change of seasons, for the sounds of running waters from melting snow in the spring, began to recede, and I started to feel that this different version of nature not only had a startling physical beauty, but its own special charm: not only could one admire it, but one could love it as well.

My friendship with Blackie and with his friend Ted, whose courtly attitude toward girls impressed me, changed for me the whole atmosphere of the last months in California. After the spring recess I went to Pasadena whenever I could get a ride there. I invited Ted to one of our dances and introduced him to several of my friends.

છ

On April 26 I received a telegram from Drozhin: "SITUATION UNFAVORABLE STAY AMERICA DROZHIN." This was really puzzling, but the intensity of my original response to his letter had passed and I was prepared to wait for an explanation, which would obviously take weeks to arrive. It never came, and must have been lost in the post.

Later that spring I received a great bundle of letters from Harbin. Among them was Father's full answer to my earlier questions, written on March 16 in the manner of a formal declaration:

WHEREAS

I feel responsible for a quick and sensible answer to a rather important and complex question, which must also be answered by everyone separately. But meanwhile I shall tell you what I think.

1. All of us (without exception) love truth and honesty. We love everybody and would be happy to sacrifice personal well-being in order that society improve living conditions for all. In other words, we all follow the bidding of our fathers, liberals and democrats of the nineteenth century, with a certain tendency to veer a little left, in keeping with your mother's legacy. We are ready to accept and be loyal to any regime which creates happiness for all the people on Earth. We firmly believe that this would occur with a raising of the

cultural level, and preservation of the cultural achievements of previous generations.

WHEREAS

2. Russia began a great movement in this direction. We were happy with that, and tried to participate in it, but fate led it along such heartless and horrific ways, to such sorrow and deceit, that we could not continue to take part, in spite of our great willingness to sacrifice all our own interests. Mother perished. By accident the children did not, but only because they were surrounded by people who followed Mother's principles, and were ready to make sacrifices too.

WHEREAS

3. When the children came to Harbin I faced the difficult problem of their upbringing. I have fulfilled it now, through my commitment to adhere to Mother's and my own guidelines: the children are raised and are ready to participate in the life of society of the extreme left, in which the basic principles above mentioned do survive. Revolution demands cruelty, and those who could have accepted that; but I could not, and I left Russia promising myself not to take up arms against a government devoted to being "creators of peoples' happiness."

WHEREAS

4. Can I deny my children's desire to help create peoples' happiness? Of course not! Not even if they wish to sacrifice themselves to that cause. The only question is the rationality and timeliness of the self-sacrifice.

WHEREAS

5. The complex political conditions of the revolution lead to one clear conclusion: now is not the right time for my children to return to Russia. All sensible, loving relatives of whatever political persuasion, having learned much through experience, firmly believe this: Brother Sasha, sisters Masha, Varya, and Zoya, all the Brullovs, Aunt Nadenka. Take note, none of them fled from the horrors of life there, and indeed many of them made a conscious decision to remain. Many

of our friends and other respected people here in Harbin are of the same opinion: Drozhin, Ustrialov, Lachinov … their names are legion. Their opinion is independent of their political convictions and reflects recent visits to the USSR, and a full knowledge of current events. The conclusion is crystal clear: now is not the right time. Such sacrifice is senseless and would result only in the loss of yet another fighter for human happiness. Even if one of you survives in the USSR, you will become coarse and will eventually abandon our basic principles.

WHEREAS

6. It is my responsibility to answer your question myself, and make it easy for all my other children to say "Father is right," and to sign their names on this sheet of paper. This will relieve them of the burden of this vexing problem, and free them for bold and honest self-improvement, in line with our principles, with the confidence to devote themselves fully to the cause of human well-being at the first opportunity. This is a heavy responsibility and only if the children agree with me can I justify my work with them in all these long years since the loss of Mother.

WHEREAS

7. Do I need to convince rebellious young heads that everything I say is right? Of course not. To do that would mean to kill their faith in the sanctity of everybody's right to work as they choose for the happiness of humanity. Is that what I want? Of course not. I only want the children to understand that this is not the right time to return to the USSR. I want the children to believe that it is necessary now to work hard on self-improvement, to prepare themselves for work for the good of the people around them, without skipping a single day. I want them to be completely ready for work everywhere they happen to live; I want them to see clearly when and where they can do maximum good in order to fulfill our ideal. I want them to believe that such a time is not far away, and that one must hasten to prepare for it.

WHEREAS

8. It was not easy for me to accept Mr. Crane's offer to send two children to America for study. But I firmly believed and believe now that the most useful work is performed by conscientious, wise, and educated people.

THEREFORE

9. I said, "Mulya and Seryozha, go there and hurry to extract the maximum from your studies, without thinking of anything else. Gather your strength. There is a time for every purpose."

10. I keep repeating: all of us shall live and work here as best we can. Lena and Tanya must finish their economics course and can then go anywhere they want. Zoya and Katya must finish at least that which seems possible now, and later the older ones will help them, if Father is unable to do so.

11. If an opportunity arises to go to America, the children must go.

I want the children to sign under items 10 and 11. ...

Agreed:

(Signed) Tanya, Lena, Zoya, Katya

12. Manya and I will stay in Harbin, until the time when Manya would be required for taking care of grandchildren. I am sure that Manya will be indispensable and will always have lots of work. She will always sacrifice her own good for those near and dear to her. She has already done a great deed by saving the children, and giving them a chance to become good and useful people.

So here was a firm and specific answer: I now had my work cut out for me, but I did not know how to begin. In any case I had to wait until I saw Mr. Crane, so that I would be able to assess what the chances were of doing something constructive about it in the near future.

CB

April 28 was the Thursday before Russian Easter. I wanted to go to a Russian church because the service of that evening, the reading of the New Testament, was my favorite. And I could not imagine an Easter without being at the Saturday midnight service. Blackie picked me up in Claremont and took me to the same Los Angeles hotel I had stayed in previously, where I remained until Easter Sunday, going to church every evening, really enjoying the services and the Russian language around me. I met bilingual children who attended a Russian school on Saturdays, and who easily switched from one language to the other. I declined an invitation to a traditional Sunday breakfast from the Women's Club. It was strange to have Easter without the *paskha,* but I wrote letters home and took a train back to Claremont on Sunday.

A week later I received from Father the answer to my letter about Drozhin's offer, dated April 9, 1932. He asked me again to be reasonable, not to rush into reckless actions. The letter was very long: four pages, single-spaced, with no margins as usual. About my wanting to sacrifice: to whom, for what? He begged me to stick to the goal I had set for myself, and to finish my education in America before thinking of anything else. This letter touched me deeply, but by the time I received it I had already come to the same conclusion myself. The whole episode seemed to me unreal: Drozhin's telegram was never explained, but I no longer needed an explanation. The situation in Harbin was such that returning there now seemed truly foolhardy.

My astronomy class was taken to see the Carnegie Astronomical Observatory at the top of Mount Wilson, where we listened to a lecture and saw the enormous telescopes, the largest in the world. We were allowed to look through the lesser of the two telescopes at the rings of Saturn. I had always been interested in astronomy and now felt a little regret that it was too late for me to change my field of specialization. We slept on the mountain-top overnight, and in the morning it was amazing to see the cloudline below us, with the peaks of other mountains like islands, surrounded by a foaming white sea – while above us the sun shone in the clear blue sky. I had never been above the clouds before.

In May I was invited to an evening of Russian poetry readings, with other amateur performances, in Los Angeles; but I found the evening not only boring and sentimental but of an appallingly poor quality. It gave me no pleasure at all to be among these émigrés, full of political intolerance mingled with homesickness for the idealized past. Their refusal to have any contact with present-day Russia made me feel that their cultural values lacked any vigor and simply were out-of-date. I was happy that most of my associations were with Americans.

The end of the school year was approaching, and Sergey would graduate with a BA degree. I hardly had any credits to show, but it did not matter, as I expected to be admitted wherever I would eventually go on the basis of my engineering credits. We planned our trip to the East Coast. I wanted to travel by boat, through the Panama Canal – it would cost almost the same as by train and it seemed to me so much more interesting. But Sergey remembered his painful seasickness and resisted. A friend of Sergey's was planning to drive east with his girlfriend in his own car, stopping at the Grand Canyon and other interesting sites. He offered to take us along if we would share the expenses. Even with hotel costs along the way it would be cheaper than going by train, and we could see more. Sergey and I could even share in the driving, since both of us had had a little practice in friends' cars, after the lessons we once took in Harbin. We decided to accept Dick's offer.

Graduation ceremonies at the two colleges were exciting, with throngs of parents in attendance. At his Sergey marched in the academic procession dressed in the usual black robe and funny hat, feeling very important. I was there among the parents to watch him, and to congratulate him as he approached me, clutching his diploma. Now he had not only caught up with me, he thought, but overtaken me, which was quite a boost to his ego. I did not really mind, for I wanted him to become independent of me – as long as he did not feel that his was the only correct opinion, and did not press me always to agree.

25

East Coast

Going East

After shipping our things to Mr. Crane's we said goodbye to our friends. Early on the morning of June 15, 1932 we were picked up by Dick and his girlfriend in their car, a two-door Ford with a rumble seat. Sergey and I added our two small suitcases to those already tied to the roof and climbed into the rumble seat.

The early morning air was fresh, but we knew that it would be rather hot in the desert after we passed the mountains. As we set off I thought with a certain regret of all the friends left behind, but it was unlike many partings in the past – there seemed to be a chance that we would meet again, either on the West Coast or in the East, for in America people seemed to move around the country quite easily. Californians warned us against Easterners: "They are not as friendly – they are snobs. You'll be in the city of Boston, 'the land of bean and cod, where Lowells speak only to Cabots and Cabots speak only to God.'" But I did not find Boston frightening: the Vernadskys said it was the cultural center of the USA and that was good enough for me. And since I had found out that MIT accepted women I looked very much forward to being there.

The wind in our faces was quite wearing, and Sergey and I slept much of the time. We arrived at the Grand Canyon late at night; it was too dark to see any of it and we were tired, so we rented cabins and went to sleep, getting up early enough to see the sun rise over the canyon. It was a magnificent sight: the early morning fog was lifting from the river below, and gradually the enormous depth of the canyon opened before our eyes. The colors were unbelievable. We stood at the edge of the drop, trying to distinguish the details of the steep pass through which several groups of tourists mounted on donkeys were descending toward the bottom.

We decided against such an excursion – it was expensive, and took several hours, which we felt we could not spare. To avoid the heat of the day we wanted to rest while we had use of the cabins, depart in the evening, and drive all night. We lunched at a restaurant at the rim of the Canyon and then slept the rest of the day.

In the evening Dick suggested that either Sergey or I should drive. Sergey was very happy to do so. Both of us had managed to obtain our driver's licenses in the spring, but we had had few opportunities to practice, and this was a wonderful chance. I was still a little timid about it, and gladly let Sergey take the wheel. The night was really cold; we put on our warm coats, while Dick and his girlfriend lowered themselves as far as they could into the narrow space of the rumble seat and packed it tightly with blankets and all the warm things we had. They could not move at all, but we hoped they would stay warm.

Sergey drove confidently. The road was two lanes wide and almost deserted; only rarely did we meet another car. The dark landscape around us was hardly distinguishable, there were no houses or any trace of human life, and I soon fell asleep. I don't know how long I had slept when a strange movement awakened me: it was the car turning over – first on its side, then upside down, then on the other side. I was thrown from the door and found myself lying on the sand by the roadside, with Sergey next to me. The rumble seat remained intact, with Dick and his girlfriend still in it – their having been wedged so far down in the seat saved them, and the heavy coats protected us.

Sergey stood up, his face feeling numb, his nose bent to one side and bleeding profusely. He instinctively seized his nose and straightened it out, which a doctor who examined him later said had been a good job indeed. Still in a daze, I got to my feet; Sergey later wrote to Father that I began to sing the toreador aria from *Carmen,* which I myself don't remember. What I do remember is that I tried to push the car upright, but Sergey pulled me away. "Stop it," he commanded, "you cannot do that!"

The others were extricating themselves from the rumble seat, dazed, but quite unharmed, asking "What happened?" Sergey explained that there had been an unexpectedly sharp curve where the road crossed a railroad track, and no warning sign. He was going too fast to negotiate the curve, and did something one is never supposed to do: he jammed on the brakes.

There was nothing we could do except wait for some passing car to come to our aid. The first shock had passed, and my back began to hurt. Sergey's face was all bloody, his hands and nose hurt. Our friends urged us to lie down on the sand and rest, which we did. They covered us with blankets from the rumble seat and collected our scattered possessions. The time was about two in the morning, and it was freezing cold. That is all I remember, for both Sergey and I either fell asleep or sank into half-consciousness.

It was nearly four in the morning when a truck finally appeared on the road, headed toward Gallup, New Mexico, some forty miles away. There were only two seats in the cab and we worried that we could not sit up all the way – our backs hurt so much. Our friends urged us to take this ride, however, because we might otherwise have to wait a long time for another. Sergey looked to be the one most hurt; and we placed him next to the driver with me by the door, so that he was supported on both sides.

It was a bumpy ride in the old truck, and my back felt each bump. In a little over an hour the driver deposited us at a filling station outside Gallup, where we waited until an ambulance came. Sergey was laid on a stretcher and I sat on a bench next to him, trying to find a position that minimized the pain in my back. In the hospital it became so severe that I fainted.

We were both x-rayed and it was found that Sergey had bruised hands, a broken nose, and a strained back, but nothing more serious. Nothing could be done with his nose at that time. I had a broken rib and a cracked vertebra and was ordered to lie in bed for at least two weeks, during which Sergey could also stay in the hospital. We really were lucky that our injuries were relatively slight. Poor Sergey kept going over all the details of the accident, feeling terribly responsible for it, and for failing to protect his sister.

Even though my back hurt terribly, and I had to lie flat without moving, my primary emotion was one of guilt. We had to wire Mr. Crane first. The answer came, wishing us a speedy recovery and assuring us that all the expenses would be taken care of. A local florist brought a bouquet of flowers from Mr. Crane into my ward, which touched me deeply.

Now we had to write home. I realized what panic this might provoke in our family, and we tried to make as light of it as we could. The awful part was that it took so long for them to get our letters, and of course we could not wire them, for that would be too alarming.

Sergey was soon allowed to walk around, and within a few days his hands were able to hold a pencil, so he went from ward to ward sketching portraits of various patients – to their great delight. Most of the sketches Sergey gave to his models, but we kept one of a little Mexican boy with a head-bandage. As soon as I could move in bed a little I began to make paper cutouts of little houses and other things, for the children lying in my ward who had nothing to amuse them. Some had working parents who could visit them only on Sundays.

Sundays were quite interesting: apparently it was a custom among the local people to visit the hospital even if they knew none of the patients there. Whole families walked through the corridors stopping at various wards. I liked their usual greeting: they would say, "I'm glad you feel better today," without asking first how you felt, just to be friendly and to make you feel better. In general what I remember of our stay in that hospital is the kindness of everyone.

We had no reading matter, for our books had been shipped to New York, and the local papers dealt mostly with the local news. We were able to follow the presidential campaign, however, Franklin Roosevelt running against Herbert Hoover. Even Father mentioned that in his letters.

We had not expected to receive any answers to our letters home while we were still in the hospital, as mail now could take anywhere from two to six weeks to reach Harbin. Letters forwarded to us in Gallup from New York were replies to our own written earlier in California. When these came Sergey and I would read them together, and for a while forget that we were alone in a hospital in New Mexico. It was not until we were quite well and settled in Cambridge that we received our first letter from the family reacting to our accident.

Later I learned from Lena that on the day after receiving our letters from the hospital Father's hair turned completely gray.

The situation in Harbin was now even more difficult than before, though the problems were different. The Japanese administration was hard on the native population of Manchuria, and on the Russians with whom they competed for influence, and whom they wished to replace. Lena reported one incident: she went to a nearby field with a Chinese laborer who was helping her to dig up some sod for the garden. A Japanese mounted policeman approached and struck the Chinese with his whip. He dropped to his knees, begging the policeman to stop, but the whipping continued mercilessly, lacerating his back. Lena stood by speechless, terrified by the brutality.

Father maintained a different perspective, with his nostalgic memories of Japan, and especially of the gentle Japanese women. He had several good Japanese friends, among them a Mr. Yagi, whose wife was Russian and who himself spoke Russian. Mr. Yagi in fact was appointed the head of the Japanese police in Harbin.

No other country but Japan recognized the government of "Manchukuo," and as a result of international concern over the Manchurian occupation an investigative commission from the League of Nations was to meet in Harbin. There had been many arrests of young men accused of sabotage, and the Japanese were preparing reports on their interrogation. Mr. Yagi, for whom Father had done translations in the past, asked Father to translate some documents into English for that commission. Father saw that in the reports the boys' answers to their interrogators gave hints of mistreatment, perhaps even torture. Translating these was very unpleasant for Father, but he hoped that an accurate rendering would make it obvious to the League how the confessions had been obtained.

The arbitrary behavior of the Japanese administration, and the unpredictable arrests, led some of our close friends still remaining in Harbin (including Drozhin, Evgenii Shmatov, and Yura Aingorn) to prepare to leave for the USSR on short notice.

Meeting Mr. Crane

It was already July when we finally arrived by train in New York, where Donald Brodie met us. On the way to our hotel he told us that Mr. Crane and his wife were still in New York and had invited us to dinner that night. They were planning to leave the next day for their summer home at Woods Hole, on Cape Cod, and wanted us to accompany them. Mr. Brodie said that Mr. Crane thought we should spend another year in college, and mentioned that at this time he was supporting about fifty different families, which was not quite fair to his own children. This alarmed me, as I had been about to ask Mr. Crane to bring Lena and Tanya to America too. But knowing now what Mr. Brodie had just told me, how could I do that? I decided to wait and see.

After cleaning up and changing we walked to 522 Fifth Avenue, where the doorman directed us to an elevator. Mrs. Crane, a gracious, rather stout lady with gray hair and a warm smile, welcomed us and asked us about our accident and the trip east. At the dinner table Mr. Crane sat quietly as we were served by a butler. I told him all about the rest of our family, about Father's futile efforts to find employment, and how without any university in Harbin I did not know what Lena and Tanya were going to do. Mr. Crane seemed interested, but made no offer to bring any of them to America. He said that there was a small cottage for us in Woods Hole, where he hoped Sergey and I could rest for a while. He asked about our plans, and I said that since MIT did after all accept women, I would like to go there and take a degree in mathematics, rather than engineering, because it would be better for Sergey and me not to compete in our search for a job. Besides, mathematics could open up a wider field of occupations to me. Sergey wanted to take his degree in electrical engineering.

After that meeting Sergey and I agreed that we could hardly hope that Mr. Crane would invite our sisters to America right away. What we had to write home would be a great letdown for Lena. In fact we did not realize just how much of a disappointment it was for both Lena and Father: only from letters that we received later did we learn what kind of suspense and anticipation the family was living in. For some reason Father was sure that at least Lena, and probably Tanya too, would be going that year to America, and he kept encouraging Lena to think so. It seemed to them that the journey was imminent, maybe a matter of only a few weeks. Even though Lena was not nearly so certain about this as Father, she was not making any plans for her education in Harbin, and had still not applied for a Soviet passport, without which she could not get a job. The new Japanese administration maintained the same agreement of "equal representation" in employment on the Railroad as the former Chinese Government, which meant that only Soviet or Manchurian citizens could work there.

Lena accepted the news remarkably well, however. Her chances of going to America had always seemed to her remote and unreal, and she had prepared herself for a negative result. Almost at once she began to make plans for the coming year for herself and the other sisters. The only possible educational institution for Lena in Harbin was a night school with two departments, economics and law. She chose economics.

Tanya seemed to have no suitable options at all for further studies. But she took typing lessons during the summer and now helped Father, he dictating his translations directly from the original while she typed, barely keeping up with him. Zoya was the only other sister who would still be in school, the Railroad Commercial School having changed into a technical school. Katya, who was under the age of admission (fifteen), would take a year off, with some private lessons. But even this reduced program had to be paid for, and Sergey and I obviously had to hurry to get our degrees, so that we could find work and help them.

The day after dining with the Cranes we took the train to Woods Hole, where we were installed in a cottage on their estate. The newspapers were full of the Roosevelt-Hoover presidential campaign. Mr. Crane, we now heard, had flown to see Franklin Roosevelt, whom he strongly supported.

During the very first week Mr. Brodie drove us to Cambridge and took us to MIT. Here was the place about which I had dreamt for at least four years. I still remember the peculiar smell of the

Charles River, separated from MIT by the wide Memorial Drive. The Charles was not yet thought to be dangerously polluted, and there was actually a public beach farther upstream. The gray MIT building with its central dome, so familiar to me now, spread its extensions like arms, facing the river and the city of Boston on the other side. Inside, it looked like a factory, with long corridors with bare floors, cement walls, and busy students hurrying to their classes or laboratories. It resembled my Institute in Harbin, and I felt right away that I belonged there.

The Registrar had never heard of Harbin Polytechnic Institute, but was willing to let us try MIT. We both wanted to be admitted to the graduate school to work for a Masters degree, which would take us one year. Sergey had no problem with his BA degree from Pomona and his four years of engineering credits. However, I had taken mathematics courses only in the first two years at Harbin, so if I wanted to pursue a degree in mathematics I had to take a summer course in differential equations, which would start in a few days. This would also show whether I could handle MIT's program. The Registrar thought that Sergey could profit from a summer course too.

M. I. T.

Sergey could be assigned a room in the dormitory, but there were no dormitories for girls, and I rented a room on the other side of the river, across the MIT Bridge. It was a gloomy room, opening onto a small inner court from which no sunlight reached my window. I had never before lived in so big a city and the noises outside at night frightened me, for they sounded like children crying. I even thought that in this sinful city someone was mistreating children; it was not until several days later that someone told me that the cries were of cats fighting.

My course work turned out to be easy. We had actually covered all of it in Harbin as integral calculus, although we did not have such interesting problems involving practical applications of the theory. Professor Struik had a remarkable way of using the blackboards, which spanned three walls of the classroom, and I thought that if

I could just photograph the blackboard, I would not need to take notes. My assignments were so simple that I concentrated mostly on the appearance of what I was turning in. I simply had fun.

Both of us did well enough in our summer courses to be admitted into the graduate school. After the end of summer school we went back to Woods Hole and spent several restful weeks on the Cranes' estate. The Vernadskys sent us the addresses of their friends, Professors Michael Karpovich in Cambridge and Pitirim Sorokin in Winchester, and suggested that we visit them when we moved back to Cambridge.

We were examined by Mr. Crane's doctor, who found that our injuries had healed completely, but that both of us needed to have our tonsils and adenoids removed for the second time. That was done the very next week, under local anesthesia. Sergey had a piece of broken bone removed from his nose, but his once handsome straight nose now looked more like that of a veteran boxer.

Mr. Crane was wonderfully attentive: he visited me in the hospital after the operation, and even called to wish me goodnight before I fell asleep. I felt shy with him and did not quite understand how to respond to such personal attention. When I came out of the hospital I received from Mrs. Crane a lovely gold ring with a large aquamarine and from Mr. Crane a little purse with a gold five-dollar coin in it. His personal interest in us both was always touching, and although I now understand that he concerned himself personally with all those whom he helped, I have also heard that the Zarudny family was one of his favorite causes.

Donald Brodie, who always took care of the business side of our relationship with Mr. Crane, told us that our support would be transferred to a charitable organization that Mr. Crane sponsored. We would each receive $1500, plus our dental and medical expenses, for one year, but this would be all. After that we would be on our own. The tuition at MIT at that time was $500, so that left us each $1000, which was quite adequate for a year. As soon as we received the check from Mr. Brodie, we sent the usual monthly sum to Harbin.

CB

In mid-September 1932 we moved to Cambridge and I found a room in a lodging house on Trowbridge Street, much nicer than what I had over the summer. The adjustment to living alone was rather hard for me, however. In retrospect, it was wise of Mr. Crane to have placed me for the first year in a small college and in a dormitory. Now, the only places where I could see and talk with people were classrooms, corridors, restaurants, or movie theaters. I had been so used to being able to invite friends to my home, to have them meet my father and sisters, to see them in large groups of other friends; but here I had no home. I was never part of a group, perhaps because mathematics students worked individually, without a laboratory or joint projects. All the students I now knew came from far away in other states.

There was a wonderful lounge at MIT for women students, but men were not allowed there. The female students were all quite young, most of them concentrating either in biology or architecture. I think there was one other female student in mathematics, none in engineering. I knew no families with children my age where I could meet young people in a home atmosphere.

So the rooming house became the nearest thing to a home for me. I fixed up my room to look like a living room, making up my bed like a sofa, but I could not serve meals there, and it was unsuitable for inviting more than one person at a time. However, I met other students living in the same house and we often visited each other's rooms. There was a fire station nearby, and I remember running to find one of my acquaintances in his room whenever I heard a siren, for I would then experience such panic, with the memory of Byeloretsk still in my mind, that I could not bear being alone; it took me more than a month to get used to this sound. I also shuddered whenever I saw a tall warehouse building with its narrow grated windows – it reminded me of the prison wall in Omsk.

Several students in our house and I breakfasted together in one of our rooms, and shared the expenses. One of the roomers was Dr. Wilhelm Jost, a physicist, one of the international fellows at MIT. He was the first young German man I had ever met, and this in itself made him seem quite intriguing.

Academically I had no difficulties. Two of my courses were given by Professor Struik,[1] who was also to supervise my thesis. His assistant was Harold Freeman, a tall, thin, shy, good-looking man, no older than I, whom I met once at the Struiks' home. The Struiks had three small daughters, and Harold was sometimes asked to look after them. It impressed me very much that a young man would take care of little girls. I had a few conversations with him and he appeared well-read, sensitive, and interesting to talk to, but I rarely saw him at MIT.

Following the Vernadskys' suggestion, soon after we arrived in Cambridge we called on the Karpovich family. Michael Karpovich,[2] whom we addressed as Mikhail Mikhailovich in the Russian manner, lectured in European and Russian history at Harvard. He and his wife, Tatiana Nikolaevna, greeted us graciously and were extremely friendly. They had four children, which made us feel quite at home in their house when we visited them. But we never met anybody our own age at their home.

Professor Sorokin,[3] on whom we called once, was quite cordial. Sergey had a long conversation with him and left full of enthusiasm about some new ideas. We were once invited for dinner there, but the relationship never developed beyond that. Probably it was our own fault.

A friend of Sergey's from California, Dwight Merrill, soon located us, and we spent much time with him and his wife. Sergey happily accepted their offer to move in with them and share the cost of their apartment and food, which would be less expensive and more pleasant than living in an undergraduate dormitory. We observed with surprise that, being Californians, the Merrills also felt strange among the Easterners, as did we.

MIT President Compton and his wife threw a party for foreign students. Mrs. Compton wanted me to meet some Soviet Russian exchange students but I thought they might not want to meet me: they were usually suspicious of recent Russian emigrants. Again I found it almost impossible to explain my peculiar position – neither "white" nor "red." Most of all I could not understand why being a Russian from China, I should be meeting Soviet Russians, or

Chileans or Indians for that matter, when what I mainly wanted was to meet Americans.

In November the national elections were held. We read about them in the newspapers and heard them discussed by our American friends, who explained the political process to us, fascinating as it was. In January Franklin Roosevelt would replace Herbert Hoover as President of the United States. Sergey looked forward to voting, as an American citizen, in the next presidential election. Neither of us had yet applied for citizenship, of course, but like all my friends, I was very much impressed by Roosevelt's program.

In Manchuria Father also followed the news from the USA. Father hoped for the best, but was afraid that Roosevelt might turn out to be too weak: he seemed like a kind person, and reminded Father of Kerensky, the head of the Russian Provisional Government that was overthrown by the Bolsheviks in October 1917. The political situation in Harbin remained complicated. The puppet government of the Manchurian Emperor installed in Mukden merely masked the complete Japanese control of the country they now called Manchukuo. The Japanese assumed that Manchukuo had inherited all the Chinese rights to the Chinese Eastern Railroad and that the Chinese-Russian agreement simply became a Manchukuo-Russian agreement, which would not affect Russians living in the Railroad Zone one way or the other. China, of course, bitterly protested this position, but at the moment was quite helpless, for in fact the Japanese controlled both the Railroad and the civilian government of the whole Zone. Japan's goal was to consolidate its position in Manchuria and to take over the Chinese Eastern Railroad entirely, and it hoped to accomplish this by arranging the sale of the Railroad by the Russians to Manchukuo. In the meantime the Japanese were using whatever means they had, including White Russian organizations, to make life uncomfortable for the Soviet administration and employees of the Railroad, as well as for the other Soviet citizens in Harbin. They also were building other railroads in direct competition with the CER, in order to reduce its economic value. All this met with vigorous protests from China and expressions of concern from the United States, France, and the League of Nations.

○ঙ

Both Sergey and I tried to live frugally. In Harbin we had been used to attending the theater, opera, and concerts quite often. Here the price of the tickets was so high that it was out of question, except on rare occasions when someone took me out, and this never happened to Sergey. But we knew that the family's income in Harbin from translations and lessons was dwindling, and it was hard to understand how Manya and Father succeeded in helping the girls, and even their friends, to keep up their spirits. Father's letters sounded increasingly desperate: he felt helpless, and he could not think or write about anything else. They all counted on our help. But here in America everyone we knew told us that with so much unemployment it was not at all certain that we could find jobs immediately after graduating We somehow had to provide for our own living until we could earn it, because unlike most of the other students, we had no family to return to. Still, once in a while we were able to send home a little more than before.

As I read the letters from home it seemed strange that they thought of our life here as glamorous. I imagined their cozy evenings with numerous friends around the table with the samovar, their going to concerts and plays which we could not afford, their visiting interesting friends at their homes, and it always made me feel homesick. I realized, however, that the great difference was that here there was a future in prospect, while in Harbin there was none.

Letters from Harbin told of an extremely rainy summer, which resulted in the greatest floods Harbin had ever known. Some of the houses near the Sungary River were completely destroyed, while the poorest parts of the city suffered most, with streets becoming rivers, and thousands of people left homeless. The floods brought epidemics of cholera and typhus, skin diseases, and injuries of all kinds. Many young people did volunteer work assembling the refugees in schools, some of which were also flooded, so that the medical personnel as well as patients had to wade through the rooms; Lena was helping in one of these schools. Luckily our house was built on an elevation, though the road to it was so deep in mud that it was nearly impassable. The house now overflowed with people instead: Lena called it a "refugee camp" in her letters. Some families paid a little rent, which for a while relieved the family's ongoing financial crisis.

Lena and Tanya had applied for Soviet citizenship but so far with no response. To improve their chances Father applied again. But my friend Yura Aingorn, who held a Soviet passport and had graduated from Harbin Polytechnic, had difficulty in being approved for a position as assistant to Prof. Drozhin, because it was known that Sergey and I, his friends, had gone to the United States. Drozhin told Father that the family should say that we were in America only for study, and that afterwards we intended to move to the USSR.

At that time an article appeared in a Harbin newspaper, headed "Marvelous luck of the Zarudny brother and sister, invited to America by an American millionaire." Though this was known to many friends, the fact of it, and the form in which it appeared in the paper, probably made it even harder for my sisters to obtain the coveted Soviet passport, and thus jobs with the Railroad. It was becoming more and more obvious that Harbin was an absolute dead-end and that every Russian must sooner or later leave it.

In November Father became ill. He coughed, and had a high temperature and heart pains. Early in December he was diagnosed with pneumonia and sent to the hospital. Lena borrowed some money from friends to pay for his stay. When we learned about this Sergey and I figured carefully to the last dollar how much money we needed to live until the last day of the school year, and sent everything over that amount to Harbin. I also wrote to Mr. Crane and he sent some money too. Father was out of the hospital in two weeks, but remained very ill. Manya learned how to take care of him; she had the natural ability, sympathy, and intelligence to make her a wonderful nurse. By Christmas time Father was said to be recovering, though still confined to bed.

About that time I began to develop a closer friendship with Wilhelm Jost. He rented a car and was able to take me riding around New England. I wrote to Father about him. Father's answer came in January. Unlike his usual typed letters, this one was handwritten;

he was not allowed by the doctor to exert himself and the family tried to keep him even from reading, let alone using the typewriter. He wrote, however, that he was able, with Lena's help, to make a little money translating. He was quite supportive of my interest in a German man, remarking that culturally the Russians are closer to Germans than to Americans. Mostly he tried to encourage me to make my own decisions, hoping that I would make the right ones, but he added that any man who wished to marry me must write to him, promising that he intended to make me as happy as possible. From the lack of chattiness in his letter it was obvious that Father was still quite ill.

Midyear exams passed without any problems and for the second term I signed up for more difficult courses. One used a German textbook, adding language difficulty to the complexity of the subject. In the other, Potential Theory, our visiting German professor's accent made it difficult for me to understand all he said; I struggled in this course, for I had never studied theoretical physics. But two graduate students in physics taking this course with me – William Shockley (who later won a Nobel Prize for his work on transistors) and Robert Richtmyer – helped me a great deal, and spent several days tutoring me before the last examination. Without their help I don't know how I would have managed it.

Robert Richtmyer, who later distinguished himself in both physics and mathematics, became a good friend. His father was a professor of physics at Cornell, and author of a celebrated college textbook, *Introduction to Modern Physics*. Bob played the violin and loved music, and he took me to several concerts. He would visit me in my room and I felt that he was interested in me, but I could not make him say so. I wished I could introduce him to my family, but he could meet only my brother, and no friendship developed between them. We remained in contact with each other, however, until his death in 2003.

The subject of my Master's thesis was continuous fractions used in the design of electric filters. My adviser was Professor Struik, together with visiting Professor Otto Szasz. During our conferences, amusingly, we spoke in three languages, native to none of us: being originally Dutch, Professor Struik spoke German to Szasz, a Slovak, and English to me, a Russian. I usually understood the German they spoke, but I replied in English.

Each day the newspapers wrote about new ways Roosevelt was trying to cope with unemployment. The Works Progress Administration was organized, and hundreds of people who had never used a shovel were cleaning streets and digging ditches; on many city squares small orchestras entertained the passing public; young men were employed to clean up national parks; and mathematicians were computing tables of mathematical functions to ten decimal places on arithmometers and primitive calculating machines.

It was about that time that I received in the mail an offer to send to me "under plain cover" a book about sex. I felt a tremendous need by this time to learn more about it. I worried a little about the cost of the book, but I knew it was important, and when I received it I read it through in one evening, unable to stop. Unlike the time when my sister Zoya enlightened me, I was now fascinated, not shocked, and ready to accept the facts – although for the time being my new knowledge remained theoretical.

My friendship with Jost gradually blossomed into a romance. He impressed me with his European manners and his wide interests reflecting his classical European education. He obviously liked me, and we seemed to have something intangible in common. As I look back on it, it may simply have been that he was the first German I knew, as Malcolm Proudfoot was the first American, their main attraction for me being their cultural difference from all others I already knew.

We agreed to consider ourselves engaged, with the understanding that when he returned to Germany I would stay in America and see to it that all my sisters were well on their way to completing their education, before moving on. Only then would I go to Germany and marry him.

At the end of January, however, the National Socialists in Germany won the elections and Hitler came into power. Jost was very concerned, but was sure that "it cannot last." I remember telling him that this was what the Russians were saying about the Bolsheviks, but his answer was "Such things can happen in barbaric Russia, but not in civilized Germany!" To me this seemed unconvincing, and his attitude toward Russia disturbed me. Jost planned to return at the end of the summer to his position of *Privat Dozent* at a German university.

A month later the Reichstag was burned in Berlin. But by then I was overwhelmed by the news we had just received from Harbin.

[1] Professor Dirk Jan Struik (1894-2000): a highly respected mathematician and an internationally acclaimed historian of mathematics.

[2] Michael (Mikhail Mikhailovich) Karpovich (1888-1959): an historian, he came to the United States on a temporary mission for the Provisional Government in the spring of 1917 and remained here after the Bolshevik Revolution. From 1927 to 1957 he was a lecturer, and subsequently Professor of History and Chairman of the Slavic Department, at Harvard University. From 1946 to 1959, he edited *Novyy Zhurnal (New Review)*, one of the most important publications of the Russian emigration.

[3] Pitirim Alexandrovich Sorokin (1889-1968): a noted, but controversial sociologist. A member of the SR, Sorokin served briefly as secretary to Prime Minister Kerensky of the Provisional Government. He was arrested by the Soviets in 1918, but released on orders from Lenin. With his wife Elena he left Russia for Prague in 1922 and soon moved to the United States. He was Professor of Sociology, and Chairman of the Sociology Department, at the University of Minnesota in the 1920s, and from 1930 was at Harvard University. A prolific writer whose works include the four-volume *Social and Cultural Dynamics* (1937), spanning 2,500 years of human history, he was elected President of the American Sociological Association in 1965.

26

Adulthood

On February 23, 1933 Sergey received a telegram from Crane's office in New York:

SORRY TO QUOTE FOLLOWING CABLE MESSAGE RECEIVED FROM HARBIN QUOTE PREPARE ZARUDNYS FATHER DIED HEART FAILURE UNQUOTE PLEASE ACCEPT OUR SYMPATHY CRANE OFFICE.

Sergey came to my room holding the telegram. He was very tender, and embraced me; we sat on my bed and cried together.

Now I finally found the courage to write to Mr. Crane that I wished to bring all my sisters to America. He generously answered that he would help us do so when Sergey and I graduated and I had a job, so that I could be their official sponsor.

The letters from Father kept coming for another month. In a way they mitigated our grief: even though we could not answer them, they fostered the illusion that Father was still with us. Even after the last letter we kept waiting for more, as if there was just a break in the correspondence. We received a long letter from Manya, who wrote:

Now we must live by his wishes that all of you should grow up and be wise, love each other, and be healthy. … Papa always said, "when I die, you need to forget about me quickly; do not torture the children," but it is so difficult for me to forget.

About three hundred people attended Father's funeral service in the Harbin cathedral; so many people had loved and respected him, through all the trials of the last years. Two horses in funeral harness drew the hearse with his coffin, and the priest and mourners walked behind it all the way to the cemetery, where the final prayers were intoned. It was a dismal sunless day with snow slowly falling over the funeral procession. A wooden cross decorated with three metal wreaths was set over his grave. Several years later, when the rest of the family was already in America, that cemetery was razed and replaced by an airport.

Father's death was a great blow to Uncle Sasha, as well as ourselves. He wrote that we should consider him our father now. He was more than ten years older than Father, and their oldest sister Masha was still living too – she and her husband would die during the siege of Leningrad in 1941-42.

In the meantime Harbin had recovered from the flood and its ensuing problems. Many more Russians were preparing to depart, but Lena had as many lessons as she could handle, and Tanya obtained a number of typing assignments. The extra money they had received from renting rooms to flood refugees before Father's death, along with his life insurance of five hundred Mexican dollars, helped them to pay off most of their debts. Tanya was counting on her sports associates to help her procure a passport and a job, and Lena wrote bravely that they could manage. She herself was taking her first-year final exams that spring.

Shortly after Easter Lena was refused a Soviet passport, and now suspected that Tanya would be no more successful. Getting a job with the Railroad looked hopeless. Lena wrote that while she was not really part of any Soviet group, she felt awkward when among the White Russian émigrés. Applying for Manchurian citizenship, however, was out of the question. The friction between the USSR and Manchukuo had been exacerbated by the Soviets moving some of the Railroad rolling stock into Russia without clearance from the CER administration. A new conflict between Japan and the USSR seemed to be brewing.

Wilhelm Jost drove me to Maine during the spring recess. One weekend we took a boat trip to Provincetown on Cape Cod. By now I felt thoroughly committed to him, although sometimes his insensitivity toward my problems made me unhappy. I also thought that he was insufficiently troubled about the situation in Germany.

My course work and Sergey's went on satisfactorily, but we both realized that we could not finish our theses before the spring graduation; we needed a few more months. No professional jobs seemed available. On the streets of Cambridge one could see horse-drawn wagons delivering ice or milk, with signs reading "Buy milk [or ice, or eggs] from an MIT graduate." Even that sort of enterprise required some money to start with, while we had none.

The Karpoviches, who were moving to a larger house on Trowbridge Place in Cambridge, kindly offered me room and board in exchange for looking after their small children in the mornings, and babysitting in the evenings whenever they went out. This was a marvelous solution for me, since it left me enough time to work on my thesis, and to look for a job. The Vernadskys offered to put up Sergey, who would draw the maps for George Vernadsky's new book.

Both of us ended the year with high grades in our courses and won strong recommendations from our professors. In a way it was good not to have finished and not to be just unemployed. The longer that period of unemployment would last, after graduation, the harder it would then be to find jobs.

On Our Own

I moved from my room on Trowbridge Street to the Karpoviches' house at the end of May. My duties were to rise in the mornings with the young children – Natasha, six years old, Serezha, four, and Marisha, three – and give them their breakfast, so that the parents could sleep a little longer. The first morning Professor Karpovich had to show me how to cook eggs and make oatmeal. Like my mother, I really knew nothing about cooking.

The Karpovich household had a relaxed atmosphere of warmth and disorganization. Both parents were extremely kind to the children, to me, and to anyone who might drop in. Tea was served at a moment's notice, but there was no routine, no system of orderliness. It seemed as though Mrs. Karpovich could not bear any pressure of that kind herself, and refused to exert it upon others. On the other hand her mother, who lived with them, was a very disciplined and rather prim lady, who ironed and repaired all the children's clothes in her own room, remaining there all day in her chair, reading English novels. Both her own parents were English, though she was born and spent most of her life in Russia.

The Karpoviches wanted their children to speak Russian at

home. Before me they had engaged an earlier Russian emigrant, but her language was such a mixture of Russian and English that they did not want the children to be exposed to it. An example of her speech: "*zakroite* window*oshki*, children*iata za* sick*uiutsia*" (close windows, children will get sick). Every root was English, but all the morphology Russian. Little Serezha spoke only Russian, and had no common language with the children he met on the street. He told me of a wonderful discovery he had made: "Mulya, do you know, that in Russia *everybody* speaks Russian!" They were charming children and I loved taking care of them.

The news from Harbin was now rather encouraging, for a change. On the basis of her application for Soviet citizenship Tanya started work on the Railroad as a messenger; it was at least a small steady income. She still hoped that her sports friends would help her toward that coveted passport. Uncle Sasha promised to try to help Lena's resubmitted application by appealing to a friend in power. Lena was in love with Vitaly, a boy who had Soviet citizenship, and they intended to marry.

Late in June the Karpoviches went to Vermont on vacation, leaving me in the house alone with a young Russian, Boris Nagashev, who occupied one of the spare rooms. He owned a car and the Karpoviches gave him room and board in exchange for driving them about when they needed it. Nagashev was a very interesting person. During the Revolution all his family died, and at the age of sixteen he traveled alone to Yugoslavia with a group of refugees. On the way there he invented an electric coil to heat water in a cup. Arriving in Belgrade, he heard that there was a call for bids to restore the electric lighting in the cathedral. The wiring was concealed in the walls, the sketches showing its location were lost, and in many places it was grounded by the damp that had got in during the war. The walls had frescoes all over them which could not be disturbed. Siemens, a large, well-known firm, made the lowest bid to put up new, unobtrusive wiring outside the walls, but Nagashev and a young friend of his offered to restore the original wiring at about one-tenth of that sum.

The underfunded government took the risk of letting these young unknowns take on the job. With a pair of earphones and a battery they succeeded in determining the location of the original wiring, poured melted wax into holes high up the walls, and thus insulated anew all the old wiring. I was told that after the cathedral lights were turned on, the Yugoslav Parliament voted them an expression of gratitude.

Someone helped Nagashev come to America, and General Electric offered him a position. He was responsible for several GE patents. Then he wanted to study. He was given a scholarship at MIT, but had a terrible time there since he knew no mathematics. He developed tuberculosis and was sent to a sanatorium, where he remained for two years, and when he came out he no longer wanted to work for anyone else. Living in the Karpoviches' house, he worked on a sound reproduction system for radio and phonograph, creating handmade loudspeakers so good that Serge Koussevitsky, the conductor of the Boston Symphony Orchestra, said that they compared to commercial ones as Stradivarius violins did to others. At that time Nagashev was installing his systems at Wellesley College and at a school for the blind in New York. He asked me to calculate for him the curves of the plywood horns that he was building for his system, since the mathematics was too hard for him. He had absolutely no money and depended on the Karpoviches' support. Nagashev's rather familiar manner, his unkempt appearance, and his bad table manners all made me want to distance myself from him, in spite of my great respect for his inventive genius. Two years later he was killed in an automobile accident in Vermont. He was then developing an idea for something resembling radar – before radar was invented – for use by the blind in navigating between obstacles.

In the summer of 1933 a World's Fair was held in Chicago. Wilhelm Jost and an English friend of his wanted to see California before returning to Europe in the fall, and on their way back would also visit the Fair. Jost offered to pay for my railway ticket to Chicago, where we would meet, see the fair, and return together. I very much looked forward to this trip. When Nagashev heard about my going to Chicago, however, where General Electric was exhibiting one of his inventions, he tried to make me ashamed of my extravagance.

"How can you spend so much money just on yourself, when you could drive there with me and give me a chance to visit Chicago? I could bring Jost, his friend, and you back here in my car, and all this travel would cost no more than your ticket alone!" I was doubtful, but Nagashev persisted. I spoke to Jost before his departure for California, and he reluctantly agreed to Nagashev's plan.

It was late in July when Nagashev and I set out for Chicago. Nagashev's car was a convertible, but more than that, it had a front windshield that could be rolled down, which Nagashev insisted on doing. My face burned from the wind, and by the time we arrived, it was so swollen that I could hardly do any sightseeing. There I received a telegram from Jost: he and his friend had begun to drive in a hired car from California but had had an accident on the way. Both were hurt, Jost's back ached, and though the local hospital said nothing was broken, they had decided to take a sleeper to Boston, only changing in Chicago and missing the Fair. I met them at one of the railroad stations in Chicago and helped them to transfer to another. Since I myself had no money left to take the train, I had to drive back with Nagashev. The only thing I remember from the Fair was a show devoted to the accomplishments of women, where among the well-known women artists was Father's sister, Ekaterina Zarudnaya Cavos, with a photograph and a list of her works.

Soon after that I helped Jost to pack and saw him off. We parted warmly, promising to correspond faithfully. I intended to go to Germany and marry him as soon as everything was settled with my sisters. I did miss him, and we wrote to each other frequently; it seemed to me that my future was settled. Letters to him and to Harbin, work on my thesis, and caring for the Karpovich children now occupied all my time.

The letters to and from Harbin maintained our family lifeline. Lena wrote more than anyone, about her thoughts, her reaction to our activities here, and their day-to-day life. She was the leader of the family now, but a gentle one: Manya sometimes wished Lena was more forceful. All of them felt the absence of Father's guiding hand.

Time was passing, if not running out, for Lena and Tanya to begin their American education. Nor could the two younger sisters be left in Harbin, and I needed to free myself for going to Germany.

Harold Freeman, 1932

Sergey, 1932

I would do all I could to bring this about, but during the rest of the summer I managed to earn only a few dollars from babysitting and other odd jobs. It paid for postage, and for traveling to two or three job interviews. Neither Sergey nor I yet had any real prospects of employment.

෬

In the fall Sergey and I registered for thesis work only. The tuition for that was minimal, but it allowed us to be considered students rather than unemployed. Sergey, living in New Haven with the Vernadskys, managed to work on his thesis unsupervised. I went to MIT every day, studied in the library, and had weekly conferences with Professor Struik. Some of my former classmates, like Robert Richtmyer, were still there, and we would meet over a cup of coffee in the physics conference room or in the student dining room. Occasionally I met Harold Freeman, who by then was teaching a course in the economics department.

MIT at that time offered foreign language courses only in German and French. Richtmyer and a few other friends told me that they might be interested in learning Russian, and wondered if I could teach them. I put up a notice on the bulletin board, and about twenty graduate students responded. As I remember, I asked each student to pay two dollars per semester. The administration of the Institute allowed me free use of an empty classroom.

We met once a week. I still missed reading Russian poetry to my friends, so I greatly looked forward to my students' progress. The only textbook I knew was hopelessly dull, so I devised my own reading exercises. Having no Russian typewriter, I wrote them by hand, using purple hectograph carbon, and duplicated them on a pad of gelatin poured onto a cookie sheet. But while I had hoped soon to share my love of Russian poetry with my students, their real progress was painfully slow, and gradually I realized how futile that hope was. By the end of the year I decided that I never wanted to teach Russian again, but instead would devote myself to perfecting my English. The next year MIT hired a Russian instructor, a Mr. Znamensky, and began to offer Russian in the language department.

Among the new foreign women that year appeared a graduate student in physics from Germany, Eva Schik. An attractive, outgoing girl, she immediately made many friends among the others. I liked her at once; her English was not much better than mine, but we had many interesting conversations. I thought her so charming that I wondered at once: if Will meets such nice girls in Germany, how can I compete? I wrote that to him.

Eva was Jewish, and told me many stories about the condition of Jews in present-day Germany. She had had many friends at the university and in her neighborhood, who frequently came to her house. When the National Socialists came to power everything changed; her friends did not visit her anymore, they did not even recognize her on the street. She was simply ostracized. From newspapers and talking to my friends I knew that this indeed was the situation in Germany, but somehow it was more chilling to hear it from one who had experienced it firsthand, and especially from someone I liked so much. In the spring I heard that Jost's professor was dismissed because he had a Jewish wife and would not divorce her. Jost was appointed in his place.

In Harbin relations between the Japanese and the Soviets continued to deteriorate. The Japanese searched the main Harbin Russian library, where they found signs of documents having been burned, and sealed off the library. There followed a number of searches of homes and arrests of Railroad employees with Soviet passports. Harbin was suddenly full of anti-Soviet posters and demonstrations put on by the anti-Soviet Russian groups, obviously encouraged by the Japanese.

Lena, whose position as family leader was now taken for granted, taught a few lessons for pay and was in the second year of the Economics School. Katya began her studies in the chemistry department of the technical school; Zoya continued at her school and had a whole crowd of young male admirers. Katya and Zoya were both awarded scholarships as sisters of a Railroad employee – Tanya. Each Sunday the house was full of friends, but to make ends meet the family was dipping into what was left of Father's life insurance, the only reserve, and waiting impatiently for Sergey and me to graduate.

In Cambridge my thesis was finished by the end of the semester. Sergey finished his, too; he lacked some mathematical textbooks for reference, but worked out what theory he needed by himself. I have to admit he was brilliant. We received our degrees, although there was no formal graduation ceremony in the middle of the year, and we would wait until spring to participate in one. It was just as well, for neither of us had an inkling yet of a job.

I wished that I could continue my studies towards a doctorate. I was not quite sure, however, that I should pursue pure mathematics, as I was better prepared for applied math. Physics was my first choice, but I had already strayed too far from it. At any rate I applied for a full scholarship at two graduate schools in mathematics. I feared, however, that Mr. Crane might feel that my being a graduate student was not quite the same as having a paying job, and he might decide against bringing our sisters to join us. With the economic situation in America so dire, competition for such scholarships was fierce, so I was not altogether disappointed when I was turned down.

I traveled to the General Electric plant in Syracuse, New York, to apply for some kind of a job. Then I went on to New York City, where Mr. Crane took me to meet the president of General Electric. I also applied to the Bell Telephone Company, for which I thought I was best qualified, and everyone there was very cordial; they took my written application and promised to let me know if any openings should occur. But there were no immediate results, and I returned to Cambridge with only faint hopes. Sergey at least had a few interviews, though no concrete offers. I continued to teach my Russian class during the spring term, but with diminishing enthusiasm and reduced enrollment. Still, I was glad that it gave me a chance to continue going to MIT. By the time the term ended most of my friends had left school.

The only young friend of the Karpoviches whom I knew was a French graduate student at Harvard, Jean-Marie Chalifour, who could speak a little Russian. We decided to exchange lessons in Russian and French conversation. We took long walks around Cambridge, speaking Russian on the outward way, and French as we returned. It was a friendship that lasted for many years.

In the summer of 1934 the Karpoviches bought a 250-acre farm in Vermont as a summer home. It later became a haven where my family as well as many Russian friends of the Karpoviches passed wonderful vacations. Among the latter was Vladimir Nabokov, who with his wife and son stayed there for parts of two summers, catching butterflies, writing, and enjoying the company; I think the spirit of this place is reflected in his novel *Pnin*. Alexander Kerensky, the head of the Provisional Government in Petrograd in 1917, was an occasional visitor, as were other Russian émigré writers, artists, and scientists. The Karpoviches invited me to stay with them there, but I felt that job-hunting required me to be near a telephone and available to move at a moment's notice. At the farm there was neither a car nor a telephone, and public transportation began miles away.

I was again left in the Cambridge house alone with Nagashev. I had twenty dollars left for the whole summer and absolutely no prospect of making any more. The Karpoviches had no refrigerator at that time and I could not afford to buy ice for the icebox; Nagashev managed without it. Jean-Marie's sister, with whom he shared an apartment near Harvard, had gone to Paris for the summer and he was also nearly broke. He suggested that we eat together, sharing the expenses, since their refrigerator was owned by the apartment house and cost him nothing; he could teach me to cook, too. I went to his place twice a day and we settled our accounts evenly at the end of each month. Before summer ended my funds were completely exhausted. But by then I luckily had a job, and was able to repay him from my first pay check.

Sergey finally was offered a temporary position as a draftsman in a factory near New Haven. He had just met a girl, Vilma Fekete, in an evening drawing class – an excellent musician, who as a child prodigy gave concerts both on violin and piano, but now was doing only a little teaching. An only daughter of Hungarian immigrants, she lived with her parents, who did everything they could for her musical education, including sending her to Europe to study. Sergey greatly respected her talent; they would marry in 1936.

At General Electric in Lynn

In August I received a letter from the General Electric River Works in Lynn, Massachusetts, offering me a job working on the thermodynamic design of steam turbines, at a salary of $25 a week. I was elated. It may well have been that my introduction by Mr. Crane to the president of the great firm brought this about, but that was never mentioned. Since I had taken a course in thermodynamics in Harbin, I hoped that I could handle the job.

Lynn is about twelve miles from Cambridge and a local train ran to North Station in Boston, so I could keep up my Cambridge contacts. I found a room in Lynn in the house of a Swedish immigrant family whose children had left home, paying ten dollars a week for room and half-board. With five dollars for lunches and incidentals, I could save ten dollars each week towards the settling of my sisters in America.

As soon as I accepted the job I wrote to Mr. Crane, and he started the procedure of bringing all four sisters, and Manya, to the United States. I had told him that Manya always took care of us and was really a part of the family, and that the younger girls especially would need her care. But I could not justify the same provision for Nanny, who was so old and sick that we all thought she would not even survive the long trip. I said nothing of Lena's and Tanya's doubts about coming here, for their hope of receiving Soviet passports was getting dimmer.

My work at General Electric turned out mostly to involve the steam chart, with which I was already quite familiar, and special formulae with approximations based on tests performed at the Works. What I did most of the day was calculate, using a slide rule, and draw charts; my slide rule was Father's, who had used it when studying in Belgium. One of my duties was to teach methods of design to the young engineers who were starting work there, and it amazed me how they would avoid simple algebraic reductions that could make their calculations more accurate, and preferred the slide rule – even when its limitations made the resulting figures meaningless. They had to learn some basic mathematical principles.

Living in Lynn was not only very dull, but terribly lonely. All the engineers were married, and in all the time I worked at GE no one once invited me to lunch or to their home, or spoke to me about anything but work. I also found my co-workers extremely uninteresting, conversing only about sports, cars, or card games. During lunchtime I would read at my desk, eating my sandwich, and I punched the clock at five p.m. and went home. After an ample supper with my goodhearted but unexciting landlady and her husband, I would retire to my room to read and write letters. Letters from Jost were nearly all I was living for. I heard nothing from Mr. Crane or his secretary about progress in bringing over my sisters, but I had confidence that something would happen.

One evening when I came home, I received an unusually thick letter from Jost, and ran to my room to read it. He informed me – as gently as he could – that he had met a new girl and intended to marry her. This struck me like a thunderbolt; never before or after did I weep so bitterly. I sobbed so loudly that my landlady came to ask what the matter was. I could not eat dinner, and cried all the rest of the evening. In my mind I had been so completely committed to him, for life, that I felt unable to reason or think about anything else: there was simply, and suddenly, no ground under my feet.

It seemed to me that I would be alone for the rest of my days, with no personal life at all. I had no chance to meet anybody in whom I could be interested. I was already almost twenty-six – two years past Mother's age when she married – and I thought I should be too. In Lynn there was no chance to meet anyone, and I would be working and living there for years to come. The thought of my sisters joining us in America did little to relieve my gloomy vision of the future, for I knew that it would increase my responsibilities, be a struggle financially, and hardly improve my situation socially: all the young men they would meet would not be interested in me, only in my sisters. I would not even have friends of my own. A lonely, loveless existence for me lay ahead.

27

Reaching the Goal

Harold Freeman

After a few weeks of utter depression I began to go back to Cambridge on weekends, in the hope of reestablishing some old acquaintances. The Karpoviches kindly let me stay overnight whenever I wanted. I would go to MIT and look for Harold Freeman, who was the only young person I still knew there. He was usually studying in his office on the ground floor, and to avoid going around to the main entrance, I would go to the window of his office, and he would open it and let me in. We sat and talked. I told him of my life and work in Lynn, about my life in Harbin, my sisters, my waiting for their arrival. I told him that I was saving money to rent an apartment for all of us. Harold did not speak much, but always seemed understanding and willing to listen. He told me very little about himself. I knew that he was an only child, that his parents lived in a coal-mining town in Pennsylvania, and that his father, an immigrant from Austria, operated a bar-room on the ground floor of the house where they lived.

One day Harold invited me to visit his apartment, if I would not object to its disorder, to show me the view from his windows. It was on Memorial Drive in Cambridge, facing the Charles River, with Boston on the other side. Newspapers were scattered all over the floor, where Harold simply dropped them after reading. I picked them all up, after which we sat at opposite ends of his large living room with the light outside waning, not even conversing, while gradually the lights of Boston came on and the city began to shine against the evening sky, which was still tinged with sunset. Then a few stars appeared, and among them lights of airplanes, landing at Logan Airport or leaving it. The river stretched like a broad ribbon between us and the city, its calm waters changing color as the sky darkened. When it became dark Harold turned on the lamps and offered to walk me home.

During the walk to the Karpoviches we talked again. He spoke
about the social problems in America, and his sympathy for the
working classes appealed to me very much. We seemed to have
similar values and social concerns, the same hope for the future,
and the same interests in scientific progress. He was the first of
his own family to attend college, or to read anything much, and
he appeared to be rather estranged from them now. How I wished
I could introduce him to mine! The more I knew him the more
appealing he seemed, with his lean figure and sensitive face with its
slender nose, and his blue eyes under their long lashes, always so
attentive. He usually had something informative and interesting to
add to whatever subject I raised.

I repeated my visit on several weekends, and I found it quite
comforting. Sometimes he would not turn on the lights at all, and
when it became quite dark I would lie on the couch and fall asleep;
if Harold noticed, he would cover me with a blanket. Soon I would
waken, and he would walk me back home. It was a great relief not
to be alone with my gloomy reflections, into which he never pried.
In his gentle way he just let me be, and seemed to understand when
I did not want to explain.

Shortly after Christmas I learned from Lena that Uncle Sasha
had died in Leningrad on the first of December. His son, our cousin
Sergey, whom I remembered as a four-year-old in Petersburg, wrote
a long letter to her about his father's last days and his funeral. On the
day after Uncle died the Leningrad Party chief Sergey Mironovich
Kirov was assassinated, an event that triggered years of repression
and arrests. Kirov's death prompted a huge demonstration of grief:
no flowers, not even wild ones, were left in the city. For hours Uncle's
funeral procession was prevented from crossing one street by the
throng behind Kirov's coffin, on its way to the railroad station and
a state funeral in Moscow.

For my sisters this was the loss of the only adult relative to whom
they felt they could turn for advice. By 1934 Uncle Sasha was the
one who connected them with Father's family and Russia. Before
his death Lena had received a letter from her boyfriend, Vitaly
Alyokhin, who had left Harbin for Moscow, and wrote that he had

visited Uncle Sasha in Leningrad and was given the address of a former friend who now held an important political post in Moscow. That friend was to help Lena obtain her Soviet citizenship. Vitaly went to the address, but the woman who opened the door told him to go away at once. Years later Lena learned that Uncle Sasha's friend had been arrested, and that his apartment was being searched at the very moment Vitaly arrived. Soon after that Vitaly too was arrested, and Lena heard (also much later) that he spent ten years in the infamous Gulag.[1]

For me, too, the last link with my parents' generation was broken: with Uncle Sasha's death my feeling of being lost and alone intensified. Harold's friendship now stood out as the only bright spot in my life. My visits to his office and to his apartment on weekends resumed, though my depression did not go away. I yearned for a whole group of young people to which I could belong, but Harold seemed not to be part of any such group, and he did not introduce me to anyone new; he was the only person I talked to. I really had nowhere else to go, but I did enjoy seeing him.

On one of our visits we sat as usual at dusk, silently, at different ends of his living room. The light had almost faded and the city lights had just started to appear on the other side of the river. Harold suddenly said, "Miss Zarudny, are you aware of the fact that I am in love with you?" I was truly startled. He had never tried to touch me or in any way to show his affection. I knew that he probably liked me, but – "in love"? I told him that I was not in a condition to respond to him, that I was recently hurt and needed time to recover. But I was touched by his admission. He somehow phrased it as if he did not require anything from me, and I was very grateful for that. Our evening walk back to the Karpoviches' house felt quite different – somehow, there was a new bond between us.

I returned to Lynn in a very different state of mind. The world did not seem so dismal anymore. To know that I meant something special to someone I liked was wonderful. I kept thinking of Harold all week, and the longer I thought, the dearer he seemed to me. By the weekend, when I came to Cambridge again, I was impatient to see him. Still, I controlled my feelings – I did not want to fall in love "on the rebound." But Harold seemed to me so much more sensitive and gentle than Wilhelm Jost, and I sensed that I could trust him, and not fear he would hurt me. I was not comparing the two men, however, for nothing remained of my affection for Jost. This was a completely different feeling.

ᘓ

During the weeks that followed Harold came several times to visit me in Lynn. He would dine with me and my landlords, and then we would sit in their parlor or even in my room and talk. On weekends I went to Cambridge; I felt that I needed his company all the time. One evening he sat down at my landlords' upright piano and began to play. I don't remember what he played, but his whole appearance changed: it was as if the piano was his own voice and he was speaking through it. At this moment I knew I was really in love with him.

When we decided to get married I told the Karpoviches right away, wrote home, and told my landlady as soon as I returned to Lynn. At work there was a lonely old Russian mathematician who had a separate office where he would work for hours at night after punching out his time card, with only his aquarium for company. He told me, "Marriage is all right provided you can live twelve miles apart!" I was somewhat shocked. Other co-workers congratulated me.

Harold bought two gold wedding rings, with money I gave him, for he had none. There was an inscription of the date inside each of them. I bought a suit in a secondhand shop in Boston. We were married on Saturday, February 25, 1935, a day after Harold moved all my things into his apartment. Our wedding was held in a Russian Orthodox church in Boston, where the priest had presented to Harold, a week earlier, a small bilingual liturgy inscribed to "my spiritual son Leo": Leo, because Harold is not a Russian saint's name, and thus cannot be used in baptism – so this was a kind of compromise.

Afterwards we returned to the apartment, and I picked Harold up and carried him over the threshold. I had heard that this is the tradition for the new husband to do with his bride, but I did not think that Harold, who was ten inches taller than me but weighed about twelve pounds less, could manage it. It never occurred to me that he might not like this, for I was sure he would be proud of having such a strong wife. After all, I assumed that he knew how great my respect was for his intellectual leadership – and wasn't that all that mattered?

We had to postpone our honeymoon until fall. On Monday I went back to work, since I had started my job only seven months earlier, and could not take time off. Harold did not tell his parents of our marriage right away. It never struck me that as Jews they might not be so happy about it. I knew nothing about the Jewish religion or tradition, but nevertheless believed that a Russian-Jewish combination was a particularly good one, for (I thought) it produced exceptionally bright children. My best friends Margarita Sechkina and Yura Aingorn had one Jewish parent, and both were baptized in the Russian Orthodox Church.

We received a few presents. Jean-Marie gave me two cake plates, and a professor in Harold's department gave us a pretty silver serving dish. One of Harold's colleagues asked him what I wanted, and I said a frying pan. It is still my favorite frying pan. I wrote to Mr. Crane that I was married and received two presents from him: a check for one hundred dollars and the opportunity to go to a tailor and order a suit. I ordered a brown flannel suit with a matching coat, which I wore for many years. With the hundred dollars we bought an old convertible, and Harold drove me to work every morning and picked me up at five in the afternoon, until I got my own Massachusetts license.

My working days were long; with the commuting time added I was away from home from seven in the morning to six at night. Harold did the shopping, and sometimes greeted me with a variety of appetizers, beautifully arranged on a tray for my dinner. I still knew very little about cooking. What I had learned from Jean-Marie was mostly how to make various salads, which Harold did not eat. Mrs. Karpovich told me that the simplest thing was to buy a whole chicken, put it into a pot with water, add salt and pepper and boil it for two hours. Then you had both the meat and the soup. I did this. I set the pot with water and the chicken on the stove and went to the living room to read for two hours. When I came back to the kitchen, I found the pot with the burnt skeleton of the chicken in it – the water had all boiled away. Harold found it difficult to trust my cooking for a long time after that.

My English was still quite shaky, particularly my writing, of which I was ashamed. I felt ignorant about so many things, and thought that my education was terribly narrow. The literature I knew was mostly Russian. What did it matter that I could integrate some differential equations or design a turbine bucket? These were not an index of culture. I looked up to Harold's knowledge of English literature, arts, politics, and especially everything about America. Now that America was to be my country I was eager to know it, to feel it, as I could feel Russia. I learned a lot from Harold about life in a small American town, about his schooling and his childhood, so utterly different from mine.

Harold often spoke about the life of the miners and other working-class people, the union organizers' struggle to improve the working conditions of laborers and the lives of their families, about slums and the people in them. My earlier thinking that life in America was too comfortable had already been considerably modified, but so far I had been just an observer; now I began to look at American life from the inside, through the eyes of a participant. I began to understand that there was a lot of work left to be done to improve the life of people, that not all the problems were solved. Most of all I started to understand something about the workings of a democracy. I admired people who were patriotic and yet could appreciate and admit to the many shortcomings of their country. When I thought of Russia I felt pain for her misfortunes and felt that a sacrifice was needed in the struggle for justice there. In America I saw the need for work and confidence in the eventual positive results of one's efforts. I still had so much to learn.

Finally, Harold wrote to his parents about us and offered to take me to visit them. I was delighted. However, he said that he would take me only as far as New York, where he had some business, and there put me on the train to Wilkes-Barre where his mother would meet me. I was a little frightened to go there alone, but was happy to have a chance to meet his parents.

It turned out to be a very satisfying trip. Harold's mother, a handsome, rather stout woman, met me at the station and enveloped me in a hearty embrace. It immediately broke the ice. She talked without stop about Harold, his growing up, his school successes. "He was born with a golden spoon in his mouth," she said several times. Harold's father greeted me formally. A stout gray-haired gentleman, he was not talkative, but very friendly. He studied me intently when he could get away from the bar, where he was waiting on his customers.

On Saturday they served a traditional chicken supper to their customers. Mrs. Freeman, whom I decided to call "Mother," cooked a vast number of chicken halves in the oven of her stove in the kitchen. Their dining room had many small tables, which started to fill up soon after I arrived. To me it seemed incredible that she could cook for and serve so many people without any help. I immediately put on an apron and started to help serving the chicken. Mother was quite proud of the fact that her "educated" daughter-in-law would wait on tables, and said so to every person she spoke to.

After the crowd left and we three sat together to eat, we talked about food. It turned out I liked all the things they liked, for most Jewish food was the same as Russian food. Mother was delighted. "You see," she said, "Russians and Jews are all the same!" From that point on I was totally accepted. It was obvious to me that I could have good relations with them; they were good warm people who loved their son very much and were ready to include me in their affection. Mother gave me a gold ring with a red stone in it. Later we received an electric toaster and a large white linen tablecloth from Harold's aunt. The toaster lasted at least forty years and the tablecloth is still in my chest.

The next day I took a train to New York, where Harold met me, and we returned to Cambridge. Not long after this I went with him to the Boston Museum of Fine Arts, the first art museum I had ever visited. He bought me a biography of Van Gogh, which I read laboriously, looking up in the dictionary the many words I did not know. Harold was a voracious reader, while I read even more slowly in English than in Russian. I stopped reading Russian in order to concentrate on improving my English. But even newspapers took me a lot of time. Harold gobbled up four or five of them every day, but did not want to review their contents with me.

Becoming an American

On April 19 Harold and I went to see the finish of the Boston Marathon. Harold used to be a ten-mile runner and was quite fascinated by the Marathon. We stood near the finish line on Commonwealth Avenue in the middle of an excited crowd. I could sense the tension of the crowd, and Harold's excitement, and found myself tensing up too. It was wonderful to be next to the one I loved yet excited about something else, to be with him and also be a part of a large group and not have to worry about anything.

After the Marathon Harold took me to Concord to see the parade of Civil War soldiers, to look at the famous bridge, the statue of the Minuteman, and the grave of the British soldiers. Still aroused by the race, I was gripped by the sense of American history around me. The quotation from a poem by James Russell Lowell inscribed on the grave of two British soldiers especially touched me:

> They came three thousand miles and died
> To keep the past upon its throne.
> Unheard, beyond the ocean tide,
> Their English mother made her moan.

This feeling of compassion for fallen adversaries moved me. Tears welled in my eyes, and I suddenly felt I loved this country, which could inscribe such words on the grave of its enemies. If they treated the British soldiers like that, after a war with them, it was obvious that they really could, and did, accept immigrants like me. I could now really be an American with my American husband; this was my country too, my home. I had always longed to belong somewhere, and now I did. I also knew now that I could show my sisters what America is about, that it could become their country, too.

April 19 remained for me a significant date.

The spring and summer passed all too quickly. Since I had been working at GE for less than a year I had no vacation time coming to me yet, while Harold, who had no teaching all summer, spent a lot of time alone. On weekends we walked along the river and occasionally took rides into the country. I learned more about Harold, as he told me about his lonely childhood.

He had always been very skinny, especially after he contracted the "Spanish" influenza, which raged in America in 1918, when his mother was also ill. Both of them survived, but the whole neighborhood was devastated – almost every household had funeral wreaths hanging on their doors. The influenza left Harold prone to many illnesses and repeated attacks of pneumonia.

He began piano lessons when still a small child, and his parents bought a grand piano for him. The men in their neighborhood were mostly miners, who worked in the local coal mines. He tried to make friends with the miners' children, but they considered him a weak, piano-playing boy, the son of a bar-keeper, whose home was out of bounds for them because liquor was sold there. After a public elementary school he attended a private preparatory school, where he did not feel he belonged, among the boys from much wealthier families. He was sent to MIT because his uncle, seeing him making complex constructions with his Meccano set, remarked: "This boy should go to Boston Tech!"

As a teenager he ran away from home one summer and picked blueberries with a group of other boys. At one time he earned money playing in the movie theaters, accompanying silent movies. He graduated from MIT with his class, even though he missed almost a year because of illness. He had not wanted to ask his parents to pay for another year, as he felt they could not afford it. After graduating, he spent a hungry year in Boston, unwilling to admit to his parents that he had no job. He worked for a short time at a shoe factory until Professor Struik gave him work grading papers.

I told Harold my stories seriously, with a touch of sentimental nostalgia about my youth. Harold, on the other hand, told his with a wonderful sense of humor. Sometimes his stories were so funny that, exhausted from laughing, I would beg him to stop. Yet I thought that his was the lonely life of a single child with parents and relatives who did not understand him, and my heart went out to him.

The Last Steps

A good deal of my free time was still taken up by correspondence with Harbin. Japan was negotiating with the Soviet Union to buy the CER, to the great concern of China, whose original agreement with Russia specified that only China could buy it. Japan's ancient ambition to expand its influence in mainland Asia seemed close to fulfillment. It looked more and more problematic for Russian émigrés to continue living in Manchuria. The Soviet Union was making it as easy as possible for Soviet citizens to return to Russia, offering advantageous passage. They were leaving in droves, with all of their possessions.[2]

During March the USSR finally concluded negotiations for the sale of the Chinese Eastern Railroad to Manchukuo, i.e., to Japan. Many of the Soviet employees of the Railroad who previously had no passports now received them, including Lena and Tanya. Evidently the Soviet authorities were trying to lure émigrés into returning to Russia, but for Lena and Tanya it was too late: they had already firmly decided upon America. But having Soviet passports allowed them to think that after some time in the US they might yet return to Russia, and made the long journey seem less of a final break with their homeland.

Manya found friends who agreed to take Nanny in. Our family's only asset – the house – would be sold, and we hoped that the proceeds would pay for Nanny's board for at least several months. In any case we promised that we would support her from the USA. The house fetched only a very low price, so it was lucky that Mr. Crane had funded the whole family's passage.

Harold and I expected their arrival in the fall, so we had to plan where to move, in order to accommodate them all. After we married we had lived on Harold's salary, and I was able to save practically all of my wages to prepare for the others. I hoped that Harold looked forward to having so many sisters-in-law. In August he began house-hunting; the lease on our expensive apartment would run out in September. Sergey's job still paid very little, and he too would be married soon, and have a wife to support, so I did not count on his help with our sisters.

Harold found a house in a lovely setting in the town of Wakefield, nearer to Lynn, and close to transport by railway to Cambridge. He always had a wonderful ability to find interesting places to live, never one that was drab, or conventional, or crowded in upon by neighbors. The rent was only fifty dollars a month, but we had to pay for heat and electricity, which later proved to be much dearer than we had expected.

Besides the living room, dining room, and kitchen on the ground floor, there were four bedrooms on the second and one more on the third. We had to furnish the house for seven people, and we owned only a bed, a couple of chairs, a couch, a small table, and a few dishes. My savings had to cover everything else: a refrigerator, five beds, five chests of drawers, four desks, mattresses, pillows, sheets, blankets, a dining table, chairs, and living room furniture. We knew no one who would give us their discards, but Harold had a friend who worked for Sears, Roebuck and we bought many things with his employee discount. Metal bed springs were put on two pieces of three-by-three-foot lumber to form beds; living room furniture of a sofa and two overstuffed chairs came from the Morgan Memorial charity second-hand store, upholstered in a cheap but new cloth; and we found crude woolen blankets at an Army and Navy store. We even bought material for drapes.

I was touched by Harold's enthusiatic sharing in these preparations. I had little time, and knew nothing about finding bargains. We spent the evenings studying the thick Sears catalogue, and he did the ordering during the day. It never even occurred to me to worry about how he would feel living with so large a family – an only child, a shy person who often wanted to be alone. But in Harbin our family often took in lonely young people, and they always seemed to feel comfortable and happy to be with us. I was still an integral part of my own family, and not yet ready to break away from it. I was simply taking Harold in.

On Labor Day weekend I decided to go to Vermont to visit the Karpoviches at their farm. Harold did not want to go, and I agreed to go alone. We had visited them on one weekend earlier, and I had seen how uncomfortable he was in that thoroughly Russian atmosphere, listening to a language he did not understand. I wished that I could help Harold accept the warmth of Russian hospitality, and appreciate the intellectual agility of these unusual and interesting people, but I understood how he felt.

That was my first long drive alone, at least four hours, through beautiful country roads. In Vermont I really indulged myself, renting a horse and saddle for a day and going riding for the first time in three years. I rode away from houses and roads and across the open fields, feeling lonely at first, but then enjoying hugely the warm day, the fragrance of the pine woods surrounding the fields, the smell of the warm horse – and even the loneliness itself, with the knowledge that it was only for a day or two.

My personal problems were solved, now that I was no longer alone. I had confidence in myself to face anything in the future. My sisters were coming, and I was sure that I would be able to help them find their way once they reached America.

Reaching the Goal

The girls and Manya left Harbin on September 22, seen off by a crowd of their friends at the station. Nanny, who had spent all her life with our family, was in despair: it was a heartrending parting for everyone. She died less than a year later, hallucinating near the end that we were all coming back.

On my advice the family crossed the Pacific by way of Hawaii, which Sergey and I never saw. They would stop first in San Francisco, and then proceed through the Panama Canal to New York, arriving (after a delay from a dock strike) at the end of October. I took a few days off from work and went to New York to meet them. Harold stayed home. The furniture was only tentatively arranged and packages of bedding and other household things were still lying about in cartons. The windows, without curtains or shades, had a vacant look, but Harold and his friend from Sears, Roebuck would try to prepare the new house as well as they could.

In New York Mr. Brodie took me to the pier where the ship was already docking. Sergey was there from New Haven, and when the crowd on the ship's deck began to thin we could see all four sisters and Manya standing in a row along the deck rail, and then shouting and jumping for joy as they recognized us. At Ellis Island, where they had to report first, Mr. Brodie negotiated the immigration procedure smoothly, and finally we were able to embrace one another. Everyone spoke at once, with exclamations, kisses, and tears. The complexity of our emotions is hard to describe. We all drove on to the Crane apartment where we rested and talked, and then dined with the Cranes before boarding a night train to Boston. On leaving New York Mr. Brodie told me that Mr. Crane would send us all two hundred dollars a month for the time being, and would take care of the girls' medical expenses. But their schooling would be our own responsibility.

The girls had had a wonderful passage, their introduction to America including Hawaii with its tropical flowers, San Francisco, the Panama Canal with its massive locks, Cuba, and at last the Statue of Liberty, looming through the fog, with the New York skyline in the background. While at sea they worked on embroidering a large cross-stitched rug in a Persian design, which they had begun in Harbin and later finished in Wakefield. Almost everyone they met on board (no Russians, so their English improved!) was put to work adding his bit to this grand project. It was their wedding present to me, and it still hangs on my wall, admired by my visitors.

All these stories came bursting out from the girls speaking at once, interrupting each other, with even Manya trying to put in a few words. But the shadow of Father was among us as well. We all sensed that, but could not talk about it until later.

We had sleeping accommodations on the train to Boston, but we hardly slept. Harold and his friend met us at the station and drove us to Wakefield, where the house was in complete order. Even the window drapes were hung, as I later found out with safety pins and unhemmed, making the house look livable and cozy. All the beds were made – Harold and his friend had finished everything late at night and slept on the floor in the living room, so as not to disturb the made-up beds.

The girls were enthralled. They ran around the house like little children again, screaming and jumping. Manya inspected the kitchen, delighted with everything she found, and immediately started thinking about how to prepare lunch.

Our new life began.

The Following Years

In the summer Mr. Crane invited the whole family to Woods Hole, letting us stay in the house of his daughter, who was away. Designed by the famous Chicago architect Louis Sullivan, it stood at the tip of Juniper Point, surrounded on three sides by the ocean and resembling an airplane, with its semicircular central section (a living room with a huge fireplace) flanked by two wings with many bedrooms. The resident maid prepared all our meals. I could visit only on weekends and during the two weeks of my GE holidays, as could Harold, and Sergey with his wife Vilma, but the girls and Manya spent the whole summer there.

Crane's grandson, Harold Bradley, occupied a small cottage nearby with his wife; they joined the girls at the beach near the bathhouse, on the second floor of which was Mr. Crane's study. He often came there, and watched over all of us as we swam. It was a glorious summer.

That fall we moved back from Wakefield to Cambridge, Harold and I settling in an apartment near MIT, and the girls in one closer to Harvard. Eventually Harold became a professor in the Department of Economics at MIT, published a number of books on statistics, and retired in 1971, though he went on writing on humanitarian and radical topics until his death in 1997. We have two sons, Arthur and Edward, neither of them parents of children. Edward, a musician, composer, and photographer, lives in Los Angeles, when he is not roaming the world in search of new subjects. Arthur is a poet, literary historian, and a dealer in rare books and manuscripts, who was formerly a professor at Boston University, and now lives in London with his wife and co-author Janet. Harold and I divorced in 1957 and never remarried. For many years I was employed at MIT as an applied mathematician, in various departmental capacities,

Five sisters, together at last

Katya, Zoya, Tanya, Lena, and Mulya
in 1998

Margaret Zarudny Freeman
Belmont, Mass., 2000

then returned to teaching Russian in the early 1960s, and retired as an Associate Professor Emeritus in 1978 – the first woman ever accorded that honor, I believe.

Sergey received his Ph.D. in physics, and until his retirement at seventy worked at the Aberdeen Proving Grounds in Maryland, the U.S. Army's premier installation for research, development, and munitions testing. He died two years later, in 1982; his wife Vilma continues to live in their home in Aberdeen. They have two daughters, Tanya and Alexandra, and four grandchildren.

Lena graduated in 1939 from Radcliffe College, having majored in English. On the day of her graduation she married Harry Levin, a Junior Fellow at Harvard who became a famous professor of comparative literature, with many volumes of criticism to his credit. Lena herself later taught at Radcliffe and translated two books, including Leon Trotsky's manuscript *Diary in Exile*. Harry died in 1994. They have one daughter, Marina, and two grandchildren.

Tanya wanted to study biology. Because her English was not as good as Lena's I advised her to go to MIT too: "It would be easiest for you," I said, "for language is not as important there!" I was sure that she would do well at MIT, and she did. After her second year she married a classmate, Robert Hull, an electrical engineering major, and they graduated together two years later. Eventually Robert became an executive of an electronics company in New York (where FM radio was developed), retired early, and moved with Tanya to Maryland. They have two daughters, Mary and Nancy, and four grandchildren. Before becoming a mother Tanya worked as a biologist, and when the children grew up and Robert retired, she became a librarian at a junior college. In her own retirement she took up photography, and became wonderfully good at it, creating inspiring portfolios of landscape and architectural images, both of America and (finally) Russia. She died in 2001.

Zoya entered the school of the Museum of Fine Arts in Boston, and performed well there both in sculpture and in painting. After two years she went to Chicago to study with Alexander Archipenko, but that did not work out well, and she moved again, to New York. There she married Robert Chambers, a medical student whom she had met in Woods Hole. Ten years later they were divorced, and she became a social worker in Brooklyn, where she still lives. She remained childless, despite an adventurous romantic career. My son Arthur remembers her admonishing him, when he was young and determined to be an intellectual, "*Arturchik*, remember, the head is only one-eighth of the body!"

Katya was admitted to MIT in the same year as Tanya, also majoring in biology. She transferred to Radcliffe the next year, and after graduating in 1941 attended several graduate schools, receiving a Ph.D. in biology from the University of Missouri in 1950. In 1952 she married a colleague, Jesse Singleton, who became a professor of biology at Purdue. He died in 1962, leaving her with one son, John. She held various positions in her field and is now retired in Providence, Rhode Island.

Manya studied English at the International Institute in Boston and there met a Ukrainian immigrant, Phillip Derricks, whom she married in 1940. She and Phillip moved to Providence, where he worked as a window-washer and took my son Arthur fishing – an affectionate companion, but a bit of a drinker. He died in 1975; Manya stayed in Providence and worked many years in a costume jewelry factory there. Having married too late to have children of her own, she remained the one fast link between all the sisters until her death in 1989, at the age of 94. She outlived Sergey and many others, and after coming to America saw eight children and ten grandchildren born into our family. And she never forgot anyone's birthday.

[1]   Vitaly Alyokhin repatriated to the USSR, was arrested and spent ten years in prison camp. After his release he moved to Fergana (Uzbekistan) and lived there to the end of his life.

[2]   As already noted in Chapter 19, note 1, most of the repatriates were arrested on their return to the USSR and spent years in the Gulag. Some were shot.

Epilogue

In 1994, with the help of the Andrei Sakharov Foundation and Elena Bonner personally, I received from Russia copies of what has been preserved in the files of the Omsk Cheka concerning my mother's case in 1921. Most of the papers and photographs that were confiscated from her at the time of her arrest were missing, but the following survived: (1) reports of her interrogations, and a report by the interrogating officer; (2) a few letters; (3) a document stating that she was sentenced to capital punishment by shooting, and another verifying that the sentence had been carried out; and (4) a statement by the Commission on Rehabilitation, seventy years later, and a document of rehabilitation, bearing on the reverse the text of the law and the list of privileges due to the survivors of imprisonment, and their children.

The report of the interrogating officer stated that Mother was guilty of belonging to an anti-revolutionary organization; that she gave shelter to two members of this group, and that she gave one of them the address of her friends in another city, whom she refused now to name; that she had passed along a parcel of stamped but unaccomplished documents; and that she received correspondence from one or two fugitives and forwarded it as requested. Her refusal to name the friends to whom she had directed the person she sheltered proved beyond doubt that she belonged to the subversive organization.

In reinterpreting the evidence, and dismissing the last interpretative leap, the Commission on Rehabilitation declared:

> In accordance with the decision of the Omsk Gubcheka of March 14, 1921 Elena Pavlovna Zarudnaya was executed by shooting. She was accused of taking part in an illegal White Guard organization aimed at the overthrow of the Soviet Power in 1920 and 1921. During the interrogation she explained that a man previously unknown to her asked her for temporary shelter in October 1920. Some people who

then visited him were also unknown to her. This man asked her permission to have mail sent to her address for him as N. P. or "Olya." To this request she responded with a joke, not giving him a positive reply. Later she received a package addressed to "Olya" with some edibles. She shared it with her maid. She received no package for N. P. She insisted that none of these people told her any details about the organization and that no one suggested that she join it or any other. Nothing else emerged during the interrogation to prove that she participated in the work of the organization. Therefore:

Zarudnaya Elena Pavlovna

is totally rehabilitated in accordance with the Law of RSFSR of October 1991, "On the rehabilitation of victims of political repression."

It took me more than two years to find the courage not only to read the documents I received from Russia, but to study them until I understood their meaning. Only the finishing of this memoir, and many discussions with friends who read it in manuscript, convinced me to do so.

Seventy-three years had passed since Mother's death. All that time we in the family believed that she had done something heroic, for which she had paid with her life. We did not know exactly what she was accused of, but were sure that she had upheld her ideals, and most likely had consciously acted against the Bolshevik government. Some of us also had the suspicion, never voiced aloud, that Mother had been so devoted to her political ideals that she not only risked her own life, but placed her children in danger.

The conclusion that I came to after studying the documents was a revelation for me: the burden of uncertainty, which had tormented me all these years, fell from my shoulders, and I finally realized that Mother had not participated in any political conspiracy at all. Her only crimes were those of compassion and risk-taking. At the age of 88, I thought for the first time of my 37-year-old mother not as her daughter, but as someone older than she. She looks at me from her prison photograph with a wan, but confident smile, and I think I understand why she is smiling.

Прокуратура Российской Федерации

ПРОКУРАТУРА
ОМСКОЙ ОБЛАСТИ

644099; г. Омск, ул. Ленина, 1

_В.ж._ 93 № ___13___

на № _____ от _____

СПРАВКА

Гр-н (ка) **ЗАРУДНАЯ ЕЛЕНА ПАВЛОВНА** _____

по приговору Омского областного суда (Западно-Сибирского краевого

суда, Тарского окружного суда, линейного суда водного транспорта

Н-Иртышского бассейна, линейного, специального суда Омской ж. д.,

военного трибунала войск НКВД Омской области), по постановлению

ГПК по Сибкраю, тройки УНКВД по Омской области (при ПП ОГПУ по

Запсибкраю, Особого совещания при НКВД СССР) **за к/рев.**

от **14 марта** 19**21**г. по с**деятельность**ук

РСФСР был (а) ~~заключен(а) в ИТЛ на~~ _____ (расстрелян(а).

В соответствии со ст. ст. 1, 3, 5, 8 Закона РСФСР от 18 октября

1991 года «О реабилитации жертв политических репрессий», он(а)

считается полностью реабилитированным(ой).

Основание: заключение прокурора области от «**23**» **04** 19**93**

До ареста работал (а) **учительницей школы №16**

преподавала на курсах "красных учителей"
г.Омск

Зам. ПРОКУРОРА
ОМСКОЙ ОБЛАСТИ **Д.А.Якунин**

Павлоградская типография, 1992 г. Заказ № 119, тир. 5000

Elena Zarudnaya's Certificate of Rehabilitation, 1993

Mother did disagree, firmly, with most Bolshevik ideas and methods. She understood what was happening in the country, and knew very well what atrocities were being committed by the Bolsheviks in establishing their regime. Nevertheless, she did not give up hope for the future of Russia. Though recognizing the extent to which most people were deceived and rendered incapable of all independent thought, through intimidation and propaganda, she regarded education as the only possible salvation, and dedicated herself totally to that, teaching from early morning till late at night, as if hurrying to do as much as humanly possible in the time remaining to her. She taught schoolchildren, she taught adult education classes, she even taught students who had just learned to read and write, but were preparing to be teachers themselves very soon.

Mother realized, of course, that most people did not share all her ideals. But she could not help sympathizing with the minority whose ideals were similar to her own, especially those who were victimized by the new regime. They were young and headstrong, and they needed guidance, which she could provide, with her experience and her sense of realities. That is part of the reason, I believe, that she gave shelter to the young man who hid in our cellar. She acted with caution, however, encouraging him to leave as soon as possible; he and his friends came at night, unobserved – she thought – by anyone; and although she did give him the address of friends in a distant city, she warned him that they would do nothing illegal (that was acknowledged in the documents).

She did not realize, I think, that she could be accused of treason, because treason was so far from her own intent. Certainly she did not seek to endanger her family, but she simply could not abandon a desperate young man. She remained true to her own principles, refusing to name her friends to the interrogator, even when threatened with death. Her heroism was in maintaining her humanity, even when it was natural to think only of saving her own life. She would have been heartsick to think of the grief that her death would cause all her family, but her confidence in the people around us allowed her to hope that her children would survive. Beyond that, she could only trust that the seeds she planted in our hearts would flourish, that we would grow up to be worthy people, and that perhaps one day we would learn she did not betray anyone.

During the seventy years of the history of the Soviet Union, millions of innocent victims perished, my mother among them. At one time I felt that she was just one of the chips that fly when the wood is cut – a familiar expression for the hapless, circumstantial victims of a revolution. But now I understand her as more than a wood-chip. In refusing to betray herself, or anyone else, she retained her human dignity and compassion to the end – even to the extent of assuring us that she was quite well, when she must have known what lay in store, and arranging proper Sunday clothes for her cellmate, and an Easter feast for all, just days from her death.

All war deprives people of their human qualities; revolution and civil war even more so. To remain human in such circumstances – *that* is heroism.

Maps

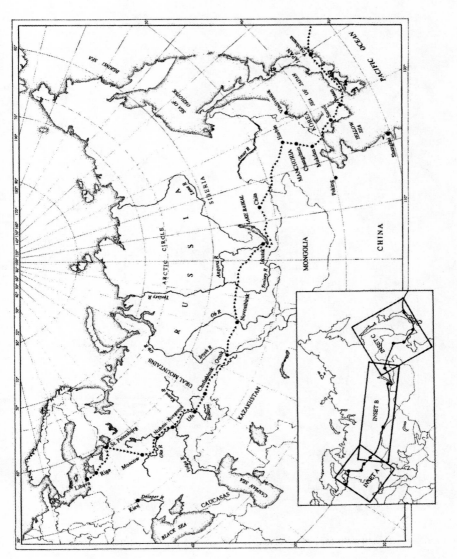

Overview

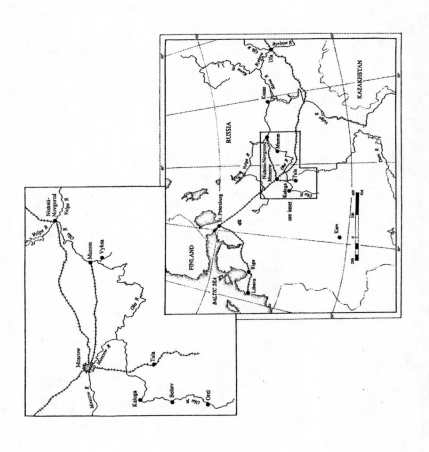

Western Russia - Inset A

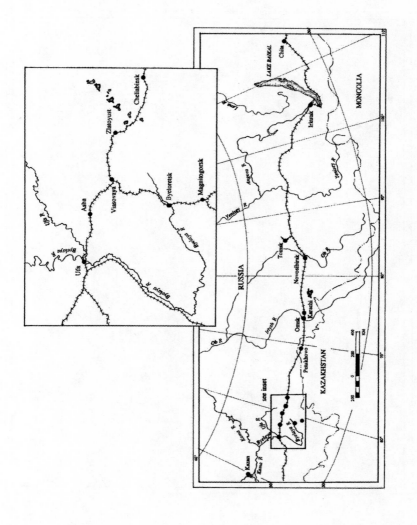

Central Russia - Inset B

The Far East - Inset C

Printed in the United States
56753LVS00002B/193-213